Also by Robert Rhodes James

Lord Randolph Churchill 1959

An Introduction to the House of Commons 1961

Rosebery 1963

Gallipoli 1965

Chips: The Diaries of Sir Henry Channon 1967

Memoirs of a Conservative: J. C. C. Davidson 1968

Churchill: A Study in Failure, 1900–1939 1970

Ambitions and Realities: British Politics 1964–70 1972

The Complete Speeches of Sir Winston Churchill 1974

Victor Cazalet: A Portrait 1975

The British Revolution: British Politics 1880–1939
Volume I 1976
Volume II 1977

PRINCE ALBERT

PRINCE ALBERT

A BIOGRAPHY

BY

Robert Rhodes James

ALFRED A. KNOPF · NEW YORK

1984

THIS IS A BORZOI BOOK PUBLISHED BY
ALFRED A. KNOPF, INC.

Copyright © 1983 by Robert Rhodes James

All rights reserved under International and Pan-American
Copyright Conventions. Published in the United States by
Alfred A. Knopf, Inc., New York. Distributed by Random
House, Inc., New York. Originally published in Great Britain
as *Albert, Prince Consort,* by Hamish Hamilton Ltd, Garden
House, 57-59 Long Acre, London WC2E 9JZ.

Library of Congress Cataloging in Publication Data

Rhodes James, Robert. [date]
Prince Albert, a biography.
Includes index.
1. Albert, Prince Consort of Victoria, Queen of Great
Britain, 1819-1861. 2. Great Britain — History— Victoria —
1837-1901. 3. Great Britain —Princes and princesses—
Biography. I. Title.
DA559.A1J36 1984   941.081′092′4 [B]   83-48934
ISBN 0-394-40763-6

Manufactured in the United States of America
First American Edition

For Kate from Papa

If ladies be but young and fair,
They have the gift to know it.

(*As You Like It*)

CONTENTS

ILLUSTRATIONS

PREFACE

It is sometimes difficult for a biographer to convey adequately, even to himself, why it is that a particular individual attracts him so powerfully that the idea of writing a biography gradually germinates and then moves from the stage of general interest to actual endeavour and then to final accomplishment. My political involvements and concerns at least partly explain my biographies of Lord Randolph Churchill, Lord Rosebery, and Victor Cazalet, and my study of Sir Winston Churchill's career between 1900 and 1939, but this new biography of Prince Albert essentially stems from many years of growing interest in a man comparable to Thomas Jefferson in the extraordinary variety and depth of his interests, who died so young and who achieved so much, but who has consistently failed to attract the serious attention of most political historians. This is all the more curious because he has received some admirable biographies, of which the first, by Sir Theodore Martin, is the most underestimated of all, but in spite of the endeavours of Sir Roger Fulford and Mr. Reginald Pound – to each of whom my debt is especially great – and my constituent and friend Mrs. Daphne Bennett, he is still inexplicably widely regarded as an enigmatic, somewhat cold, and not very significant participant in the life and reign of Queen Victoria, some of whose biographers have given him a rather minor role.

He is a man from whom contemporaries and subsequent commentators have seemed to derive much pleasure in calculatingly denigrating, and, it must be admitted, with considerable effect. The grotesque portrait presented by Lytton Strachey, with its sneers and false innuendoes – 'owing either to his peculiar upbringing or to a more fundamental idiosyncrasy he had a marked distaste for the opposite sex' is a notably unpleasant example – has left its mark. So, also, have the strictures of Arthur Ponsonby, who wrote in his essay on Queen Victoria in 1933 that Prince Albert 'was not an English gentleman, he was unmistakably a German, rather professorial, shy,

cold, and formal. He lacked the warmth and geniality which may
often overcome adverse prejudices ... he was a foreigner and a
pedant'. While it was perhaps inevitable that there should be a
reaction against the somewhat overdone memorials to 'Albert The
Good' it is entirely wrong that such crude and inaccurate portraits of
a remarkably complex character should remain unchallenged.

Indeed, so wide, and so many, were Prince Albert's interests and
abilities, packed into a very short life, that the real difficulty con-
fronting his biographer is that of giving a fair balance to each of
them. As with Jefferson, he merits a volume as architect, designer,
farmer, and naturalist. His influence on English music and art
appreciation is only now being fully recognised – not by the few, who
have long realised it, but by a much larger audience as the result of
Sir John Plumb's and Sir Huw Wheldon's superb *Royal Heritage*
television programmes and book. Very few men in modern times
have made such a lasting and permanent mark in such an astonishing variety of fields, from the popularisation of the Christmas Tree to
the saving of Cleopatra's Needle and its placing on the Thames
Embankment; the spectacular revival of Cambridge University from
medieval slumber to a world eminence it has never surrendered;
the foundations of Imperial College London were his work, as are the
museums in South Kensington, the carved lions at the base of
Nelson's Column in Trafalgar Square, the extension to the National
Gallery and its glorious early Renaissance paintings whose purchase
he inspired and of which twenty-two are his personal gift, the idea of
the Royal Balcony on the façade of Buckingham Palace, the concept
of the Model Village, and the inspiration for the Victoria Cross as
the highest award for gallantry in battle, to be awarded regardless of
rank. It is to him that we owe the tragically destroyed Crystal Palace,
the great frescoes in the Royal Gallery in the Palace of Westminster,
the exact manner in which the Koh-i-Noor diamond was cut, the
abolition of duelling and the final defeat of slavery. And this is not
the complete list of what he did for his adopted country. *Si monu-
mentum requiris, circumspice* has an absolutely literal meaning in his
case. Osborne and Balmoral are better known, but represent only a
small part of his artistic contribution.

Nonetheless, I have found that I cannot accept the judgement of
my mentor and inspirer, Sir Roger Fulford, who, in 1947, at Barbon
Manor, first introduced this then schoolboy to the wonders of Prince
Albert, when he wrote of him that 'in politics and affairs of state he
did his best, but ... not readily, and largely from a sense of duty'.
Although the sense of duty, as the husband of the Queen, was indeed
important, I believe that there was much more to it than that. Thus,
it is the *politician*, whose influence upon the history of his time and

on the development of the British Constitutional Monarchy is often misunderstood, and to which role he devoted by far the greatest amount of his intellect and energies, who should command the larger attention. As I have emphasised in my account, he early sought, and eventually achieved, political position of major importance – and this was not accidental. His other activities – which included the organisation of Queen Victoria's papers in the Royal Archives, to the gratitude of the researcher – must be regarded as peripheral to his essential achievements, which were political and constitutional.

As my interest in this remarkable individual grew over the past twenty years it became obvious to me that no serious new assessment could be attempted without access to the Prince Consort's formidably substantial archives in Queen Victoria's papers. Although other biographers and historians since Martin have discovered and used new and important material from the Royal Archives and other sources I felt that there could be no real justification for a new venture without such access. I am profoundly grateful to Her Majesty the Queen for graciously giving me her permission to inspect and use documents in the Royal Archives at Windsor.

Inevitably, my interpretation corrects or modifies some of the judgements of my predecessors, but this study represents my honest endeavour to fulfil Edmund Gosse's classic definition of biography as 'the portrait of a soul in his adventures through life'.

Shortly after this project began in 1976 I was elected to Parliament for Cambridge, and it has accordingly been very formidably delayed by the substantial burdens of political life, and has often had to be set aside for the paramount concerns of my generous and staunch constituents and the work of the House of Commons. It has, therefore, taken infinitely longer to research and write than anyone had expected, and I am deeply grateful to Her Majesty the Queen, the ever-helpful Royal Librarian Sir Robin Mackworth-Young and his colleagues at Windsor, and my British and American publishers, for their patience and understanding.

The list of those to whom I am indebted for much kind assistance is very substantial, but I am especially grateful to Sir Oliver and Lady Millar, Miss Jane Langton, Mr and Mrs de Bellaigue, Miss Dimond, and Miss Cuthbert who have been unvaryingly helpful.

When I contemplate the evidence of my intense activity as a Member of Parliament for a particularly demanding marginal constituency I marvel that this biography has been written at all, but it has been a solace at times of disappointment and frustration, a source of refreshment and exhilaration when current problems have

PRINCE ALBERT

ONE

PROLOGUE

The sagas of dynasties, of the rise and fall of families and confederations, remain one of the most fascinating, and yet the most perplexing, of historical phenomena. Out of apparent total obscurity there emerges an individual, or a generation linked by blood and descent, of outstanding capacity and achievement, but the light they shed is often limited to that generation and thereafter to fade, although sometimes to have a magnificent and surprising recrudescence much later. An English family such as the Cecils, with lustre in virtually every generation for three centuries, is rare; but also uncommon is the Churchill family, alternating dizzily between brilliance and obscurity. But what of a Napoleon or a Metternich? –a blaze confined exclusively to one individual, thereafter to vanish for ever, leaving the chronicler of their fortunes baffled by the mystery of the sources of their genius, and seeking in their parents and ancestors some clue to its resolution, and finding none. And yet, a clue there must be in their heredity to explain the presence of intellect and confidence which can be shaped, but not completely formed, by the physical experience of childhood and life.

In this quest the historian is too often confronted only with a procession of names. Fragments may come to him of their personalities and achievements; there may be some physical likenesses, of whose fidelity he cannot be certain; but usually there are only the simple factual records of birth, marriage, and death – tantalising shadows haunting the historian in his search, but shadows remaining.

The struggles for land, possessions and titles throughout Europe in the sixteenth and seventeenth centuries afford relish and pleasure to a limited number of students of those remote controversies. Most of the boundaries which the participants contested so fiercely have themselves vanished, as have so many of the buildings and palaces they constructed and the wealth that some acquired. The tramp of armies, the vagaries of circumstance, the frowns of fortune, new attitudes to religious passions, and the attrition of Time have, either singly or collectively, swept away those Duchies, Palatinates, Princedoms and Principalities that men sought to acquire, did acquire, and ruled after their fashion. Some titles have survived, but in a void. Out of the disparate, competitive, and sometimes warring factions in Northern Europe there were to emerge single confederated nations, of which Germany was to become the most substantial and by far the most formidable. And yet, even at the height of that sombre unity at the end of the nineteenth century, the old territorial and tribal differences remained, and defiantly remain to this day. The harsh twentieth century's terrible ravages of war, defeat, foreign occupation and division have literally transformed the physical structure of that part of Northern Europe, although thankfully not totally, but have not conquered that long-established sense of difference, of a separate local identity and loyalty, which goes back down the years and the centuries to those times when their forebears were gathering themselves under separate and competing banners, intent upon aggrandisement or simple preservation of their hard-won possessions.

In these contests the sword was less employed than the hallowed political artifices of guile, negotiation, territorial barter, and the potent weapon of dynastically and politically inspired marriage. By such methods and stratagems, skilfully deployed, did some Houses rise, and by their ineptitude at these subtle and crucial crafts of constructive statesmanship did others fade or fall. With success went reputation, influence, and loyal support. Rarely did the Princes of Germany resort to oppression or tyranny over their fiefdoms; the true measure of success was contentment and prosperity, the effective cultivation of the soil, and the profitable expansion of business and commerce.

The Napoleonic government of Germany – which constituted over a hundred small states and principalities when that ferocious Corsican carved his imperious swathe – was one important factor that made the concept of German federation conceivable. Another was Goethe, who had welcomed the advent of Napoleon, but whose entire life and endeavour was dedicated to the belief that it was through the truly artistic qualities, and which included the pursuit of scientific truth, that mankind could discover its true destiny. In one of those mysteries of history which the historian can catalogue, but cannot adequately explain, the quality of German literature, science, scholarship, and music was dominant in the first two decades of the nineteenth century.

It was one of those glittering periods that nations experience, in which there is that magical combination of circumstances, personalities, and ideas which occur so seldom, and which is impossible to recapture. The fragmented States of Germany sensed in themselves, for all their differences, something of that unity and excitement that had inspired and enthralled the English at the end of the sixteenth century. There was a new confidence, there was happiness, and there was the love of learning for its own sake. Prince Albert was the child of this amazing and wonderful surge of endeavour.

The House of Saxe-Coburg-Gotha was, by the end of the exhausting Napoleonic Wars in 1815, one of the conspicuous, if minor, survivors of those centuries of endeavour and varied fortunes. It was one of the numerous branches into which the ancient House of Wettin had been divided, and it had ruled over Meissen and the adjoining districts since the eleventh century, to which had been added Upper Saxony and Thuringia. In the sixteenth century Frederic The Wise, Elector of Saxony, was the heroic protector of Martin Luther. Of this remarkable man – described by his descendent, Prince Albert, as 'the first Protestant' – it has been written that he was 'one of those men who, without being either powerful or in any way brilliant, influence history from the respect which they inspire, and by the opportune exercise of a kindly and paternal moderation. A mild, prudent, peace-loving ruler, proud of his chapel choir, his pictures and his castles, and of the University of Wittenberg, of which he was the founder, and much occupied with pious Biblical exercises, Frederic gave to the new movement (the Lutheran Church) just that encouragement which was most necessary to carry it through the critical early stages of its growth'.[1]

The House subsequently divided into the senior, Ernestine, and junior, Albertine, branches. The victor of this division was the junior one. The Ernestine branch surrendered the Electorate of Saxony, and after the Battle of Muhlberg in 1547 the Kingdom itself. It retained several Duchies, under complex circumstances of inter-marriages and agreements and divisions and sub-divisions, which labyrinthine bargaining demonstrated by their results that these shadowy Saxe-Coburgs did not lack patience, resource, or the acquisitive urge. On the death, in 1679, of Duke Ernest The Pious, the Duchies were further divided, and the modest one of Saxe-Coburg-Saalfeld fell to the youngest son, John Ernest. It was to be patiently preserved until 1825, when Saalfeld was surrendered for the Principality of Gotha. Of his sons, Ernest succeeded him as Duke in 1764, and the youngest, Frederic, was an eminent soldier who commanded the Allied armies in the Netherlands at the beginning of the French revolutionary war – a contest which was to last far longer,

[1] H. A. L. Fisher: *A History of Europe*, p. 504.

and to be infinitely more bloody, than any had anticipated at its beginning. The Coburgs' success was, however, very limited, and was not to be remotely compared with that of the House of Hanover, which became linked to the British monarchy on the death of Queen Anne in 1714; henceforth – until, indeed, the accession of Queen Victoria (the Hanovarian monarchy limited to the male line) – the English sovereign and the Electorate of Hanover were closely joined, to the greater advantage of the latter.

Out of the shadows the Coburg family begins to emerge in clearer delineaments. Ernest Frederic died in 1800, and his son – Francis Frederic – only lived six years to enjoy his title and his possessions in Coburg and the surrounding territories. But he left behind him seven remarkable children – Ernest, born in 1784, who became Duke of Coburg in 1806 and was to be the father of Prince Albert; Ferdinand, who was to marry the heiress of the Hungarian possessions of the Kohary family, and whose son was to become King Consort of Portugal; Leopold; Sophia, who married Count Mensdorff-Pouilly; Antoinette, who married Duke Alexander of Wurtemberg; Julie, who contracted – at 15 – an unhappy marriage to the Grand Duke Constantine of Russia; and Victoire Marie Louise, who was married first, and not happily, to the Prince of Leiningen, and who was widowed with a daughter and son in 1814.

Of the sons, the most notably handsome and able was Leopold, the eighth child, born in Coburg on December 16th 1790, and a particular favourite of his strikingly beautiful and talented mother, Augusta. Ernest, although a greatly loved and affectionate heir, was unsophisticated and somewhat narrow, and was to prove a disappointment. In marked contrast, Leopold was not only highly capable and intelligent, and received an enlightened education of remarkable scope, but he also possessed a drive and ambition that were to take him to the verge of the throne of England, to the offer of the Kingdom of Greece, and to the possession of the Kingdom of the Belgians. In the process of his advancement he served as a fighting soldier, negotiated in 1807 with Napoleon, and made a considerable impression at the post-war Congress of Vienna, where the Ernestine princes received full recognition of their status as sovereign entities of the Germanic Confederation.

There were now five such entities, whose total population was barely three hundred thousand people, and the Dukedom of Coburg could not be regarded as possessing great wealth or influence, let alone power, in the post-Napoleonic settlements. Even compared with Hanover or Bavaria, the position of Coburg was humble. That of Leopold, a younger son, was particularly lowly. This situation was to be dramatically transformed by a succession of marriages which were to make the Coburg dynasty of immense influence outside its modest borders.

In 1814, Leopold, attending the victory celebrations in London, met the beautiful but deeply unhappy Princess Charlotte, daughter and only child of the Prince Regent and his estranged wife Caroline of Brunswick, and, after him, heiress to the throne of England. Their love incensed her father. Princess Charlotte was in effect incarcerated in a house in Windsor and all correspondence between the two was banned. But, through the involvement of her loving and loved uncle, the Duke of Kent, the couple was able to correspond, awaiting the time when the bitter opposition of the Prince Regent might abate.

It is a wise man who, embarking upon a career of political advancement, draws into his camp an adviser of sagacity and trust, linked to his fortunes not by avariciousness or vanity but by affection and regard. In 1814 Leopold found such a man, under improbable but deeply significant circumstances.

Christian Friedrich Stockmar was born at Coburg on August 22nd 1787, the second child, and first son, of Johann Ernest Stockmar, a successful lawyer, also well known for being highly cultivated and a bibliophile of distinction. Stockmar's mother, his son was to write, 'lives in our memories as a clever, humorous woman, a lover of poetry, and given to moralise on human affairs. She liked to put her ideas into a proverbial form, and one of her favourite sayings was, "Heaven takes care that the cow's tail shall not grow too long"', a particular saying that was a source of special amusement to Leopold when he came to know her. Stockmar was devoted to her, and valued her wisdom and basic common sense – a fact in itself which emphasises that she must have been a remarkable woman.

Stockmar's childhood was spent in and near Coburg; he was educated at the Coburg Gymnasium, and subsequently was a medical student at Wurzburg, Erlangen, and Jena. A close friend and contemporary wrote of him that 'he thus acquired his real science and art, which, even after he had given up their practical pursuit, yet remained for life the foundation of his scientific thought and critical action. Even later in life, as a statesman, he was fond of looking upon a crisis in political or domestic affairs, from his own medical point of view; always anxious to remove as fast as possible every pathological impediment, so that the healing moral nature might be set free, and social and human laws resume their restorative power. And still more clearly, perhaps, did he show his medical antecedents by the way in which he was able at once to recognise the existence of such social diseases or accidents by his power of penetrating at one glance the whole man or the whole situation of things by the help of single expressions and acts; regulating, at once, his own acts and conduct according to that diagnosis'.[1]

Stockmar himself subsequently believed that his medical training had been crucial in developing his abilities to assess people and human situations. No doubt it did, but from a relatively early age he impressed teachers and contemporaries by a fundamental common sense and practicality which later prompted Lord Melbourne to remark of him that he was 'one of the most sensible men I have ever met with'. But he was also sensitive, and he felt the humiliation of his country under Napoleonic domination very acutely. At one stage he was prepared to join an assassination attempt on Napoleon, but was quietly dissuaded by an old Prussian officer, who advised him to 'trust to the natural course of events'. Stockmar, accordingly, returned quietly to Coburg to practise medicine.

In 1812 he took the step that was to change the entire course of his life, and was to have such profound and lasting influence upon history. He founded a military hospital at Coburg, which was rapidly filled with French, Allied, and Russian sick and wounded. Typhus took possession of it, which Stockmar fought by keeping all windows and doors open, even in mid-winter, but unavailingly. At one stage, only he and one other doctor remained at their posts, and in November 1813 Stockmar himself caught the disease. He recovered by the beginning of 1814, after an acute but brief illness, and then accompanied the Saxon Ducal Contingent to the Rhine as principal physician. It was at the military hospital at Worms that the crucial episode occurred.

The hospital was full of wounded French troops when a large number of German victims arrived. The senior medical officer ordered Stockmar to give priority to the Germans. Stockmar refused, declaring that he would deal with all the wounded in strict priority, regardless of their nationality. A fierce argument ensued, in which Stockmar held his ground and won his point. Leopold heard of this event, was deeply impressed, and made his acquaintance. Thus began a relationship of vital importance to Leopold, Stockmar, and the British Monarchy.

In March 1816 Stockmar was again practising medicine in Coburg when he received an invitation from Leopold who was now in London, the Regent's hostility to his daughter's engagement having been at last modified, to become his personal physician. He

[1] Stockmar: *Memoirs*, xl–xli.

accepted, and travelled to London, which enraptured him. In his
Diary he recorded:

> The country, the houses, their arrangement, everything, espe-
> cially in the neighbourhood of London, delighted me, and so
> raised my spirits, that I kept saying to myself, 'Here you must
> be happy, here you cannot be ill'.

There are several mysteries about Stockmar, and one of them is
why, at apparently an early age, he had become dedicated to the two
great political causes of his life – the liberation and unification of
Germany, and strong links between Germany and England. The
first is explicable, but the second, which seems to have preceded the
Anglo-Prussian coalition that eventually defeated Napoleon, is more
difficult to comprehend. It was clearly not simply that Britain was
the most powerful nation in the world, because Stockmar's liberal
faith did not inspire him with admiration for the dissolute and
unpopular British Monarchy or Britain's political leadership.

Perhaps the reason was the one he put simply to Prince Albert in a
letter on August 9th, 1857: 'the English people surpass all others in
Europe in energy and vigour of character.'

And, then, whence did the liberalism come? He himself ascribed it
to his literary father and tolerant mother, and to the good-natured
and relaxed atmosphere of Coburg; but, whatever the causation, it
was central to his character, and utterly dominated his approach to
politics. In the words of his son:

> Whilst the statesmen of Europe since 1815 followed various
> arbitrary aims and tendencies, arising from narrow egotism or
> pedantry, despotically fought against the natural bent of politi-
> cal circumstances, and strove to restrain or remodel the natural
> growth of the people by artificial arrangements, he, to his latest
> breath, was devoted with his whole soul to a national liberal
> development, and worked for it with all his powers.

What was surprising about Stockmar's personality was that it
contained remarkable contrasts between periods of almost excessive
zest, gregariousness, and bubbling good humour with others of
heavy seriousness, coldness, and iron self-control. These moods were
partly the result of recurrent ill-health and a marked tendency to
hypochondria and deep depression, but physical causes alone are
unlikely to provide the full explanation. Thus, the most merry of
companions – 'it is good that you are so often ill, or there would be no
bearing your exuberant spirits', as a particularly close friend once
remarked to him – could swiftly become lugubrious and sharp-
tongued. These interludes did not, however, affect that aspect of his

character that had first impressed Leopold, and was to impress so
many others, and which can best be described as a fundamental
humanity and willingness to serve others with warmth and loyalty.
Perhaps the key to Stockmar can be found in words he wrote shortly
before he died:

'Were I now to be asked by any young man just entering into life,
What is the chief good for which it behoves a man to strive? my only
answer would be, Love and Friendship! Were he to ask me, What is a
man's most priceless possession? I must answer, The consciousness
of having loved and sought the truth – of having yearned for the truth
for its own sake! All else is either mere vanity or a sick man's dream'.

The young doctor who had stood up to his commanding officer on
behalf of the French wounded with such vehemence was the real
Stockmar, and no comprehension of this remarkable man can begin
without appreciating this basic fact. He was not solely respected by a
wide variety of serious people; he was also greatly and genuinely
loved and trusted by them. Thus, he was to become something very
considerably more than a political counsellor and *eminence grise*, but a
beloved friend and companion. It was this very unusual combination that at first puzzled so many, and was then recognised by the
most sensible as not affecting the basic decency and humanity of the
man. It was from these elements that his political liberalism essentially stemmed.

The marriage of Princess Charlotte and Prince Leopold, achieved
after so many difficulties, was one of supreme happiness, in which
Stockmar joyfully shared. Leopold quickly removed him from his
post as physician and made him his chief personal adviser and
assistant – posts he was to hold until 1831.

Princess Charlotte had known little happiness in her short life,
caught as she had been between the growing and intense bitterness
between her parents.

It was small wonder that Princess Charlotte, the only child of
the marriage, should suffer from the hatred between her
parents. She had been the pawn of each, in turn, in the ruthless
family politics. Her mother had naturally claimed her, her
father quite as naturally protested that Caroline was not fit to
look after her, and the King [George III] had determined to
control the upbringing of the child who would no doubt one day
ascend the throne. Charlotte had suffered from all three. No
childhood could have been more disturbed than the childhood of this little girl who so needed emotional stability. Her

governesses and ladies-in-waiting had been frequently changed; for years she had no friends of her own age. She had lived in growing isolation in a harsh adult world.[1]

She came to despise her parents equally, with the balance of dislike being principally placed on her father, an opinion sedulously encouraged by perhaps the most gifted yet grievously flawed man of his generation, Henry Brougham,[2] who sought in the bitter divisions between Caroline and her husband personal advancement and revenge upon a man who he believed was an implacable obstacle to his political fortunes. But Brougham, although frustrated and erratic, was a powerful and astonishingly articulate advocate. From the genuine unhappiness of her circumstances, marriage offered the only possibility of escape, and in December 1813 she had become engaged to the Prince of Orange at their first meeting, at the age of 17. Brougham is hardly an impartial witness, but his report in March 1814 that 'she agreed to the match as a mere matter of convenience and *emancipation*, caring for the Prince of Orange literally nothing' is confirmed from other sources. The news was initially received with some approval in both countries, but Charlotte soon began to entertain serious doubts, which turned out to have been wholly merited. She later told Stockmar that 'there was nothing Princely about him', but there were other practical objections. Each was, after all, heir-presumptive to their respective thrones, and neither had the slightest intention of renouncing them. What would be the situation of any sons of the union? Where would they live? Charlotte refused to contemplate living in the Netherlands, and her mother was strongly opposed to the marriage. While political negotiations continued, the unfortunate Princess gradually appreciated that the marriage was impossible, and the Parliamentary opposition became publicly hostile.

Breaking off this engagement was complicated by the fact that it had now become a State agreement, but Charlotte insisted that the marriage contract contained full security, sanctioned by Parliament, that she should never be removed or kept away from England. On this insistence the engagement foundered, although the critical event was the refusal by her father to permit her mother to attend any of

[1] Joanna Richardson: *George The Magnificent*, p. 145.
[2] A brilliant lawyer and accomplished Lord Chancellor, he was to be excluded from the 1835 Whig Government and never held public office again. In the words of Justin McCarthy: 'He thought he knew everything and could do anything better than any other man. His vanity was overweening, and made him ridiculous almost as often as his genius made him admired', (*A Short History of Our Own Times* (1910), p. 7) a terse portrait on which it is difficult to improve.

the victory celebrations in June. But it was also during these –
somewhat premature – festivities that Charlotte met Leopold. The
combination was fatal for the engagement, which was then decisively broken off.

The rage of the Regent took characteristic form. He dismissed
Charlotte's entire household, ordered her to leave Warwick House
and to go to Cranbourne Lodge, Windsor. She fled to her mother's
house in Connaught Place, only to be brought back by her uncle, the
Duke of York, and taken to Cranbourne Lodge. All correspondence
between her and Leopold was prohibited, but the Duke of Kent was
a willing intermediary. Through his hands the lovers' correspondence continued for two years until the Regent unhappily relented.
Charlotte and Leopold were deeply grateful to the man who not only
rendered this service to a girl who 'was really treated as a sort of
prisoner' in Leopold's words, but who was also, as Leopold
expressed it, 'the chief promoter of the marriage'. By January 1815
Charlotte was writing that she had 'perfectly decided and made up
my own mind to marry, and the person I have decisively fixed on is
Prince Leopold.... At all events I know that more *worse off*, more
unhappy and wretched I *cannot* be than I *am now*, and after all if I end
by marrying Prince L., I marry the *best* of all those I *have seen*, and
that is some satisfaction'.

It was from this exile that she was rescued by Prince Leopold and
love, and was married, amid continued severe parental difficulties,
on May 2nd 1816. In August they moved to Claremont House, near
Esher, in Surrey. Stockmar went with them for what he subsequently
regarded as an idyllic interlude in his life. The happiness of the
young couple, their great and growing public popularity, the feeling
of a brilliant future for the young heiress to the throne of England,
now so suddenly and magically happy and radiant, were never
forgotten by either Stockmar or Leopold, and it was in this tragically
brief period that their relationship moved into deep and abiding
friendship and trust.

The diarist Gronow has described Charlotte as 'a young lady of
more than ordinary personal attractions; her eyes were blue, and
very expressive, her hair was abundant, and of that peculiar light
brown tint which merges into the golden; in fact, such hair as the
middle-age Italian painters associate with their conceptions of the
Madonna'. Not all English perceptions of Leopold were favourable,
but there was a general view that he was a vast improvement upon
Prince William of Orange – derided as 'young frog' by Brougham –
and Lady Ilchester described him, somewhat condescendingly, as
being 'like an Englishman in all but the ease, elegance, and deference
of his manners', but she considered him cultured, handsome, and

'positively interesting'. Thus, although she quite understandably
exaggerated when she wrote that 'Indeed there is not a soul that is
not in ecstasies at my fate and choice', the fact that the necessary
legislation to naturalize Leopold passed through Parliament with
remarkable speed and approval and that he and his future wife were
voted £60,000 a year – with a lifelong sum of £50,000 for him in the
event of her death – had their significance. In short, it was generally
considered an admirable marriage, with very fair prospects.

Not surprisingly, Princess Charlotte was a difficult young woman.
Her moods were very variable, a clear sign of the insecurity of her
childhood and adolescence. Her education had been fair, but she
was very impulsive, and sometimes thoughtless. Her warmth of
personality and genuine kindness touched all who worked with her,
but existence with her brought frequent, and sometimes tumultuous
storms. 'My first impression was not favourable', Stockmar recorded, but he gradually warmed to her, and she to him. By October he
was writing that she was 'astonishingly impressionable and nervously sensitive, and the feeling excited by a momentary impression
not seldom determines at once her opinion and conduct', but he also
noted with approval that Leopold's influence on her had notably
increased her 'calmness and self-control', although 'She never for a
moment forgets the king's daughter'.

The marriage between Prince Leopold and Princess Charlotte,
with the faithful Stockmar at hand, was an event of remarkable
historical importance. Leopold was in effect learning the difficult,
and unprecedented, task of how to become a future Prince Consort of
the Queen of England – and a highly headstrong and determined
future Queen at that. Already Stockmar had begun to develop his
concept of the role of the Monarchy, which was wholly different from
that of the Royal Family, whom he collectively and individually
despised, and on whom his contemporary comments were understandably sulphurous.

The public reputation of the never greatly loved Hanoverian
dynasty was at its lowest point. King George III, long mad and
isolated, was a distant and melancholy figure, his otherwise not
unsuccessful reign irretrievably shadowed by the loss of the
American Colonies. His heir, the Prince Regent, had many qualities,
but public frugality, political wisdom, and uxoriousness were not to
be included among them. Of the Regent's brothers, the notorious
Royal Dukes, Cumberland was the most hated, and none was
esteemed. Most ominous of all, in Stockmar's unsparing analysis of
their defects, was the blatant political partisanship and meddling of
the Regent, unbuttressed by any evidence of genuine popular support. Fears of violent revolution were exaggerated, although under-

standable, but no thoughtful or perceptive observer of the English political situation in 1816 could come to the conclusion that the position of the Monarch and his Regent and successor was high in the estimation of an increasingly hostile and articulate Press and ambitious politicians.

Stockmar's bleak assessment of the condition of the English Monarchy also recognized the fact that Britain had emerged from the Napoleonic Wars as the most powerful nation in the world. In the immediate aftermath of the wars contemporaries were concerned by the impact of the short-term slump in trade, the sharp increase in the population, and the immense strains caused by the growth of towns and cities. But Britain's 'industrial revolution' had a much more positive aspect. New wealth was being rapidly created, for the first time in the island's history, from within. Foreign trade remained crucial, and agriculture prospered, but now the availability of cheap energy, the development of steam power, new expansion in technology, and the best transport system in the world – even before the coming of the revolution of the railways – had begun to transform not only the economy but the face of Britain. 'All the way along from Leeds to Sheffield it is coal and iron, and iron and coal' wrote Cobbett wonderingly in 1830. Foreign visitors were amazed by the spectacle of the Manchester spinning mills, the growth and prosperity of London, and the expansion and wealth of the industrial Midlands and the port towns.

It was a lively, individualistic, and unruly society, but although often turbulent – and especially in the period of immediate distress after 1815 – the development of wealth and employment, and the emergence of a prosperous middle class gave a ballast to the nation at a time of genuine and serious difficulty which was infinitely more crucial than the use of military force to curb disturbances or the negative reaction of politicians to the discordant calls for social and electoral reform. Historians have tended to devote more attention to the obvious evils of the process of rapid industrialisation and urbanization than to the substantial benefits of an unprecedented prosperity that gradually converted any movement towards revolution into demands for reasonable reform and change. The new wealth may have been poorly distributed, and the conditions of employment and housing often horrific, but Britain was developing with startling rapidity into the most advanced and rich nation in the world.

Stockmar rejoiced that Princess Charlotte was now detached from the evil influences of her family, and particularly that her marriage to Leopold was in such total contrast with that of her parents and the blatant womanising and extravagance of so many of her close relatives. He saw that it was this fact, above all others, that gave the

Princess her increasing popularity. 'In this house', he wrote conten-
tedly, 'reign harmony, peace and love – in short, everything that can
promote domestic happiness. My master is the best of all husbands in
all the five quarters of the globe; and his wife bears him an amount of
love, the greatness of which can only be compared with the English
national debt'. In August 1817 he wrote: 'The married life of this
couple affords a rare picture of love and fidelity, and never fails to
impress all spectators who have managed to preserve a particle of
feeling'.

Princess Charlotte herself was endearingly aware of her volatility.
To Sophie Mensdorff she wrote: 'Don't think that one is necessarily
changeable or unsteady, when one is quick and even a little carried
away at times. The enchanting voice of Leopold and, above all, its
sweetness, always unfailingly brings me back and recalls me. It is
quite certain that he is the only being in the world who would have
suited me and who could have made me happy and a good woman. It
is his celestial character, his patience, his kindness, and nothing else
would have succeeded ... In fact, he has all my confidence, he is
master of all my thoughts, of everything that I do'.

But what would the role of her husband be? To Mme de Poigne
Charlotte was characteristically extreme, but significantly so:

> She [Charlotte] spoke of the great gratitude which she owed to
> Prince Leopold for his willingness to marry the heiress to a
> kingdom. She drew with much gaiety, archness, and wit a picture
> of the 'Queen's husband', but she added with emphasis:
> 'My Leopold shall not be exposed to such humiliation, or my
> name is not Charlotte ... Should they wish to cross my will, I
> would rather renounce the throne and find a cottage where I can
> live according to the laws of nature, in submission to my
> husband. I will and cannot reign over England except upon the
> condition that he shall reign over England and myself... Yes, he
> shall be King or I will never be Queen. Do not forget what I am
> now telling you'.

Stockmar's chief concern was less with the Princess than with
Leopold, he having already discerned the obvious weaknesses of
the British Monarchy. It was markedly, and publicly, dissolute and
not respected, heedless of Parliamentary and popular reaction to its
excesses, public quarrels, and coarseness of language and behaviour.
But it was also unaware of the even greater perils of behaving as
though it were still a virtually absolute monarchy, free to involve
itself in partisan politics, and always intervening on the side of
reaction and delay. Stockmar very quickly detected the strong
stirrings of public disaffection, which could easily develop into a

genuinely revolutionary mood that would imperil not only the Monarchy but all other established institutions. Stockmar was in many senses a radical, and he was blessedly possessed of a strong social conscience, but was never a revolutionary.

Already, Stockmar had begun to develop his remarkably sophisticated and clear concept of a subtly yet substantially changed version of the British Constitution. It is not clear when this began to formulate in his mind, although it is plain that it had done so before he came to England. His view was a remarkable admixture of an idealistic view of the role of the Constitutional Monarch with a wide application, and with a thoroughly practical understanding of the peculiarly English difficulties.

Leopold proved to be a very receptive pupil and listener. As he wrote:

> Our life is arranged on principles of great moderation. Amongst other things, we do not visit Society in the capital and we have announced that we have nothing to do with [political] parties . . . The father, and especially the Queen, began to meddle in all sorts of domestic affairs, but I very courteously and respectfully declined to have it.

He had learned prudence the hard way in his relatively short life, and the fact that he had secured the eventual approval of the Regent to his engagement and marriage demonstrated his personal negotiating skills. A pragmatist, not at all devoid of ambition, he shared Stockmar's bleak assessment of the current position of the British Monarchy; and the fact that Stockmar rose so rapidly in his estimation – and that of Princess Charlotte – is a notable tribute to each of them. Stockmar was often alone, with his books and thoughts, and sometimes unhappy, but his intellectual power, combined with his common sense, warmth of personality, and political shrewdness quickly made him far more than a functionary at the small Court at Claremont. Charlotte, also, understood the strength of Stockmar's advice. 'Believe me, at a moment like this, when the country is far from being in a quiet state', she wrote to a close friend, 'a good example of morality is not only very necessary, but highly important'. Charlotte was, in the words of a contemporary observer, 'a singular Princess, but a most interesting creature'. Advised and influenced by two such remarkable and shrewd confidants, she might have become a most interesting Queen.

The news in February 1817 that the Princess was pregnant – after two rumoured but unconfirmed miscarriages[1] – excited such an

[1] Sir Jack Dewhurst: *Royal Confinements*, 110.

extent of political and public interest that it is only explicable in the context of a blind and insane King and a widely loathed heir. Princess Charlotte may have been – and was – a headstrong and opinionated young woman, but the circumstances of her childhood, and the obvious happiness and respectability of her marriage, combined to stir hopes for the future that are difficult to quantify today, but which were very substantial. Stockmar noted sardonically on August 26th 1817 that there was heavy betting on the sex of the child, that the Stock Exchange had calculated that the birth of a son would raise the funds by 6%, whereas a daughter would only increase them by 2½%, and that 'the ambassadors of the highest Powers have paid me, the poor doctor, the most friendly and obliging visits'.

Unhappily, Stockmar was not the doctor. That he was not so was largely his own decision, as he felt that a foreigner should not be the personal physician of the future Queen of England. Subsequently, he bitterly regretted his decision, while standing by his political assessment, which would have blamed any misjudgement upon 'the incapacity of the German doctor. And in my hypochondriacal state I should perhaps have myself believed in the accusations of others, and self-reproaches from within would have raised the burden of sorrow pressing upon me from without to an unbearable degree'.

The English doctors were Dr. Matthew Baillie and Dr. John Sims, with Sir Richard Croft as accoucheur. Croft and Baillie believed firmly in the current doctrine of treating pregnant women by low diets and some bleeding, which inevitably greatly weakened the Princess in her final weeks of pregnancy.[1] There were no apprehensions of an unfortunate result. Princess Charlotte experienced her first pains at seven in the evening of November 3rd 1817, yet they ceased at two in the following morning. Labour progressed very slowly throughout the next day and night, and it was not until nine o'clock on the evening of November 5th that, in Stockmar's own words, 'the Princess was delivered of a fine large dead boy'. She had been in labour for over fifty hours.

Stockmar's poignant account in the Royal Archives of subsequent events deserves to be recorded in full.

Immediately after the birth the Princess appeared quite well. The news of the death of her child had apparently not affected her. This state of apparent well-being only lasted until midnight.

[1] See F. Crainz: *An Obstetric Tragedy* for the most detailed account.

Then Croft came to my bedside, took my hand, and said the Princess was dangerously ill, the Prince alone, I must go and inform him of the state of things.

The Prince had not for three days left his wife's room for an instant, and had now, after the birth of the child, retired to rest.

I found him resigned to the death of the child, and he did not appear to understand that the state of the Princess was very serious.

In about a quarter of an hour Baillie sent to say that he wished I would see the Princess. I hesitated, but at last I went with him.

She was in a state of great suffering and disquiet from spasms in the chest and difficulty in breathing, tossed about incessantly from one side to the other, speaking now to Baillie, now to Croft.

Baillie said 'Here comes an old friend of yours'. She stretched out her left hand eagerly to me, and pressed mine twice vehemently. I felt her pulse, which was very quick; the beats now full, now weak, now intermittent. Baillie kept giving her wine constantly. She said to me, 'They have made me tipsy'.

For about a quarter of an hour I went in and out of the room, then the rattle in the throat began. I had just left the room when she called out loudly, 'Stocky! Stocky!' I went back; she was quieter, but the rattle continued.

She turned more than once over on her face, drew her legs up, and her hands grew cold. At two o'clock in the morning of November 6th 1817 – therefore about five hours after the birth of the child – she was no more.

Leopold had not been present at his wife's death, as he had been totally exhausted by his vigil, and had not appreciated how desperate the situation really was. Now, Stockmar had to gently waken him, but Leopold still did not realise that his wife had died, and it was some time before the reality came to him. Stockmar's account describes Leopold's reaction:

He thought it must be a dream; he could not believe it. He sent me once more to see about her; I came back and told him it was all over. Then he went to the chamber of death; kneeling by the bed, he kissed her cold hands, and then raising himself up, he pressed me to him and said, 'I am now quite desolate. Promise never to leave me'.

'As long as his grief found no expression, I was much alarmed for his health [but] now he is relieved by frequent tears and moans', Stockmar wrote on November 7th of his master. On November 19th he recorded of Leopold that 'he is too good, too resolute, too devout to give himself over to despair, though life seems already to have lost all value for him, and he is convinced that no feeling of happiness can ever again enter his heart'. When he was 72, Leopold wrote that he had 'never recovered the feeling of happiness which had blessed his short married life'.

The death of Princess Charlotte and her son immediately transformed the succession situation, but for Leopold and Stockmar the tragedy meant the end of a brief chapter of their lives. The unhappy Croft, consumed by remorse, committed suicide three months later, and Leopold was only narrowly dissuaded by Stockmar from returning immediately to Coburg. As Stockmar pointed out, he had established a position of influence, and the fact that Parliament had settled upon him £50,000 a year for life required that he should remain in England, at least for a while.

Princess Charlotte's parents were stricken by the death of their only child, and for a while Leopold was in high favour with the Regent. He moved to a house near Dorchester, and then to Weymouth 'because the poor Princess liked it'. Stockmar wrote of him that 'he possesses in the activity of his innate, early-developed scientific taste an admirable preservative from a dreamy absorption in his sorrow. He studies English history most perseveringly in its original sources'. Foolishly, at the height of the embittered trial for adultery of his mother-in-law Caroline in 1820 he tried to see her and enraged her husband – now King George IV – and also found that his popularity had waned considerably. He was regarded by some as a bore, by others as too ambitious. His annual Parliamentary allowance now roused criticism and his style was censured. His fall from fame and grace appeared to be complete.

Stockmar sardonically wrote that 'The death of Princess Charlotte, in opening up the prospect of succession to the throne to the younger sons of George III, had inspired them with the desire to marry'.

As the Prime Minister, Lord Liverpool, publicly put it: 'The great and general question which everyone asks himself and asks his neighbour is how will this event operate of the succession to the throne?' This was a rhetorical exaggeration, but for everyone involved in politics the death of Charlotte opened up dismal prospects. Brougham recorded that Charlotte's death had stunned the nation 'as if by an earthquake at dead of night'. 'I never looked into a blacker political horizon than is now around us', J. W. Croker reported to Sir Robert Peel immediately after Charlotte's death. The highly unpopular Regent was 55, separated but not divorced from

Queen Caroline, and his 'marriage' with Mrs. Fitzherbert was illegal: of his three married brothers the Dukes of York and Cumberland had no children while the two marriages of the Duke of Sussex – the first of which had produced a son and a daughter – had not received the sovereign's permission and, under the Royal Marriages Act, were void so far as the succession was concerned. This left the unmarried Dukes of Clarence, Kent, and Cambridge. The unpopularity of the Regent and his brothers was such that Wellington described them to Creevey as 'the damnedest millstone'.

Clarence, 52, had produced ten illegitimate children by the actress, Mrs. Jordan, but his attempts at contracting a financially advantageous marriage had been unsuccessful. Cambridge was the only one without severe financial problems, was mildly agreeable, had only demonstrated a fleeting interest in matrimony – when he had proposed to the lady who married his brother Cumberland – and was a more familiar, and certainly far more popular, figure in Hanover than in London.

Kent was 50 and had had a mistress for 27 years, but was regarded as by far the most intelligent of George III's sons after the Regent, whose very real qualities of mind and artistic sensitivities and flair were fatally obscured by his lamentable defects of character. Kent was Charlotte's 'favourite and beloved uncle', but he was grievously in debt and his military reputation was that of a hard and often merciless martinet, which brought his career to an abrupt end in 1804 when he commanded the Gibraltar garrison with such ferocity that it was regarded as intolerable even in that harsh age. But Kent's financial situation was so desperate that matrimony approved under the Royal Marriages Act, and which would at least provide him with an increased Parliamentary grant, was the only solution, and by the time of Charlotte's death he had been engaged on that quest for two years, and had proposed to – but had been rejected by – the widowed sister of Leopold, Victoire, who was 31 and had a son, Charles, aged 12, and a daughter, Feodora, who was ten. 'Nature had endowed her with warm feelings', Stockmar wrote approvingly of his master's sister, 'and she was naturally truthful, affectionate, and friendly, unselfish, full of sympathy, and generous'.

After Charlotte's death, opining that if the Duke of Clarence did 'nothing as to marrying' it would be his duty 'to take some measures' himself, Kent again mentioned Victoire's name in December 1817 to the diarist, Creevey, in Brussels 'from the circumstances of Prince Leopold being so popular with the nation'. It is not clear whether the grieving Leopold or the concerned Stockmar were deeply involved in the subsequent hurried engagement and marriage. Although Leopold strongly favoured it, little scheming from outside was in fact

required. Charlotte and Leopold's gratitude and affection for the
Duke of Kent were well known to Victoire; he had a very high
opinion of Leopold; and although she had rejected his first proposal
he had made a good impression; but there were difficulties over the
guardianship of Victoire's children, and there was no formal engagement by the time Charlotte died.

Princess Charlotte was buried with her son at Windsor on November 16th 1817; the Prince Regent made it known that he strongly
favoured his brother's marriage to Victoire, although the couple had
only met once; all difficulties were swiftly resolved, and the Duke of
Kent married Princess Victoire on May 27th 1818 at Coburg. On
July 13th there was a second ceremony at Kew Palace, in which the
Kents were joined by Clarence, who married Princess Adelaide of
Saxe-Meiningen; this was a loveless, organised affair, yet was to
prove a happy marriage, but with no surviving children. There were
miscarriages – one of twins – a daughter who lived only a few hours,
and another who died at four months. 'My children are dead',
Princess Adelaide wrote to the Duchess of Kent, 'but your child
lives, and she is mine, too'.

On May 24th 1819 the Duchess of Kent gave birth to a daughter,
Princess Victoria. In the following January the Duke died, and her
brother Leopold's fortunes had suddenly changed. Although he
wrote, and believed, that 'My fate is bound up with that of England',
new and severe tensions arose with his former father-in-law – now
the King – and it seemed expedient for him to travel widely in
Europe, to buy a house in Vienna, and to revisit Coburg, where
Louise, the wife of his brother, Ernest, Duke of Coburg, had given
birth to a second son shortly after the birth of Princess Victoria, the
Duchess having the same accoucheuse as the Duchess of Kent. He
was Princess Victoria's first cousin, and the subject of this biography.

TWO

'A Good and Useful Man'

The marriage of Prince Ernest of Saxe-Coburg, then aged thirty-three, to Princess Louise, the sixteen-year-old daughter of Duke Augustus of Saxe-Gotha-Altenburg, on July 31st 1817 at Gotha had certain similarities to that of the Duke of Kent to his sister a year later, the dominant motivations being political and dynastic, although it began glowingly. Biographers and historians have tended to take a bleak view of this handsome, extrovert, selfish and self-indulgent man, but contemporary opinions, although often morally censorious, were considerably more tolerant. Ernest's sons certainly revered him, and his mother-in-law, the formidable but warm-hearted Dowager Duchess of Gotha, does not appear to have blamed him for the eventual failure of the marriage, although it is evident that he was far from blameless. If he certainly lacked the intelligence, caution, and ambition of his younger brother, Leopold, there was a compensating warmth and spirit in his character that emerge clearly from his own letters and the memories of his two sons. His portrait is not easy to give, but the principal features are clear enough, and are not without their attractions.

His young wife is less difficult to discern. She was small in stature, widely regarded as singularly pretty, vivacious, and intelligent. She was precocious and vital, and was a sensitive and accomplished musician, a quality which her two sons – and particularly the younger – were to inherit. She was also of a romantic disposition, and there seems no doubt that she was genuinely in love with the dashing Prince Ernest. Her surviving letters give an impression of somewhat artless warmth, and her mother-in-law wrote of her immediately after the marriage that 'It is a charming, tiny being, not beautiful but very pretty, through grace and vivacity. Every feature of her face has expression; her big blue eyes often look so sad from under her black lashes, and then again she becomes a happy wild child'. To a close friend Louise wrote after her marriage 'to tell you how happy and contented and joyous I am ... If one loves an Angel, one's master and husband, one is much softer and more tender, more susceptible, and warmer also for friendship'. For Ernest's part, in spite of the fact that marriage was a necessary requirement to preserve the Protestant succession to Coburg, his affections seem to have been fully engaged.

Late in 1817 the Duke of Saxe-Coburg died, and Ernest succeeded to his titles. Their first son – Ernest – was born in Coburg at the Ehrenburg Palace on June 21st 1818. The noise of the town in her confinement distressed Louise, and her mother-in-law insisted that her next should be in the family country home, The Rosenau, some few miles outside the town. There, on August 26th 1819, the Princess gave birth to her second son, subsequently christened Francis Charles Augustus Albert Emmanuel, but known in the family from his birth as Albert.

Many years later, dark rumours circulated both in Coburg and London as to whether this child was in fact the Duke's son, and one rumour, of which Coburg had an inordinate quantity, selected the Court Chamberlain, the Jewish Baron von Meyern, as the real father. In July 1820 one of the ladies in waiting told the Duke that Louise was in love with a Count Solms, which she vehemently denied and which reduced the Count to derisive laughter. Ernest's reactions were more ominous. 'If he had been sensible', Louise wrote to a close friend, 'he would have laughed also, but he took it seriously and was angry with me. We talked about it and it all ended in tears ... Now he watches me, which he has never done before'.

The first published allegation that Albert was not the legitimate son of Duke Ernest appears to have originated in a vicious anti-Semitic work by one M. L. W. Foss, published in Berlin in 1921, which stated that 'Prince Albert, the Prince Consort, is to be described without contradiction as a half Jew', and in the following year Lytton Strachey dealt with this wholly unsubstantiated statement with characteristic felinity:

> There were scandals: one of the Court Chamberlains, a charming and cultivated man of Jewish extraction, was talked of ...'[1]

The letters from Louise's mother-in-law to her daughter, the Duchess of Kent, clearly indicate that the marriage was a happy one until Prince Albert was at least two years old, and Louise's subsequent affair with Lieutenant von Hanstein appears to have been the only actual case of her infidelity; it was certainly the only one cited in Duke Ernest's divorce petition, and, as Hector Bolitho has

[1] Strachey: *Queen Victoria*, pp. 97–98.

emphasised, 'there exists no fragment of evidence in the letters
written by either Louise's enemies or her friends to prove or even
suggest that she was unfaithful until the Princes were grown children'.[1]

There is no evidence that the marriage of Ernest and Louise was
under any serious strain at this time until the rumours about Solms
in 1820. But Ernest's suspicions received justification subsequently
when he discovered that she did have a lover, a young army officer,
Alexander von Hanstein, on which discovery he demanded a separation, and despite popular clamour for a reconciliation she left
Coburg for ever in September 1824, when Albert was five years old.
Louise neither admitted nor denied the charge of adultery, but there
was a divorce in 1826, after which she immediately married von
Hanstein, who had become Count von Polzig.

Although Louise was sixteen years younger than Duke Ernest,
and had a reputation, possibly, but not certainly, justified, for being
flirtatious, no contemporary account that survives accuses her of
being promiscuous, and her love for von Hanstein was clearly real.
Whether Ernest's own conduct with other women was as bad as
some have claimed, and his frequent absences from Coburg and
neglect of his wife gave her justification for her loneliness and
infidelity, is a matter on which it is impossible to adjudicate. What
does appear clear is that the allegations about the doubtful paternity
of the second son circulated only after Louise's subsequent liaison
with von Hanstein was exposed, and developed when Albert's
character grew into a very different one from that of his elder
brother. Accordingly, everything points to the emphatic conclusion
that Albert was indeed the second son of Ernest, Duke of Coburg,
and the rumours that gave him a Jewish father and a promiscuous
mother may be safely rejected. Albert was not unaware of these
rumours, which later became widely current in London and were
crudely hinted at in hostile political tracts. Although he was to
become sternly censorious of sexual licence, it was not with the glum
intolerance of which he has been accused. One who came to know
him well subsequently wrote that the presence of what he regarded
as evil 'depressed him, grieved him, horrified him. His tolerance
allowed him to make excuses for the vices of individual men; but the
evil itself he hated'. His lifelong devotion to his mother's memory
and name was one evidence of this tolerance.

Prince Albert loved his parents deeply, and always honoured and
treasured them. After the death of his father in 1844 he and Ernest
had his mother's body brought back to Coburg to rest in the same
mausoleum as that of his father, which the brothers had had built

[1] *Albert The Good*, pp. 17–18.

specially for them. This action has not often been remarked upon by Albert's biographers; its significance may be regarded as very considerable. It may also be considered significant in any assessment of Duke Ernest's own reputation, which has been somewhat harshly portrayed on occasions as that of a debauched and odious profligate. His elder son was to write of him that 'he took the keenest interest in anything and everything which concerned our bringing up. A more beautiful bond between a father and his sons it would be difficult to find'. All the evidence justifies this tribute. Duke Ernest's inadequacies and failings were many, but he received and always held the devotion of his sons.

The Duchess of Gotha wrote joyfully to the Duchess of Kent on August 27th 1819 from The Rosenau:

The date will of itself make you suspect that I am sitting by Louischen's bed. She was yesterday morning safely and quickly delivered of a little boy. Siebold, the accoucheuse, had only been called at three, and at six the little one gave his first cry in this world, and looked about like a little squirrel with a pair of large black eyes.[1] At a quarter to seven I heard the tramp of a horse (in the courtyard at Ketschendorf). It was a groom, who brought the joyful news. I was off directly, as you may imagine, and found the little mother slightly exhausted, but *gaie et dispos*. She sends you and Edward [the Duke of Kent] a thousand kind messages.

Louise is much more comfortable here than if she had been laid up in town. The quiet of this house, only interrupted by the murmuring of the water, is so agreeable. But I had many battles to fight to assist her in effecting her wish. Dr. Müller found it inconvenient. The Hof-Marshal thought it impossible – particularly if the christening was to be here also. No one considered the noise of the palace at Coburg, the shouts of the children, and the rolling of the carriages in the streets ...

How pretty the *May Flower* [Victoria] will be when I see it in a year's time. Siebold cannot sufficiently describe what a dear little love it is. *Une bonne fois*, adieu! Kiss your husband and children.

> Augusta.

Albert was christened in the Marble Hall at The Rosenau on September 19th, the address being delivered by Pastor Genzler

[1] They were in fact blue.

(whose daughter later married Albert's tutor, Florschütz) and who
had also officiated at the marriage of the Duke and Duchess of Kent.
'The good wishes with which we welcome this infant as a Christian,
as one destined to be great on earth, and as a future heir to
everlasting life, are the more earnest when we consider the high
position in life in which he may one day be placed, and the sphere of
action to which the will of God may call him'.

Louise wrote of her children on May 22nd 1820:

> Ernest est bien grand pour son âge, vif et intelligent. Ses grands
> yeux noirs pétillent d'esprit et de vivacité ... Albert est superbe
> ... d'une beauté extraordinaire; a des grands yeux bleus, une
> toute petite bouche – un joli nez – et des fossettes à chaque joue
> – il est grand et vif, et toujours gai. Il a trois dents, et malgré
> qu'il n'a que huit mois, il commence à marcher.
>
> In July, 1820: Albert est toujours beau, gai et bon, et a sept
> dents. Il marche déjà, quelquefois tout seul, et dit 'papa et
> maman'; n'est-ce pas un petit prodige pour dix mois?

When Albert was two:

> Albert adore son oncle Léopold, ne le quitte pas un instant, lui
> fait des yeux doux, l'embrasse à chaque moment, et ne se sent
> pas d'aise que lorsqu'il peut être auprès de lui ... Il est
> charmant de taille, et yeux bleus. Ernest est très fort et robuste,
> mais pas la moitié si joli. Il est beau, et a des yeux noirs.

A few months later:

> Mes enfants ont faits les délices de leurs aieuls. Ils sont
> beaucoup et deviennent très amusants. L'aîné surtout parait
> avoir de l'esprit, et le petit captive tous les coeurs par sa beauté
> et sa gentillesse.

From an early age, Louise made Albert her particular favourite,
and as their tutor, Florschütz, later recorded:

> Endowed with brilliant qualities, handsome, clever, and witty,
> possessed of eloquence and of a lively and fervid imagination,
> Duchess Louise was wanting in the essential qualifications of a
> mother. She made no attempt to conceal that Prince Albert was
> her favourite child. He was handsome and bore a strong
> resemblance to herself. He was, in fact, her pride and glory. The
> influence of this partiality upon the minds of the children might
> have been most injurious.

Albert was not as physically strong as he appeared. He had a slow
and somewhat feeble pulse, low blood pressure, and even as a child

fatigued easily. He was to develop into a boy, and then into a man, of quite remarkable application and intellectual energy in what was in reality a weak physical frame.

In 1839 Ernest wrote that 'from our earliest years we have been surrounded by difficult circumstances of which we were perfectly conscious and, perhaps more than most people, we have been accustomed to see men in the most opposite positions that human life can offer. Albert never knew what it was to hesitate. Guided by his own clear sense he always walked calmly and steadily on the right path'.

Queen Victoria later wrote of her (and Albert's) grandmother, the Dowager Duchess of Coburg ('Grandmother Coburg'):

> She was a most remarkable woman, with a most powerful, energetic, almost masculine mind, accompanied with great tenderness of heart and extreme love for nature ... She was adored by her children, particularly by her sons; King Leopold being her great favourite.
>
> She had fine and most expressive blue eyes, with the marked features and large nose inherited by most of her children and grandchildren. Both the Prince [Albert] and his brother were exceedingly attached to her, and they lived much with her in their younger days.

It was the Dowager Duchess' great ambition that Albert – interestingly, not Ernest – should marry his cousin, Victoria, but she died when Albert was twelve years old.

Of all her children, Leopold was the favourite, and he subsequently wrote of her that 'she was a woman in every respect distinguished; warm-hearted, possessing a most remarkable understanding, and she loved her grandchildren most tenderly'.

The Dowager Duchess kept her daughter, the Duchess of Kent, fully informed of the Coburg cousins, particularly about Albert. 'He is not a strong child' (February 10th 1821); 'Little Alberinchen, with his large blue eyes and dimpled cheeks, is bewitching, forward, and quick as a weasel. He can already say everything. Ernest is not nearly as pretty ... ' (July 11th 1821); 'Leopold is very kind to the boys. Bold Alberinchen drags him constantly about by the hand. The little fellow is the pendant to the pretty cousin [Victoria]; very handsome, but too slight for a boy; lively, very funny, all good nature, and full of mischief ... ' (August 11th 1821).

The Duchess of Saxe-Gotha-Altenburg ('Grandmother Gotha'), the boys' step-maternal grandmother (the second wife of Duke Augustus who was father of Louise) was equally devoted and beloved. In the summer of 1822 the boys stayed with her when their

parents were away. Their mother wrote in their album that 'Ernest is
very much grown. He is not as handsome as his father, but he will
have his good figure. Albert is much smaller than his brother, and
lovely as a little angel with his fair curls'.

Grandmother Coburg recorded on February 14th 1823:

> The little boys have interrupted me, for you know how little one
> can do during such a visit. A couple of boys always find means
> to be noisy, which, and the loud talking, calls for many a
> scolding from grandmama. They are very good boys on the
> whole, very obedient, and easy to manage. Albert used to rebel
> a little sometimes, but a grave face brings the little fellow to
> submit. Now he obeys me at a look.

She wrote to the Duchess of Kent on May 9th 1823:

> The boys are very wild, and Ernest flies about like a swallow ...
> Do not yet tease your little puss with learning. She is so young
> still.

In 1823 the boys – aged five and not yet four respectively – were
put under the care and tuition of Herr Christoph Florschütz of
Coburg.

This development was the direct result of the intervention of
Stockmar, whom Leopold had asked to report upon the young
Princes and their education. Stockmar had gone to Coburg, conducted his investigation, and reported favourably on the boys. He was
struck by the fact that although Albert was aggressive and
self-confident with other children in their games, and particularly
when playing soldiers, he was strangely quiet and quick to cry at
home, a difference which Stockmar considered 'very marked'. He
became convinced that the boys needed a male tutor, and Herr
Florschütz, tutor to Alexander and Arthur Mensdorff, youngest sons
of Emmanuel, Count of Mensdorff-Pouilly and his wife Sophie, sister
of the Duchess of Kent and Leopold, was engaged. It was an inspired
choice, one of Stockmar's most remarkable, even by his standards.

Apparently Albert had disliked being under the care of women,
and was happy at the event, despite his long-standing affection for
his nurse, Miss Müller. Grandmother Gotha, solicitous for their
health ('Albert being so subject to attacks of croup') opposed the
development, but was swiftly reconciled to the conscientious and
devoted Florschütz.

After Louise left Coburg for von Hanstein in 1824 she never saw
her children again, and died seven years later. 'Leaving my children
was the most painful thing of all', she wrote. 'They have whooping
cough and said, "Mamma cries because she has to go now, when we

are ill". The poor lambs, God bless them. The Duke was friendly towards me. We came to an understanding and parted with tears, for life. I am more sorry for him than for myself'. There were no subsequent contacts of any kind between her and her sons, which was part of the divorce agreement. Her stepmother wrote: 'I told her that it was impossible for them to forget their mother, but that they were not told how much she suffered, for this would make them suffer also'. 'The Prince never forgot her', Queen Victoria later wrote, 'and spoke with much tenderness and sorrow of his poor mother, and was deeply affected in reading, after his marriage, the accounts of her sad and painful illness. One of the first gifts he made to the Queen was a little pin he had received from her when a little child'. Florschütz subsequently recorded that when the Duchess left Coburg 'there was no cheerfulness or happiness here'.

With singular heartlessness, Duke Ernest left Coburg immediately after his wife's departure for a shooting holiday with Leopold and remained away for his birthday (January 6th), to the dismay and sadness of his sons. So powerful was Prince Albert's desolation at this double separation that it remained vivid to Florschütz forty-five years later.

Grandmother Gotha wrote to Duke Ernest on July 27th 1831:

> The sad state of my poor Louise bows me to the earth ... The thought that her children had quite forgotten her distressed her very much. She wished to know if they even spoke of her. I answered her that they were far too good to forget her; that they did not know of her sufferings as it would grieve the good children too much.

When Louise died of cancer, Grandmother Gotha wrote to the Duke:

> This also I have to endure, that that child whom I watched over with much love should go before me. May God soon allow me to be reunited to all my loved ones ... It is a most bitter feeling that that dear house [of Gotha] is now quite extinct.

Thus the brothers, deprived of their mother, grew up at The Rosenau. Florschütz later recollected the great affection between them – which was to endure despite many vicissitudes – but also recorded:

> Even in infancy, however, a marked difference was observable in their characters and dispositions. This difference naturally became more apparent as years went on, and their separate paths in life were definitively marked out for them; yet far from

leading at any time to any, even momentary, estrangement, it seems rather to have afforded a closer bond of union between them.

Florschütz found Albert an eager pupil – 'to do *something* was with him a necessity' – and an enthusiastic athlete, although at this time 'he was rather delicate than robust, though already remarkable for his powers of perseverance and endurance'.

All accounts of Albert's early life, contemporary and subsequent, speak glowingly of Florschütz. He was only twenty-five when he assumed his responsibilities, but had already established himself in the family and thereby had come to the attention of Stockmar. He spoke English fluently, so that his charges became familiar with it from a very early age. An admirable teacher, exceptionally well read, and with a deep interest in science as well as literature and languages, he encouraged the boys to widen their own interests. Both were fascinated by natural history, and Florschütz arranged for regular instruction by an expert; their collection of rock specimens was later established as the Ernst-Albrecht Museum, and is maintained to this day. Albert's love of music was also encouraged, and Florschütz became a guide, mentor, and companion as well as tutor, and his influence upon Albert was immense and beneficial.

Albert's Journal in 1825 recorded his daily life with considerable vivacity and warmth (he was not yet six). There are frequent references to tears: 'When I awoke this morning I was ill. My cough was worse. I was so frightened that I cried' (January 23rd 1825); 'we recited, and I cried because I could not say my repetition, for I had not paid attention . . . I was not allowed to play after dinner, because I had cried whilst repeating' (January 26th); 'During our walk I told the Rath [Florschütz] a story. When I came home I played with my companions. But I had left all my lesson-books lying about in the room, and I had to put them away: then I cried, but afterwards I played again' (February 20th); 'I cried at my lesson today, because I could not find a verb: and the Rath pinched me, to show me what a verb was. And I cried about it' (February 28th); 'I wrote a letter at home. But because I had made so many mistakes in it, the Rath tore it up, and threw it into the fire. I cried about it' (March 26th). But there are happy references to expeditions and walks, and trips with 'dear Papa', including a visit to Ketschendorf where 'I drank beer, and ate bread and butter and cheese'. On April 10th he recorded: 'I had another fight with my brother: that was not right'.

His tutor later wrote that 'In his early youth [childhood] Prince Albert was very shy, and he had long to struggle against this feeling. He disliked visits from strangers, and at their approach would run to the furthest corner of the room, and cover his face with his hands; nor was it possible to make him look up, or speak a word. If his doing so was insisted upon, he resisted to the utmost, screaming violently'. At a children's fancy dress party, when he was five, Albert was dressed 'as a little Cupid' and urged to dance, but adamantly refused, 'and his loud screams were heard echoing through the rooms'. What was regarded by others as obstinacy and aloofness was rightly discerned by Florschütz as a profound shyness and unease with strangers, while with those he knew and trusted 'the distinguishing characteristics of the Prince's disposition were his winning cheerfulness and his endearing amiability. His disposition was always to take a cheerful view of life, and to see its best side. He was fond of fun and practical jokes'.

Grandmother Gotha visited Coburg in June 1824, and recorded:

> The dear children are, thank God, perfectly well, and as happy and merry as one could wish. They delight so much in driving and walking about that, if one were to ask them, they would say they never wished to go home.

In July 1825, when the boys were staying with her:

> They had a very simple and regular life, and are out in the open air as much as possible. They are so good and gentle, and give me great pleasure ... The 'Rath' really does all he can for them, and you have a real treasure in him.

She wrote to the Duchess of Kent, on August 17th 1826, that she had noted a report in the papers that King George IV had seen Princess Victoria at Virginia Water: 'The little monkey must have pleased and amused him. She is such a pretty, clever child ... Alberinchen looks rather pale this summer. He is delicate; the heat tries him, and he grows fast'.

After the extension of the Duchy, the pattern of the boys' lives – centred in Coburg in the winter and The Rosenau in the summer – was changed in that Gotha and Reinhardsbrunn were added to their regular homes. But The Rosenau was their true home, 'the place he most loves', as his future wife subsequently wrote in her Journal. She also described the frugal circumstance of their childhoods: 'It is quite up in the roof, with a tiny little bedroom on each side, in one of which they both used to sleep with Florschütz their tutor. The view is beautiful, and the paper is still full of holes from their fencing; and the very same table is there on which they were dressed when little'.

Grandmother Gotha wrote to the Duke, after a visit by the children, on January 30th 1828: 'I cannot say enough in praise of their good behaviour, and I shall feel the separation from them very much

... Do not let them take much medicine, nor hear much about their health; it only makes them nervous. A well-regulated diet and mode of life is much better than medicine, and as much air as possible'.

Arthur Mensdorff wrote in 1863 that: 'Albert, as a child, was of a mild, benevolent disposition. It was only what he thought unjust or dishonest that could make him angry ... Albert thoroughly understood the naïveté of the Coburg national character, and he had the art of turning people's peculiarities into a source of fun. He had a natural talent for imitation, and a great sense of the ludicrous, either in persons or things; but he was never severe or ill-natured ... '

The portrait that we receive from all quarters – and including Albert's own notes, letters, and fragmentary Journal – is that of a happy and privileged childhood. It is, accordingly, strange to find his eldest daughter, Princess Victoria, writing many years later that 'Papa always said that he could not bear to think of his childhood, he had been so unhappy and miserable, and had many a time wished himself out of this world', as this is in complete contrast with all contemporary evidence, and Prince Albert himself later told his wife – perhaps somewhat tactlessly – that his childhood was the happiest period of his existence.

No doubt there was some loneliness, and periods of unhappiness that seem inseparable from all childhoods, and particularly one in a broken home. But the brothers were devoted to each other, the grandmothers were close and dedicated to them, and Duke Ernest emerges from all contemporary accounts as a genial, affectionate and indulgent father, whose enjoyment of his sons' company severely interrupted Florschütz's careful plans for their education. Neither the Gotha nor the Coburg grandmothers found fault with Albert, and this biographer is baffled by references in biographies of Queen Victoria to Prince Albert's 'stressful and unhappy childhood' and 'the traumatic experiences of his youth', which 'left him permanently wounded'. The loss of a mother under particularly sad circumstances obviously left its mark, and the gap could not be filled wholly by the delightful and loving grandmothers, but the gaiety and cheerfulness of the boy – to which so many contemporary accounts refer – belie these portraits of misery.

Grandmother Coburg wrote to the Duchess of Kent, on March 23rd 1829, that 'Ernest is beginning to grow handsome ... Albert is very good-looking, very clever, but is not so strong as his brother'. Again, after the death of George IV in 1830, and very shortly before her own death:

God bless Old England, where my beloved children live, and where the sweet blossom of May may one day reign! May God yet for many years keep the weight of a crown from her young head! and let the intelligent clever child grow up to girlhood before this dangerous grandeur devolves upon her!'

Leopold became King of the Belgians in 1831. Leopold owed his success as the British candidate for the throne of the somewhat artificial and highly divided nation principally to British dislike of the King of Holland, coupled with the realisation that the failure of the concept of a United Netherlands under the King's sovereignty was a definitive political reality. When a French candidate – the Duc de Nemours – entered the lists the British went firmly for Leopold's candidature, and King William IV's doubts about Leopold were far less powerful than his detestation and profound suspicion of the French. An acute European crisis passed, and by the spring of 1833 the independence of the new state of Belgium was assured by the major Powers. It was not a particularly glittering position to have achieved in some respects, but a significant advancement for a younger son of the small House of Coburg. In the summer of 1832 Ernest and Albert visited him at Brussels, which, according to Florschütz, made a great impression upon them. In the autumn of that year their father remarried, to Princess Mary of Würtemburg, but not happily, and her relations with her stepsons were distant.

Prince Albert was now marked by his tutor and his uncle Leopold as an exceptionally advanced, serious, and capable boy, with a remarkable range of interests and formidable self-discipline. He demonstrated, Florschütz noted, 'rather too strong a will of his own, and this disposition came out at times even in later years. Surpassing his brother in thoughtful earnestness, in calm reflection and self-command, and evincing, at the same time, more prudence in action; it was only natural that his will should prevail'. Albert wrote in his Journal when he was eleven that 'I intend to train myself to be a good and useful man'.

At the age of fourteen he drew up his own work programme. One day's regime was as follows:

6 – 7	Translations from the French
7 – 8	Repetition and Preparation in History
8 – 9	Modern History
10 – 11	Ovid
11 – 12	English
12 – 1	Mathematics
6 – 7	French
7 – 8	Latin Composition

The Prince's education was particularly strong in languages, history, the natural sciences, and music, with rather less attention to

the classics and mathematics. It was also significant that the programme included five hours specifically set aside for outdoor activities and recreation.

The reality, however, was not as Prince Albert or his tutor had
wished, and the principal difficulties were caused by Duke Ernest,
now 'much occupied with his new and splendid possession of Gotha'
in the words of Leopold, but also delighting in the company of his
sons. The trouble was that he insisted on their company for breakfast
– and later for lunch – when he was staying in Coburg, and the boys
were at The Rosenau. As Roger Fulford has written so succinctly
about Duke Ernest, he 'was not a pleasant character, for he was fired
with political ambition which he lacked the capacity to realise and in
personal habits he was selfish and extravagant'.[1]

As he grew older Albert began to realise more clearly the deficiencies of his father, which were to be inherited to the full by Ernest, but
his devotion to both of them was total and unwavering, even when
they strained his patience greatly in later life. But Duke Ernest's
devotion to his sons meant that breakfast was taken between nine
and ten with the Duke whenever he was at home, and the travelling
involved often meant that, as Florschütz complained, 'the greater
part of the forenoon was inevitably wasted, to the interruption of
useful studies and occupations. The Duke, however, was indifferent
to this, and we can only wonder that the Princes, notwithstanding,
retained their love for study'. Albert, also, was highly impatient at
these interruptions in spite of his affection for his father, and Queen
Victoria later wrote that he had often referred to this dislocation of
his studies. Some of Prince Albert's biographers have taken his plans
and Florschütz's schedule rather too literally, describing it as
'relentless', 'unvarying', and 'inhumanly severe', when in fact it was
not excessive in terms of hours, and was varied with other activities,
holidays, and companionship with other boys of the area. Furthermore, Albert loved Coburg, but particularly The Rosenau, and the
glorious countryside around it, which he subsequently called 'the
paradise of our childhood'. That countryside has now become
somewhat ravaged, but it is not difficult to recreate in one's mind
how beautiful it must have been. On The Rosenau itself, judgement
may be more critical. 'A lovely spot', as one English visitor recorded,
' – but the house, oh, so dreary and uncomfortable!'

Albert, who rose very early, also always retired early. In Florschütz's words: 'An irresistible feeling of sleepiness would come over
him in the evening, which he found difficult to resist even in after life;
and even his most cherished occupations, or the liveliest games, were
at such times ineffectual to keep him awake. If prevented from going

[1] Fulford, *The Prince Consort*, p. 21.

to bed, he would suddenly disappear, and was generally found sleeping quietly in the recess of the window – for repose of some kind, though but for a quarter of an hour, was then indispensable'.

After he was eleven the programme became even more difficult to maintain, as the brothers regularly lunched with their father at three in the afternoon ('the place of dinner being as uncertain as that of the breakfast', as Florschütz sourly commented), and the time for regular lessons seldom exceeded five hours a day for six days a week, hardly an exceptionally severe regime, but interesting in its careful planning, balance, and Florschütz's insistence on time set aside for 'bodily exercises, also regulated at fixed hours, and amusement'. Although a carefully trained and excellent shot, Albert demonstrated little real interest in the great shooting expeditions so beloved by his father and the German gentry. The exercise, fresh air, and company appealed to him far more than the actual sport, and Florschütz was pleased that 'The active life which the Prince thus led in the open air strengthened alike the mind and the body. His thirst for knowledge was kept alive and indulged, while under the influence of his bodily exercises he grew up into an active and healthy boy'. In fact his looks rather belied the reality; although never seriously unwell, his constitution was not a strong one, and his surviving grandmother was constantly concerned about the effects of fatigue upon him, as, subsequently, was his wife.

Florschütz also believed very much in what he called 'self-imposed' studies, at which Albert was particularly assiduous. The total of five hours a day formal learning was, accordingly, only a part of the whole.

Albert was devoted, and deeply beholden, to the kind and critical Florschütz, who was the dominating and beneficent influence of his childhood and early youth. These emotions were warmly returned. Many years later Florschütz wrote that Albert's outstanding qualities were 'his eager desire to do good and to assist others; the other, the grateful feeling which never allowed him to forget an act of kindness, however trifling, to himself'. Stockmar, characteristically, was much more critical of the boy and doubted the reality of his application and constancy: 'He has the same mobility and readiness of mind [of his mother]', he severely noted, 'and the same intelligence, the same over-ruling desire and talent for appearing kind and amiable to others, the same tendency to espiéglerie, to treat things and people in the same amusing fashion, the same habit of not dwelling long on a subject'.

It was at Albert's specific request that he and Ernest were confirmed together on Palm Sunday (April 12th) 1835. It was an elaborate event, in which the two brothers had their public examination in the Giants' Hall of the castle in Coburg on the 11th, in the presence of their father, Grandmother Gotha, relations, ministers, officials, and invited members of the public – but in the conspicuous absence of their step-mother. 'The dignified and decorous bearing of the Princes', it was recorded, 'their strict attention to the questions, the frankness, decision, and correctness of their answers, produced a deep impression on the numerous assembly'. The actual ceremony was conducted by Pastor Genzler, and was followed by a special service in Coburg Cathedral, and on April 13th there was a grand banquet of celebration in the Giants' Hall, when Florschütz was presented with a diamond ring in tribute to his devotion to the Coburg sons.

This event was more dominated by Albert's devotion to his brother than to his actual piety. He was never, as a child or a man, excessively interested in religion, and was totally indifferent to abstract theology. He recorded Church quarrels in Bonn with a refreshingly sardonic amusement, and the subsequent endeavours to portray him as possessed of a profoundly religious character were categorised by his brother as for public consumption, and 'suited him certainly even less than it did me' – which is perhaps to take a good point too far, although an excellent example of what Roger Fulford describes as 'that gentle malice which belies his very dull book of Memoirs'.[1] Leopold took the view that 'the real spirit of Christianity demands that man shall work every moment during life', with which interpretation Albert was well content. His faith was real enough, and Florschütz described him as 'instinctively devout'; certainly he had little interest in the formalities of religion, and his intellectual scepticism was to be fortified by the influence of Karl Gottlieb Bietschneider, an eminent and highly controversial critical theological scholar, at University. His subsequent composi- tions – and particularly his enchantingly colourful and warm *Jubilate in A* – testify to the minimal impact of the somewhat glum Pro- testantism in which he was confirmed. One detects in the tributes to his piety after his death by his contemporaries and friends, under the virtual command of Queen Victoria, an exaggerated note.

If formal religion was of relatively small significance, it is difficult to understand Prince Albert without an appreciation of the deep importance of music in his life and personality. This was partly as a result of family influences. Leopold was extremely knowledgeable, and was regarded as a singer of professional quality, while Ernest's coarseness of character was partly redeemed by his compositions, of which one was an opera that enjoyed considerable popular and

[1] Fulford, op. cit., p. 28

critical success in Germany. For his part, Albert's interest and pleasure had been attracted early; he was a genuine scholar as well as a gifted organist, and his own compositions – especially his *Jubilate in A*, but also his *Chorale*, the tune now generally known as *Gotha* – demonstrate not only his real gifts as a musician, with much tenderness and warmth, which were perhaps seen to their best effect in his *Lieder und Romanzen*, of which he composed twenty-six, but also that gaiety in his personality which his family and close friends knew, but which was less obvious in many of his relationships with strangers, and particularly English strangers. After his marriage he was to obtain special pleasure from planning concerts of his favourite works and most esteemed performers, and a contemporary subsequently wrote that:

> They seemed to take him into a dream-world, in which the anxieties of his life were for the moment forgotten. He would often stand apart in the Drawing Room, while some great work of Beethoven, Mozart, or Mendelssohn was being performed, rapt in reverie, but with a look on his face, which those could best understand, and most loved to see, who knew by it the pressure on a brain often too severely taxed was for the moment removed.

The confirmation of the Princes was followed by a visit to Berlin with their father to be presented formally at the Prussian Court, and thence on a tour to Dresden, Prague, Vienna, and Budapest. Grandmother Gotha was concerned that the schedule was too intense and the travelling too constant, and Albert wrote to his new step-mother that 'It requires a giant's strength to bear all the fatigue we have had to undergo. Visits, parades, rides, déjeûners, dinners, suppers, balls, and concerts follow each other in rapid succession, and we have not been allowed to miss any of the festivities'.

To the Director of the High School at Coburg Albert wrote on February 5th 1836:

> In spite of all the distractions of our life here at Gotha, in spite of innumerable visits, in spite of the howling of the wind and storm, in spite of the noise of the guard under our windows, I have at length completed the framework of my Essay on the Mode of Thought of the Germans, and I send it with this for your perusal, begging you not to judge too severely the many faults which your critical eye will doubtless discover in it.
>
> You have my work without head or tail. I have sketched no form of introduction or conclusion, thinking it unnecessary, for my desire is to trace through the course of History the progress

of German civilization down to our own times ... The conclusion will contain a retrospect of the shortcomings of our time, with an appeal to every one to correct these shortcomings in his own case, and thus to set a good example to others.

On March 12th he reported that 'the work on the History of German Literature gets on but slowly, owing to our Gotha engagements'. 'It is painful', he wrote from Brussels in December, 'to see the mean idea which the French and Belgians, and even the English, have of our German literature.'

The position of King Leopold in the childhoods of Princess Victoria and Prince Albert was crucial. To each he was a trusted and loved uncle, to Victoria virtually a surrogate father, and his accession to the throne of Belgium had added not only to his formal position but to his glamour and attractiveness. The fact that he was at that time disliked and distrusted by the British Royal Family did not diminish his stature in her eyes, and always there was the influence and presence of Stockmar, in whom particularly Princess Victoria had begun to place much trust in a difficult childhood surrounded by swirling jealousies, personal antipathies, and political machinations. For some time Leopold had thought seriously of Victoire Kohary as a possible future wife for Albert, and it was only gradually that the idea of attempting to arrange a marriage with the eventual heiress to the English throne began to develop.

It was natural that such an ambition should have long been harboured by the children's mutual grandmother, the Duchess of Coburg, but it is wholly excessive to state that 'The plan of a marriage between the two first cousins existed from the moment of Prince Albert's birth ... Marriage to Princess Victoria was to be his vocation and he accepted it, never considering anything else'.[1] There is no evidence whatever that Albert was even faintly aware of the possibility until he was nearly seventeen, and it is the fact that Leopold, although concerned about the uncertain prospects of the younger son of the Duke of Coburg with his little reasonable hope of succession to any title or possessions, and who was genuinely devoted to his English niece, was only slowly drawn even to the possibility of a marriage between Albert and Victoria. Mythology is a strong barrier to the biographer, but, however frequently this particular myth has been repeated, the facts are that Prince Albert and Princess Victoria did not even meet until they were both

[1] C. Woodham-Smith: *Queen Victoria*, p. 37.

seventeen, and that although Leopold did eventually arrange this meeting the results, as will be related, were not totally successful.

It should also be remembered that there was no inevitability about Princess Victoria's succession to the English throne until early 1830, and Leopold was on very bad terms with the British Royal Family. He kept his links open with Kensington Palace, and particularly with Princess Victoria, for whom his deep devotion was warmly returned, but even here the bitter disputes at Kensington Palace were as disagreeable to Leopold as they were labyrinthine. Leopold, moreover, was now a Continental monarch with more and substantial responsibilities, and the possibility of capturing the very considerable Kohary fortunes for the family was a very alluring one.

These ambitions were changed by two factors. The first was that it became gradually clear that Princess Victoria was virtually certain to become Queen of England, and was by far the greatest prize in Europe. The second was that Stockmar, whose experience with Leopold and Charlotte had had such a profound influence on him, had maintained his English political contacts very thoroughly and had developed a very real affection and admiration for England, where he was well-liked, respected, and taken seriously by intelligent politicians. As he wrote to Prince Albert in 1854:

> I love and honour the English Constitution from conviction. I think that, with judicious handling, it is capable of realizing a degree of legal civil liberty which leaves a man free scope to think and act as a man. Out of its bosom singly and solely has sprung America's free constitution in all its present power and importance, in its incalculable influence upon the social condition of the whole human race; and in my eyes the English Constitution is the foundation-, corner-, and cope-stone of the entire political civilization of the human race, present and to come.

Such emotions effectively countered King Leopold's disgust with the Royal Family, and also played upon his feelings of responsibility for his fatherless niece and motherless nephew. Leopold was a schemer, and a calculating man, but he was much more than this. A marriage between Albert and Victoire Kohary was straightforward *Realpolitik*; a union between Prince Albert and Princess Victoria was a very different matter, and it was only gradually that Leopold became convinced of its feasibility. He also recognised that although Prince Albert might be relatively docile and be persuaded by his sense of duty, Princess Victoria was a quite different proposition.

· · ·

The childhood of Princess Victoria was not happy. Her father had died on January 23rd 1820, Stockmar having been summoned by the Duchess of Kent too late to do little more than console the distraught widow. Kent had been, as Stockmar wrote, 'a chivalrous husband', but he died deeply in debt. Leopold had to come to the rescue of his sister and niece, as the new King George IV – the Prince Regent succeeded his father nine days after the death of the Duke of Kent – was not only indifferent to their fate but was actively anxious for them to leave the country. Leopold relieved them from hopeless penury, but their circumstances were, and remained, difficult and humiliating, while Leopold received little commendation for his generous assistance either from his sister or Parliament. Meanwhile, the ambitious and avaricious Captain John Conroy, the Duke's Equerry, made himself so essential to the Duchess' existence that she was unheeding of warnings about his immense personal ambitions and doubtful financial probity. Her relationship with the King and his brother, Clarence, the heir to the throne, degenerated from the embittered to the sulphurous. For the growing Princess Victoria the visits to her Uncle Leopold at Claremont were 'the brightest epoch of my otherwise rather melancholy childhood'.

Another brightness was provided by an equally controversial personality, Louise Lehzen, who became the governess of both Victoria and her step-sister, Feodora, and was devoted to the child –a devotion warmly reciprocated. But Lehzen did not lack ambition either. It was at Conroy's instigation that she was raised to the rank of a Hanoverian Baroness, while he became a Knight Commander of the Hanoverian Order. It was only gradually that Princess Victoria realised how she had become the object of Conroy's ambitions that had nothing to do with her well-being, beyond her survival to become Queen of England. Leopold's influence on his sister diminished sharply, and it was uncharacteristically unfair for Prince Albert to blame his uncle subsequently for the evil influence on the Duchess of Kent that the adventurer Conroy obtained: the truth was that the Duchess demanded too much of her brother Leopold and was impatient of his caution and difficulties, that he himself was deeply out of favour with the Royal Family and was the object of heavy criticism in Parliament and the popular Press, and Conroy poisoned the Duchess' mind against him by alleging that he was seeking the Regency – if the Crown became vacant before Victoria inherited – for himself.

Princess Victoria grew up, principally in Kensington Palace, in unhappy and difficult circumstances, surrounded by intrigue, and never permitted to be alone. Her guardians were always adults – her mother, Lehzen, or Conroy – and it was a childhood of intense loneliness. But her surviving Journals give a clear indication of a fresh, sometimes critical and even acerbic personality, with much warmth and zest and enthusiasm and spirit, which had survived a singularly complex and lonely childhood.

But there was a severe price to be paid. She became understandably alienated from her mother and bitterly hostile to Conroy, and her devotion and gratitude to her uncle Leopold leap endearingly and movingly from her letters and her early Journals – the few originals that have survived the appalling holocaust after her death. But she also became a young woman with intense feelings and prejudices, so often the fate of an only child with no father or stable family life. Like Charlotte, she was headstrong and emotional, and, although talented, was hardly to be described as having notable intellectual qualities. She could be intolerant, was usually uninterested in the circumstances of others outside her immediate circle and concerns, and was not only ignorant through her education of the actual conditions of the nation she gradually realised she was likely to rule but at that stage remarkably lacking in serious inclination to learn more of them. In this sense, her surviving Journals make very revealing but somewhat depressing reading; there is an artless shallowness about them that reveals not only a selfishness, which is not uncommon, but a melancholy lack of imagination and sympathy for people outside her immediate knowledge. Individuals, towns, cities, and large tracts of the British countryside are bleakly assessed and curtly dismissed. As she grew up, and in spite of the severe restrictions of Conroy's 'Kensington System', she acquired not only a precocious self-confidence but something very close to arrogance and personal vanity. None of this was to be wondered at, but her often over-sympathetic biographers have tended to minimise the unattractive aspects of this otherwise graceful, vivacious, and endearing girl brought up under unpleasant circumstances.

No fair estimation of the young Princess Victoria can exclude certain realities about her personality. She was highly emotional and very impressionable, was by no means a good judge of people, was often lacking in gratitude, and was profoundly self-centred and highly susceptible to flattery. She had a hard common sense, but even this was variable when it did not affect her own personal interests.

The similarities with Princess Charlotte are remarkable, both in circumstances – in effect both fatherless, and hostile to their mothers – and in personality, and it was not only Stockmar who commented upon the several common factors. The many portraits of Princess Victoria printed and published during the early years of her reign are mainly derivative, and the few drawn from life are clearly

somewhat flattering. She was very small and Lady Wilhelmina
Stanhope (later Lady Dalmeny, and the mother of the future Prime
Minister, Lord Rosebery), who was one of her train-bearers at her
Coronation, wrote that she 'never, at any time, could have been
called pretty, but when she came to the throne she was distinctly
attractive: her small fair head well set on extremely pretty shoulders,
singularly graceful in all her movements, with a great charm of
manner, the brightest and gayest of smiles, and a remarkably clear
and musical voice'. But, for all her warmth, enthusiasm, and
attractiveness, contemporaries also detected a coldness and an
element of ruthlessness that troubled them. She had grown up in a
hard school, and it appeared to many that this fundamental tough-
ness and intolerance would remain her principal characteristics.
And so they might well have been, had it not happened that she was
temporarily released from the influences of her childhood, upbringing, and heredity by the warmth and ability of the one person whose
quality she wholly appreciated and loved, and whose wise advice she
eventually followed.

That King Leopold had decided that marriage between Princess
Victoria and Prince Albert would be highly desirable, and a further
major advance in the Coburg family fortunes, is incontestable. What
would be wrong would be to conclude that his actions were dominated by calculation and cynicism. For one thing, his devotion to
Princess Victoria was as strong and as genuine as hers to him. 'What
a happiness was it for me to throw myself in the arms of that *dearest* of
Uncles', she wrote in her Journal on September 29th 1835, 'who has
always been to me like a father, and whom I love so *very dearly!*'
Moreover, Leopold was acutely aware of his own personal unpopularity in England, the keen dislike of the Coburg influence, and the
increasing rift between his sister the Duchess of Kent and his niece
Princess Victoria. These were not propitious circumstances, and
certainly not made easier by his marriage in 1832 to Louise Marie,
Princess of Orleans, the daughter of King Louis Philippe of France,
and a Roman Catholic. His letters to his niece were addressed to 'My
dearest love', and, although they often contained earnest advice
radiated an affection that is manifestly sincere. He was also unsure
about his nephew, Prince Albert.

Leopold's visit to Coburg early in 1836 was deliberately planned
by him and Stockmar to assess Albert's development and to establish whether Florschütz's enthusiastic reports were justified. Both
were acutely aware of the low reputation of Duke Ernest and his
entourage, and were genuinely – and very understandably –

concerned at the possibility of moral and intellectual contamination
from a Coburg hedonism. As Albert wrote to his brother in 1840,
'You well know the events and scandals that had always happened in
Coburg castle and in the town, and just this knowledge has made you
indifferent to morality.' Prince Albert was evidently not contaminated in this sense, but while Stockmar was impressed by Albert's
character and ability he considered that he was, not surprisingly,
very deficient in his understanding of contemporary European
political affairs – in which he demonstrated little interest – and was
manifestly ill-at-ease with strangers. Albert's shyness and reserve
did not greatly trouble Leopold, and he shrewdly realised that they
were not the result of lack of confidence and were also very attractive
to women. Nonetheless, he agreed with Stockmar that Albert was
not yet fully developed, and that there were gaps which had to be
filled.

Stockmar's assessment is so interesting that it deserves to be
quoted at some length.

> He is a handsome youth who, for his age, is tolerably developed,
> with pleasant and striking features; and who, if nothing
> interferes with his progress, will probably in a few years be a
> well-built man with a pleasant, simple, and yet distinguished
> bearing. Externally, therefore, he has everything attractive to
> women, and possesses every quality they find pleasing at all
> times, and in all countries. It may also be considered as a
> fortunate circumstance that he has already a certain English
> look about him ...
>
> He is said to be prudent, cautious, and already very well
> informed. All this, however, is not enough. He must not only
> have great capacity but true ambition, and a great strength of
> will. To pursue so difficult a political career a whole life through
> requires more than energy and inclination – it demands also
> that earnest frame of mind which is ready of its own accord to
> sacrifice mere pleasure to real usefulness. If simply to fill one of
> the most influential positions in Europe does not satisfy him,
> how often will he feel tempted to regret what he has undertaken.
> If he does not, right from the start, regard it as a serious and
> responsible task upon the fulfilment of which his honour and
> happiness depend, he is not likely to succeed.

This was a severe assessment indeed, and may be partly explained
by Stockmar's obstinate perfectionism. But it was an absolutely
honest portrait, characteristic of the man and his relationship with
Leopold. Furthermore, Stockmar was as worried about Princess
Louise's wayward character as he was about Duke Ernest's

reputation, and was alarmed that aspects of it – the charm, intelligence, and wit unaccompanied by application to any subject for very long – were evident in the younger son. Neither he nor Leopold trusted the influence of Duke Ernest, particularly when he had taken his sons to Berlin after their confirmation, a city whose materialism and low moral standard both men deplored. In this matter they had no need to trouble themselves; Prince Albert had hated it as well.

Stockmar was right to be cautious. The Coburg atmosphere was narrow, claustrophobic, gossip-ridden and at best amoral; Florschütz's talents might have been considerable, but his range was necessarily and humanly limited; neither of Prince Albert's parents were, in Stockmar's eyes, estimable people, and Stockmar's sense of heredity was as strong as his revulsion from scandal and loose moral and intellectual standards. Judged by these criteria, Albert was unpromising material for advancement in political life, and it was wholly characteristic of Stockmar that he laid these concerns and apprehensions clearly before Albert's uncle. But he also detected some signs that were hopeful, and indeed the fact about Prince Albert that most surprised and impressed him was that so fine a developing character should have survived such a background, and 'with such a father and such a brother, both equally unprincipled'. But at the time his hesitations were real, were merited, and are very understandable.

Albert was not his pupil, nor his protegé, as Leopold had been, and his admiration for Florschütz – although considerable – was qualified. What Stockmar could not discern in Prince Albert was the presence of any intellectual and moral strength behind a very agreeable and charming façade. Above all, Albert seemed to lack – and indeed at that time did lack – any ambition or resolution. He was evidently a genuine and natural scholar and devoted countryman, an accomplished musician and linguist, well read and clearly highly intelligent and well educated, but he was in Stockmar's eyes a somewhat *gauche*, unsophisticated, cheerful and amusing sixteen-year-old boy. In tendering his advice to Leopold, Stockmar had a heavy responsibility to bear. He did not conceal his doubts, and they were fully justified. His portraits were sharp, but also fair. Between Florschütz's eulogies and Stockmar's severities one sees the clear portrayal of a talented and engaging boy of sixteen, but still reserved and immature.

Nevertheless, in spite of all reservations, time was pressing, and Prince Albert and Princess Victoria – who was now almost seventeen and might inherit the English Throne at any time – had never even met, and knew very little of each other. On this meeting Leopold was now determined, and Stockmar, despite his qualified approval of

Albert, completely agreed for political reasons, as there were now other challengers in the field. When Prince Adalbert of Prussia advanced his claims to be included 'in the list of those who pretend to the hand of HRH the Princess Victoria' in May 1837 the Duchess of Kent sent the magnificent reply to Lord William Russell, the British Minister in Berlin who had communicated this possibility: 'If I know my duty to the King, I also know my maternal one, and I will candidly tell your Lordship that I am of opinion that the Princess shall not marry until she is much older. I will also add that, in the choice of person to share her great destiny, I have but one wish – that her happiness and the interests of the country be realised in it'. 'From this time onward the connection [between Victoria and Albert] was regarded as the one aim to which all energies should be directed', Charles Prince of Leiningen, Victoria's half-brother, subsequently recorded in a memorandum specially written for Albert in 1841, but although this was now the Coburg intention – certainly that of Leopold and the Duchess of Kent, with Stockmar giving his cautious support and advice – the actual difficulties remained formidable, and not the least of these was the tempestuous character of Princess Victoria herself.

But there were other problems in England. By this stage, King William IV was 71 and clearly ageing rapidly, but his intense hostility to the Duchess of Kent, Conroy, and to the Coburgs in general had not abated. These vehement emotions were wholly understandable, particularly where they concerned the ambitious and tactless Duchess of Kent and the even more ambitious and obnoxious Conroy. The King's most recent biographer has admirably summarised the attitude of the Duchess:

> The Duchess of Kent seems to have considered his reign as an undesirable and inconsiderately protracted interregnum between the black wickedness of the Georges and the radiant paradise to open with the accession of Queen Victoria.[1]

The attitude of the Duchess prompted the King to urge his Ministers to 'keep a watchful Eye upon the Designs of the Duchess of Kent, who may not scruple to sacrifice the Interests of this Country to personal Considerations'. Greville recorded a dramatic outburst by the King at Windsor in August 1836 when, in the presence of the Duchess of Kent and her daughter and a large assembly, he expressed the vehement hope that there would be no Regency and that the Royal authority would not be vested, even briefly, 'in the hands of a person now near me [the Duchess] who is surrounded by

[1] P. Ziegler: *King William IV*, p. 277.

evil advisers and who is herself incompetent to act with propriety in the station in which she would be placed'.[1]

The King's ambition to marry off Princess Victoria to one of the sons of the Prince of Orange, the eldest son of the King of the Netherlands and the man rejected by Charlotte for Leopold, was eagerly shared by the Prince of Orange himself, who, after Leopold had become King of the Belgians now had a particular additional cause of hatred against Leopold. 'Voilà un homme qui a pris ma femme et mon royaume' he would remark with venom, and Leopold fully returned his antipathy. Thus, when it became known at Kensington Palace that the King was inviting the Prince of Orange and his two sons to London, the Duchess at once urged Duke Ernest to accelerate his proposed visit, and indeed to come at once.

A ferocious storm ensued. The King ordered the Foreign Secretary, Lord Palmerston, to prevent the Coburgs from coming, but the Duchess of Kent stood firm. Palmerston's relations with the King were markedly lacking in harmony, and the King had to accept the fact of the forthcoming visit, but with a very bitter grace.

King Leopold was incensed, and wrote to Princess Victoria to tell her what was afoot. It was an angry letter, but also a very shrewd one. 'The relations of the King and Queen therefore are to come in shoals', he wrote, 'when *your relations* are to be forbidden ... Really and truly I never heard anything like it, and I hope it will a *little rouse your spirits* ... I have not the least doubt that the King, in his passion for the Oranges, will be *excessively rude to your relations*, this however will not signify much, they are *your* guests and not *his*'. The point was not lost on the Princess. In spite of all the endeavours of the King and the Prince of Orange, she viewed the two Dutch sons with bleakness. 'The boys are both very plain', she wrote to the intensely relieved Leopold, 'and have a mixture of Kalmuck and Dutch in their faces, moreover they look heavy, dull, and frightened and are not at all prepossessing. So much for the *Oranges*, dear Uncle'.

Leopold also wrote at length to Lehzen, asking her to convey the contents to Princess Victoria. After emphasising their link of deep loyalty to the Princess amidst all intrigues, and reminding Lehzen with some bluntness that she owed her continued presence at Kensington Palace to him, he went on:

> The Princess's 17th birthday marks an important stage in her life: only one more year and the possibility of a Regency vanishes like an evil cloud. This is the perfect time for us, who are loyal, to take thought for the future of the dear, dear child.

[1] Greville: *Dairies*, iii, p. 309.

An immediate alliance is out of the question; she must reach her 18th birthday, perhaps even more – her health must decide that; but the Princess might perhaps do well, for the sake of composure and peace of mind, to find a choice and firmly anchor herself to it ...

Thus, in May the Coburg Princes travelled to England with their father from Rotterdam. 'It must be a *sine qua non*', Stockmar wrote to Leopold, 'that the object of the visit must be kept strictly from the Princess as well as from the Prince, so as to leave them completely at their ease'.

Victoria's account in her Journal (May 18th, 1836) of her first meeting with Albert deserves to be given in its entirety:

At a ¼ to 2 we went down into the Hall, to receive my Uncle Ernest, Duke of Saxe Coburg Gotha, and my cousins, Ernest and Albert, his sons. My Uncle was here, now 5 years ago, and is looking extremely well. Ernest is as tall as Ferdinand and Augustus; he has dark hair, and fine dark eyes and eyebrows, but the nose and mouth are not good; he has a most kind honest and intelligent expression in his countenance, and he has a very good figure. Albert, who is just as tall as Ernest, but stouter, is extremely handsome; his hair is about the same colour as mine; his eyes are large and blue, and he has a beautiful nose, and a very sweet mouth with fine teeth; but the charm of his countenance is his expression, which is most delightful; *c'est à la fois* full of goodness and sweetness, and very clever and intelligent.

Albert's immediate reactions on meeting Victoria are not recorded, but they can hardly have been as enthusiastic, to judge by his letters. The crossing had not been agreeable – 'the journey to England has given me such a disgust for the sea that I do not like even to think of it', he wrote – and he wrote to his step-mother on June 1st that he had been suffering from a bilious fever. 'The climate of this country, the different way of living, and the late hours, do not agree with me'. Nor did the succession of dinners, concerts, and levées to which the young Princes were invited and compelled to attend. 'You can well imagine that I had many hard battles to fight against sleepiness during these late entertainments', he reported with feeling. This disability for public life was to prove enduring; 'he never took kindly to guest dinners, balls, or the common evening amusements of the fashionable world; and went through them as a duty which his position imposed upon him, than as a source of pleasure or enjoyment', his first biographer and secretary wrote, on which Queen Victoria commented defensively: 'Yet nothing, at the same time, could exceed the kind attention he paid to every one, frequently standing the whole evening that no one might be neglected'.

The Duchess of Kent gave 'a brilliant ball here at Kensington Palace' at which the Duke of Wellington was present. The Princes visited the Duke of Northumberland at Sion House, and saw 'at last some of the sights of London'. 'Dear Aunt [Kent] is very kind to us, and does everything she can to please us; and our cousin [Victoria] also is very amiable', Albert recorded, with a conspicuous lack of enthusiasm.

Princess Victoria was pleased and impressed by her cousins whom she described as 'very amiable, very kind and good, and extremely merry, just as young people ought to be; with all that they are extremely sensible and fond of occupation. Albert is extremely good-looking, which Ernest certainly is not, but he has a most good-natured, honest and intelligent countenance'. Her half-sister, Princess Feodora, preferred Ernest to Albert, but Ernest – perhaps as a direct result of the strongly expressed views of Leopold and Stockmar – was never seriously considered as a possible suitor by anyone except himself.

It was on this first visit to England that Albert met Benjamin Disraeli. His views have not been recorded, but they were probably very similar to Ernest's, who commented upon him as 'a vain young Jew of remarkably radical tendencies. He carried his left arm in a black sling, which peculiarity was sneered at by his enemies, who said that he only did it to make himself interesting'.

Prince Albert made an immediate and excellent impression on others – and not least upon King William, who both liked him and referred to him as one of the most handsome young men he had ever met. Indeed, the more one studies this neglected Monarch, the more one warms to him. Rough and blunt he may have been – and was – but his kindnesses to his obvious successor were unaffected by his loathing for her mother, and his equal detestation for the Coburgs did not prevent him from quickly developing a fair and very generous opinion of Prince Albert. For the King's goodness towards her, Victoria was always deeply grateful. 'He had a truly kind heart', she wrote of him many years later, ' ... and of his kindness to herself and his wish that she should be duly prepared for the duties to which she was so early called, the Queen can only speak in terms of affectionate gratitude'. The formal meeting between the King and Albert – at a Royal Ball – reflected immense credit on the very nervous and unwell young German Prince and the tired, suspicious, anti-Coburg and irascible King. They liked and respected each other at once.

1a   Prince Leopold and Princess
      Charlotte, by Dawe

1b   Baron Stockmar, by Partridge

2a   Princess Louise, mother of Prince Albert, after Ruprecht

2b, c Prince Albert and Prince Ernest as children, by an unknown artist

3a   The Duchess of Kent and
     Princess Victoria, 1821,
     by Beechey

3b   Prince Albert, aged thirteen,
     by an unknown artist

4a   Lord Melbourne, by Partridge

4b   The Duke of Wellington and
      Sir Robert Peel, by Winterhalter

5   Queen Victoria, 1838, by Ross

6a   The arrival of the Coburg Princes at Dover, February 7th, 1840, by Knell

6b   The wedding of Queen Victoria and Prince Albert, by Hayter
      In the front row, third and fourth from the left, are Prince Albert's
      brother, Ernest, and his father, and Queen Adelaide; Lord Melbourne is
      immediately to the right of the Queen, and the Duchess of Kent is to the
      right of the officiating Archbishop of Canterbury

7   Queen Victoria's watercolour sketch of Prince Albert, c1840

8a Prince Albert, 1842, by Ross

8b Queen Victoria, 1843, by Ross

Princess Victoria was impressed by the fact that both her cousins played the piano excellently, and that Albert was a gifted amateur artist. But there are two particularly interesting aspects of Victoria's comments on Albert. As a person particularly susceptible to beauty, she was very struck at once by the fact that Albert was a very handsome young man, although not yet as handsome as he was to become. But also, in a life that conspicuously lacked fun – 'I am very fond of *pleasant* society', she had written to Leopold on March 14th 1837, 'and we have been for the last three months immured within our old [Kensington] Palace. I longed sadly for some gaiety' – she responded with especial warmth to Albert's lively humour combined with a seriousness and reflectiveness which she noted in contrast with Ernest. Both were '*very, very* merry and gay and happy, like young people ought to be'. Those who remorselessly insist on the alleged misery of Albert's childhood must avert their gaze from these, and many other, indications of the opposite.

The visit was marred by the knowledge of the King's deep anger against the Coburgs and by Prince Albert's inability to cope with the whirl of the celebrations and the insupportable late hours which the strange English kept. At the birthday ball itself he nearly fainted – 'turned as pale as ashes', as Princess Victoria recorded – and took to his bed for a day; on at least two other occasions he had to excuse himself and leave early, prompting Victoria to write to Leopold, 'I have only now to beg you, my dearest Uncle, to take care of one, now *so dear* to me'. It is not difficult to detect a clear note of disappointment, even of disapproval, in Victoria's accounts of Albert's regular ailments and disappearances. 'I am very sorry to say', she wrote somewhat tartly to Leopold, 'that we have an invalid in the house in the person of Albert, who, though much better today, has had a smart bilious attack. He was not allowed to leave his room all day yesterday, but by dint of starvation, he is again restored to society, but looks pale and delicate'. She immensely enjoyed the celebrations, and after another Ball, when she danced until dawn, she felt herself 'all the better for it next day'. 'Poor dear Albert', however, did not. 'Poor dear Albert came to breakfast without eating anything, looking weak and delicate'; 'Poor dear Albert was unable to leave his rooms'.

Prince Albert's emotions on this, his first visit to England, were understandably very mixed. He was evidently now aware of the strong hopes of the Coburgs and Stockmar, and could not have been unconscious of the fact that Ernest was extremely interested himself in marriage with Victoria – an interest that had to be emphatically suppressed by Leopold and Stockmar. The clear and resolute hostility of King William to his aunt and uncle, and the harsh intrigues in the British Royal Family also shadowed the occasion. Beyond the political difficulties he disliked the food, the weather, and the succession of formal dinners with their associated dreadful hours. His English, although technically excellent, had never been tested so severely before. But it is also clear that he enjoyed the company of the young people invited for the celebrations, and was very struck by Victoria's vivacity and attractiveness. There is no evidence at all that his feelings for her went beyond this point at this stage. For her part, Victoria wrote to Leopold that Albert 'possesses every quality that could be required to make one perfectly happy', but, also, one only detects cousinly affection, pleasurable amusement, and regard.

Thus, on neither side were there any indications of deeper emotions. As Prince Albert subsequently wrote in a personal memoir: 'Princess Victoria and myself, both at the age of 17, were much pleased with each other, but not a word in allusion to the future passed either between us, or with the Duchess of Kent'. Victoria wrote to Leopold after Albert's departure, saying that she accepted him as the husband whom he had selected for her, but did not consider herself bound to marriage in the near future. It was a tactful letter, pleasing to Leopold, yet clearly guarded, and Victoria subsequently made it clear that she did not consider herself committed to Albert at all. 'He is so sensible, so kind and so good and so amiable too. He has besides the pleasing and delightful exterior and appearance that you could wish to see'. Leopold – and Stockmar – clearly understood that cousinly affection, although successfully created by this first meeting, was all that had been achieved.

Indeed, the visit had confirmed Stockmar's doubts about the maturity of Prince Albert, and his inability to withstand the physical pressures of the entertainment and difficulty in casual social intercourse had been very marked. Thus, while it can hardly be regarded as a total failure, the meeting between the two cousins had fallen very far short of the most hopeful expectations.

It must be emphasised again that Princess Victoria's life was at this time tedious and strained. Her half-sister, Feodora, later wrote: 'When I look back upon those years, which ought to have been the happiest of my life, from fourteen to twenty, I cannot help pitying myself. Not to have enjoyed the pleasures of youth is nothing, but to have been deprived of all intercourse, and not one cheerful thought in that dismal existence of ours, was very hard'. It was an exaggerated portrait, but not one devoid of truth, and it made Princess Victoria especially receptive to the occasional exposure to pleasure and the company of young people, and particularly young men. The visit of her other Coburg cousins, Ferdinand and Augustus, in March 1836, had been equally welcome to her, and their departure –

and particularly that of Ferdinand – had evoked much sadness. Nonetheless, Albert and Ernest *had* made a considerable impression. 'Dearly as I love Ferdinand and also good Augustus', Victoria wrote in her Journal, 'I love Ernest and Albert *more* than them, oh, yes, MUCH more ... Though I wrote more when Uncle Ferdinand and Augustus went, in my Journal ... I feel this separation more deeply, though I do not lament as much as I did then, which came from my nerves not being strong then. I can bear more now'.

But while she wrote dutifully to Leopold thanking him for 'the prospect of *great* happiness you have given me in the person of dear Albert' the memory of his visit quickly faded. He occasionally wrote to her; she very rarely to him. There was no question even of an 'understanding' between the young couple, and certainly none whatever of an engagement.

Her interest in him was reduced even further when she became Queen on the death of William IV on June 20th 1837. The King's last satisfaction was that Princess Victoria had come of age on May 24th, and the dreaded fear of a Conroy-dominated Regency had been averted. But he had achieved much more. When George IV had died in June 1830 *The Times* had commented that 'no monarch will be less generally mourned'. The brief reign of William IV had been one of tempestuous political activity and tension, which had included his dismissal of two Administrations – one Whig, one Tory – and the passage of the 1832 Reform Bill, and yet when Alexis de Tocqueville came to England a year later he was struck by the absence of revolutionary feeling. William IV was no radical, but he had shrewd political sense, always sought sensible compromise, and in the public view was certainly not an enemy of Reform. His popularity had varied greatly, but at crucial moments he had actually *been* popular, which was in itself a striking novelty for the Hanoverians. 'He inherited a monarchy in tatters, he bequeathed to his heir the securest throne in Europe' is a fair assessment of his notable contribution.[1]

The new Queen was unaware of what had been done. 'She is surrounded with the most exciting and interesting enjoyments', Greville noted with truth; 'her occupations, her pleasure, her business, her Court, all present an unceasing round of gratifications. With all her prudence and discretion she has great animal spirits, and enters into the magnificent novelties of her position with the zest and curiosity of a child'. Bewitched by her Whig Prime Minister, Lord Melbourne, who disliked change and Germans and saw no need for an early marriage, Albert appears to have virtually

[1] Ziegler, op. cit., p. 294.

vanished from her thoughts. In her own words, 'the freedom, the gaiety and the excitements of becoming Queen at eighteen' drove all thoughts of marriage away.

Three years were to elapse before the cousins were to meet again. Prince Albert's education was resumed.

The next stage of that education was a period of ten months in Brussels, being prepared for entry to the University of Bonn by a Baron von Wiechmann, a retired German officer, to the dismay of Grandmother Gotha, who wrote to Duke Ernest to lament that 'it makes me sad to think that you are coming back without them, and I cannot reconcile myself to this long separation from them'. This decision was not at all to the liking of the other German noble families, and represented a considerable triumph for Leopold and Stockmar. Prince Albert now came under the tutelage of the very eminent mathematician Quetelet, who subsequently shrewdly remarked that Prince Albert did not think enough of his own talents whereas Leopold never forgot his. There was also the influence of the Reverend William Drury, who had conducted a lengthy correspondence with Byron, but most subtle of all was the liberal atmosphere of Brussels itself and the close proximity of Leopold and Stockmar, with Florschütz still in close attendance. To his father, Albert wrote that 'we live in a small but very pretty house, with a little garden in front, and though in the middle of a large town, we are perfectly shut out from the noise of the streets. The masters selected for us are said to be excellent, so that everything is favourable to our studies, and I trust there will be no lack of application on our part'. Their period with Baron von Wiechmann included visiting manoeuvres with Leopold and to Waterloo, where their tutor had fought, and a warm invitation by his father to spend Christmas at Coburg was politely declined by Albert on the grounds that 'our course of study would be quite disturbed by such an interruption'.

Von Wiechmann was of a stiff and restricted personality, whose relationship with his young charges was not smooth. Albert's gift for mimicking and his acute sense of the ridiculous evidently did not assist this relationship. In April 1837 the Princes entered Bonn University – 'in search of more wisdom', as Albert wrote – staying in a house specially rented for them under the approving eye of Florschütz, who reported that Albert 'maintained the early promise of his youth by the eagerness with which he applied himself to his work, and by the rapid progress which he made, especially in the natural sciences, in political economy, and in philosophy ... Music also, of which he was passionately fond, was not neglected, and he had already shown considerable talent as a composer'. He became consumed by what his brother later described as a 'reading rage'. He also demonstrated great talent as a fencer, winning a University competition, and developed a close and enduring friendship with Prince William of Löwenstein, who was particularly delighted by Albert's mimicry of the professors, his irreverent caricatures and bubbling humour. 'Music was also a favourite pursuit of the students', Prince William later recorded. 'To the despair of Colonel von Wiechmann, we hummed several students' songs, and even practised the "Glocke" of Romberg for four voices. In spite of many false notes, we went resolutely on and passed many an evening in song. Prince Albert was looked upon amongst us as a master of the art', as he was in improvised amateur dramatics, in which 'Prince Albert was always the life and soul'.

This was one of the most supremely happy periods of Prince Albert's life. The University of Bonn was perhaps the most advanced and enlightened in Europe, matched only by Edinburgh in its standards and spirit of liberal scholarship. He had his studies, which absorbed him, his music, his new student friends, and, followed by his beloved greyhound Eôs, went on walking expeditions with his friends. 'He liked above all things to discuss questions of public law and metaphysics', Prince William wrote, 'and constantly, during our many walks, juridical principles or philosophical doctrines were thoroughly discussed'. But Prince William's abiding memory was of Albert's merriment and the excellence of his company. 'The Prince's humour and sense of the ludicrous, found a natural counterpoise in his other great and sterling qualities; and the great business of his later life, the many important duties he had to fulfil, soon drove into the background the humorous part of his character, which had been so prominent at the University'. Another contemporary wrote shortly afterwards that 'Prince Albert is kind, affable, and gay; joining freely in the mirth of those about him; sensible to any committed absurdity, but showing in his laughter that it proceeds from a really good-humoured temper'. It should not be forgotten that Princess Victoria had been particularly attracted by Prince Albert's sense of humour, cheerfulness and merriment when they had first met.

When King William died Prince Albert wrote a courteous letter to his cousin, now Queen of England, in English.

My dearest cousin,
    I must write you a few lines to present you my sincerest felicitations on that great change which has taken place in your life.

Now you are Queen of the mightiest land of Europe, in your hands lie the happiness of millions. May Heaven assist you and strengthen you with its strength in that high but difficult task.

I hope that your reign may be long, happy, and glorious, and that your efforts may be rewarded by the thankfulness and love of your subjects.

May I pray you to think likewise sometimes of your cousins in Bonn, and to continue to them that kindness you favoured them with till now. Be assured that our minds are always with you.

I will not be indiscreet and abuse your time. Believe me always, your Majesty's most obedient and faithful servant,
                                        Albert.

In Queen Victoria's and Prince Albert's voluminous and meticulously maintained papers there is no record of any acknowledgement or reply to this letter.

The persistent but wholly unfounded rumours that Prince Albert and Queen Victoria were in effect engaged were a source of real embarrassment to them both, and even to Leopold, who advised Albert to undertake a long tour through Switzerland and Northern Italy to divert speculation and attention that were not only undesirable and unwelcome but also could have been deeply injurious to Leopold's own plans and ambitions. As Queen Victoria herself subsequently noted with severity of these rumours, 'nothing was then settled'. At the time, her emotions were considerably more vehement. She had just become, at the age of eighteen, Queen of England. She had not been greatly impressed by her wan cousin at the occasion of their only meeting. She did not particularly wish to be married. Of her cousin Albert she wrote bleakly to her uncle Leopold in July 1839 that 'one can never answer beforehand for *feelings*, and I may not have the *feeling* for him which is requisite to ensure happiness. I *may* like him as a friend, and as a *cousin*, and as a *brother*, but not more; and should this be the case (which is not likely) I am *very* anxious that it should be understood that I am not guilty of any breach of promise, for *I never gave any*'. Also, all that Albert heard about England from Leopold displeased him. 'United as all parties are in high praise of the young Queen', he wrote to his father, 'the more do they seem to manoeuvre and intrigue with and against each other. On every side there is nothing but a network of cabals and intrigues, and parties are arranged against each other in the most inexplicable manner'. Prince Albert accepted Leopold's advice that he should temporarily 'disappear' on a lengthy and unpublicised journey, and found his reasons 'imperative and conclusive'.

The journey through the Alps and into Northern Italy with Ernest and Florschütz was in itself a great and enjoyable success. Albert carefully kept a small album, which in fact was a scrapbook of his journey, which he sent to Victoria, who was both surprised and touched. 'Nothing had at this time passed between the Queen and the Prince', she later wrote about what she described as 'one of her great treasures', 'but this gift shows that the latter, in the midst of his travels, often thought of his young cousin'. There is little evidence of this, beyond the gift of the scrapbook.

The Princes returned to Bonn in November 1838. 'How tall and handsome Albert is grown', Grandmother Gotha noted, but he was already concerned and saddened by the prospect of his inevitable separation from his brother, and the extreme uncertainty about his own future after he left Bonn in the summer of 1838. For the first time the real possibility of marriage with Victoria had been brought home to him as a result of a conversation with Leopold in March, but the report from London was, Albert wrote to his father, that 'the Queen had in no way altered her mind, but did not wish to marry for some time yet'. Leopold wrote to Stockmar of Albert's reaction that: 'He looks at the question from its most elevated and honourable point of view. He considers that troubles are insepar-able from all human positions, and that therefore if one must be subjected to plagues and annoyances, it is better to be so for some great or worthy object than for trifles and miseries. I have told him that his great youth would make it necessary to postpone the marriage for a few years ... I found him very sensible on all these points. But one thing he observed with truth. "I am ready," he said, "to submit to this delay, if I have only some certain assurance to go upon. But if, after waiting, perhaps, for three years, I should find that the Queen no longer desired the marriage, it would place me in a very ridiculous position, and would, to a certain extent, ruin all the prospects of my future life" '.

From Leopold's point of view the reality was even less promising. The young Queen, riding high, had grown cold towards him; 'dear Uncle is given to believe that he must rule the roast (sic) every-where', she tartly noted. Leopold, clearly sensing the tone of Queen Victoria's letters, wrote cautiously to her (April 13th 1838) 'con-cerning the education of our friend Albert' and assuring her that 'on one thing you can rely, that it is my *great anxiety*, to see Albert a *very good* and *distinguished young man*, and *no pains will be thought too much* on my part if this end can be attained'. Victoria's letters to Leopold over the following months are notable in their absence of reference to Albert, and Leopold responded by never referring to him. In a somewhat voluminous correspondence, replete with family references, these omissions are noteworthy.

In London, Stockmar was concerned by her unexpected arrogance, her refusal to accept any advice 'which does not agree with
her opinion', and a temperament 'as passionate as a spoilt child'. But
matters were in fact even worse than they realised. The Queen had
become deeply suspicious of Leopold's ambitions for her, 'so as to be
able to rule the niece through the husband'. She sent to Stockmar a
letter from Albert '*to show how badly he writes*', which Stockmar
admitted. Before she became Queen she and Albert had maintained
a very intermittent correspondence, which now virtually ceased. She
was absorbed by her new position, by the persuasive Melbourne, by
her enthralling independence – all of which, as she later wrote, 'put
all ideas of marriage out of her mind, which she now most bitterly
repents'. Victoria thought Albert too young, and her heart had not
been captured. Nor had Albert's. His father attended Queen
Victoria's Coronation in June 1838 by himself, when he was made a
Knight of the Garter; there was no invitation to the two Coburg
Princes – nor to King Leopold.

In October, while they were staying at the Coburg Palace after
leaving Bonn, the Princes were involved in a fire when a stove ignited
material left on it, and which was eventually suppressed by them and
Albert's devoted valet, Cart, who had been in his service since 1830.

There were other indications of the end of childhood and adolescence. Albert was keenly and genuinely disturbed by the separation
from Ernest, now destined for military training. 'The separation will
be frightfully painful to us', he wrote to Löwenstein. 'Up to this
moment we have never, as long as we can recollect, been a single day
away from each other. I cannot bear to think of that moment'. To
Ernest he wrote immediately after the separation: 'You cannot
imagine how empty it seems to me since you left. I felt a lump in my
throat and it was only with difficulty that I could hide my tears. It is
the first separation; and it will not be the last. But I console myself
with the old saying, "There must be a valley between two hills" '.
'The thought of the separation of such fondly attached brothers quite
breaks my heart', Grandmother Gotha wrote, while Albert lamented
to her after Ernest had left for Dresden:

> Now I am quite alone. Ernest is far off, and I am left behind, still
> surrounded by so many things which keep up the constant
> illusion that he is in the next room. To whom could I turn, to
> whom could I pour out my heart, better than to you, dear
> Grandmama, who always takes such interest in everything that
> happens to us; who also know and understand us so well? ... I
> must now give up the custom of saying *we* and use the *I*, which
> sounds so egotistical and cold. In *we* everything sounded much

softer, for the *we* expresses the harmony between different souls, the *I* rather the insistence of the individual against outward forces, though also confidence in its own strength.

The departure of Ernest also brought to an end the role of Florschütz in their upbringing. Since the boys were five and four respectively he had been their tutor, guide, constant companion, and eventually their close friend. Their gratitude and affection for him were strong and enduring, and it was to him even more than to his beloved father and grandmother that Prince Albert was subsequently to ascribe the true happiness of his childhood and youth.

After Ernest's departure 'in order to sacrifice himself to Mars', as Albert wrote to Löwenstein, Albert travelled to Italy in the sombre and significant company of Stockmar at the end of 1838. Stockmar's presence was far from coincidental, as his scepticism about Albert – not yet eradicated – remained. Leopold, however, was by now convinced. 'If I am not very much mistaken', he had written to Stockmar in March 1838, 'he possesses all the qualities required to fit him completely for the position he will occupy in England. His understanding is sound, his apprehension clear and rapid, and his feelings in all matters appertaining to personal appearance are quite right. He has great powers of observation and possesses much prudence, without anything about him that could be called cold or morose'. Stockmar also accompanied Albert at the specific request of Queen Victoria, conveyed in a letter to Leopold on April 4th 1838, as 'he knows best my feelings and wishes on that subject'. Stockmar had become one of Queen Victoria's most respected counsellors. Invited by King William to deal with a possible Regency *coup* by the Duchess and Conroy he had acted swiftly and successfully, and had earned her profound gratitude. When she did become Queen he was in almost constant attendance with calm and sensible advice. Her impatience with Leopold's attempts to interfere did not extend to Stockmar, on whom she had leaned at a very difficult time and in which he had not failed her.

This was a strange interlude. Stockmar faithfully reported to the Queen on their travels. It was a somewhat lengthy journey, and in Florence, at Leopold's request, Albert was joined by Francis Seymour, later General, whose brother was to be in Prince Albert's personal entourage for twenty-one years. Seymour was an agreeable companion who was to become a close friend. The real purpose of his presence was to keep an eye open for any signs of dissipation and indiscretion on the part of Albert, a fact which caused Victoria much indignation when she learned of the fact many years later. 'God knows, vice itself would have recoiled from the look alone of one "who bore the lily of a blameless life" '. Seymour was impressed by Albert, and noted his impatience with meals, considering that 'eating was a waste of time', a refrain that was to become very familiar to his future wife. Albert wrote to Löwenstein with mingled enthusiasm and sarcasm: 'Oh! Florence, where I have been for two months, has gathered to herself noble treasures of art. I am often quite intoxicated with delight when I come out of one of the galleries. The country round Florence, too, possesses extraordinary attractions. I have lately thrown myself entirely into the whirl of society. I have danced, dined, supped, paid compliments, have been introduced to people, and had people introduced to me; have spoken French and English – exhausted all remarks about the weather – have played the amiable – and, in short, have made "bonne mine à mauvais jeu". You know my *passion* for such things, and must therefore admire my strength of character that I have never excused myself – never returned home till five in the morning – that I have emptied the carnival cup to the dregs'.

The remainder of this odyssey was hardly less successful. He disliked Rome ('but for some beautiful palaces, it might just as well be any town in Germany') and had a curious audience with Pope Gregory XVI:

'The old gentleman was very kind and civil. I remained with him nearly half an hour, shut up in a small room. We conversed in Italian on the influence the Egyptians had had on Greek art, and that again on Roman art. The Pope asserted that the Greeks had taken their models from the Etruscans. In spite of his infallibility I ventured to assert that they had derived their lessons in art from the Egyptians'.

In fact, the audience was even more comical. To Albert, the Pope looked 'like a Pagoda', and one devout Catholic who accompanied them tried to kiss the Papal toe. He lay down flat on the floor and grabbed the Pope's ankle; the startled Pontiff was thrown off balance, and kicked the ardent supplicant hard in the mouth, to the barely-concealed delight of the Protestant Prince, Albert recording the scene for Florschütz.[1]

He attended the Pope's blessing of the people from the Vatican balcony, 'amidst the ringing of bells, firing of cannon, and military music'. He found the occasion impressive, although the ceremonies which followed the blessing were tedious 'and savoured strongly of idolatry'.

Naples was little better; 'the sky and the sea are so dull and grey that one might fancy oneself transported to the North Sea'. There then followed the lengthy journey north, eventually returning to

[1] Fulford, op. cit., p. 32.

Coburg in the early summer. 'Italy is truly a most interesting country', he wrote, 'and an inexhaustible source of knowledge. One contrives, however, to taste extraordinarily little of the enjoyment which one there promises oneself. In many, many respects the country is far behind what one had expected. In the climate, in the scenery, in the study of the arts, one feels most disagreeably disappointed'.

'Albert is much improved', Leopold wrote to Stockmar on September 12th. 'He looks so much more manly, and from his "tournure" one might easily take him to be twenty-two or twenty-three'. But he remained deeply concerned about Victoria's insistence upon postponing any decision. 'If he waits until he is in his twenty-first, twenty-second, or twenty-third year, it will be impossible for him to begin any new career, and his whole life would be *marred* if the Queen should change her mind'. For his part, Prince Albert noted that 'my sphere of observation has been doubled', a singularly cool comment on his exposure to the wonders of Italian civilisation.

What was to prove of real importance was that Prince Albert's other companion was Ludwig Gruner, only slightly older than himself, but already regarded by his tutors as an outstandingly sensitive young appreciator of art and design. The two young men became close friends, and it was Gruner who opened Albert's eyes to the glories of the Early Renaissance, then much ignored, and indeed despised in fashionable artistic circles. Thus began a friendship and a collaboration of incalculable value to English art and architecture.

The return to Coburg was marked by the joint coming-of-age of himself and Ernest – by special legislation – and the consequent public celebrations. 'I am now my own master, as I hope always to be, and under all circumstances', Albert wrote. To Stockmar, however, he wrote somewhat flippantly that he would follow his advice to 'accustom himself more to society' and 'pay more attention to the ladies'. He was then obliged to accompany his father to Carlsbad before returning to The Rosenau 'in order to enjoy some days of quiet and regular occupation'.

This letter was written to Stockmar on September 6th 1839. His respite was short-lived. Shortly afterwards his father told him that the Coburg trio was to travel to England at the invitation of the Queen. She had conveyed to Leopold by special courier a cold reminder in July that there was no understanding of an engagement, that there was '*no anxiety*' in the country for her marriage – which was a highly questionable statement, considering that her heir was her Uncle Cumberland, King of Hanover – and that there was no question at all of any marriage for two or three years. To Florschütz

Albert gloomily wrote that 'Victoria is said to be incredibly stubborn
... she delights in court ceremonies, etiquette, and trivial formalities. These are gloomy prospects'. Without any discernible enthusiasm whatever, Prince Albert prepared himself for his second
meeting with his mercurial young cousin, absolutely resolved that a
definite decision, one way or the other, must be reached.

Arthur Mensdorff later wrote to Queen Victoria:

> Albert confided to me under the seal of the strictest secrecy that
> he was going to England in order to make your acquaintance,
> and that, if you liked each other, you were to be engaged. He
> spoke very seriously about the difficulties of the position he
> would have to occupy in England, but hoped that dear Uncle
> Leopold would assist him with his advice.

To his brother, Albert wrote on August 26th:

> I am now twenty years old and it is the first time that I do not
> spend my birthday in your company. In the morning, when the
> well-known, touching hymn awoke me in The Rosenau, I
> thought you must come to my bed. I can well feel what you write
> and I thank Heaven that we were allowed to go side by side
> through the greater part of our lives. Our childhood is over, at
> least not to return here on earth; yet I can say that I retain my
> childlike soul, and this is the treasure that everyone should take
> with him into his future life. Let us try all the more to attain
> something perfect – general education, elasticity of the brain.
> That is what gives great men such power to rule over others.
>   You were born for a position that required such qualities.
> Fate seems to have chosen me for a similar or rather more
> difficult position. Whatever may be in store for us, let us remain
> one in our feelings. We have, as you correctly say, found what
> others seek in vain, during all their lives: the soul of another that
> is able to understand one, that will suffer with one, be glad with
> one: one that finds the same pleasure in the same aspirations.

From this commitment Albert never wavered. He loved his
wayward and often dissolute brother as fervently as he did his
parents, and his forgiveness had no element of sanctimoniousness.
He accepted them as they were, and although angered by their
financial importunities and dismayed by their blatant promiscuity
was never censorious. When Ernest contracted an 'illness' almost
inseparable from his dissolute habits in 1841 his brother wrote:

> The cause of it made me very sad. So also did the death-blow
> which your reputation received, at least in this country. Yet, it

would never occur to me to curse you or take away from you the love I owe you as my brother.

That love was reciprocated, and no documents in Albert's papers are more genuine and moving than Ernest's letters to Victoria about him during his lifetime and after his death. In them, if only for an instant, one feels the authentic note of love between these very different brothers and their veneration for their ill-starred parents.

It was thus with reluctance that Prince Albert agreed to return to England and to meet his cousin again.

THREE

BETROTHAL

The conditions of British politics had changed very significantly since the end of the Napoleonic wars, although to contemporaries the full importance of what had happened between 1815 and the accession of Queen Victoria was not generally recognised. The resignation of the Tory Administration of the Duke of Wellington in November 1830, which led to that of Lord Grey and the passing of the first Reform Bill two years later, was remarkable in that although Wellington and his Ministers had the full confidence and support of the King the Government fell in the House of Commons. The influence of the Sovereign remained, as William IV demonstrated, but the failure of the first Government of Sir Robert Peel in 1834 also emphasised that it was upon Parliamentary majorities rather than on the support of the Monarch that Ministries henceforth depended for their power. This can now be seen as the most significant shift in power between the Crown and Parliament since the seventeenth century.

Lord Grey's Administration described itself, and was regarded as, a Whig Government, but the British political process had not reached anything approximating to the modern understanding of separate political parties vying for majorities at elections, the winner taking Office. What political organisation existed was local, and elections, even after the reforms of 1832, continued to be dominated by influence, wealth, venality, corruption, and sharp practice of various kinds, and, to some extent, individual personality. The Grey reforming Ministry was a confederation of individuals and groupings drawn together by hostility to the Wellington Government and support for electoral reform. After 1832 these unifying elements began to fade, and after Melbourne became Prime Minister in 1834 the Whig Government became markedly hostile to popular agitation for social and political reform, becoming in many respects notably more reactionary than its opponents, who gathered themselves, with varying degrees of enthusiasm and

expectation, behind the sombre combination of the Duke of Wellington and Sir Robert Peel.

It was out of the crisis over the Reform Bill that there was
gradually created the nucleus of a modern political party. The work
of F. R. Bonham as a national agent concentrating not on Parliament
but the constituencies, and the founding of the Carlton Club in 1832,
were indications that the Tory confederation recognised the new
realities with greater clarity than their opponents. Bonham was
helped in the constituencies by dislike of Whig alliances with Daniel
O'Connell's Irish M.P.s, and anger at alleged, although much
exaggerated, Whig indifference to the problems of agriculture. In
addition, there had been those who had regarded themselves as
Whig supporters who disliked the radicalism of the Reform Act and
were fearful of possible new measures on similar lines. These were
not mollified by the statement of Lord John Russell in the autumn of
1838 that the 1832 Act represented the furthest increase in the
franchise that he could accept, thereby earning himself the sobriquet
of 'Finality Jack'. Russell's domestic liberalism was now out-
matched by Palmerston's unexpected demagogic espousal of liberal
causes abroad. Thus, the Tories began to acquire new support from
those who were alarmed by Whig radicalism and others who were
hostile to its negative attitudes to social problems. We can see, if only
faintly, the beginnings of that extraordinary admixture of dedication
to the *status quo* and appetite for radical reform that was to be the
decisive collective appeal and strength of the modern Conservative
Party.

In retrospect it can be seen clearly that Peel, a professional
politician of a type more easily recognizable today than it was then,
was the natural and obvious leader of this new grouping, but it was
neither obvious at the time to himself or others. In spite of his regular
protestations in public and private of his keen desire to quit politics
he was too deeply enmeshed in them, and too fascinated by them, to
take such an irrevocable step. Yet these statements were not entirely
false. In Ireland, and in the harsh struggles to achieve Catholic
Emancipation in 1828, in addition to the fierce controversies over the
Reform Bill, he had made many enemies in the Tory confederation.
The county M.P.s, and the magnates who put them into Parliament,
viewed him with suspicion, and in many cases a keen dislike that was
sincerely reciprocated by this tense and sensitive man. In background and class he was conspicuously different from the bulk of the
Tories, and his somewhat cold and precise manner did not create a
wide circle of intimate friends and admirers. But his unrivalled
experience, his outstanding Parliamentary skills, his national prominence and even fame as the creator of the modern metropolitan

police force, and his unquestioned ability compelled him to be the
real leader of the Tories. By 1835 all the important strands of the
national party organisation were firmly in his hands.

It would be unwise to make the claim that the Tories were, by the
accession of Queen Victoria, a political party on a national scale,
with agreed policies and leaders. What they did have – as not all
realised – was a national political party in embryo, composed of
diverse factions and interests, and individuals eager for Office,
patronage, and preferment. Of all those interests the agricultural
one remained the most powerful, wealthy, and selfish, but Peel
himself, and the young William Ewart Gladstone, first elected in
December 1832, represented significant new strands in Toryism,
while the enfranchisement of the industrial boroughs in 1832 opened
the way for others whose background was that of industry and
commerce, the first substantial beneficiaries of the new wealth that
was beginning to burgeon in the northern cities.

There is no evidence that Stockmar clearly perceived the full
extent of this change. His veneration for the British Constitution was
intense, but so was his determination to maintain, in new circumstances, the power and position of the Monarchy. What deeply
worried him was that the impressionable and headstrong young
Queen was obviously capable of harming that development by her
reckless partisanship and political innocence. His forebodings were
justified more swiftly than he had appreciated.

The glorious and hopeful beginning of the reign of Queen Victoria,
when so many were enchanted by her youth, attractiveness, vivacity,
and dedicated application, and she herself was an enthralled and
exhilarated recipient of lavish affection and adulation which she had
never experienced, was unhappily not of long duration. By the
spring of 1839 she had become deeply embroiled in a major and
sustained political crisis which seriously affected not only her public
popularity but the respect of many who had welcomed her accession
so warmly.

It is easy to see why there was such high public enthusiasm for the
young Queen, and what heady wine it was for her to be suddenly so
independent, so important, so admired, and so apparently powerful.
'She conducts herself with surprising dignity: the dignity which
proceeds from self-possession and deliberation', as Greville wrote on
November 14th 1837, but all the early golden opinions could not
obscure the fact that she was an inexperienced, emotional, volatile,
and in many respects immature young woman with very limited
understanding both of politics and the nation whose Sovereign she

now was. This was not to be wondered at, and she was to develop rapidly, but by the beginning of 1839 the initial lustre had faded almost completely, and she was learning for herself the bitter truth of the Byronic warning:

> ...*All the world looked kind,*
> (*As it will look sometimes with the first stare,*
> *Which youth will not act ill to bear in mind*).

Queen Victoria's new-found and delightful independence of her mother and her coterie had been far from complete. The Duchess, Conroy, and their adherents moved physically from Kensington to Buckingham Palace, and continued their intrigues. 'It is a hard and unfair trial of the Queen, whose mind and health should not be exposed to such absurd vexation and torment', Lord Liverpool reported to Stockmar. For her part, the Queen was implacable in her hostility to Conroy, with consequent distressing appeals, scenes, and correspondence with her mother. This was not only wearying, and made her 'sick and miserable', but the continued presence of the Tory Conroy and his malignant machinations had significant political consequences, and not least in the abrupt decline in the Queen's estimation of Leopold, which had a considerable importance for the immediate fortunes of Prince Albert and the Coburg family.

There were difficulties and public embarrassments over the settlement of the Duchess' considerable debts, which had to be partially resolved not only by a special vote in Parliament but also by the Queen's careful management of her own income. But the Duchess' spendthrift, feckless ways continued, and 'plagued' Victoria at a time when she was conscientiously attempting to learn the intricacies of domestic and international politics and was preparing for her own Coronation. This took place on June 28th 1838 amidst a certain amount of cheerful chaos, during which the Archbishop of Canterbury forced the ring on to the wrong finger, the Bishop of Bath and Wells ended the ceremony prematurely and it had to be re-started, the altar in St. Edward's Chapel, as Melbourne noted, was 'covered with sandwiches, bottles of wine, etc.', and the lack of rehearsal was very evident. The young Benjamin Disraeli maliciously recorded that 'Melbourne looked very awkward and uncouth, with his coronet cocked on his nose, his robes under his feet, and holding the great sword of state like a butcher'. As has already been related, Duke Ernest of Coburg was invited, but his sons were not.

Meanwhile, the injudicious award of a baronetcy and a pension to Conroy in a clumsy attempt to buy him off— 'surely never was such a blunder committed as letting this man have the most unlimited means of intriguing against the Queen's Government', Liverpool remarked with valid vehemence to Stockmar – was arousing public attack, notably from *The Times*, to which Conroy responded with an action for criminal libel, and writs flew bitterly. Stockmar, who unhappily found himself subpoenaed in this bizarre and demeaning episode, became very alarmed by the reactions of Queen Victoria to these difficulties, reporting to Leopold that she had become 'as passionate as a spoilt child, if she feels offended, she throws everything overboard without exception'. She had become impatient with Leopold's frequent attempts to guide and advise her, and Lehzen's suspicions about Leopold's ambitions for a marriage with Albert were fortified by those of Melbourne, to the point that Stockmar himself urged Leopold to amend his attitude and style of approach to the Queen – wise advice which Leopold, equally wisely, followed. Stockmar reported that she 'had begun to take ill every piece of advice . . . which does not agree with her own opinion, and to see it as unjustified and undeserved criticism. On these occasions I have also found in her an underlying feeling that resembles the wounded pride of a person so highly placed that she says to herself "in normal circumstances these admonitions might be appropriate, but for me they are out of place" . . . and Lehzen encourages her. Just like the nurse who hits the stone that tripped the child up'. 'This year I did not enjoy pleasure so much', Queen Victoria wrote.

An additional, and major problem was that Victoria now had only one adviser whom she truly trusted and revered – her Whig Prime Minister, Melbourne. It was not at all surprising that the Queen became besotted by Melbourne. He was 58, handsome, worldly, amusing, and genuinely devoted to her service; 'he *alone* inspires me with that feeling of great confidence and I may say *security*', she wrote, 'for I feel *so safe* when he speaks to me and is with me'. 'He has *such* stores of knowledge; such a wonderful memory; he knows about everything and everybody; *who* they were and *what* they did . . . it does me a *world* of good, and his conversations always *improve* me greatly'. Noting this remarkable relationship, Greville wrote that the Queen's feelings 'are sexual, though she does not know it', and that Melbourne's 'province [is] to educate, instruct, and form the most interesting mind and character in the world'. Hobhouse described the relationship more accurately and shrewdly as that of a child to a father, and Creevey tartly commented that 'the part she at present plays is putting herself unreservedly into the exclusive management of Melbourne, without apparently thinking of anyone else'. Lord Aberdeen wrote to Princess Lieven that 'no minister in this country, since the days of Protector Somerset, was ever placed in such a situation . . . He has a young and inexperienced infant in his hands, whose whole conduct and opinions must necessarily be in complete

subservience to his views. I do him the justice to believe that he has
some feeling for his situation ... but in the nature of things, this
power must be absolute, at least at Court'.

In many respects Melbourne was an admirable first Prime Minister for a very young and politically naïve Queen; as Greville wrote,
'He treats her with unbounded consideration and respect, he con-
sults her tastes and her wishes, and he puts her at her ease by his
frank and natural manners, while he amuses her by the quaint,
queer, epigrammatic turn of his mind, and his varied knowledge
upon all subjects'. But however great the benefits of Melbourne's
excellent company, consideration, and sardonic observations –
'none of the Pagets can read or write, and they get on well enough' –
the fact was that he was a Whig Prime Minister, and a particularly
reactionary, cynical, and insensitive one. When taxed by Queen
Victoria about his irregular attendance at Church and his doubtful
full-hearted commitment to religion he retorted that 'I am a *quietist*',
and this honest self-description had significant application to his
political attitudes. 'You had better try to do no good, and then you'll
get into no scrapes' was not only his advice to the young Queen, but
his entire philosophy.

In her Journal she meticulously noted his observations.

' "All depends on the urgency of a thing", said Lord M. "If a thing
is very urgent, you can always find time for it; but if a thing can be
put off, why then, you put it off." ' (September 21st, 1838). On
September 28th he told her that 'I like what is tranquil and stable'.
And to these commentaries and views the very young Queen responded very eagerly. When Greville wrote that she was 'blinded by her
partialities', it was only too true.

But these were not quiet times.

The Chartist movement, whose first meeting was held only a few
weeks after the Queen's Coronation, sprang from several sources of
discontent and concern, involving alike the desperately poor in town
and country and middle class reformers who believed that the 1832
Reform Act was only the first step in substantial political peaceful
change. When the People's Charter was eventually produced its
famous Six Points – manhood suffrage, annual Parliaments, vote by
secret ballot, abolition of the property qualification for Parliamentary candidates, payment of Members of Parliament, and the creation of equal electoral districts – clearly emphasised its essentially
peaceful and constitutional nature. This was not the general reaction
of Parliament or the Melbourne Government, and the fact that
serious urban and rural violence was linked with the aspirations of
the Chartists did not lessen their dismay and fear. In the words of
Justin McCarthy, 'an ignorant panic prevailed on all sides'. Today,

with all the points except annual Parliaments accepted and established as major features of the British Constitution it is perhaps
difficult to appreciate the extent and fierceness of the controversies,
and the vehemence with which the established political confederations denounced the Six Points and successfully prevented their
introduction for a generation. In the Queen, they had a strong,
determined, and convinced ally, in every respect far closer to
Melbourne's distaste for any reform and change than to Russell's
commitment to modest but genuine liberalism and Peel's pragmatic
Toryism. When she described Peel in her Journal as a 'nasty wretch'
she meant it.

Queen Victoria's complex personality at this time has never been
better described than by A. C. Benson:

> She was high-spirited and wilful, but devotedly affectionate,
> and almost typically feminine. She had a strong sense of duty
> and dignity, and strong personal prejudices. Confident, in a
> sense, as she was, she had the feminine instinct strongly devel-
> oped of dependence upon some manly adviser. She was full of
> high spirits, and enjoyed excitement and life to the full. She
> liked the stir of London, was fond of dancing, of concerts, plays,
> and operas, and devoted to open-air exercise. Another impor-
> tant trait in her character must be noted. She had strong
> monarchical views and dynastic sympathies, but she had no
> aristocratic preferences; at the same time she had no democratic
> principles, but believed firmly in the due subordination of
> classes.[1]

With the latter principles Melbourne was in emphatic agreement,
and her personal dependence upon, and reverence for, Melbourne
dangerously included his political attitudes and those of his Party.

Melbourne had been Home Secretary in 1834 when six Dorset
farm labourers in Tolpuddle, whose employers had reneged on a
modest wage increase, formed a Friendly Society, and were arrested.
Melbourne wholly approved and took advice about which statute
should be employed to prosecute; under the Secret Oaths Act of
1797, passed to combat the naval mutiny at the Nore, the men were
prosecuted and sentenced to seven years' deportation. This savage
treatment of desperately poor men in a starving village aroused an
intense reaction and several heated debates in the Commons. Melbourne was indifferent to mass petitions and marches, but his
colleague Lord John Russell took a different view, and at his
insistence the sentences were remitted and the men given a free

[1] Introduction to *The Letters of Queen Victoria*, Vol. I, pp. 27–28.

passage home. But the episode of the 'Tolpuddle Martyrs', although the legend has become embellished, was of truly historic magnitude, and the fact that the Government had been forced to bow before the storm was significant. As has been wisely remarked, 'the reforming energy was in the time, and not in the Ministry'.[1] By the time Victoria became Queen Melbourne's reactionary instincts had become even more firmly entrenched.

The Melbourne Government had no real majority, no policy save that of maintaining a precarious *status quo*, amid notably little public or political esteem, facts which Melbourne appreciated clearly, with great regret and some incomprehension, but which Queen Victoria did not. 'I am sure that there are some times of trouble approaching for which Your Majesty must be prepared', he wrote to her in October 1838. 'Your Majesty is too well acquainted with the nature of human affairs not to be aware that they cannot very well go on as quietly as they have gone for the last sixteen months'. But Queen Victoria did not share Melbourne's melancholy and physical weariness – features which were now becoming notably significant in his conduct of affairs, and increasingly obvious to his colleagues, opponents, and political commentators, but not, unhappily, to the Queen.

The Queen's enthusiasm for Melbourne did not wholly extend to his outspoken and flamboyant Foreign Secretary, Lord Palmerston. A notorious womaniser, with a number of illegitimate progeny to testify to the fact, he had late-developing and surprising gifts of demagoguery and a leaning to liberalism at home and abroad that had been unsuspected in his previous political career, which had begun in 1809 when he had entered Parliament at the age of 25 after several unsuccessful endeavours and had been at once offered Cabinet office as either Chancellor of the Exchequer or Secretary for War, a commentary more on the grievous dearth of talent available rather than on a visionary appreciation of his future eminence. In the event he became Secretary for War outside the Cabinet, and since then had been a standard fixture in almost every Administration. Regarded by politicians as a poor orator but a notably hard-working Minister he also gave an appearance of flippancy, while his many

[1] A very good example of this was Rowland Hill's revolutionary proposal in 1837 for a uniform charge of one penny for a half-ounce letter without reference to distance. In 1839 the Government proposed four pence, but under pressure retreated, and in January 1840 the 'penny post' was introduced. Letter-writing ceased to be the expensive prerogative of the rich; in 1839 the total number of letters in Great Britain and Ireland was eighty-two million, by 1875 it was over a thousand million. Combined with the dramatic expansion of the railway system, and consequently national newspapers, this was a revolution indeed.

female conquests were regarded with that mixture of shock and admiration that the English affect on such matters. But Palmerston was a professional politician, and the first to grasp and use the new weapon of the Press. He arranged for the Whigs to secretly buy their own newspapers, and wrote unsigned anonymous leading articles and commentaries. He developed a populist approach to foreign affairs; his formidable Parliamentary skills, although they burgeoned relatively late, were beginning to mark him as a coming man. Melbourne was nervous of him, and so was the Queen, but her disapproval of his deplorable private life was overridden by the fact that he was a Whig, and Melbourne's choice as Foreign Secretary. These were sufficient lines of credit at that time.

Queen Victoria's blind devotion to Melbourne, his Government, its attitudes, and the Whig Party, now deeply imperilled her own position. She was not only young, emotional, ill-prepared, pre-judiced, reckless, imperious, and totally politically inexperienced, but she was, above all, *alone*, without access to any impartial political advice – Lehzen being a vehement Whig – and quite unaware of its necessity. Even Stockmar's former special authority was temporarily severely clouded by his close relationship with Leopold, with whom Queen Victoria had lost patience. This was particularly unfortunate, as his advice at this difficult time was very wise. 'You are too clever not to know', he wrote carefully on January 16th 1838, 'that it is *not* the being *called* Queen or King, which can be of the *least consequence*, when to the title there is not also annexed the power indispensable for the exercise of those functions. All trades must be learned, and nowadays the trade of a *constitutional Sovereign, to do it well, is a very difficult one* ...' In her Court, she leant only on Lehzen and her Whig ladies, but on them far less than on Melbourne. Her attitudes were implacable and open. At her very first levée a Whig renegade, Lord Lyndhurst, was in attendance; when she saw him, Creevey recorded, she drew herself up 'as if she had seen a snake'. She thought she knew her friends; she thought she knew her enemies, and her apparent popularity and power had gone to her head. All this was very human, very understandable, but very dangerous. As Stockmar realised from afar, she was frighteningly vulnerable, and in her personal obsessions wholly unaware of the fact.

The Tory Arbuthnot wrote angrily that 'with the young foolish Queen against us we can have but little hope. She seems to be full of power for evil – and to be full of weakness for good', a sentiment which accurately enough represented Tory impatience at the man-ifest partisanship of the Monarch. This was not a new phenomenon at all; what made Queen Victoria's partiality so unfortunate was that the real hopes that had been felt on her accession that a

genuinely disinterested and politically unbiassed Sovereign had
arrived had proved unfounded. Peel had remarked to Greville
immediately after her first meeting with the Privy Council that 'how
amazed he was at her manner and behaviour, at her apparent deep
sense of her situation, her modesty, and at the same time her
firmness'. But although Peel himself was cautious, 'the great body of
the Tories, on the other hand, are thirsting for office', as Greville
wrote; '... they are chafing and fuming that they can't get in, and
would encounter all the hazards of defeat for the slightest chance of
victory. It is only the prudent reserve of Peel (in which Stanley and
Graham probably join) that restrains the impatience of the party
within moderate bounds'.

This was written immediately after the Queen's accession. By the
Spring of 1839 the position had become infinitely worse. Melbourne's Whig administration clung precariously on to Office with
highly unreliable Radical and Irish supporters in the House of
Commons, increasingly unpopular, querulously divided in Cabinet,
and dominated solely by a passion for survival, which the Queen
vehemently shared. Lord Howick wrote that 'Lord Melbourne
adhered to the "stationary system", cannot bear adopting any new
measures unless he is absolutely compelled to do so, and thinks it
quite enough to deal with the difficulties which immediately press
upon him without looking to those which are likely to arise hereaf-
ter'. Following the dictum, 'Why do you bother the poor? Leave
them alone', the Melbourne Government found itself assailed with a
crisis in Canada – partially resolved by the dispatch of Lord
Durham, whom Melbourne detested – the evident continuance of
slavery in spite of its technical abolition, urban and agrarian unrest,
the rise of public education – not a subject at all close to Melbourne's
heart – and the first serious indications of the emergence of a national
campaign for the repeal of the Corn Laws.

Few issues in modern British politics have aroused such passions,
and had more notable political consequences. The Corn Law of 1815
banned the import of grain until the price of home-grown grain
reached eighty shillings per quarter; Customs Duty, subsequently
amended with a sliding scale whose effect was to reduce the duty on
imported wheat as the price of home-grown rose, and thereby gave a
double protection to the grower. Behind the Anti-Corn Law League,
whose roots were essentially in the Midlands, and especially in
Manchester, was the cause of Free Trade, espoused with an almost
messianic fervour by its advocates, of whom the most notable was
Richard Cobden, first elected to Parliament in 1841, but for some
time beforehand the outstanding populist champion of what Disraeli
described as 'the School of Manchester', one of his many phrases

that almost at once entered, and remained in, the political vocabulary. Cobden's principal lieutenant was John Bright, who brought to Cobden's sweet reason and mastery of statistics an oratorical power that Cobden lacked; they were, on platform and in Parliament, a most formidable combination. But the landed interest, as dominant in the Whigs as in the Tories, was implacable on the Corn Laws. It might be possible for politicians such as Russell and Peel to flirt with the principle of Free Trade in generalities, but not with the Corn Laws. On this matter Melbourne was as vehement as any Tory – 'I doubt whether property or the institutions of the country can stand it [repeal]' – but his tactics were to procrastinate, to express formal concern, and to calm those of his Ministers who were beginning to give evidence of some sympathy with the League. He also had a characteristically shrewd judgement that Peel, the leader of the Corn Law protectionist Tories, was already more persuaded of the need for reform – if not repeal – than he was prepared to admit even to himself, let alone to his followers.

The Cabinet by the beginning of 1839 was, as Lord Tavistock wrote, 'disunited, dissatisfied, and disgusted'. 'Lord Melbourne cannot but consider that affairs are in a most precarious state', he reported to the Queen on February 10th, 'and that whilst there is so much discontent fermenting within the Cabinet itself there must be great doubt of Lord Melbourne's being much longer to hold the Administration together'. A new Member of Parliament was the Tory, Benjamin Disraeli, whose maiden speech on December 7th 1837 had been a famous disaster, redeemed only by the final declaration, 'I sit down now, but the time will come when you will hear me'. He wrote in *Coningsby* (published in 1844) that the death of King William 'was a great blow to what had now come to be generally styled the "Conservative Cause"', and he subsequently admirably described the position of the Melbourne Government:

> The Ministerial majority became almost minimal, while troubles from all quarters seemed to press simultaneously upon them ... The extreme popularity of the Sovereign, reflecting some lustre on her Ministers, had enabled them, though not without difficulty, to tide through the session of 1838; but when Parliament met in 1839 their prospects were dark, and it was known that there was a section of the extreme Liberals who would not be deeply mortified if the Government were overthrown.[1]

[1] Disraeli: *Endymion* (1881).

At this point the Tories' impatience and frustration found a new target – the Queen herself. It is a measure of the abrupt fall in her popularity that they felt they could exploit this issue so bluntly and effectively.

The Lady Flora Hastings affair has been often related, but it has a supreme importance not only in British political history but in the life of Prince Albert, at this stage virtually forgotten by Queen Victoria but not at all unhappy in his scholarship and companions.

Lady Flora was 32 years of age, a lady-in-waiting to the Duchess of Kent, a Tory, and a vehement, astringent, and unwise ally of Conroy in the interminable and ferocious battles that had now moved from Kensington Palace to Buckingham Palace. Victoria regarded her as a Conroy spy and disliked her intensely, thereby causing another abrupt decline in her relationship with her mother, which subsequently gave her so much anguish. 'Oh! I am so wretched to think *how, for a time, two people most* wickedly estranged us', she wrote on her mother's death in 1861; '... it drives me *wild* now'. At the time, her feelings were very different, and very antagonistic.

In the autumn of 1838 Lady Flora and Conroy travelled together to Scotland, and on her return to Court in November both the Queen and Lehzen noted that her figure had suspiciously enlarged, and drew the obvious conclusion; 'we have no doubt', Victoria wrote, 'that she is – to use the plain words – *with child*!!' Also, she had no doubt that the cause was 'the Monster and Devil Incarnate, whose name I forbear to mention'. When Lady Flora indignantly refused to submit to a full medical examination by the Queen's physician (and that of the Duchess), Sir James Clark, the Queen's conviction seemed, not surprisingly, to have been confirmed, to her great pleasure. By this stage the matter was being discussed freely in Court and political circles, and Lady Flora did eventually submit to an examination which revealed that she was not, and never had been, pregnant. A public certificate to that effect was published, and Greville wrote that 'The Court is plunged in shame and mortification at the exposure ... The Palace is full of bickerings and heart-burnings, while the whole proceeding is looked upon by society at large as to the last degree disgusting and disgraceful'. Queen Victoria was appalled, and endeavoured to make amends to her mother and Lady Flora, but any hope of a reasonable conclusion to the episode was destroyed by Conroy, the Hastings family, and the Tories.

At the centre of the attack was the persistent demand as to who had initiated and circulated the calumnies against Lady Flora. Suspicion was levelled against Lehzen personally and the Whig ladies of the Court, and specifically, those 'of the bedchamber'. Lady Flora herself ominously blamed 'a certain foreign lady' but also the conspiratorial machinations of the Whig ladies in a letter to her uncle, Hamilton Fitzgerald, which was published in *The Examiner*; the Dowager Marchioness Hastings sent her correspondence with Melbourne to *The Morning Post*. The Tories were in tumult, the newspapers were in full cry, and there was a call for a special committee of enquiry into the alleged diabolical activities of the Whig ladies.

The public hubbub was immense, and deeply unnerving for the young Queen. No one in public life enjoys criticism, and particularly the first experiences are deeply discomfiting and hurtful. The Queen had got used to ecstatic huzzahs from Parliament and the newspapers, and reacted violently against the unexpected hostility, derision, and harsh innuendo to which she was now subjected. Melbourne wisely ignored her imperious demands that criticism of the Sovereign should be legally prohibited, and – although vainly – urged a philosophical acceptance of the disagreeable aspects of public service. Melbourne's advice on the handling of the Hastings affair had been lamentable, but the Queen did not blame him for his ineptitude and poor advice – as she could very reasonably have done – but clung to him all the more strongly. '*I* am but a poor helpless girl, who clings to him for support and protection – and the thought of ALL ALL my happiness being possibly at stake, so completely overcame me that I burst into tears and remained crying for some time'. Unhappiness and loneliness were also accompanied with anger against her mother, Conroy, the Hastings family, and the unspeakable Tories with their vicious newspapers and scurrilous allegations. In these bleak and unhappy circumstances the slender Parliamentary majority of the Government eroded to only five on the proposal to suspend the Constitution of Jamaica. This was on May 7th, and Melbourne informed the Queen that the Cabinet considered that the vote 'leave your Majesty's confidential servants no alternative but to resign their offices into your Majesty's hands'.

This event, coming at the height of the tumult over the treatment of Lady Flora Hastings, was a shattering blow to the Queen. The loss of 'Lord M.' would have been difficult to bear under any circumstances, but under these they were seen by her to be catastrophic. Her reactions were emotional and personal, but the political – and personal – consequences were to be momentous.

Most historians have been highly censorious of what then ensued; a few have taken Queen Victoria's side, but the key factor is the context in which the crisis took place. The Queen's hostility towards the Tories was now intensely augmented by the furore over Hastings. She felt herself to be virtually alone and was deeply estranged from her mother. The Tories were her bitter enemies, Melbourne and Lehzen and the Whig ladies at Court her only allies. 'I clung to someone and having very warm feelings,' she described her relationship with Melbourne in later years; 'Albert thinks I worked myself up to what really became quite foolish'. He was right, but the political fact in the summer of 1839 was she was indeed 'worked up'.

The Queen was not in an emotional condition to see the situation calmly, nor did she. She was distraught, and particularly responded to Melbourne's advice, which developed from 'Your Majesty had better express your hope that none of your Majesty's Household, except those who are engaged in politics may be removed', to the much stronger statement that 'they'll not touch your ladies', to which the Queen replied that 'I said they dared not and I never would allow it'. Thus was the scene set for the next stage of the crisis.

The Duke of Wellington, when summoned, declined the offer of the Premiership and advised the Queen to send for Peel. The Duke had no enthusiasm whatever for the Tories, and doubted whether he would serve in the new Ministry unless it were absolutely necessary. Under such forbidding circumstances did the Queen reluctantly summon Sir Robert Peel. This meeting was hardly a notable success. Victoria thought him 'embarrassed and put out', which was hardly surprising, considering that she subjected him to a eulogy on the virtues of Melbourne; she considered him a 'cold, unfeeling, disagreeable man', and was infinitely depressed by 'the awful incomprehensible change'. 'Oh! how different, how dreadfully different to that frank, open, natural and most kind warm manner of Lord Melbourne!'

Melbourne had warned her not 'to be affected by any faultiness of manner which you may observe. Depend upon it, there is no personal hostility to Lord Melbourne nor any bitter feelings against him. Sir Robert is the most cautious and reserved of mankind. Nobody seems to Lord Melbourne to know him, but he is not therefore deceitful or dishonest. Many a very false man has a very open sincere manner, and vice versa'. But even if Peel had possessed formidable resources of personal warmth and charm, nothing could have availed him at this moment with the Queen. He was a Tory; therefore he was her enemy. Peel's natural reserve, and the uncomfortable nature of the audience and its attendant circumstances, clearly did not assist matters, but it was not really important. When she made the point about the Household Ladies, he was non-committal. Melbourne, with whom she was in close, and doubtfully proper, correspondence, advised her 'to use this question of the Household strongly as a matter due to yourself and your own wishes; but if Sir Robert is unable to concede it, it will not do to refuse and put off the negotiations upon it'.

The fact was that the Ladies of the Household were totally partisan, and several were closely related to leading Whig families, and this point had been made several times during the Flora Hastings controversy, which was still raging. Lady Lansdowne, wife of the Lord President of the Council, was First Lady of the Bedchamber; one sister of the Irish Secretary was Mistress of the Robes and another was a Lady of the Bedchamber, as was Lady Normanby, the wife of the highly controversial former Lord Lieutenant of Ireland. Queen Victoria's own experiences led her to the very real – and by no means unwarranted – fear that the new Government would remove Lehzen as well as her Whig allies, and give Conroy his final and complete triumph. Thus, her passionate personal desire to see Melbourne return as her chief adviser had another aspect – the need to defeat Conroy and retain the limited independence and authority for which she had had to fight so hard. If there had been no Flora Hastings scandal and no Conroy-encouraged Tory demands for the wholesale removal of the Whig ladies there well might not have been any crisis over the position of the Ladies of the Bedchamber.

The Queen now took this up as *the* issue with Peel. It was her first experience of dealing with this remarkable man, and she was fortunate that he was to prove himself a man of honour and discretion, with complete loyalty to the Throne. 'Sir Robert Peel', Disraeli was to write of him in a celebrated passage, 'had a bad manner of which he was sensible; he was by nature very shy, but forced early in life into eminent positions, he had formed an artificial manner, haughtily stiff or exuberantly bland, of which, generally speaking, he could not divest himself'. The Queen's intransigence, now proof against even the pleadings of Wellington and the warn-ings of Melbourne, completely disconcerted him. She informed him that she intended to keep all the Ladies, and would not budge from this position. Even Melbourne was doubtful about the propriety of taking so intransigent an attitude, particularly as Peel himself never proposed the kind of sweeping changes that the Queen feared – or claimed to fear. Melbourne's colleagues, however, took a more robust view, and Melbourne himself swiftly saw the personal and political advantages. The Queen stood her ground, and Peel consi-dered that his position was hopeless. In reality, he was not deeply disappointed politically, although wounded personally by the Queen's attitude to him. He was very well aware of his own difficulties within his Party, and was perhaps over-conscious of national problems, particularly with regard to Ireland. Wellington could not conceal his relief that a serious obstacle to a Tory Government had been discovered. The Tories panted for Office, their leaders were more wary, but even if they had shared their followers' hunger the Queen's attitude would not have been much different. 'Do not fear that I was not calm and composed', she wrote to Melbourne. 'They wanted to deprive me of my ladies, and I suppose they would deprive me next of my dressers and my house-maids; they wished to treat me like a girl, but I will show them that I am Queen of England'. To Melbourne she also wrote that 'The Queen of England will not submit to such treachery'. On May 10th Peel gave up, and Melbourne and the Whigs were back.

The Tories were outraged, but were so astounded by the turn of events and the collapse of their own leader that the gunfire of their fury ranged on a considerable number of targets. Brougham launched a three-hour philippic in the Lords against Melbourne and the Queen which was, as Greville wrote, 'received by the Tory Lords with enthusiastic applause, vociferous cheering throughout, and two or three rounds at the conclusion', but Brougham characteristically went too far, and Wellington pointedly would not support him. Greville considered that 'He looks to the Crown of England, and not to the misguided little person who wears it', but Wellington's game was deeper than this. For the moment the Tories were utterly discomfited and felt outmanoeuvred by a subtler foe rather than simply by the implacable partisanship of the Queen. It was fortunate that they did not know the whole truth, or realise how deeply their own abuse of her over the Hastings affair had alienated her. They were also not to know that this was the last occasion on which a British Sovereign was able to prevent the formation of a Ministry which was politically uncongenial to the Monarch.

Such was the famous Bedchamber Crisis – or, as Disraeli called it, the Bedchamber Plot. Although it was a major victory for the Queen, it was very dearly bought. Disraeli, writing – very fortunately for his future relations with the Queen – under a pseudonym in *The Times* denounced her attitude and actions in an open letter to her: 'You will find yourself with the rapidity of enchantment the centre and puppet of a camarilla, and Victoria, in the eyes of that Europe which once bowed to her, and in the hearts of those Englishmen who once yielded to her their devotions, will be reduced to the level of Madrid and Lisbon'. Stockmar was appalled: 'The late events in England distress me', he wrote. 'How could they let the Queen make such mistakes, to the injury of the monarchy?'

'It is a high trial of our institutions when the caprice of a girl of nineteen can overturn a great Ministerial combination', wrote Greville, 'and when the most momentous matters of Government and legislation are influenced by her pleasure about her Ladies of the Bedchamber ... This making the private gratification of the Queen paramount to the highest public considerations: somewhat strange Whig doctrines and practice!' But Greville also saw – as did many others – the real impropriety of Victoria's conduct, dealing simultaneously with a resigned Ministry as though it had not resigned and with marked hostility to the incoming one as though it were not the constitutional alternative to the former one.

The crisis only lasted for four days, but the blatantly partisan conduct of the Queen was not forgotten or forgiven by the bitterly disappointed Tories. When Lady Flora Hastings died in July from a tumour on her liver, their fury and scorn reached new levels of virulence. Queen Victoria was hissed at Ascot, was derided as 'Mrs. Melbourne', and the feelings were so intense that she told Melbourne that 'if I were a private individual I should leave the country immediately, as I was so disgusted at the perpetual opposition'. Greville wrote that 'The Libels in the *Morning Post*, so far from being stopped, have only been more venomous since her [Lady Flora Hastings'] death and this soi-disant conservative paper daily writes against the Queen with the most revolting virulence and indecency'. Melbourne publicly denied that he had given the Queen any advice 'whatever' on the matter of the ladies, and that he had resumed office 'solely because I will not abandon my sovereign in a situation of difficulty and distress', and Peel behaved with great dignity and loyalty. Under such lowering circumstances the Whig-Irish-Radical combination renewed its very precarious and highly unpopular existence.

After the crisis had subsided, more sensible counsels prevailed. There could be no early reconciliation between Victoria and her mother, but the Court could and should include Ladies of Tory family; this was done gradually. ('Flies are caught with honey, not with vinegar', as Melbourne sagely told her, as he, somewhat belatedly, tried to cool her partisan passion against all Tories). Melbourne remained disturbed about the circumstances in which he had returned to Office, and from this moment whatever zest he had for politics noticeably declined. Lassitude fell upon him, and even the pleasure of the Queen's company was inadequate compensation for the weariness of continuing an unpopular minority confederation in office. His health began to deteriorate, he tired quickly, and his weary cynicism became increasingly evident. 'I do not dislike the Tories', he told the Queen, 'I think they are very much like the others: I do not care by whom I am supported; I consider them all as one: I do not care by whom I am helped as long as I am helped'. He no longer seriously feared Revolution. And thus, very slowly, his influence upon the Queen began to fade.

Although she had triumphed in retaining the Whigs, Queen Victoria's self-confidence had been seriously shaken by the combination of the Hastings affair, the continuing troubles over her mother and Conroy, and the Bedchamber Crisis. In April, for the first time, she spoke to Melbourne seriously about the possibility of marriage – emphasising that '*my* feeling is quite against ever marrying' and describing it to him as 'the shocking alternative' to dependence upon her mother – and mentioned Leopold's 'great wish' that she should marry Albert. Melbourne at once tackled the political point – would he take the side of the Duchess? The Queen 'answered him he need have no fear *whatever* on that score'. Melbourne was not enthusiastic about first cousins marrying, and they spoke of other possible alternatives to the Coburg connection which Melbourne, like his former master, King William, so detested. But Melbourne's lack of enthusiasm was easily matched by Queen Victoria's: 'I said I dreaded the thought of marrying; that I was so accustomed to have my own way, that I thought it was 10 to 1 I shouldn't agree with anybody'. The only definite decision was that a proposed visit to England by Duke Ernest and his sons in October would still take place. When Victoria asked Melbourne whether he had heard of Albert's habit of falling asleep after dinner he replied that 'he was very glad to hear of it'.

It was at this time that she sent to Leopold the bleak warning to which reference has already been made on page 52, but her situation and attitude were both changing. By August Melbourne's lack of enthusiasm was still very marked, but while Queen Victoria's distaste for two of her Saxe-Coburg uncles remained – she described Duke Ferdinand as the 'stingy one', and Duke Ernest as 'the difficult one', and resented their constant applications to her for money – she reacted with some imitation of Melbourne's coolness, remarking that she 'heard Albert's praises on all sides, and that he was very handsome'. But there were other factors, which at the time she perceived, as her discussions with Melbourne demonstrate. Her initial popularity had virtually disappeared; the political situation was very ugly; she was utterly estranged from her mother; and she was surrounded by considerably older people, in few of whom she reposed any confidence or affection. She was suddenly desperately lonely, and subsequently wrote: 'A worse school for a young girl, or one more detrimental to all natural feelings and affections, cannot well be imagined, than the position of a Queen at eighteen, without experience and without a husband to guide and support her'.

But there had been one major, and immensely important and beneficial consequence of the combined Hastings and Bedchamber crises. Conroy resigned his position in the Duchess of Kent's household on June 1st. A certain mystery remains as to who, or what, precipitated this very desirable event, and the claims of the Duke of Wellington that he was the principal instigator may well have been true. 'The Duke as usual has been called in, for in desperate cases he is always the Doctor they rely on', Greville noted on June 1st, and Wellington subsequently reported to Melbourne that 'That fellow's going', and, Melbourne told the Queen, was 'in great joy at it'. Both the Queen and Melbourne were sceptical about the finality of Conroy's departure, but in fact it was to be the last – or almost the last – of this sinister and deplorable man. He carried with him into his exile a deep bitterness against Leopold and Lehzen but not, it would appear, against the Queen herself; but she was to remain implacable in her hatred for him and the ill-service he had rendered to herself and her mother. The enormity of Conroy's misappropriation of other people's money was only fully appreciated later, but it may be that he considered it expedient to leave England before matters came to light. In any event, Conroy was gone, and the dark shadows that had so deeply afflicted Victoria's relations with her mother slowly began to lift.

There were other signs, in addition to the discussions with Melbourne over the possibility of marriage to Prince Albert, that the Queen's mood had been substantially changed by the torrid events of the spring and summer of 1839. Her relations with Melbourne, although still immensely warm, began to show certain signs of her awareness of the decline in his own spirits. In June she confessed that she had found an evening in his company to be actually dull; on other occasions it was even more apparent that, as the Queen grew up with such rapidity in her new position, she was developing attitudes to which Melbourne did not respond. His flippancy, which had once so delighted her, now sometimes shocked her. His unrepentant dislike of religion – 'I think there will be a great deal of persecution in this country before long, people interfering with one another about going to Church, and so on' – was only one, if significant, area of difference. In a neat juxtaposition of their relationship, her admonitions on his eating, drinking, and sleeping habits became severely maternal and censorious. 'I fear that I was sadly cross with Lord Melbourne', she wrote after one of these episodes.

But there was something else. Victoria's bleak childhood had contained very little enjoyment and few contacts with her contemporaries, and particularly with young men. As she later wrote, she had had 'no scope for my very violent feelings of affection.' She found that in this aspect being Queen had not greatly improved her situation, and her unalloyed enjoyment of a visit by the youthful Alexander, Grand Duke of Russia, in the summer and with the subsequent feeling of deflation when he was gone was an indication of her growing interest in young men, in fun, and in laughter. As she remarked wistfully to Melbourne after the Grand Duke had departed, 'a young person like me must *sometimes* have young people to laugh with'. She was delighted by the visits of her 'Ferdinand' Coburg cousins Augustus and Leopold and the shy and handsome Alexander Mensdorff-Pouilly, son of Princess Sophia. Alexander made a deep impression, even more than the Grand Duke, which both Melbourne and Leopold – with very different motives – hastened to remove. Eventually the young man wrote to Victoria a gentle letter of farewell which one doubts was a wholly spontaneous one. Alexander was indeed a handsome young man, and, as the Queen remarked with charming candour, she was 'not insensible to beauty'.

Elizabeth Longford has described this aspect of Queen Victoria's character admirably:

> The Queen's susceptibility to beauty was one of her most interesting characteristics. Whether in men, women, children, animals, landscapes, houses or clothes, she hailed it with an enthusiasm unexpected in one who set such store by sterling worth. Just before her marriage she frequently emphasised her admiration for male beauty, often discussing the handsome figure of one or other of her courtiers. Melbourne tried to damp down this ardour, perhaps because he feared no suitable consort would come up to the Queen's romantic ideals. But she was set on a love-match and beauty was one of the essentials'.[1]

It is too much to say that 'King Leopold had thus cleverly set the stage for Prince Albert and a renewal of warm Coburg family life'.[2] All he had achieved was to arrange the visit of the Princes in October, which Queen Victoria had tried to cancel in July. Neither she nor Albert were at all sanguine about the prospects, and the chilling words that 'I might like him as a friend, and as a *cousin*, and as a *brother*, but not *more*', emphasised the absence of her commitment. To her credit, she was troubled about the effect on her cousin,

[1] Longford, *Queen Victoria*, pp. 127–8.   [2] Ibid., p. 127.

and recorded in her Journal (July 12th) a discussion with Melbourne:

> Talked of my fearing that too many of my relations had come over this year, which Lord M. didn't think, and said there had been no remarks made about it. Talked of my Cousins Ernest and Albert coming over – my having no great wish to see Albert, as the whole subject was an odious one, and one which I hated to decide about; there was no engagement between us, I said, but that the young man was aware that there was the possibility of such a union; I said it wasn't right to keep him on, and not right to decide before they came; and Lord M. said I should make them distinctly understand anyhow that I couldn't do anything for a year; I said it was disagreeable for me to see him though, and a disagreeable thing. 'It's very disagreeable,' Lord M. said. I begged him to say nothing about it to anybody, or to answer questions about it, as it would be very disagreeable to me if other people knew it. Lord M. I didn't mind, as I told him everything. Talked of Albert's being younger. 'I don't know that that signifies,' said Lord M. 'I don't know what the impression would be,' he continued, 'there's no anxiety for it; I expected there would be.' I said better wait till impatience was shown. 'Certainly better wait for a year or two,' he said; 'It's a very serious question.' I said I wished if possible never to marry. 'I don't know about *that*', he replied.

Her lack of enthusiasm for Albert was reciprocated. The young man's impatience and annoyance at his position were very sympathetically viewed by Leopold and Stockmar when he was told that the Queen had said that there could be no discussion on the matter for two or three years 'at the *very* earliest'. It was, as the Queen later completely admitted with great remorse an impossible and humiliating position for a young man, and one that he justifiably strongly resented.

But the reality of the situation was far more propitious than anyone realised. 'The stage of schoolgirl hero-worship was passing', as David Cecil has written of Queen Victoria, 'and there had begun to stir uneasily within her the desire for a more mature emotional fulfilment'.

Although in retrospect there appears to be a certain inevitability about the love between the young Queen and Prince Albert, none existed when they approached their second meeting, which they each viewed with doubts and apprehensions, and on Albert's side

with some degree of annoyance. He subsequently wrote to
Löwenstein on December, 6th that 'I went therefore [to Windsor]
with the quiet but firm resolution to declare on my part that I also,
tired of the delay, withdrew entirely from the affair. It was not,
however, thus ordained by Providence'.

Albert and Ernest arrived at Windsor Castle in pouring rain on
the evening of October 10th after another terrible crossing of the
Channel, cold, ashen, dishevelled, and without their luggage, which
had been mislaid. Victoria, waiting for them very nervously at the
top of the staircase, was not prepared for the change in Albert since
she had last seen him. 'It was with some emotion that I beheld Albert
– who is *beautiful*', she wrote that evening. Word was communicated
to him that he had 'made a favourable impression', but although she
told Melbourne on the 13th that she had not made a decision no one
at Windsor had any doubt that she had fallen deeply in love. As
Melbourne wrote to Lord John Russell on the 13th, 'A very strong
impression is evidently made ... and I do not know that anything
better could be done. He seems a very agreeable young man, he is
certainly a very good looking one, and as to character, that we must
always take our chance of'.

Queen Victoria's admiration for Albert's 'beauty' dominates her
Journal and letters even more than on their first meeting, when she
had written that 'Albert is so very handsome, and has such a
beautiful and delightful expression' (Journal, June 4th 1836).
'Albert', she wrote now in her Journal on October 11th, 'really is
quite charming, and so extremely handsome, such beautiful blue
eyes, an exquisite nose, and such a pretty mouth with delicate
moustachios & slight but very slight whiskers: a beautiful figure,
broad in the shoulders & a fine waist; my heart is quite *going*'. To
Leopold she wrote that 'Albert's beauty is *most striking*, and he is so
amiable and unaffected – in short, very *fascinating*'. Leopold wrote in
turn, with skilful restraint, that 'Albert is a very agreeable companion. His manner is so gentle and harmonious, that one likes to have
him near oneself. . . may Albert be able to strew roses without thorns
on the pathway of life of our good Victoria! He is well qualified to do
so'. The interesting point for Prince Albert's biographer is that he
was making an equally strong impression upon more detached
observers. Lady Cowper – shortly to marry Palmerston after a long
and star-crossed liaison – wrote that 'Albert of Coburg, of whom
there is so much talk, is a very charming young man, very well
mannered and handsome and gay, and said to be very well informed
and sensible'. Melbourne was impressed by him at once, although
with certain reservations, and when he saw the Queen on October
14th and found that her mind was completely made up he urged her

to marry quickly, and together they planned the timetable, the Parliamentary procedures for an allowance for Albert, and honours.

Albert did not keep a Journal during these hectic days (or if he did, it has disappeared, with his other diaries), but from his letters and subsequent comments one has a clear picture of a shy young man at first bewildered and then deeply moved by Victoria's passion. 'How is it that I have deserved so much love, so much affection?' he wrote to her, signing his letter 'In body and soul ever your slave, your loyal Albert'. Lytton Strachey stated in his study of Queen Victoria that 'he was not in love with her' – only repeating, it is fair to point out, the comments of some contemporaries, including the waspish Duchess of Bedford – and implied, as others have done, that he was stampeded into matrimony by a scheming uncle and a passionate girl experiencing her first real love. But although Prince Albert was indeed understandably bewildered and confused by the pace of events and the turmoil of Queen Victoria's feelings, we have enough evidence to realise that, beneath his reserve and reluctance to demonstrate his emotions to others, his heart had been deeply touched by Victoria's warmth, ebullience and attractiveness. Although of a volatile nature, the young Queen had a sparkle and physical beauty which had affected many other men, who had also found her gaiety and zest irresistible. Thus, although Albert's letters to her were somewhat less frenziedly excited than Victoria's to him, she had no doubt that her love was fully returned.

Prince Albert's shyness and reserve in public was in such contrast with his real personality that his friends have had difficulty in conveying their pleasure in his company. Stockmar's son wrote that 'In his intercourse with persons to whom he was intimate, the cheerfulness and amiability of his youth never ceased, as well as a childlike pleasure in jokes, and a rare talent in producing or representing what was comical. In larger circles, on the other hand, he appeared formal, measured, and reserved, and, as many thought, cold and stiff'.

On October 15th Albert was summoned to a famous private audience, which Victoria related in her Journal:

'I said to him that I thought he must be aware *why* I wished them [the brothers] to come here, and that it would make me *too happy* if he would consent to what I wished (to marry me); we embraced each other over and over again, and he was *so* kind, *so* affectionate; Oh! to *feel* I was, and am, loved by *such* an Angel as Albert was *too great delight to describe*! he is *perfection*; perfection in every way – in beauty – in everything! I told him I was quite unworthy of him and kissed his dear hand – he said he would be very happy 'das Leben mit dir zu zubringen' and was so kind and seemed so happy, that I really felt it was the happiest brightest moment in my life, which made up for all I had suffered and endured. Oh! *how* I adore and love him, I cannot say!! *how* I will strive to make him feel as little as possible the great sacrifice he has made ... I feel the happiest of human beings'.

'The openness of manner in which she told me this quite enchanted me, and I was quite carried away by it', Albert wrote to his grandmother.

The references to Albert's 'sacrifice' are frequent in the Queen's Journal and letters of the time of her engagement. While he demurred at the description, she always appreciated, with acute sensitiveness and sympathy, Albert's evident uneasiness in England. It was, after all, only his second visit to this cold, sea-tossed island with its peculiar food, uncongenial hours, chaotic politics, and deep suspicions of foreigners, and particularly Germans. 'While I shall be untiring in my efforts and labours for the country to which I shall in future belong', he assured his grandmother, 'and where I am called to so high a position, I shall never cease to be a true German, and true Coburg and Gotha man'.

Nor did he have any illusions about the other difficulties that would arise as consort of the Queen of England. 'My future position will have its dark sides, and the sky will not always be blue and brilliant', he wrote to Löwenstein. '... My future lot is high and brilliant, but also plentifully strewn with thorns' was another comment, while to his grandmother he wrote: 'Oh, the future! does it not bring with it the moment when I shall have to take leave of my dear, dear home, and of you? I cannot think of this without being overcome by a feeling of profound melancholy'. Grandmother Gotha, while delighted at his personal happiness, was 'very much upset', as she told Duke Ernest: 'The brilliant destiny awaiting our Albert cannot reconcile me to the thought that his country will lose him for ever! and, for myself, I lose my greatest happiness ... I hope the Queen will appreciate him ... I *cannot* rejoice'.

The Court tensions in London were only too obvious, and for someone to whom separation from his brother had been such an agonising experience the prospect of living permanently in a foreign country clearly had severe difficulties, and of which Prince Albert – and Stockmar – were acutely aware.

It was characteristic of Queen Victoria to realise this immediately, and perhaps even more to her credit that although it would be excessive to say that she never forgot it, she constantly reminded herself of it, and was consequently even more devotedly grateful. For his part, Prince Albert at once assumed a protective attitude towards his adoring fiancée, immediately deeply conscious of her need for such protection and companionship. Few marriages begin with such mutual sensitivity and respect, and these, rather than natural physical attraction between two very attractive young people, was the rock on which their love and their marriage was truly based.

The day after his engagement Prince Albert wrote to Stockmar:

'I am writing to you today on one of the happiest days of my life to send you the most joyful possible news. Yesterday in a private audience V. declared her love for me, and offered me her hand, which I seized in both mine and pressed tenderly to my lips. She is so good and kind to me that I can scarcely believe such affection should be mine. I know you take part in all my happiness, and so I can pour out my heart to you. For the present the event is to remain a secret, and is to be announced to the nation before being communicated to anyone else, at the meeting of Parliament. What grieves me is that my aunt[1] to whom this important step by her daughter touches so nearly is not to know of it. But as everyone says, she cannot keep her mouth shut and might even make bad use of the secret if it were entrusted to her, I quite see the necessity of it.

'V. wishes that the wedding shall take place as early as the beginning of February, to which I gladly agreed as the relations between a betrothed pair, when the fact is public property, may often appear indelicate.

'I cannot write further or on more serious matters – I am in too great a state of confusion for

Das Auge Sieht den Himmel offen
es Schwimmt das Herz in Seligkeit.[2]

Stockmar's letter of reply was, although warmly congratulatory, replete with advice and warnings, to which Albert responded meekly but with some firmness that 'I have laid to heart your friendly and kind-hearted counsels as to the true foundation on which my future happiness must rest, and they accord entirely with the principles which I had already thought out on that subject for myself'.

The secret of their engagement must have been extremely difficult to keep. For the next month the brothers stayed at Windsor, and Victoria and Albert were alone together so often in the Blue Boudoir that it was remarkable that even the Duchess of Kent was unaware of what had happened. It was indeed 'a halcyon month', as Roger Fulford has described it. There was no question at all that the Prince was now passionately devoted to Queen Victoria, but acutely conscious that his letters were stilted compared to hers. 'I reproach

---

[1] The Duchess of Kent.
[2] 'The eye sees Heaven open,/The heart floats on a sea of blessedness' (Schiller: *Song of the Bell*).

myself so often', he wrote movingly to her, 'because compared to
yours my letters are so cold and stiff, and yet I shrink from boring
you with my outpourings'. But this was perhaps excessive self-
criticism; in another letter he wrote that: 'Thinking of you makes me
so happy – what a delight it must be to walk through the whole of my
life, with its joys and storms, with you at my side. Love of you fills my
whole heart'. In a singularly moving letter Ernest told Queen
Victoria that 'Setting aside that he is my brother, I esteem and love
him more than any man on earth. You will smile, perhaps, if I speak
to you of him in such high terms of eulogy! but I do it in order that
you may feel still more what you have gained in him! As yet, you are
most taken with his manner, so youthfully innocent, his tranquillity,
his clear mind – this is as he appears at first acquaintance. Knowledge of men, & experience – one would read less in his face; and
why? because he is pure before the world and before his own
conscience; not as if he did not yet know sin, the earthly temptations,
the weakness of men – no, but because he knew and still knows how
to struggle with them, supported by the incomparable superiority &
firmness of his character'.

From Prince Albert's letters and her enchantingly artless and
touching account, they lived only for each other during that month,
to the point when the Queen apologised to Melbourne for being
unable to think of anything else than her own happiness (to which
Melbourne tactfully replied, 'Very natural'). 'He seems perfection',
Victoria wrote to Leopold, 'and I think that I have the prospect of
very great happiness before me. I love him *more* than I can say, and
shall do everything in my power to render this sacrifice (for such in
my opinion it is) as small as I can ... These last few days have passed
like a dream to me, and I am so much bewildered by it all that I know
hardly how to write; but I do feel very happy'. There were frequent
dances, which Albert subsequently remembered with joy when 'I
was flying with you through that lovely ballroom', and on one
occasion Victoria showed him her Journal for the day of their
engagement which deeply moved him. There was much passionate
kissing, laughter, conversation, and happiness. The glow from
Queen Victoria's Journal is almost palpable. As Cecil Woodham-
Smith has rightly written: 'One of the most celebrated romances in
history had begun, the Queen had fallen in love'.[1] So, also, had
Prince Albert. 'Yes – I am now actually a bridegroom!' he wrote to
Löwenstein, 'and about the 4th of February hope to see myself
united to her I love!'

[1] Woodham-Smith, op. cit., p. 182.

FOUR

'Only the Husband'

With his engagement still a closely kept secret, Prince Albert left London on November 24th and discussed his situation, and specifically the arrangements for his future establishment, with Leopold and Stockmar at Wiesbaden. Leopold reported to Queen Victoria that her fiancé was looking particularly well: 'It proves that happiness is an excellent remedy, and keeps people in better health than any other. He is much attached to you, and modest when speaking of you. He is besides in great spirits, full of gaiety and fun'. Stockmar, for so long so critical of Prince Albert, now wrote to Lehzen on December 15th that 'the more I see of the Prince the better I esteem and love him', and, while he did not underestimate the difficulties facing Albert now believed that 'if he really possesses the love of the Queen and the respect of the nation, I will answer for it, that after every storm he will come safely into port'. One promising sign was the warmth of the letters to Albert from the Duchess of Kent; well aware of the severe tensions between her and Victoria, Albert's letters were masterpieces of affection and tact. To Queen Victoria herself he wrote that 'That I am the object of so much love and devotion often comes over me as something I can hardly realise. My prevailing feeling is, What am I, that such happiness should be mine? For excess of happiness it is for me to know, that I am so dear to you'.

The public announcement in London of the engagement on November 23rd was greeted with enthusiasm in Coburg and Gotha – where Prince Albert arrived at the end of November – with the conspicuous exception of grandmother Gotha, who was, Albert reported to Victoria, 'red-eyed' when he went to see her. But in England, after the initial excitement, there were less favourable popular reactions than in Coburg. This was not to be wondered at, although the Queen was astonished and angered. She accepted Melbourne's strongly worded advice that Albert should not receive the title of King Consort, which she had proposed, but the criticism of her choice for her husband was wholly unexpected. Prince Albert was not generally regarded as an appropriately important husband for the Queen of England, and his youth, the fact that he was Queen Victoria's first cousin, was German, and a Saxe-Coburg at that, was the nephew of the Duchess of Kent and King Leopold – those highly controversial and not widely popular personalities – was without any wealth, and was generally unknown beyond these unflattering facts generated considerable hostility and critical questioning.

Stockmar arrived in England, as the Prince's Plenipotentiary, to negotiate the marriage contract and arrangements with Palmerston. 'The ultra-Tories are filled with prejudices against the Prince', he noted, 'in which I can clearly trace the influence of Ernest Augustus of Hanover. They give out that he is a Radical and an infidel, and say that George of Cambridge, or a Prince of Orange, ought to have been the Consort of the Queen. On the whole, however, the mere determination of the Queen to marry, and the satisfaction thereby given to what was a very universal desire (for the idea that the King of Hanover and his line might succeed to the throne was very distasteful to the people) has raised the Queen's popularity, and will for a while lend some strength to the very weak Ministry. The public is tolerably indifferent as to the person of the bridegroom; but I hear it generally complained that he is young'.

Even more seriously, it was rumoured that the Prince was a Roman Catholic and had 'Papalistic' tendencies, as the Declaration of the marriage prepared by Ministers had unwisely, but deliberately, omitted to mention that he was a Protestant Prince. The Queen told Albert (November 21st) that the Declaration was 'very simple and nice', but although it had been courteously received when she read it, with great nervousness, to the Privy Council on November 23rd the glaring absence of reference to Prince Albert's Protestantism had been swiftly noted.

The uproar must be seen in its context. A vast and fundamental convulsion had gripped the Church of England when John Henry Newman, the saintly and influential Vicar of St. Mary's Church, Oxford, published Tract Number 90 of a series of 'Tracts for the Times' whose contributors included Keble, Pusey, and Richard Froude, brother of the historian. Although the 'Tractarian' movement had caused widespread controversy, it was Number 90 that had caused the greatest excitement and division, because Newman's fundamental point was that it was possible for an individual in all honesty to subscribe to the articles of the Church of England while yet holding many of the doctrines of the Church of Rome. Oxford responded violently to this heresy, the Vice-Chancellor and heads of houses meeting in solemn conclave to denounce and censure

Newman, and the reverberations of the long and bitter battles over
Catholic Emancipation in the 1820's once again thundered, and not
least in Parliament. Prince Albert was the unwitting, and totally
innocent, victim of the deep fears of the Protestant Establishment.

The Prince himself set out the impeccable Protestant and non-
Catholic history of his family on this matter in a long letter to Queen
Victoria on December 7th, and Leopold had warned her to make this
clear in public as any doubts would 'give rise to interminable
growling. On religious matters one cannot be too prudent, because
one can never see what passionate people will make of such a thing'.
But, looking nervously over their shoulders at their crucial Catholic
Irish votes, Melbourne and his colleagues took a different view. As
Prince Albert's uncles, Ferdinand and Leopold himself – in his
second marriage to Princess Louise d'Orleans, daughter of Louis
Philippe, King of France – had married Catholics, the fears were not
wholly groundless. The result was that the matter was fiercely
debated in both Houses of Parliament, and in the Lords Wellington
successfully moved an amendment to the Congratulatory Address to
insert the word, 'Protestant', justifiably charging the Government
with attempting to placate their Irish supporters in the Commons by
the deliberate omission. He did not raise himself in the Queen's
estimation by adding that 'It appears to me that the public ought to
know something beyond the name of Prince Albert', although it was
in fact a characteristically blunt and fair point. So heated did the
matter become that Palmerston wrote urgently to Stockmar 'in great
haste' to seek categorical assurances on the matter, which were at
once given. 'God knows', Stockmar later wrote, 'with the prevailing
fanaticism, what horrible absurdity might not have resulted'.

This was a dismal beginning, which reflected considerable dis-
credit upon Melbourne and his Ministers and plunged him and
them even lower in Albert's estimation, although not in that of the
Queen, while also significantly increasing his already considerable
and understandable unhappiness at the prospect of leaving his
country, family, and friends. This gloom, which dominates his
letters at this difficult time, was certainly not eased when a storm
arose over the issue of his future income.

Again, the Melbourne Government bungled the matter wretch-
edly. Taking the precedents of recent consorts, including that of the
much-criticised Leopold, Ministers proposed to Parliament an
annuity of £50,000 for Prince Albert without consulting the Opposition leaders, and the dismayed Albert accordingly found himself the
victim of the intense passions of British party politics yet again. The
Whigs accused the Tories and Radicals of lack of devotion to the
Crown, while the latter responded with considerable vehemence on

the fruitful topics of the arrogance of Ministers and their insensitiveness to the economic distress in the country.

There was clearly another factor, with Leopold's example still very much in the public memory, and unkindly exposed in a broadsheet:

> *He comes the bridegroom of Victoria's choice,*
> *The nominee of Lehzen's vulgar voice;*
> *He comes to take 'for better or for worse'*
> *England's fat Queen and England's fatter purse.*

A motion by the Radical, Joseph Hume, to reduce the grant to £21,000 was defeated in the Commons, but one to fix it at £30,000 proposed by the flamboyant Tory Colonel Sibthorp was carried by 262 votes to 158, with Peel and his Tory colleagues on the front bench voting for the reduction. As Melbourne frankly admitted to Stockmar, 'The Prince will be angry at the Tories. But it is not the Tories only whom the Prince has to thank for cutting down his allowance. It is rather the Tories, the Radicals, and a great proportion of our own people'. The Queen, however, said that the episode and the Press comments had made her hate the Tories even more. She wrote in her Journal for January 1st 1840: 'From the Tories, good Lord deliver us'.

Even worse was to come. The Government calmly presented to Parliament a Bill to grant Prince Albert naturalisation, but it also accorded him precedence for life after the Queen in Parliament or elsewhere as she might decide. This was Queen Victoria's direct personal wish, after Melbourne had ruled out her proposal that he should be 'King Consort', but again there had been no attempt at Party consultation, and what was constitutionally a difficult situation that should have been recognised as such at the outset and seriously discussed before legislation was introduced now became, again, a political matter. As Prince Albert would rank above the Princes of the Royal Blood, the consent of Queen Victoria's uncles was necessary. Sussex and Cambridge did agree, although not immediately, but Cumberland, now King of Hanover,[1] violently objected, and persuaded Cambridge to withdraw his consent while also stirring up the Tories.

Wellington, supported by Brougham, now implacably hostile to Melbourne, opposed the Bill in the Lords on the absolutely justified

---

[1] The Kingdom of Hanover, under the Salic law, could not pass to a woman, so Cumberland had inherited it on the death of his brother King William, and was, until Queen Victoria had a child, heir to the British throne. It was this fact which tempered popular opposition to the Queen's engagement, and had a considerable influence upon politicians.

constitutional grounds that such sweeping powers should be granted
by Parliament and not simply by the Queen. Ministers were disconcerted and the debate hurriedly adjourned. Unreasonably, the
Queen again blamed the 'abominable infamous Tories'. 'I grew
quite frantic', she wrote in her Journal, 'declared I never would
forgive it, never would look at the Duke again, etc. 'Don't be angry',
Lord M. said calmly. I was quite furious and raged away . . . As long
as I live I'll never forgive these infernal scoundrels, with Peel at their
head'. She considered it an 'act of personal spite!!' by the 'vile,
confounded, infernal Tories', and resolved that Wellington should
not attend her wedding. Melbourne was more phlegmatic, but the
Queen's wrath was intense:

> I was perfectly frantic – this wicked old foolish Duke, these
> confounded Tories, oh! may they be well punished for this
> outrageous insult! I cried with rage . . . Poor dear Albert, how
> cruelly are they ill-using that dearest Angel! Monsters! You
> Tories shall be punished. Revenge! Revenge!

Eventually it was agreed to drop the offending section from the Bill
and, at the suggestion of Greville, by Letters Patent issued on March
5th – this time, with all-Party agreement – it was provided that
Prince Albert should henceforth 'upon all occasions, and in all
meetings, except when otherwise provided by Act of Parliament,
have, hold, and enjoy place, pre-eminence, and precedence next to
Her Majesty'. He was to receive no title, and it was not until July
1857 that he formally was granted, again by Letters Patent, the title
of Prince Consort – long after it had become his universal, but wholly
unofficial, title.

The Queen had had little intimation that matters would be so
difficult. 'Your rank will be settled just before you come over, as also
your rank in the Army', she had written confidently to Albert on
November 21st; 'Everything will be very easily arranged'. She
strongly resisted Leopold's suggestion that he should receive a
Peerage, and wrote to him with severity on November 26th that 'the
English are very jealous at the idea of Albert's having any political
power, or meddling with affairs here – which I know from himself he
will *not* do'. To Albert she wrote directly on November 27th on the
same lines, but admonitions such as these – which read somewhat
strangely in the light of later events – were very different from the
issue of the position and rank of her future husband. Thus, she
regarded the disputes over this matter as not only personally insulting to herself and to her fiancé but also as demeaning to the position
of the Sovereign. A complex woman, who in private was not only
amusing but also modest, she was very different when the status of

the Sovereign was involved, and the refusal of her clear wishes – only resolved by Greville's opportune memorandum on the use of the Letters Patent procedure – was seen by her as a manifest attempt by political opponents in Parliament to diminish her powers.

Prince Albert had been reasonably philosophical about the cutting of his annuity, remarking sadly that it would tend to limit his opportunities of assisting artists and men of learning and science, which he had already marked down as a personal priority, but the uproar over his title angered and upset him intensely, while the Queen was incensed. 'The Tories really are very astonishing', she informed Albert (January 21st); 'as they cannot and dare not attack us in Parliament, they do everything that they can to be personally rude to me . . . The Whigs are the only safe and loyal people, and the Radicals will also rally round their Queen to protect her from the Tories; but it is a curious sight to see those, who as Tories, used to pique themselves upon their excessive loyalty, doing everything to degrade their young Sovereign in the eyes of the people . . .'. 'We had much difficulty on this subject', she wrote in 1856, 'much bad feeling was shown, several members of the Royal Family showed bad grace in giving precedence to the Prince, and the late King of Hanover positively resisted doing so'. This was to cause endless difficulties and several embarrassments abroad. 'The only legal position in Europe, according to international law, which the husband of the Queen of England enjoyed', the Queen wrote 'was that of a younger brother of the Duke of Saxe-Coburg, and this merely because the English law did not know of him. This is derogatory to the dignity of the Crown of England'.

It was also another stinging rebuff to the Melbourne Government, although not seen as such by Queen Victoria, and, coming immediately after the fiascoes over the allegations about the Prince's religion and his annuity, demonstrated that the forthcoming marriage and the monarchy itself were seriously unpopular. Not unreasonably, Albert – who first read of the annuity vote in a newspaper in Aix – drew the ominous personal conclusion that 'the people of England were not pleased with the marriage' and particularly with himself, and wrote to Victoria of 'the very unpleasant effect produced upon me by the news', but he added touchingly, that, 'while I possess your love, they cannot make me unhappy'.

Less serious, but considerably more significant, were the difficulties over the Prince's Household, a matter on which he and Stockmar felt strongly. Melbourne undertook the detailed negotiations with Prince Albert under the evident impression that he, the experienced Prime Minister, was dealing with a young German Prince with little understanding of English politics and customs, who would be deeply grateful for the Prime Minister's thinly veiled orders, courteously conveyed as advice. By the conclusion of their correspondence Melbourne had learned rather more about the future consort of the Queen than he had expected, and perhaps particularly cared for. Albert made his position clear to Victoria (December 10th):

... The maxim, 'Tell me whom he associates with and I will tell you who he is' must here be especially not lost sight of. These appointments should not be mere 'party rewards'. Let them be either of very high rank, or very rich, or very clever, or persons who have performed important services for England. It is very necessary that they should be chosen from both sides – the same number of Whigs as of Tories; and above all I do wish that they should be well-educated men and of high character. I know you will agree with my views ...

The Queen certainly did not, and on December 20th Prince Albert opened his assault on Melbourne:

My dear Lord Melbourne,
    Since my return from England I have repeatedly and most seriously reflected on the new state into which I am about to enter, and in many respect my future position will appear to me very difficult. I am so full of it, that I am sorry that the space of a Letter forbids me to expound to you completely all I have thought and felt on the subject. Don't think however that the serious examination I have put frequently to my new State and myself have had the effect of rendering me diffident for at the end of all my meditations *one conviction of a comforting nature* presents itself invariably to my mind, viz. that *if earnest and honest intentions have something to do with Success*, I may almost feel assured of a happy result.
    Before I finish, I take the liberty of recommending one point in particular to your mature consideration, I mean the composition of my future Establishment or Household. In the very *just* demand upon me, that I shall carefully abstain from Party Politics on one hand, and in the possible appointment of gentlemen, who from their actual position in Life must necessarily belong to a party on the other hand, I see a glaring contradiction which I cannot reconcile to my Logick. In consequence I have proposed to the Queen that in my absence the most necessary appointments should be made only, and that the rest should be put off till my presence in England.
    Pray, my dear Lord, assist me in this proposition and believe me to be, with the truest and greatest regard,
                Your Lordship's Sincere and obliged friend,
                        Albert

As Melbourne and the Queen had already prepared the names for Albert's Household, including Melbourne's private secretary, George Anson, this declaration of independence was not welcome. Melbourne wrote warningly to King Leopold on December 23rd:

> ... I have every expectation that everything connected with this affair will pass off here well and easily and in good humour. But I may venture to say, that I think your Majesty would do well to prepare both the Duke [of Coburg] and the Prince [Albert] for the possible admixture of something of a contrary nature and character.
>
> This match does not come off at quite a good moment. The times are somewhat unpropitious. Party spirit runs high, commerce suffers, the working classes are much distressed, and your Majesty well knows how the feelings of nations, which have the power of manifesting public opinion, are affected by these circumstances.
>
> If upon the score of the public accounts there is a surplus of 3 or 400,000 pounds, there is nothing Parliament will not vote and the people applaud the voting of it. – If, on the contrary, there is a similar apparent deficiency everybody thinks himself ruined and is unwilling to give a farthing ...

In the meanwhile Albert had written to Victoria about Anson:

> ... As for your proposition concerning Mr. Anson, I confess to have my doubts. I am quite sure that he must be an intelligent and a strictly honest man, else he would not be Secretary to Lord Melbourne, but to take a man for a confidential Servant is another thing. This requires confidence, and confidence grows only out of time, self observation, and trial.
>
> It is my nature, dearest beloved V, to trust only upon a thorough knowledge and self conviction of a person's worthiness, and I must acknowledge that I feel unwilling to deviate in an important point from a maxim congenial with my character. . Besides that, I know nothing personally of Mr. Anson, except that I have seen him dance a Quadrille.
>
> I give you to consider, dearest love, if my having the Secretary of the Prime Minister as Treasurer would not make me from the beginning a partisan in the eyes of many? ...
>
> I hope you will, dearest Victoria, agree with me that all these appointments are in no way so urgent, and that it will be in every way more safe for You and Myself not to make more than absolutely necessary, and rather to put off the rest, till I am on the spot.

This would not do, as the Queen and Melbourne emphatically agreed. They had decided that Anson would be his secretary, and Victoria had already written to her fiancé to inform him of this fact, adding that she 'was very much in favour of it, because he is an excellent young man, very modest, very steady, very well informed and will be of much use to you'. Albert was also informed that Anson's uncle, Sir George Anson, a very prominent Whig, would be Groom of the Bedchamber. Now, faced by his rebellion, she wrote with some tartness:

> ... as to your wish about your gentlemen, my dear Albert, I must tell you quite honestly that it will not do. You may entirely rely upon me that the people who will be round you will be absolutely pleasant people of high standing and good character ... You may rely upon my care that you shall have proper people and not idle and not too young, and Lord Melbourne has already mentioned several to me who would be very suitable ...

Leopold, who was not ill-informed about this sharp difference of opinion, wrote with some feeling to Melbourne:

> ... The position of a husband of a Queen, who reigns in her own right, is a position of the greatest difficulty for *any person* and at *any time*; and if you recollect what my position in England was from the year 1816 to that of 1831, you will at once admit that I ought to know something about it.
>
> Albert, altho' young, is steady much beyond his years, has very good common sense and an equally good judgement. He is pure minded and well behaved, has a decided turn for scientific occupations, and from a natural gay, candid and amiable disposition, he seems very little inclined to forget himself and to meddle with affairs which are neither not his own, or of which he understands nothing. From this, it might appear that there is a good deal of that in him which will enable him to manage the task which has fallen to his lot.
>
> But the success *we all desire* will depend on the good sense and right feeling *not of one alone*, but of both parties. It is my most intimate conviction that a really sensible husband may be the most *useful*, the safest and *the best friend a Sovereign Queen can have*.
>
> To enable any man to become this, it seems however necessary that the Queen herself do *take from the very beginning a correct view of* her married position. She ought to see clearly that from the moment of her marriage even her political success will greatly depend upon her domestic happiness, and that by

endeavouring to ensure the latter she *increases herself* by her own *power and arguments the chances of a prosperous and honourable reign.* She ought then to be imbued with a strong and deep conviction that it is *as well her own* as *the Prince's interest* to make *common cause and to live well together.*

That on a matter of such vital importance *truth* may as soon as possible arrive at the Queen's ears I take to be of the highest consequence, not only for the sake of my Niece, but also for the sake and honor of Old England itself.

You, my dear Lord, in whose honor, loyalty, and devotion my Niece very justly places unbounded Confidence, you are *now the only man* who can fully speak out to her, and by doing so, establish *in time* in *her young mind* a *proper* and *correct view* of the *true sense and high importance of the union she is about to form* – for I verily believe that any mistake committed by her in this respect would be more seriously visited [on her] by the Nation than any error the Prince might have the misfortune to fall into.

Let her then, before everything, *be just* to Albert's difficult position, and by being so, give him a fair chance to fulfil his chief and paramount duty, viz: to cultivate the Queen's love, esteem, and confidence, by all possible manly and proper means ...

This was an admirable, sensible, and sensitive letter, but on the matter of the Prince's Establishment the Queen and Melbourne were adamant. On December 29th Melbourne wrote to Prince Albert a letter in which condescension and cynicism struggled for predominance and which, although Melbourne did not appreciate until too late, helped to seal his fate in the eyes of the recipient. But it did set out the views of himself and the Queen in such clarity that it should be recorded at length:

Your Serene Highness is entering no doubt upon a state & situation of some difficulty, inasmuch as it is one of a peculiar and extraordinary character, and of which there has been little experience and but few precedents; but depend upon it, Sir, the difficulties are not as great nor so formidable as they appear, nor are there any which, as Your Royal Highness well expresses it 'earnest and honest intentions' joined with prudence and courage will not surmount and overcome.

The means of preventing embarrassment are in my opinion very short, very clear, very easy and very simple. The main and principal object is to avoid the reality, the appearance, and the suspicion of anything like division or difference of opinion between Your Serene Highness and Her Majesty. Public differences in the Royal Family are always *pro tanto* a weakening and diminution of the authority of the Crown. How much more must this be the case if any discrepancy should exist or be thought to exist between Your Serene Highness and Her Majesty.

Your Serene Highness says truly that it will be demanded of you that 'you should carefully abstain from Party Politics'. It will be certainly prudent that Your Serene Highness should not take an active part in those political questions which divide Parties in this Country, but it will be absolutely necessary that Your Highness should be considered as sanctioning and countenancing the policy pursued by the actual Government of the Queen, however that Government may be constructed. I earnestly counsel Your Serene Highness to take your stand from the beginning on this principle and never to depart from it.

Your Highness will not suspect me of giving this advice because I am at present the Minister. I should urge the same, if those who may be considered to be my political opponents, were at this moment in possession of the chief offices of the State.

I should apply this principle, which in my opinion ought to be the general guide of Your Serene Highness's whole conduct, to the formation of your Establishment. To compose your Household of Persons, who are neither themselves nor by their relations connected with political Parties, is impossible. So many neutral persons fit for the purpose do not exist, and would form a strange assemblage if they could be found.

Your Serene Highness's Household should in my opinion be constituted of Persons of rank and Character, as many of them as possible Members of neither House of Parliament in order to avoid the[m] being pressed to change upon the change of Administration, but still with a decided leaning to the opinions of the present Government, otherwise the conclusion will at once irresistibly prevail that Your Serene Highness is adverse to Her Majesty's Ministers and you will find yourself in spite of yourself taken up by the party in Opposition and elevated to the Post of the Leader of the Tories.

I should also think it better that the appointments should be generally known, if not actually made, previous to your arrival or at the moment of it. If so, they will be considered as having been recommended to you; if otherwise you will be held responsible for them, and every sort of conclusion as to Your Serene Highness's views and opinions will be drawn from those of the Persons selected. The inconvenience of this I have already pointed out ...

The Prince was deeply hurt by her sharp rejection of his arguments – 'I am distressed to be obliged to tell you what I fear you do not like, but it is necessary', she had written to him on December 23rd – but recognised he was powerless against the combined strength of the Queen and her Prime Minister. But he did not surrender without spirit, as his letter in response to Melbourne's unyielding lecture revealed, and it is crucial to any understanding of what subsequently occurred.

My dear Lord Melbourne,

Accept my best thanks for your kind letter of the 29th of Dcr. I am very glad that you have explained to me your opinions concerning my future position in England and you may be sure that I feel most grateful for them. I am in consequence induced to enter more closely upon the subject, & more particularly in reference to the latter part of your letter, namely the establishment of my Household. I must at the same time confess that I can not agree with you in this last matter – indeed I see in the affair *two* & two ways only of considering the question.

Either the establishment is formed according to *my* views & wishes and then I have a mixed household of whigs and tories, who remain with me during *every* administration, in order to prove therby [sic] to the nation that *I will belong to no party*. As I form it, so I will be responsible, it stands and falls with me.

Or, the establishment is formed according to the views and wishes of the ministry. In this case my household will be composed to persons wearing the ministerial color in order to advertise to the nation that *I will always support the Government of the Queen for [the] time-being*. This household then of course cannot be a permanent one, it stands and falls with the ministry who are responsible for it.

A combination of both these systems, as your Lordship argues, is in my opinion impossible (which indeed I could never consent to) as it is putting forward the two above mentioned principles (one of always supporting the government of the day, and the other of showing myself of no party) and drawing but half the consequences of it, & if realized, would throw the benefit on one party and all the onus on the other.

I hope your Lordship will not misunderstand me and pardon me if I have spoken quite without reserve, but in so serious a matter I consider a frank statement as the safest.

Pray, my dear Lord, to be with the truest and greatest regard,
Your Lordship's sincere and obliged friend
Albert.

There was no possibility of misunderstanding this letter, but Prince Albert was defeated, only gaining the limited concession of obtaining a lowly post for his personal secretary, Doctor Schenck. To Queen Victoria he wrote with evident pain:

> ... I am very sorry that you have not been able to grant my first request, the one about the gentlemen of my household, for I know it was not an unfair one ...
>
> Think of my position, dear Victoria; I am leaving my home with all its old associations, all my bosom friends, and going to a country in which everything is new and strange to me – men, language, customs, modes of life, position. Except yourself I have no one to confide in. And is it not even to be conceded to me that the two or three persons who are to have the charge of my private affairs should be persons who already command my confidence? ...

But even this appeal was unavailing, and there is a certain triumph in Victoria's report to Leopold that her fiancé 'I am glad to say, consents to my choosing his People'.

This was an uncomfortable prelude to a marriage in which it was already obvious that Albert's position was certain to be very difficult, and it left its mark on him. Unquestionably he was right, and the Queen and Melbourne were wholly in the wrong, but the fact – ironically – that Anson turned out to be an admirable, devoted, and trusted assistant was not only largely fortuitous but did not undermine the essential validity of Prince Albert's arguments. He lost on this occasion; he was rarely to lose again.

Thus, in the aftermath of these unhappy episodes, and with deep melancholy at leaving his country and family, Prince Albert departed from Gotha for England and his marriage. His sombre mood cannot have been lightened by his fiancée's bleak and somewhat irritated response to his suggestion for a honeymoon at Windsor. 'You forget, my dearest Love', she wrote on January 21st, 'that I am the Sovereign, and that business can stop and wait for nothing. Parliament is sitting, and something occurs almost every day, for which I may be required, and it is quite impossible for me to be absent from London. I am never easy a moment, if I am not on the spot'. Leopold found him 'rather exasperated about various things, and pretty full of grievances' when Albert and his party stayed briefly at Brussels on their way to Calais, adding that 'He is not inclined to be sulky, but I think he may be rendered a little melancholy if he thinks himself unfairly or unjustly treated'; but he added that 'he looks well and handsome, though rather inclined to surrender himself to Morpheus' (Leopold to Victoria, January 21st 1840).

He had been invested with the Garter at Gotha on January 23rd by his father, on the orders of the Queen, and reached Dover on February 7th after another 'terrible' Channel crossing arriving, in his own words, 'with the color of a wax candle', with deep forebodings about his welcome, and still under the sadness that afflicted him in his last days in Coburg and Gotha. Colonel Charles Grey, who had travelled with Lord Torrington with the Patent for investing Albert with the Garter, described the departure from Gotha on January 28th 1840:

> The streets were densely crowded; every window was crammed with heads, every housetop covered with people, waving handkerchiefs, and vying with each other in demonstrations of affection that could not be mistaken. The carriages stopped in passing the Dowager Duchess's, and Prince Albert got out with his father and brother to bid her a last adieu.
>
> It was a terrible trial to the poor Duchess, who was inconsolable for the loss of her beloved grandson. She came to the window as the carriages drove off, and threw her arms out, calling out 'Albert, Albert!' in tones that went to every one's heart, when she was carried away, almost in a fainting state, by her attendants.

At the frontier they found that 'an arch of green fir-trees had been erected, and a number of young girls dressed in white, with roses and garlands, and a band of musicians and singers who sung a very pretty hymn, were assembled to bid a final 'God Speed', as he left his native land behind him, to the young Prince. It was a pretty sight, but bitterly cold. A hard frost and the ground covered with snow, with a bitter north-east wind, were scarcely in keeping with white muslin gowns and wreaths of flowers'.

Albert and his party arrived at Dover on February 7th, and he wrote at once to her:

> Now I am in the same country with you. What a delightful thought for me! It will be hard for me to have to wait till tomorrow evening. Still, our long parting has flown by so quickly, and to-morrow's Dawn will soon be here. Our recep-

tion has been most satisfactory. There were thousands of people on the quay, and they saluted us with loud and uninterrupted cheers.

The reception had indeed been tumultuous, but the passage from Calais had taken over five hours in the kind of weather that he had now gloomily come to accept as normal for the Channel. In spite of his sea-sickness the large and friendly crowds were a considerable relief to Prince Albert as he progressed to London, although the route was so curiously arranged that large crowds that had gathered at the expected vantage points never saw him. He arrived at Buckingham Palace at half-past four on the afternoon of February 8th. Queen Victoria admitted to feeling agitated, but the sight of her fiancé's '*dear dear* face again put me at rest about everything'. They exchanged presents, and then the Lord Chancellor administered the oaths of naturalisation. Some observers considered that Albert was uneasy at this ceremony, and this is unquestionably true; his assurance to his grandmother that he would 'never cease to be a true German' was sincere, and this particular price for his marriage and his new eminence was a heavy one. Walter Bagehot, who was present, doubted whether Prince Albert's heart was 'in the matter', naturalisation, and his observation was right.

The wedding was to be on February 10th, and Albert stayed at Buckingham Palace, an alleged impropriety that dismayed the Duchess of Kent and even surprised Melbourne, but Victoria dismissed 'that nonsense' with fierce scorn.

On his wedding morning Albert received a gentle note:

Dearest, how are you today, and have you slept well? I have rested very well, and feel very comfortable today. What weather! I believe, however, the rain will cease. Send one word when you, my most dearly loved bridegroom, will be ready. Thy ever-faithful VICTORIA R.

To his grandmother, he wrote:

In less than three hours I shall stand before the altar with my dear bride! In those solemn moments I must once more ask your blessing, which I am well assured I shall receive, and which will be my safeguard and my future joy! I must end. May God help me!

There is no doubt that each approached the marriage with apprehension, which was perfectly natural, but with confidence in their love. Lady Lyttelton remarked that Queen Victoria's eyes 'were much swollen with tears, but great happiness in her counte-

nance', while Lady Wilhemina Stanhope commented that Prince
Albert – now with the title of Royal Highness – 'appeared awkward
from embarrassment and was a good deal perplexed and agitated in
his responses', but this was not the opinion of others present at the
Chapel Royal in St. James's Palace, and certainly not that of Queen
Victoria. There was one particularly jarring note at the ceremony –
the almost total absence of Tories, at the Queen's insistence. Indeed,
it had been difficult for Melbourne to persuade her to invite the Duke
of Wellington, so intense were her feelings. 'She had been as wilful,
obstinate and wrong-headed as usual about her invitations', Greville
wrote, 'and some of her foolish and mischievous Courtiers were
boasting that out of above 300 people in the Chapel there would only
be five Tories'. A bride is indeed entitled to invite whom she wishes
to her wedding, but a Queen should be more careful, and the adverse
comments on the invitation lists – which were not confined to
Greville – were not unmerited. She did at least have the advantage of
knowing most of the guests, whereas Albert was surrounded by
complete strangers, knowing only his bride, his father and brother,
the Duchess of Kent, and Melbourne, who could hardly be described
as an intimate friend. The ceremony over, the couple left in pouring
rain for Windsor, in what Greville caustically described as 'one of the
old travelling coaches, the postillions in undress liveries, in a very
poor and shabby style'.

After Victoria had changed she joined Albert in his room. He
embraced her and 'was so dear and kind. We had our dinner in our
sitting room, but I had such a sick headache that I could eat nothing,
and was obliged to lie down ... but ill or not I NEVER, NEVER spent
such an evening!! My DEAREST DEAREST DEAR Albert sat on a
footstool by my side, and his excessive love and affection gave me
feelings of heavenly love and happiness I could never have *hoped* to
have felt before! He clasped me in his arms, and we kissed each other
again and again! His beauty, his sweetness and gentleness – really
how can I ever be thankful enough to have such a *Husband*! ... to be
called by names of tenderness, I have never yet heard used to me
before – was bliss beyond belief! Oh! this was the happiest day of my
life! – May God help me to do my duty as I ought and be worthy of
such blessings!'

Thus began one of the most remarkable of all marriages. Victoria's pre-marital nervousness was replaced with total happiness, to
which she added an acute sensitivity to her husband's loneliness in a
strange country and surrounded by new faces which he found
difficult to remember in the first days.

She was astonished to find her husband in tears after he had said
farewell to his father after the wedding, and the episode left a deep

and abiding impression upon her. She wrote in her Journal: 'Oh, how I did feel for my dearest, precious husband at this moment! Father, brother, friends, country – all he has left, and all for me. What is in my power to make him happy I will do'. Prince Albert found it difficult to acclimatize himself, and disliked the constant entertainment and late hours. He hated London and 'Society', and yearned for the country. Soon after his wedding he had to listen to twenty-seven addresses of congratulation from civic leaders and other notables and to make a suitable response. He found himself a husband with only limited formal public duties, no political position, and with only the faithful Stockmar to hand – at Albert's direct request – as a confidant and adviser. His dislike of Lehzen was early, and strong, and he was firmly barred by Queen Victoria from audiences with her Ministers. His request to know 'everything connected with public affairs' was ignored. 'What is to become of Prince Albert!' Princess Lieven enquired of Lady Palmerston. 'Will he always remain at his wife's side? It will be a dreary situation'.

One of Prince Albert's first, and most acute, difficulties was to learn whom to trust, a dilemma with which anyone who has been in public life will at once sympathise. Apart from Stockmar, whose presence in England became increasingly intermittent, he was sur-rounded by complete strangers, some of whom were obvious sycophants and Court careerists, others politicians with whose names he was familiar but whom he did not know, and other individuals who moved in Court circles but whose allegiance and reliability – especially to him – were doubtful. The Paget family, thanks to Melbourne and Lehzen, seemed everywhere, and the head of what Roger Fulford has rightly called 'the Paget faction' was Lord Uxbridge, who installed his mistress at the Palace, and had become Lord Chamberlain in 1839. Lehzen even attempted to prevent Prince Albert riding with the Queen in the State Carriage to Parliament and questioned his right to sit in the House of Lords with her; his confidence in Anson's complete fidelity and reliability only grew gradually through experience.

The Queen had never thought of him becoming involved in her official political duties, which she continued to conduct in long conversations with Melbourne, Prince Albert not being invited. 'Rested and read Dispatches – some of which I read to Albert', is a particularly significant Journal entry shortly after their marriage, as is 'Albert helped me with the blotting paper when I signed'. Anson commented on his 'constitutional timidity', which was wholly understandable. 'I know it is wrong', Victoria said to Melbourne in this difficult early period, 'but when I am with the Prince I prefer talking on other subjects'. Not until November did Victoria arrange for him to have his own key for 'the Secret Boxes'; Anson considered this 'an important advance', but in reality it was only a modest one, so long as Melbourne was Prime Minister and Lehzen held sway.

By nature shy, these restrictions made Prince Albert more cautious and taciturn than ever in company he did not know, giving an impression of cold hauteur and even dim-wittedness which was eagerly spread abroad by those who hated the Coburgs, or disliked the Queen's politics, or who despised foreigners, or who simply wished to cause trouble. Some years later a chance remark in what he thought was a private conversation that 'the Poles are as little deserving of sympathy as the Irish' was repeated and published, to no little embarrassment to Albert and Ministers. Episodes such as this only served to increase his caution, nervousness in unfamiliar company, and suspicion of all whom he did not know or trust. None of this increased his popularity, and gave a gloomy Teutonic impression. More importantly, it greatly increased his own sense of insecurity and deep loneliness.

His frustration and unease were at least partially compensated by the profound happiness in his relations with his wife, whom he described as 'the most delightful companion a man can wish for'. Malicious gossip alleged that the joy was confined to the Queen, but Lady Palmerston was right when she wrote that 'it is quite impossible for any two people to be more happy'. The only shadow for the Queen – and a considerable one – was when she realised she was pregnant; she had written in her Journal that having babies was 'the ONLY thing I dread', and the realisation made her unhappy and morbid, with the fate of Princess Charlotte heavily in her mind. Albert and Victoria were passionate in all their relations, and Victoria's intense dislike of pregnancy and child-bearing – 'the shadow side of marriage' – should not mislead either her biographers or Albert's. They conceived nine children, and after his death she wrote to her eldest daughter 'Oh! it is too, too weary! The day – the night (above all the night) is too sad and weary'. Albert's attempts to lift her from her pregnancy depression were only partly successful, although he gradually brought her into a more hopeful mood. But it was clearly a most difficult time for them both.

The principal strain was upon the Prince. Stockmar was deeply critical of him, accusing him of intellectual laziness and political apathy, while making insufficient allowances for his caution and insecurity in a new environment and the difficulties of the early months of his marriage. The charge was, moreover, peculiarly unfair, for, as early as May, Albert was complaining to Victoria of her lack of confidence in him 'on all matters connected with the politics of this country', but Stockmar told Anson that Prince Albert

was being unnecessarily impatient: 'The Queen has not started upon
a right principle. She should by degrees impart everything to him,
but there is danger in his wishing it all at once ... The Queen is
influenced more than she is aware of by the Baroness [Lehzen]'. Of
this last fact Albert was only too conscious. Stockmar bombarded
him with earnest memoranda and long discussions of his inadequacies, which Albert bore with estimable equanimity and patience.
Stockmar's son later wrote that it had been his father's task to
'arouse and strengthen in the Prince ideal aspirations and the sense
of duty', while at the same time – with some inconsistency – urging
him not to press the Queen too hard for political influence. 'In my
home life I am very happy and contented', Albert wrote to
Löwenstein; 'but the difficulty in filling my place with the proper
dignity is that I am only the husband, not the master, in the house'.

The relationship between Prince Albert and his appointed secretary,
George Anson, had not opened propitiously, and promised to be
very uncomfortable. Anson recorded in February that Albert had
said to him:

> Wished to have an opportunity of telling you that I was
> determined not to appoint you. I felt that it was committing
> myself by taking one who was confidentially placed about the
> Prime M. The Q. insisted upon your app. – & resented my
> opposition.
>   Baron S. had heard a good deal of you, & after my arrival
> persuaded me to confirm the appointment which had been
> promised [to you].

Although this was honest, it was highly unpromising, as were
Albert's admonitions to him shortly afterwards, again carefully
noted by the secretary.

> Necessity of caution in the extreme & discretion in the Society of
> a Court.
>   Constantly subject to the influence of petty intrigue &
> jealousy. The less the intercourse with all save with your
> Principal the better your chance of escaping difficulty & of
> producing mischief. Avoid all in a general way as much as
> possible. Always [be] an attentive listener, but avoid giving an
> opinion as much as possible, & never volunteer it.

But by April 15th the Prince had clearly developed enough trust in
Anson to expound to him his somewhat superficial understanding of
British politics:

I do not think it is necessary to belong to any Party. Composed as Party is here of two extremes, both must be wrong. The exercise of an unbiassed judgement may form a better & wiser creed by extracting the good from each.

The Whigs want to change *before* change is required. The love of change is their great failing. The Tories on the other hand *resist change* long after the feeling & temper of the Times has loudly demanded it, & at least make a virtue of necessity by an ungracious concession. My endeavour will be to form my opinions quite apart from politics & party, & I believe such an attempt may succeed.

This was a remarkably crude, and in fact seriously inaccurate, judgement, and an Administration more hostile to social change of any kind than the Melbourne Government would be difficult to imagine, while Peel's Conservative federation was already demonstrating signs of pragmatic radical thinking that was anathema to the Whig Party. The new English Prince had much to learn.

From the beginning he was working out in his own mind, and in his talks with Anson, how his personal position was to develop. Anson wrote after one such discussion:

Uncertainty of Position –

Under all natural probability must exercise great influence on all State affairs, tho' that influence ought never to appear – in cases of difficulty, who so fit to advise as the Husband – often in Illness the only person who can or ought to approach.

These assumptions were, also, naïve. So long as Melbourne was Prime Minister and Lehzen was close to the Queen, the position which he regarded as his by right was strongly challenged, and it was only gradually that he realised it had to be fought for. In this contest Anson became his strong personal, and trusted, adherent and guide. Stockmar's letters of advice – always long, often very perceptive, sometimes portentous – came from a distance; Anson was the daily companion and strategist.

The more Anson worked with the Prince the more baffled he became by the extraordinary difference in his character when compared with those of his father and brother, something that had also aroused Stockmar's great interest when it became clear that his earlier fears that he might also have inherited some of his mother's passionate ways were clearly unfounded. Stockmar realised, as Queen Victoria had found to her delight, that Albert was indeed a passionate man, but with the strong self-control that was so conspicuously absent in his father and brother Ernest. In discussion with

Anson 'S. put it down to his fundamental purity of mind, but it was well that he had been removed from the Coburg influence'.

This was not the only puzzle in this extraordinary young man for whom Anson not only worked but felt an affinity that took their relationship to an unusual one for men in their positions. This puzzle has best been expressed by Albert's brother:

> His mild amiability went hand in hand with a critical severity. The greatest warmth and self-sacrificing love would sometimes change to painful coldness. His constant thought was how to make people happy, and he could [also] be as hard as possible to those same people.

It was indeed these contrasts that gave the majority of people an impression of humourless earnestness which made him the mockery of London Society, and the 'Upper Ten Thousand', to whom he was an insufferable German Puritan on the make, another Coburg adventurer like Leopold, and a boring adventurer at that. And yet to his step-sister in law, Feodora, he was the provider of family fun and laughter, and she took particular joy in the family breakfasts, when Albert's gift of mimicry, on which all his friends and family placed great emphasis, was used to make mock of pompous Court officials, politicians, and guests. 'Albert always so merry', Victoria wrote happily, and one of the Ladies, the Hon. Georgiana Liddell, later Lady Bloomfield, wrote of a dinner of much talk and laughter when she and the Duchess of Kent joined Victoria and Albert. Observers from afar often found – particularly if they were writers, artists, musicians, scientists, or other kindred souls – a jolly, friendly, and humorous young man, in complete contrast with what they had expected. But in uncongenial company, or even on occasion with family and friends, there would be a sudden and unexpected switch to an intimidating sternness. All who really knew him *liked* as well as respected him, and found real pleasure in his company. He was a thoroughly nice and manifestly kind young man, with great consideration and generosity, even to his father and brother, however sorely they tried him. His fear of scandal was partly based on the clear calculation that if it came near the Throne it would do immense harm to his ambition to strengthen its position, but it was not based, as has so often been assumed, on prudery or what one biographer of Queen Victoria has called his 'horror of sex'. He was in fact very tolerant of frailties of the flesh, including drinking; when Home Secretary Sir James Graham expressed criticism of a tipsy courtier Albert dismissed the matter as one of no importance. Years later the annual Ghillies' Ball at Balmoral was not noted for its complete sobriety. But he was determined to keep the Court as morally pure as was humanly possible, and here the bad reputation of the Coburg Court – as well as that of George IV – had a strong and ineradicable influence on him.

As Anson realised, he had a very complex young man as his master, and also a very under-utilised one, and in this context there was a significant conversation between him and Melbourne on February 19th, 1841:

> ... Ld M. said the Prince is indolent, & it would be better if he was more so, for in his position we want no activity. I replied the Prince *may* be indolent, but it results from there being no scope for his energy. If you required a cypher in the difficult position of Consort of the Queen you ought not to have selected the Prince, having got him you must make the most of him, & when he saw the power of being useful to the Queen he will act. He is not ambitious, he wishes for no Power, except such as will enable him to support & assist the Queen ...

Indolence was not the problem; boredom and frustration were, and Anson was quickly to realise that he severely underrated Prince Albert's political ambitions, although there are other indications in his papers that he was beginning to appreciate this fact rather more than this conversation might indicate. In short, one suspects a diplomatic rather than a strictly truthful approach to the Prime Minister.

In the meanwhile, Lehzen blocked the way. Albert mused to Anson on February 17th 1841 that he believed 'that the Queen has more fear than love for the Bss & that she wd really be happier without her, tho' she cd not acknowledge it'. When, in April, the Queen was incensed by Uxbridge 'but dreaded his outbursts of temper' Albert at once undertook the task of rebuking the Lord Chamberlain, although Melbourne feared that, as he told Anson, it 'would place implacable enmity on Uxbridge's part against the Prince'. Surrounded as he was by these vipers, it is not to be wondered at that Albert told Anson that 'I give every person about me credit for the best intentions & honesty of purpose until they prove themselves unworthy of my confidence. I applied this my general rule to the Bs. She has lost it by repeated instances of animosity'. The reality was that he came to hate her as an evil but potent influence on his wife, constantly causing difficulties and scenes between them, impeding his work to reform and reorganise the Court and the appallingly ill-managed Royal finances, and deliberately setting the Court against him. He saw her not only as a political schemer and a Court meddler but as a real threat to his relationship with his wife. Anson, although a Whig himself, and a

Whig appointee, took Prince Albert's side. Melbourne's faculties may have been failing, but the crafty politician in him saw no value whatever in increasing Prince Albert's influence at the expense of his and Lehzen's. So long as Melbourne was Prime Minister, Albert could receive no help from that quarter. Thus, to an extent that it is doubtful he or Anson fully appreciated – although they certainly did later – Prince Albert's personal and political interests depended upon a change of Government, and a smooth and uncomplicated transition of power in which the Queen would not be politically implicated. The Prince had, accordingly, a real and personal stake in the advent of a Tory Government and the ending of the Whig domination over the Court and his wife.

It is surprising that this crucial point has been so consistently overlooked by so many. Prince Albert remained formally aloof from Party politics as such, but already he was personally involved in them in fact. His early high-minded protestations of complete impartiality had had to be amended very severely in the light of harsh experience at the hands of Melbourne, Lehzen, the insufferable Pagets, the arrogant and avaricious Whigs; and his totally partisan wife. A Tory Government under Peel offered the only way out of this unhappy morass, which threatened his happiness, his usefulness, his unfulfilled energies, and even possibly his marriage. Anson, and others, were to discover for the first time that when Albert's interests were concerned he could change very rapidly from the humorous, charming, merry and cheerful companion and master to a strong-willed and resolute politician.

Queen Victoria's many qualities did not include an acute social conscience, and, preoccupied as she always had been with her own world she was strikingly unaware of, and lacked real interest in, the issues of wealth, poverty, and social reform that were inexorably becoming the principal issues of contemporary Britain. Here, the negative aspect of Melbourne's influence was most conspicuous, but his indifference to such matters was shared by the Queen, and his cynicism fell on receptive ears. The Factory Act of 1833 to reduce the appalling exploitation of child labour had been only a modest step towards limiting these abuses, while the Poor Law of 1834 had not improved the condition of the very poor, but had actually made them worse. 'If paupers are made miserable', as Thomas Carlyle cuttingly wrote, 'paupers will needs decline in multitude. It is a secret known to all rat-catchers'. A bad harvest and a sudden slump in trade in 1837 made matters even worse, and combined to give The People's Charter a substantial popular support. When it was disdainfully rejected by Parliament fierce rioting broke out in Birmingham, swiftly followed in other towns and in the hitherto peaceful country-side. Although the temper subsided, the cause of the Chartists did not. The Queen vehemently supported the Government, but Prince Albert was more doubtful.

His first public speech was on June 1st 1840 to the Society for the Extinction of the Slave Traffic and the Civilization of Africa at Exeter Hall, in the Strand. As it was an open public meeting there was an immense demand for tickets, and although Albert was intensely nervous his brief speech had a bite that was somewhat unexpected, and left no one in any doubt as to his strength of feeling on the subject of humanity and justice, which was the theme of his remarks. Although he confined himself strictly to the slave trade – 'the blackest stain upon civilized Europe ... a state of things so repugnant to the spirit of Christianity and to the best feelings of our nature' – the significance in a national context only became publicly evident rather later.

In 1838 he had told Stockmar, to the latter's dismay, that he had little interest in politics, and at that stage it was true. His general impressions of British politics had not been improved by the disputes over his income and title, and the furore over his religion. He now found himself carefully excluded from his wife's duties as Queen, with the jealously protective Lehzen denying him even the position of Private Secretary. When he suspected that Lehzen had diverted £15,000 of the Queen's income into the coffers of the Whig Party he raised the matter, in considerable concern, with Melbourne, who merely remarked that this was nothing compared with the sums that King George III had spent on elections, an observation that did nothing to assuage Albert's alarm about the political independence of the Monarchy or his dislike for Lehzen. Characteristically and fairly, he did not blame Melbourne; it was the 'Kensington System' that still survived, and which he was determined to end.

With Stockmar's strong support, he plunged himself into study of his new country, its politics, and its problems. By this stage Stock-mar's knowledge of these subjects was detailed, and probably unrivalled, and his lack of personal involvement in active partisan politics made him a uniquely trusted figure. His approach has been best described by himself:

> If you are consulted by Princes to whom you are attached give your opinion truthfully, boldly, without reserve or reticence. Should your opinion not be palatable, do not, to please or conciliate him, deviate for a moment from what you think the truth. You may in consequence be some time out of favour,

treated with neglect or coldness; and when they come back (for back they will come, if you remain honest and firm), never complain of the treatment you have received, never try to make them own how right you were, and how wrong they have been. It must be enough for you that you should, for their good and the good of the country, act upon the principles, the soundness of which is thus acknowledged.

In Albert he found somewhat stronger material than he had expected, and which had already so surprised, and impressed, Melbourne. Prince Albert had developed a considerable regard for Melbourne, which was reciprocated, although not totally on either side. Their relationship, after their initial correspondence, was courteous but wary. In a sense, each was competing for the ear and attention and support of the Queen, although this should not be exaggerated. What was more fundamental was that Melbourne, although devoted to Queen Victoria and her interests, remained a Whig politician precariously hanging on to Office, while Albert was obsessed by his wife's and Lehzen's Whig partisanship and its attendant dangers, and the discovery that Lehzen might have been channelling Royal income to the Whigs brought home to him how perilous the situation actually was. Also, Queen Victoria had gradually mellowed her original strict views on personal morality under Melbourne's subtle influence – 'times have changed, but I do not know if they have improved' – and had become markedly more tolerant of personal peccadilloes, a feature of her character that always existed and which was to be both enduring and endearing. Her stern censures on her 'wicked uncles' were firmly resisted by Melbourne ('but they were such jolly fellows, Ma'am') until they were a topic of amused and engaging interest. This was emphatically not the view of Stockmar and Prince Albert, with such acute experience of the libertine activities of Duke Ernest and his elder son, and the Queen's comment to Melbourne that 'the Prince is much severer than me' has a critical and somewhat wistful note. Albert's eagerness to extricate the Court from any hint of scandal was very understandable, and also clearly understood by Melbourne, but his cry 'This damned morality will ruin everything!' after a session with Albert emphasises the gulf between them. But the fact that they admired and liked each other should be recorded to the credit of each, particularly as although Albert's political influence over the Queen slowly grew, as David Cecil has rightly written: 'It was still not to be compared with Melbourne's'. *This* was the problem.

At this stage, in effect only given the task of organising the Royal finances and households – into which he threw himself with much

energy and with immediate and enduring benefit – Prince Albert
had not worked out his own role for himself, but he had already
established the principles of political neutrality, to which his wife
became reconciled only gradually, and the need to strengthen the
real influence of the Crown. Ten years later he set out his purposes in
a letter to the Duke of Wellington which can be inserted at this point.
These were, he wrote,

> to sink his own individual existence in that of his wife – to aim at
> no power by himself, or for himself – to shun all ostentation – to
> assume no separate responsibility before the public – to make
> his position entirely a part of hers – to fill up every gap which, as
> a woman, she would naturally leave in the exercise of her regal
> functions – continually and anxiously to watch every part of the
> public business, in order to be able to advise and assist her at
> any moment in any of the multifarious and difficult questions
> brought before her, political, or social, or personal. To place all
> his time and powers at her command as the natural head of the
> family, superintendent of her household, manager of her private
> affairs, her sole confidential adviser in politics, and only assis-
> tant in her communications with the officers of the Govern-
> ment, her private secretary, and permanent Minister.

These were indeed awesome objectives, aimed at a degree of
personal power unparallelled by any Consort, and drawing into his
hands the reality of political knowledge and influence. These purposes took some time to achieve, but it is clear that they were present
from the outset. The campaign to remove Lehzen from her position
was only the beginning, but a highly significant one.

Equally important was the establishment of his title as Regent in
the event of Queen Victoria's death while her child was still a minor.
In view of the extreme difficulties over Parliament's hostility to him
only a few months before, this step – vehemently opposed by the
Duke of Sussex – could have run into serious difficulties, but these
were swept aside by an episode on June 10th best described by
Albert himself:

> Dear Grandmama,
>   I hasten to give you an account of an event which might
> otherwise be misrepresented to you, which endangered my life
> and that of Victoria, but from which we escaped under the
> protection of the watchful hand of Providence.
>   We drove out yesterday afternoon, about six o'clock, to pay
> Aunt Kent a visit, and to take a turn round Hyde Park. We
> drove in a small phaeton. I sat on the right, Victoria on the left.

We had hardly proceeded a hundred yards from the Palace, when I noticed, on the footpath on my side, a little mean-looking man holding something towards us; and before I could distinguish what it was, a shot was fired, which almost stunned us both, it was so loud, and fired barely six paces from us. Victoria had just turned to the left to look at a horse, and could not therefore understand why her ears were ringing, as from its being so very near she could hardly distinguish that it pro-ceeded from a shot having been fired. The horses started and the carriage stopped. I seized Victoria's hands, and asked if the fright had not shaken her, but she laughed at the thing.

I then looked again at the man, who was still standing in the same place, his arms crossed, and a pistol in each hand. His attitude was so affected and theatrical it quite amused me. Suddenly he again pointed his pistol and fired a second time. This time Victoria also saw the shot, and stooped quickly, drawn down by me. The ball must have passed just above her head, to judge from the place where it was found sticking in an opposite wall.[1]

The many people who stood round us and the man, and were at first petrified with fright on seeing what happened, now rushed upon him. I called to the postillion to go on, and we arrived safely at Aunt Kent's. From thence we took a short drive through the Park, partly to give Victoria a little air, partly also to show the public that we had not, on account of what had happened, lost all confidence in them.

To-day I am very tired and knocked up by the quantity of visitors, the questions, and descriptions I have had to give ... My chief anxiety was lest the fright should have been injurious to Victoria in her present state, but she is quite well, as I am myself. I thank Almighty God for His protection.

Your faithful grandson,
                              Albert.

The name of the culprit is Edward Oxford. He is seventeen years old, a waiter in a low inn – not mad – but quite quiet and composed.

This near-tragedy transformed the situation. The Queen's waning popularity was entirely restored, and the question of the Regency was handled with great tact and skill by Stockmar. The key was that Albert had already convinced the Tories of his genuine impartiality – 'The Tories are very friendly to me, as I to them', he

---

[1] In fact the ball was never found. Oxford was found guilty but insane and committed for life.

wrote to his father – and although Prince Albert gave the credit to Stockmar, the fact was that the politicians had been impressed by the warm reception given to his slavery speech by the audience and the newspapers, and the public reaction to the assassination attempt demonstrated that it would have been politically highly unwise to have opposed the Bill. Melbourne was right when he told the Queen that 'three months ago they would not have done it for him'.

This having been achieved, Stockmar considered that his task was over and he returned to Coburg, having briefed Anson carefully before his departure. His reservations about Albert remained, and he was to be an active and wise counsellor from afar to whom Albert often turned. But the relationship had definitely changed. In the course of a long and solemn letter on September 2nd Stockmar suddenly wrote, in complete contrast with the rest of the letter:

> ... One day on my way up the Rhine I was made very sad, but only for a short time, by reading in a newspaper that you had had a bad fall from your horse. At that moment I felt how sincerely I love you.

The first year of any marriage is a difficult one. In the case of Queen Victoria and Prince Albert this crucial period of adjustment was not made any easier by Albert's frustration at the ambiguity of his formal position, Victoria's early pregnancy, acute political difficulties with the fading and unpopular Whig Government, the assassination attempt, and a heavy programme of Court and other functions and duties. The Queen was extremely busy, Lehzen hovered and intrigued possessively, Prince Albert was deep in his studies and reorganizing the chaotic condition of the Royal administration, feeling acutely his situation as a foreigner, and with no real friends in a strange country. And yet it was clearly a time of much happiness for both, as Queen Victoria began to discover the extraordinary width and range of her husband's interests and knowledge, and not least in music and art. He organised and directed his first public concert in April, which was a revelation to the small minority of serious musicians who had long despaired of informed interest in their field from anyone in public life. The scurrilous jokes and sneers in London Society continued, but it was appreciated by a few people that here was a man of remarkable capacities. For his part he had realised the essential truth of Melbourne's comment on Queen Victoria: 'She is the honestest person I have ever known. The only difficulty is to make her see that you cannot always go straight forward, that you must go round sometimes'. The same point was

made by Greville in 1842: 'Her chief fault (in little things and in
great) seems to be impatience; in a sea phrase, she always wants to *go
ahead*'.

But it was not only as a lover but as a husband, friend, and
companion that Victoria's deep dependence upon him began in that
first year. Subsequently, she recalled how he quietly organised their
day:

> At this time the Prince and Queen seem to have spent their day
> much as follows:
> They breakfasted at nine, and took a walk every morning
> soon afterwards. Then came the usual amount of business (far
> less heavy, however, than now); besides which they drew and
> etched a great deal, which was a source of great amusement,
> having the plates *bit* in the house.
> Luncheon followed at the usual hour of two o'clock. Lord
> Melbourne who was generally staying in the house, came to the
> Queen in the afternoon, and between five and six the Prince
> usually drove her out in a pony phaeton. If the Prince did not
> drive the Queen, he rode, in which case she took a drive with the
> Duchess of Kent or the ladies.
> The Prince also read aloud most days to the Queen. The
> dinner was at eight o'clock, and always with the company. In
> the evening the Prince frequently played at double chess, a
> game of which he was very fond, and which he played extremely
> well.

Queen Victoria 'tried to get rid of the bad custom, prevailing only
in this country, of the gentlemen remaining, after the ladies had left,
in the dining room.' But Melbourne advised against it, and the
Prince himself thought it better not to make any change. The
compromise was that the gentlemen were permitted only five
minutes at the table after the ladies withdrew. What Albert did
change, however, were the hours of such dinners, and he gradually
achieved his objective of eliminating the, to him, loathsome practice
and custom of the English of sitting and conversing after dinner until
the early hours of the morning. To the dismay and surprise of many,
matters concluded by eleven at the latest. He was elected to the
Royal Society, and made a Privy Councillor on his twenty-first
birthday ('my thoughts were naturally much at The Rosenau', he
wrote); his earnest studies in English law and politics continued, as
did his firm pruning of the Household and the lazy and indifferent
Royal staff. From these activities he made substantial savings, and
his energies also made the Windsor Home Farm a profit-making
concern. In this period Prince Albert made some enquiries about the

state of the finances of the Duchy of Cornwall, which revealed that the income was £36,000 a year, of which £12,000 was spent on administrative costs. Stockmar (September 13th) advised him 'to avoid going too deep into details, which will only bewilder you. It is for *you* to *give only the impulse*, to establish sound principles, and this once done *to hold fast*, in everybody's dispute, *to these principles with steel-like sternness.* . . . The fundamental principle to which you have to hold fast is that the Duchy is altogether a private affair with which neither the Government nor its ministers have, or ought to have, anything to do.' The Prince followed this counsel closely, and with Anson's advice began to drastically improve the income, and reduce the administrative costs, of the Duchy of Cornwall.

There was another aspect about life in England that baffled him, and which he disliked – the English Sunday, whose gloomy boredom irked him. He was worried by 'the want of amusements for common people of an innocent class', the lack of pleasure grounds, and public entertainments. 'One thing I am sure of', he wrote to Sir Robert Peel in 1846, '& that is, that the English *people* generally can enjoy themselves with propriety & are not so dull & cold as the Saints of the day wish to represent & make them'. When the opening of Osborne was celebrated with a huge dinner to the workmen and their families he organised music and dancing, and he recorded with pleasure 'that everybody seemed in the highest spirits, shouting & laughing'. Even at this early stage he was thinking of steps that could open up to ordinary people the pleasures of music, art, and gardens then the privilege of the very few. Unhappily, the English Sunday was to defeat him, and also Queen Victoria, whose dislike of 'a *Sunday Face*' became well known in her Court. But he was to make progress in his other objectives. 'Albertian England', far from being calculatedly earnest and glum, was intended to be cheerful and relaxed. No one can understand the Great Exhibition of 1851, or Prince Albert, without grasping this essential point.

Buckingham Palace had replaced St. James's as the Sovereign's London residence, and after years of disputes between patrons and architects, considerable press and Parliamentary criticism, and very heavy expenditure, was habitable when Queen Victoria came to the throne, but was neither comfortable nor secure. A twelve year old boy was found in the Palace in 1838 having lived there for a year without having been discovered, and in December 1840 Edmund Jones, aged seventeen, was discovered asleep under a sofa in the Queen's sitting room, and it was not his first intrusion. Indeed, after severe punishment of three months' imprisonment and spells on the still-preserved barbarity of the treadmill he broke in again, was captured again, returned to the treadmill and eventually sent into the Navy. With the Queen the target of assassination attempts, and the possibility of any of the Royal children being kidnapped, these episodes reflected well neither on the Royal servants nor the ramshackle building itself.

The situation had its elements of pure farce. The Lord Steward and the Lord Chamberlain had their functions, however ill-defined, that were in practical terms irreconcilable. Territorial disputes were common; the Lord Chamberlain allegedly had control of the rooms at Buckingham Palace, while the Lord Steward dominated the kitchens. The insides of the windows were cleaned by the minions of the Lord Chamberlain or the Lord Steward, whereas the outsides were the responsibility of the Office of Woods and Forests. When Queen Victoria asked for a fire she was told that the Lord Steward's functionaries laid it but that the Lord Chamberlain's lit it. The result was that the Queen of England had no fire. And there was another authority – that of the Master of the Horse, to whom the footmen and junior servants of the Palace owed their allegiance. Prince Albert discovered an item called 'Red Room Wine', which transpired to trace back to the days when the Red Room at Windsor Castle had been used as a guard room and wine had been provided at the public expense to the officer on duty. The list of petty corruptions, ancient and profitable usages, and incompetence was very formidable.

The gradual transformation of the Palace from what Queen Victoria reasonably described as 'a sad state' was lengthy, expensive, and controversial. The Prince's minatory letters to Ministers about the Palace – 'a disgrace to the Sovereign and the nation' he described it to Peel – were detailed and frequent. The problem was, as always, money, and Albert noted that whenever he raised the matter Peel 'puts on his wooden face'. But although Ministers were grudging, and there was a constant barrage of criticism from Radical M.P.s in the Commons and in the newspapers, improvements were made under Thomas Cubitt and Edward Blore in the 1840s and by James Pennethorne in the early 1850s[1] which resolved the most acute difficulties, provided much better accommodation for the Royal Family, their staff, and State visitors, but it was never admired architecturally nor loved by its occupants. The removal of the Marble Arch from outside the Palace to its present position, when the somewhat gloomy new façade was completed, and Penne-

---

[1] The changes to the façade overlooking the Mall included the famous balcony, first used by the Queen and Prince to respond to the crowds at the opening of the Great Exhibition in 1851. The balcony was Prince Albert's suggestion.

thorne's new Ball Room, were perhaps the most significant artistic external improvements, and Prince Albert was to achieve much with the interior and the grounds. But it was never to be regarded by any of the family as 'home'.

The administration of the Palace was chaotic. Uxbridge was regarded by Albert as indolent and insolent and overbearing, and as long as Lehzen reigned there would be problems. But there were others, of temperament. Prince Albert was a countryman, with a quickly formed and abiding dislike of London, its Society, its entertainments, and late hours, and the condition of the Palace was not calculated to diminish these hostilities. 'In a small house', he wrote somewhat wistfully to Ernest in March 1841, 'there is more cheerfulness to be found than there is in the big cold world, in which most people have hearts of stone'. Victoria, in total contrast, did not initially share Albert's profound feeling for nature and a pastoral and quiet life. She was the Queen, she was young, she was attractive, and she loved dancing and flattery. Her subordination of what to her were real pleasures to her husband's craving for a calm, ordered, and rural routine was to be a major personal sacrifice, but she also shared Albert's strong preference for Windsor, which became their real home. If Buckingham Palace was, regarded from any consideration of comfort, efficiency, or attractiveness, notably deficient, George IV had left to his successors a transformed Windsor Castle. He and his chief architect Sir Jeffrey Wyatt – who had with the King's puzzled permission, changed his name to Wyatville to mark the signal honour – 'found a workhouse and left a palace.' He found 'the coldest house, rooms and passages that ever existed'; he left a warm, dry, comfortable, well-appointed house.[1] To describe George IV's Windsor Castle as 'a house' is somewhat misleading, when one contemplates the magnificence of the State and private apartments, the glittering Waterloo Chamber, and the pictures and furniture and statues that George IV acquired and which Wyatville used to such wonderful advantage. George IV saw it as 'his Versailles', a palace appropriate for the Sovereign of England, where, as has rightly been written, 'he brought together once more in one great building the royal medieval past, the long centuries between, and the living present.'[2] There has been no need to make any significant change from George IV's time to this. It is unquestionably, the finest and most satisfying of all the palaces of the British monarchy. When the Court left Windsor to return to the draughty, uncomfortable, and lamentably ill-managed Buckingham Palace on January 2nd 1841

[1] Owen Morshead: *Windsor Castle*, p. 96.
[2] J. H. Plumb and Huw Weldon: *Royal Heritage*, p. 242.

the Queen noted the event with keen and heartfelt regret. This was, on the surface, a small victory for Albert; it was to prove an enduring one.

But perhaps the most important of his achievements in this early period was to reconcile his wife with her mother, a difficult task – made even more difficult by Melbourne's views, soured by his experience of the Conroy faction, and which prompted him to describe the Duchess to her daughter as 'a liar and a hypocrite' – which he achieved with great delicacy and skill, and the eventual removal of Lehzen. As it had been Lehzen who had been a major cause of the rift – and certainly symbolised it – the latter should have stemmed naturally from the first achievement, but did not. Lehzen told Anson, that the Prince 'had slighted her in the most marked manner and she was too proud not to resent it'. Albert actually told her to leave, but she refused on the grounds that he had no power to turn her out of the Queen's house – a peculiarly infuriating and offensive response. Prince Albert referred to her in correspondence as 'the House Dragon spitting fire', and, when she had jaundice, somewhat cruelly, as 'the Yellow Lady'. Leopold backed Albert strongly, as did Anson but Melbourne advised caution. To this Anson responded that Lehzen 'was always in the Queen's path, pointing and exaggerating every little fault of the Prince, constantly misrepresenting him, constantly trying to undermine the Queen's affections and making herself appear a martyr, ready to suffer and put up with every sort of indignity for the Queen's sake. The effect of this state of things cannot be viewed but with alarm'. There is no question that Anson faithfully reflected his master's views. But, so strong were Queen Victoria's memories of Lehzen's loyalty in difficult times that she emphatically supported the Baroness against her husband, and the subject became one of such tension between the couple that Albert decided to bide his time. Leopold wrote to Victoria to say that Charlotte had always regarded him as 'her lord and master', and, Ernest, who stayed for two months after the wedding, noted that they 'could not yield to each other'. Prince Albert informed Stockmar that 'I have come to be extremely pleased with Victoria during the past few months. She has only twice had the sulks', but the reality, as Anson noted, was of two strong-minded young people deeply in love and yet engaged in a battle of wills. 'Victoria is annoyed that I should disturb her with such quarrels, she takes everything about the Baroness so much to heart and feels she ought to be her champion'. It was Melbourne's view that if Prince Albert made the matter a choice between himself and Lehzen the Queen, with her 'determination and obstinacy of character', would choose Lehzen. This was unquestionably a gross exaggeration, but there was sufficient truth in it to make Prince Albert and Anson draw back – for the present.

The remarkable year of 1840 ended with the birth, on November 22nd, of, in Victoria's words, 'a perfect little child ... but alas a girl and not a boy, as we both had so hoped and wished for. We were, I am afraid, sadly disappointed'. 'I should have preferred a boy', Albert wrote frankly to Ernest, 'yet as it is, I thank Heaven'.[1] Albert was deeply solicitous, his wife recovered rapidly from her confinement, and the baby – christened Victoria Adelaide Mary Louisa at once and always known as Vicky, on February 10th 1841, the anniversary of their marriage – was healthy.

Their first Christmas together was spent at Windsor Castle, with Christmas trees, decorations, and presents. The former German custom was little known in Britain until it was popularized by Albert, to the point that it became believed that he had actually introduced it into his adopted country, when in fact that credit belongs to Queen Charlotte. The Queen had begun to relent in her attitude to the political position of her husband, and in a brief flurry of excitement and tension over the chronic Eastern Question in August had, on Melbourne's advice, shown Albert all the dispatches, and he had submitted detailed memoranda to the Prime Minister; 'he seldom answers me', Albert wrote to his father, 'but I have the satisfaction of seeing him act entirely in accordance with what I have said'. After the birth of his daughter he had been given full access to Cabinet and other confidential papers for the first time, and had become, in Anson's words, 'in fact, tho' not in name, Her Majesty's Private Secretary'. Lehzen was resisting strongly; 'in her', Anson wrote, 'we must be always subject to troubled waters'.

But it was a very happy first Christmas, with skating on the frozen pond at Frogmore, Christmas trees, presents, and the new baby. In her Journal Queen Victoria reflected with emotion on 'the solid pleasures of a peaceful quiet yet merry life ... with my inestimable husband and friend'.

[1] His irritation both with the formalities of religion and obsequious courtiers was never better demonstrated than in his testy exchange with a Canon of Windsor who sought permission to offer a special prayer for the Queen in labour.
  'You pray five times already; it is too much'.
  'Can we pray, Sir, too much for Her Majesty?'
  'Not too *heartily*, but too *often*'.

FIVE

THE TURNING-POINT

The struggle for supremacy between Prince Albert and Lehzen caused the darkest hours in his marriage with Queen Victoria. It coincided with the decline and disintegration of the Melbourne Government and the rise of the accursed Tories, and Queen Victoria's morale was lowered further when she discovered that she was pregnant again very soon after the birth of Vicky. 'You cannot *really* wish me to be the Mama d'une *nombreuse famille*' she wrote to Leopold with some feeling on January 5th 1841, and many years later she wrote to Vicky herself that 'what made me absolutely miserable was to have the first two years of my married life utterly spoilt by this occupation'. 'Victoria is not very happy about it', Albert wrote to Ernest in March, informing his brother of the news, with considerable understatement. 'One feels so pinned down – one's wings clipped', she wrote.

Low and depressed as she was, there were also signs, which Melbourne noted with concern, of jealousy at her husband's developing position, and particularly his contacts with the Opposition Tories. Prince Albert and Peel, each shy and awkward men of exceptional ability, seriousness, and dedication, had already developed a strong and enduring regard for each other which Queen Victoria, still obsessed by her Whig prejudices and memories, neither comprehended nor shared. 'I study the politics of the day with great industry', Albert wrote to his father in April. 'I speak quite openly with the Ministers on all subjects, so as to gain information ... and I endeavour to be of as much use to Victoria in her position as I can'.

It was with considerable dismay that she viewed the political situation at the beginning of 1841. In the inimitable phrase of Kitson Clark: 'It was in February that the Government began to give signs of collapse, like the first menacing cracks of a hewn tree'.[1] Its

[1] *Peel and the Conservative Party*, p. 463.

position in Parliament became more precarious as the Conservatives won a series of by-elections, and the dilemma of whether or not to capitalise on the popular fervour of the Anti-Corn Law League exercised Ministers throughout the Spring. The problem here was that very few of the masses who attended the rallies of the League had votes, and in the counties the landowners and farmers who had votes were alarmed and hostile to the campaign of the League, now fortified by the Report of the Committee on Import Duties, which was widely circulated by the League and made an immediate impact on the Chancellor of the Exchequer, Francis Baring, and a larger one on Peel. Eventually, both political parties prevaricated. Baring proposed reductions in the duties on imported sugar and timber, and after Lord John Russell had unsuccessfully put forward a sliding scale for imported corn, it was decided to propose a lower fixed duty. Seeing the trap, Peel attacked on the issue of sugar and dodged the much more lethal one of corn. When Ministers proposed a debate at the beginning of June on the Corn Laws to flush Peel out he at once tabled a motion of no confidence which had priority, and on which the debate began on May 27th.

The real fact was that although the Free Trade against Protection issue stirred many passions the Whig Government was tired, its Ministers jaded, its reputation low, and its Party organisation non-existent. The authority of Melbourne had long gone; it was a Ministry living on borrowed time, as it well knew, and now resorted to desperate expedients and calculations of opportunism as to the advantages of an early or later election that are the infallible indications of a Government in terminal decline.

Prince Albert saw this clearly; Queen Victoria found it difficult to accept. It was clear, even in Coburg, that the Melbourne Government, so long a-dying, was on the verge of breathing its last unlamented sighs, and both Albert and Stockmar were determined to avoid any repetition of the Bedchamber shambles. Stockmar wrote to him on May 18th:

> ... If things come to a change of Ministry, then the great axiom, irrefragibly one and the same for all Ministries, is this, viz: The Crown supports frankly, honourably, and with all its might, the Ministry of the time, whatever it be, so long as it commands a majority, and governs with integrity for the welfare and advancement of the country. A King, who as a Constitutional King cannot or will not carry this maxim into practice deliberately descends from the lofty pedestal on which the Constitution has placed him to the lower one of a mere party chief. Be you, therefore, the Constitutional genius of the Queen; do not con-

tent yourself with merely whispering this maxim in her ear
when circumstances serve, but strive also to carry it out into '
practice at the right time and by the worthiest means.

Prince Albert was already carrying out every part of this advice.
On his instructions, and with Queen Victoria's knowledge,[1] Anson
had entered into secret discussions with Peel on May 10th to remove
the possibility of any difficulty over the Ladies. Then, when the
Government was defeated by one vote on June 3rd, Albert had been
directly involved in the detailed discussions that had taken place in
May on the very difficult question of whether Ministers should
resign or Parliament – which had three years to run – be dissolved.
But although the omens looked bad for the Whigs (a point on which
Queen Victoria did not agree) there were members of the Cabinet
who strongly favoured this course rather than resign.

The actual occasion for the Government's fall had been the defeat
on May 18th on that part of the Budget reducing the foreign sugar
duties, which had prompted Peel's motion of no confidence. To
Melbourne's horror, Palmerston and Russell now advocated the
extension of the principle of reducing the duties on the import of
sugar to the total abolition of the duties on the importation of foreign
corn. To Melbourne, the Corn Laws were an essential feature of the
Constitution, and the protection of English agriculture against
foreign competition an article of the most profound faith. The idea of
a general election on this issue – 'the most insane proposition that
ever entered the human head', as he described the repeal of the Corn
Laws – made him favour resignation. Russell and Palmerston were
for dissolving at once, and retaining Office until the new Parliament.
The Queen, who believed that the Whigs must win, and was not
particularly interested in the Corn Laws, agreed with them. Parliament was prorogued on June 23rd and dissolved on the 29th.

The advice given to Queen Victoria and Prince Albert had been
very contradictory, but the principal factor in Queen Victoria's
mind was that it was far preferable to sending for Peel. Her view,
expressed to Melbourne on May 17th, and recorded in her Journal,
was that 'the Government would gain by a dissolution'; Melbourne

---

[1] Fulford, op. cit., p. 67, repeated by Longford, op. cit., p. 156, states that the
Queen did not know. In fact she had told Melbourne on May 5th, who reported
the fact to Anson, that 'she was prepared to give way upon the ladies if required,
but much wished that that point might be previously settled by negotiation with
Sir R. Peel, to avoid any discussion or difference'. (Memorandum by Anson,
May 5th 1841). On May 12th Queen Victoria wrote in her Journal that
Melbourne 'gave me the copies of Anson's conversations with Peel'. Thus,
although Anson was the intermediary, both the Queen and the Prime Minister
were fully informed.

was more doubtful. On the 19th she repeated her clear preference for an immediate election, and the majority in the Cabinet agreed. After Peel and the Conservatives had won the elections easily, and she had no choice but to send for him at the end of August, she felt very differently.

On June 11th Anson was the dismayed witness of an unpleasant scene between the Queen and her husband, whose immediate cause was the resignation of the Duchess of Bedford; her letter, significantly, had been sent to the Queen through Lehzen. Anson recorded:

'The Q. said I always felt that you and Ld Melbourne had compromised me, & There you have it. I never wished to give up 3 Ladies. The P. said you must be very cautious & well reflect. The Q. said the Tories would say if she submitted to this that she had been vanquished & lowered before the world.

The P. said I fear the Ladies' gossip again getting about you. The Q. on that burst into tears which could not be stopped for some time – & said she could Not force the Duchess to resign – they could not make her do that & that she would never appoint any Tories. 2 Ladies were more than any Minister ought to have given her.

The P. said, in this moment all shd be done to quiet you & get you over difficulties & it was shameful on the part of those who attempted to convert her mind. She said No – it was very well meant, Ld M. would not see that she was wrong in what she had agreed to but he would come round bye & bye – & nobody knew of the transaction & she therefore could act as she pleased.

In a moment of great excitement she said she did not know whether she should show to P. that letter. The P. added she might do that as she liked. The Q. after some reasoning of the Prince – the Duchess may resign but she must do bye & bye – or else it has the appearance of giving way.

On which the P. said on the contrary if she says she dislikes staying on with the Tories & resigns at once there is *no* appearance ...

The Q. was the whole day much depressed & said it weighed heavily on her mind, & felt she had been over hurried & compromised by the P. and Ld Melbourne'.

Melbourne was studiously unhelpful. When Anson put to him the dangers of another Bedchamber Crisis 'in its full force' on June 12th Melbourne 'said, Why not let it alone till the time for action arrives? I said the objection to that was that it kept the Q's mind in perpetual agitation, when it ought to be perfectly calm, & that under existing circumstances this excitement might be attended by serious consequences'. In spite of Anson's closeness with Melbourne, he found the Prime Minister indifferent to the serious possibilities, about which

Albert was deeply concerned. So were the Tories, Lord Ashley warning Anson that 'the Conservatives felt there was a great danger to be apprehended, to Sir R. Peel's coming into office, from the Intrigues of the Baroness Lehzen who they felt was ready to plunge everything into confusion, regardless of, or perhaps blind to, the consequences for the Queen, they dreaded her violence & intemperance, they felt that she used an influence against them by misrepresentation & false reports, & thereby unfairly prejudiced the Queen's mind'.

Had the Conservatives known that Lehzen was strongly supporting the Whig campaign their reaction would have been even more strong, but Ashley warned Anson that any repetition of the events of 1839 would 'destroy the position of the Queen, & it would be impossible to foresee the effect of it upon the Country. He said he feared that Peel would be some time before he could place entire confidence in the disposition of the Queen towards him – that no man had ever been so deeply cut by the conduct of the Q. towards him than he had been, & if it had been proposed to him to take office 6 months after that intrigue he was certain that nothing wd. have induced him'.

To the dismay of Prince Albert and Anson, the Queen resolutely continued a copious private correspondence with Melbourne. Not discouraged by Lehzen, she felt she had been somehow tricked into a wrong decision, and faced the prospect of seven years of Peel and the Tories with unconcealed and articulate gloom. 'What *is* to come hangs over me like a baneful dream' she wrote to Leopold on August 3rd when the elections already showed a distinct reversal for the Whigs, and on the 24th, when the Conservative victory was assured she referred to 'my present heavy trial, the heaviest I have ever had to endure' and reproached Leopold for not condoling with her. Stockmar fully shared Albert's admiration for Peel, but it took a considerable time before the Queen became reconciled to him. When she did, it was characteristically total, but the movement was slow and uneasy.

The elections contained their usual ingredients of bribery, intimidation, corrupt practices of all kinds, and much expenditure. Elections at that time were not for the squeamish or high-minded, and 'the will of the people' – very few of whom could actually vote – was strangely manifested. The Conservatives did well everywhere, but particularly in the English counties, where 22 seats changed hands, and the result was an emphatic victory for Peel and his confederation. Ministers awaited the recall of Parliament before resigning.

It was Prince Albert's first experience of this turmoil, but his reactions were of amusement rather than censure. The election, he wrote to his mother-in-law, 'empties purses, sets families by the ears, demoralises the lower classes, and perverts many of the upper, whose character wants strength to see them straight. But then, like other things, comes to an end, and so does not bring the body politic to ruin, as it might otherwise do'.

In spite of a series of successful visits in the late summer and early autumn, in which the young couple was genuinely surprised by public enthusiasm and warmth at a time of acute social difficulties and angry popular disturbance, Queen Victoria's distress at the loss of the Whigs, her unwanted pregnancy, and the continued shadow of the unresolved Lehzen issue, made it a difficult period. She told Anson at dinner on October 2nd about 'Sir R. Peel's awkward manners which she felt she could not get over' and his 'ignorance of Character was most striking & unaccountable', and a month later he found her still complaining about her new Prime Minister: 'He could not even look at her with ease'. It does not seem to have occurred to her that he had been deeply wounded by her treatment of him in the past, that she had allowed herself to become publicly, personally identified with his opponents, and that he was very suspicious – and with very good cause – of the activities of Lehzen. 'The Baroness is very mad just now', Anson wrote on November 19th, and, on December 5th, 'She has been moving her malevolent spirit with great activity lately'. Meanwhile, to the alarm of Albert, Stockmar, and Anson, Victoria continued her correspondence with Melbourne. In fact, their fears were groundless, and the letters were of no political significance, but the possibility of one going astray and falling into hostile hands, or the very fact of the correspondence becoming public knowledge made Stockmar tell Anson that he was 'very apprehensive that Evil will spring out of the correspondence carried on between the Q. and Ld M. He thinks it is productive of the greatest possible danger'. He was absolutely right to be so worried, but the letters, and the fact of their existence, were secure. But it was a nervous time for the Queen's advisers and her anxious husband.

Her letters and Journal contain constant references to her low spirits at the loss of Melbourne and her forthcoming confinement – 'very *sad*, and God knows! very wretched at times for myself and my country', complained of 'constant headaches' and her 'severe trial', and even on August 30th reminded Albert how abominably the Tories had treated him over his annuity and in effect forbade him from seeing them 'at all events for some time'.

Matters deteriorated further after the birth, on November 9th, of their first son, Albert Edward, from the beginning known as 'Bertie'. It had been a difficult and painful confinement, Victoria was low and wretched – 'Lord Melbourne entreats Your Majesty to pick up your spirits', her alarmed mentor had written to her in August – and then Vicky became seriously unwell, to the point when Albert became desperately alarmed.

It is clear that the Queen was suffering from acute post-natal depression, not lessened by Albert's anger at Lehzen's insistence on having a major role not only in the new baby's christening arrangements but in everything affecting the children. On December 26th Anson wrote of her mood on Christmas Day:

> The Q. was not at all well again yesterday – being again troubled with lowness ... The Baroness lets no opportunity of creating mischief & difficulty escape her – to keep an influence over the Nursery underlings is one of her great aims, which she succeeds in doing through the usual channels. I trust as another year closes we shall not be subject to her indefatigable meddling – & that she will not longer reside in the House.

Vicky's illness was the event that caused the explosion, and its intensity can be recognised from Albert's terrible note to Victoria on January 16th:

> Dr. Clark has mismanaged the child and poisoned her with calomel and you have starved her. I shall have nothing more to do with it; take the child away and do as you like and if she dies you will have it on your conscience.

There is relatively little surviving correspondence between the couple, as they were so constantly together. The loss of their diaries is irreparable for their biographers, and only their very occasional separations give the evidence of their love. On August 28th 1841 Victoria wrote to Leopold that 'I expect [Albert] back at about eleven tonight. He went at half-past eleven this morning. It is the first time that we have ever been separated for so long since our marriage, and I am quite melancholy about it'. But the Lehzen crisis was an exception to their sparse correspondence.

Viewed calmly in retrospect, far removed from the unhappy atmosphere of intrigue, jealousy, disappointment and tiredness that enveloped the participants and made life at Windsor and Buckingham Palace odious for all, it can be dispassionately observed that everyone behaved badly. Queen Victoria owed Lehzen much, and her husband should have been more solicitous of this fact and of her low spirits after her difficult confinement; Lehzen herself, by seeking the revenues of the Duchy of Cornwall and constantly causing difficulties between husband and wife, sought too much, including total influence over the Royal children, which was bound to inflame Albert further; also, she exaggerated the value of her undeniable popularity at Court, 'much beloved by the women and much esteemed and liked', as Greville wrote; Victoria's judgement, and her language to her husband, were alike injudicious; Anson's role, as Albert's vehement champion, was questionable. But, as in most power struggles – for this is what it was – many passions were aroused, and much folly was committed.

Fortunately in their distress, both Queen and Prince turned to Stockmar in January 1842. Albert wrote to him (January 16th) in considerable bitterness of Lehzen as 'a crazy, stupid intriguer, obsessed with the lust of power, who regards herself as a demi-God, and anyone who refuses to recognise her as such is a criminal ... I declare to you, as my and Victoria's true friend, that I will sacrifice my own comfort, my life's happiness to Victoria in silence, even if she continues in her error. But the welfare of my children and Victoria's existence as sovereign are too sacred for me not to die fighting rather than yield them as prey to Lehzen'. The Queen was deeply upset, and wrote to Stockmar that 'my tears flow always afresh. I feel so forlorn and I have got *such* a sick headache! I feel as I had had a dreadful dream. I do hope you may be able to pacify Albert. He seems so very angry still. I am *not*'. But Albert was very angry indeed, as his next letter to Stockmar (January 18th) dramatically reveals:

> ... Victoria is too hasty and passionate for me to be able often to speak of my difficulties. She will not hear me out but flies into a rage and overwhelms me with reproaches of suspiciousness, want of trust, ambition, envy, etc. etc. There are, therefore, two ways open to me: (1) to keep silence and go away (in which case I am like a schoolboy who has had a dressing down from his mother and goes off snubbed; (2) I can be still more violent (and then we have scenes like that of the 16th, which I hate, because I am so sorry for Victoria in her misery, besides which it undermines the peace of the home) ...

The appalled Stockmar fully appreciated that the peace of the home had indeed been grievously undermined, and the 'scene' of the 16th had included Victoria accusing Albert of wanting to drive her out of the nursery and telling him that he 'could murder the child [Vicky] if he wanted to'. Stockmar at once wrote to express his dismay and shock – 'Language has not sufficient power to declare with what despondence he looks to the future if he allows for a moment that such violent emotions could be produced again from the same causes' – and it was Victoria who was contrite; Albert 'must not believe the stupid things I say like being miserable I ever married and so forth which come when I am unwell ... Dearest Angel Albert, God only knows how I love him. His position is difficult, heaven knows, and we must do everything to make it easier'.

In her fury, and poor health, the Queen had hurled accusations at Albert that were cruel, deeply wounding, and hurtful to any husband, but particularly one in his difficult position. His emotions were those of bitter resentment and anger, but hers, after the initial storm, of genuine remorse and shame; 'my being so passionate when spoken to', she wrote to Stockmar, 'this I fear is irremediable as yet, but I hope in time it will be got over. There is often an irritability in me which (like Sunday last which began the *whole* misery) makes me say cross and odious things which I don't myself believe and which I fear hurt A., but which he should not believe'. At the end came this noble sentence:

> Our position is tho' very different to any other married couples. A. is in my house and not I in his. – But I am ready to submit to his wishes as I love him so dearly.

Thus did sunshine and happiness return after the storm. Bertie was christened at St. George's Chapel, Windsor, on January 25th 1842. Lehzen was handsomely pensioned off to Germany, Victoria and Albert were totally reconciled, and although there were to be further difficulties, tempers, and strains in this marriage between two such determined young people nothing so serious or embittering was ever to cloud their marriage as this incident did. Both became more cautious and sensitive to each other's feelings, and out of near-disaster there came a greater strength, a deeper mutual understanding, and an increased love. 'Poor Lehzen', Queen Victoria recorded some years later, 'how ill everything went while she was here'. And, on another occasion: 'I shudder to think what my beloved Albert had to go through ... it makes my blood boil to think of it'.

Family problems remained, however. In spite of her reconciliation with her daughter, the Duchess of Kent was not an easy woman, was quick to complain of neglect or any other failings, and had as fiery a temper as her daughter. It was fortunate that she was so genuinely devoted to Albert, and he to her, as it was sometimes his duty to deny her wishes. Her deep affection for her nephew was usually mixed with expressions of her grievances against the lack of consideration shown towards her, as when she told Anson (April 26th 1841) that 'She thought the P. was not properly supported in his very difficult position, & she had not the influence to assist him in any way which a mother's authority ought to give. She felt there was a want of little attentions towards her, which she was less indifferent on her own account than for the opinion of the public which she felt would blame her Child'. Anson defended both Victoria and Albert in this discussion, but when the Duchess pleaded for Conroy to be forgiven and reinstated he had to say that this was impossible. It was some time before she accepted this fact, and did so with such reluctance and unhappiness that the reader of her letters is left in no doubt about her emotional dependence upon him, and which long survived his disgrace and exile, both of which she constantly attempted to reverse until she realised that the venture was without hope. On this matter, Prince Albert was implacable.

Early in January 1843, to take one example, she wrote to ask for a favour, an apartment in Hampton Court, for a member of the Conroy family. He replied:

... I have not informed V. of your wish, for I should be sorry if she saw that you still retain a certain tender attachment for a family to whom the peace and quiet of the whole of her earlier life was sacrificed. In spite of that, Victoria does more for Sir John than she does for anyone, and I am afraid that even you in your limited circumstances impose privations on yourself and deprive yourself of the pleasure of doing something to relieve the situation of your own children, who really love you, I mean Karl and particularly Feodora, in order to heap favours on a man to whom you feel under an obligation, whereas it is he who owes you endless gratitude for raising him up from nowhere, and he who bears the guilt for so much of the suffering to which you were exposed and are still daily exposed ...

The Duchess wrote back on January 12th:

My dear Albert,
   Your answer to the wish I expressed to you has UPSET me VERY MUCH; I cannot say how much I regret that I wrote to you about it. Your remark that the *peace* and *quiet* of V's earlier life was sacrificed to this family WOUNDED me VERY MUCH! it was too *strong* and unjust. I intended to leave your letter unanswered, but I could not bring myself to do so. Had Stockmar not told me last year that V. was not disinclined to grant her former playmate this favour which costs her *nothing*, I should not have mentioned it again.

As to the remainder of your letter, I will only remark that Sir John was in the service of the late Duke; – and that I help Feodora as much as I now can.

Your answer surprises and upsets me! I must repeat how deeply I regret having written to you about this matter.

Your

true

Mother

Albert's response illuminates their relationship:

I am deeply sorry that my letter wounded you, which truly was not my intention. But I considered it my duty to place the naked truth before you, as we are always more or less inclined to harbour illusions, and I am the only person whose relationship to you makes it possible to do this, and who can speak impartially and dispassionately of matters in which he was not involved.

I should not be fulfilling my duty as a son, nor showing you true devotion, if out of fear of upsetting you for a moment I flinched from telling you the truth about a situation which has already caused you so much suffering and which daily continues to do so.

This difference was quickly resolved, and the Duchess's letters resumed their pattern of 'My beloved Albert' (*Mein theurer geliebter Albert*), and ending 'Your truly loving Mother' (*Deine dich innigst liebende Mutter*). He was sensitive to her need for small tokens of her position as mother of the Queen – the 'little attentions' for which she craved – and frequently was able to achieve them. Her rebukes – 'I fear you and Victoria are not missing your Mama very much; that is how it is as life goes on', and 'Grandmamma send you both her love; she complains a little that you do not write to her very often, but I have defended you' – are mild enough, and in one case had absolutely no effect:

... As you seem to have sworn death to all pheasants, I beg you to *spare* the poor Frogmore pheasants, they come up under my window now, and Sir George claims that partridges come quite close too, and he told me that in the course of 15 months 40 cats had been shot in the garden ...

The essential problem had been that there was too little for Prince Albert to do. He busied himself intensely with reorganising the Court and its finances to the point that Peel became worried about

the possibility of 'a cheap Court', to which Albert responded sympathetically, but pointed out that the existing system 'works so that
neither regularity, comfort, or security, nor outward dignity is in the
Queen's Palace'. This was tedious work which, Albert wrote, 'hung
about me like an ever-present weight', and made him highly unpopular with politicians and others who had relations or friends at
Court. The Queen was not greatly interested in these matters, and
Peel, although very sympathetic, had to address himself to the
political aspects of the Prince's constant searches for economies and
reforms. As late as 1844 he minuted warningly to the Prince that
'Reforms in the Royal Household are not very palatable to either of
the great political parties of the State . . . The *esprit de corps*, the fear of
reductions, the hope of profiting by lavish expenditure, unite all,
whatever be their party attachments, by a sense of common interest'.
Eventually, to Albert's intense relief, complete authority was given
to the Master of the Household of his own choice, and he was wholly
freed from these vexations. The reforms were indeed long overdue,
and of great benefit, but it was poor – if onerous – employment for a
man of his abilities. The fact that he did it at all, and did it so well, is
greatly to his credit, but gave him neither pleasure nor satisfaction.
In a far more interesting and rewarding area he addressed himself to
the affairs of the Duchy of Cornwall in meticulous detail, to their
lasting advantage.

But after his skilful steering of the Ministerial transition of 1841 he
now attended audiences with the Queen with her Ministers. 'I must
alone be her adviser', as he told the departing Melbourne. He was
increasingly informed about political and official business. He took
charge of the Royal papers, read widely and deeply, was an indefatigable correspondent, a devoted husband and father – and yet, as
Melbourne and Anson noted, was bored and dissatisfied. Queen
Victoria shared neither his intense feeling for nature nor his pleasure
in the company of intellectuals, which Melbourne – probably rightly
– ascribed to her sense of inferiority in their presence. Long evenings
playing chess or at official functions were infinitely tedious to him,
and his inability at 'small talk' often gave others the impression of
aloofness, coldness, and even arrogance, when the simple fact was
that he was ineffably bored.

Victoria frankly liked to be amused and entertained, and was far
from hostile to the pleasures of the table – 'A Queen does not drink a
bottle of wine at a meal', Stockmar wrote censoriously – she loved
London and its excitements, was certainly not interested in 'a cheap
Court', intensely resented her pregnancies, and had so little in
common with her husband's intellectual concerns and activities that
the strength of their marriage becomes even more remarkable. It was

a real sacrifice for her to abandon London life for 'the solid pleasures of a peaceable, quiet, yet merry life in the country', yet one she did make on his behalf. Also, always sensitive to his 'sacrifice' in leaving Coburg, she was increasingly concerned about his status. At the end of 1841 she wrote in her Journal, touchingly, that he 'is above me in everything, really, and therefore I wish he should be equal in rank with me' and tentatively proposed again to Stockmar the idea of creating him King Consort. Stockmar, while understanding the motive, again strongly advised against such a step at so early a stage, and Peel agreed. Prince Albert had no knowledge of this proposal, which the Queen shelved but never abandoned. Both Albert and Stockmar strongly resisted the proposal that he should succeed Wellington as Commander-in-Chief after Wellington's death, and very wisely.

The key to his happiness lay not in titles or status, but in his political influence with the Queen and her Ministers. It had taken some time for Queen Victoria to realise this, and then she had resisted strongly. But the departure of Melbourne, the arrival of the far more amenable – to Albert – Peel, and the removal of Lehzen transformed his position, and his happiness. 'He is now all-powerful', Greville recorded; ' ... Melbourne told me long ago that the Prince would acquire unbounded influence'. Stockmar, summoned by Albert to assist him in resolving the intractable problems of the Royal Household and finances, noted the difference in April 1843:

> The Queen is well, the Princess wonderfully improved [in health], round as a little barrel, and the Prince of Wales, though a little plagued with his teeth, is strong upon his legs, with a calm, clear, bright expression of face. The Prince himself is well and happy, though he frequently looks pale, worried, and weary. He is rapidly showing what is in him. He is full of a practical talent, which enables him at a glance to seize the essential points of a question, like the vulture that pounces on its prey and hurries off with it to his nest.

Lehzen's departure not only led to the complete reconciliation between Victoria and her mother but to one between the Duchess and Queen Adelaide; Albert did not exaggerate when he told Ernest that it had required 'the skill of a diplomat and the delicate touch of a tightrope walker, but patience and perseverance have won the day'. Thus, the bitter acrimonies which Queen Victoria had known all her life, and which had been a major part of it, were suddenly and dramatically replaced by harmony and love. It was in some respects Prince Albert's greatest single contribution to his wife's happiness in the first years of their marriage.

There are few fates so melancholy for a man of ability, ambition, and political interests and skills to be placed in a political situation in which he is only a tentative participant, and is reduced to the position of an impotent observer. This had been Albert's fate for the first year of his marriage, and had created the frustration which was the real cause of the explosion of January 1842, especially after his role in the smooth change of Government the previous summer. From this time his political role as the Queen's chief counsellor, secretary, and sole confidant, although never formally defined, became understood and accepted by her and by her Ministers. His really useful and significant work could now begin.

After this sad, but perhaps inevitable, and indeed even necessary, crisis, 1842 became a year of peace and happiness for the Royal couple, made especially memorable by their first visit to Scotland. Apart from a brief but very successful visit by George IV in 1822, no reigning monarch had visited Scotland since the unfortunate precedent of Charles I. The Royal couple went to Edinburgh, Perth, Taymouth and Stirling. Their reception was ecstatic, they were fascinated by the country and the people, and Albert, who was very struck by the similarities with the land and towns around Coburg, was introduced to the skills of deer-stalking, which he described as 'one of the most fatiguing, but it is also one of the most interesting of pursuits'. They departed on September 15th with real regret. 'As the fair shores of Scotland receded more and more from our view', Queen Victoria related as their ship left the Firth of Forth, 'we felt quite sad that this very pleasant and interesting tour was over; but we shall never forget it'. It was not until later that the idea of buying property in Scotland occurred to them, but this first venture across the Border left an indelible mark on both, and they returned in 1844.[1]

It must be emphasised that in political as well as in personal terms their marriage was a partnership, and a most remarkable one. They worked together, with adjoining desks, whether at Buckingham Palace or Windsor, and, later, Osborne and Balmoral, and the sheer

---

[1] In September 1842 Peel had responded immediately and favourably to the Queen's tentative suggestion that a ship might be provided by the Navy for her use on her Royal visits abroad, and to Scotland and Ireland. In February 1843 the matter was put to the House of Commons, and approved without opposition. The ship was named the *Victoria and Albert*, and as the Royal Yacht served the Queen and the Prince on many of their visits. Always prone to sea-sickness, even in the most mild conditions, Albert was never as enthusiastic about the new acquisition as the Queen.

volume of the official and private documents they read and wrote demonstrates how hard and conscientiously they did work. But there was also laughter and enjoyment, as there was whenever they were together, save in the moments of sharp disagreements, which became fewer and fewer as their love and mutual respect deepened.

It is because they worked together as a team that it is dangerous – except in certain clear and specific cases – to give the credit or otherwise to either of them individually. Although Albert's influence on the Queen's attitudes and opinions became immensely strong, to the point when she almost always – although not always – took his advice, her own judgements and opinions had their influence on him. She never entirely accepted his harsh views about Palmerston and his policies, although on this she often deferred to Albert and took his cause, and, as subsequent events proved, was more in instinctive sympathy with Palmerston's English nationalistic view of the world than with her husband's essentially pacific international-ism, which she admired and supported, but with obvious inner qualifications. She was proud of her husband's growing, and even-tually very high, reputation among intellectuals, but did not really share his pleasure in their company. Her assessments of people may have often been impulsive and wrong, but they stemmed from a warm personality, and were an invaluable corrective to his, which often tended to place too heavy an importance on cerebral and moral qualities – although, as has been emphasised, this latter aspect in his character has been consistently exaggerated. Thus, in the case of Peel, Victoria's uneasiness at his bleak and awkward manner initially led her – in addition to her Whig sympathies – to under-estimate his many other qualities, but she was not entirely wrong in sensing that there was something lacking in his personality, and an inner coldness that his admirers fervently deny but which certainly existed. For his part, Albert's admiration for Peel's brain, experi-ence, and unblemished character took him too far in accepting his judgements as almost automatically right. It was their *combined* assessment that was so interesting, and, so far as any human judgements on other humans are correct, was very close to the truth.

This was also to happen over Palmerston, for whom Albert was to develop a very grudging, halting, but definite respect after years of intense and sometimes even bitter animosity – and which was wholly reciprocated. Here again, it was the combination of their characters and minds that brought the couple to a collective opinion that was eventually balanced, fair, and sensible.

The quality and clarity of the Queen's handling of business after Albert died – and most notably in the over-criticised period of withdrawal immediately after his death – is evidence enough that although she had learned much from him, and relied heavily upon his judgements, she herself had a mind to be admired, a firm application to work, however disagreeable, and much common sense and a shrewd understanding of human nature. Thus, it was the *combination* of these two remarkable minds and personalities that gave such formidable and growing strength to the political position of the Crown. The achievements, and the errors, were those of the team, working together in loving and happy collaboration at their linked desks.

On November 25th Albert was so struck by a passage on King William III in Hallam's *History of England* which he had been reading that he copied it out and sent it to Anson. It read: 'The demeanour of William, always cold, and sometimes harsh, his foreign origin (a sort of crime in English eyes) conspired to keep alive this disaffection'. Anson and he then discussed the matter, and Albert said that while he could easily understand such antipathy, he had not experienced it personally.

There was truth in this, but the fact was that his growing popularity was limited. His campaign to abolish duelling in the Army was not well received in traditional circles, and his open hostility to London Society was keenly resented. 'He was not made to shine in commonplace society,' it was well written by a contemporary. 'He could talk admirably about something, but he had not the gift of talking about nothing, and probably would not have cared much to cultivate such a faculty ... Thus it happened that he remained for many years, if not exactly unappreciated, yet not thoroughly appreciated, and that a considerable and very influential section of society was always ready to cavil at what he said, and find motive for suspicion in most things that he did'.

By this stage Albert had definitely influenced Victoria's attitude to town life, to the point when she had come to resent almost as deeply as he did the time they had to spend in London. Artists and musicians – most notably Mendelssohn – were welcome guests at Buckingham Palace and Windsor. Albert in effect became the Master of the Queen's Musick, added strings to the wind instruments of the Queen's Private Band, transformed its repertoire, and made it give the first performance in England of Schubert's C Major Symphony. Peel's appointment of him as President of the Fine Arts Commission gave him particular pleasure. He greatly increased and extended Victoria's interest in music, and encouraged her painting, for which she had real ability, and installed etching equipment at the Palace. With their storms past, Lehzen gone, his wife and her mother totally reconciled, this was a period of much contentment. Vicky, called 'Pussy', was a great joy, and Bertie was thriving.

The popularity of the couple was again substantially increased by two more assassination attempts in London. In May 1842 they were shot at in their carriage by a John Francis. Albert saw Peel at 6 pm on the evening of the 29th in the garden of Buckingham Palace to describe how he had seen 'a man of the age from 26 to 30, with a shabby hat and of dirty appearance, stretch out his hand and snap a small pistol at the carriage window.' The pistol was about a yard from the window. 'The noise of the snap was distinctly heard by the Prince, and confirms his impression that he could not possibly be mistaken, that that which the man held in his hand was a pistol.' He described his position, and his appearance as 'that of silliness amounting almost to idiocy.' A boy of 14, George Pears of 7 Castle Street, Holborn, reported seeing a man at the scene who muttered to himself 'they may take me if they like, I don't care, I was a fool that I did not shoot,' and a mysterious 'elderly gentleman' whom he followed to St James's. As he was not apprehended, the Royal couple deliberately drove out again later to draw his fire. 'You may imagine', Albert wrote to his father, 'that our minds were not very easy. We looked behind every tree, and I cast my eyes round in search of the rascal's face'. Francis – 'a little, swarthy, ill-looking rascal', in Albert's account – did shoot again, missed, and was arrested. This episode can be regarded as one of extraordinary courage or extraordinary folly. Contemporary opinions emphatically favoured the first interpretation.

Prince Albert believed at once, although both Anson and Stockmar were very doubtful, that the King of Hanover was behind these attempts on the Queen's life, and he took very seriously an affidavit by a Mrs. Blow who claimed she had overheard a conversation between 'a female, a tall dark man [with] large black Moustachios, and a third person a shorter man of a shallow complexion' several months before, in November 1841 in London, and that the latter had said 'the Queen's life must be decided upon before the birth of the Child, as there must be no Prince *borned*, he made use of that exact term ... One of the men said remember, remember that the £30,000 is the sum. He then added when do you suppose will be the time, alluding to the Queen's confinement, because I must go to Hanover first. There seemed a deal of determination about him.' Mrs Blow claimed that she saw the woman and one of the men in the Park just before Francis' attempt. After careful investigation Mrs Blow's account was dismissed as maliciously fraudulent by the police and Home Office, and Albert, after his initial keen interest in the possibility that Hanover was behind the assassination attempt, came to the conclusion on July 1st, that the 'proneness of the People to commit (sic) attempts upon the person of the Sovereign

is increased in our times by the increase of democratical & republi-
can Notions & the licentiousness of the Press.'

The aftermath was interesting and instructive. Queen Victoria
regarded attempts on her life with remarkable tolerance, almost as
an inevitable aspect of the job she had inherited. She was always
casual about her personal security, rode openly in her carriage in
London, Windsor, and on the couple's 'expeditions' around the
country – much of which was in violent, if sporadic, ferment – and
spurned anything approximating to the security which nervous
monarchs throughout Europe insisted upon. Of all her qualities,
perhaps that of her physical courage has received less attention than
it merits, and it was certainly a major element in the restoration of
her popularity. No previous modern Sovereign, not even King
William IV, had travelled so openly or frequently, and with such
manifest enjoyment. She liked this freedom, and enjoyed being
cheered; she never forgot being hissed at Ascot, and always regarded
her reception as her carriage went down the course on the opening
day of the summer meeting as a touchstone of her popularity. It was
natural, human, and unfeigned. It was Prince Albert who transformed the security at Buckingham Palace and Windsor – especially
for the children – and was constantly worried, and with good reason,
about the dangers to her life. But he also understood and respected
her attitudes, and her admirable, if perilous, indifference to
danger.

Francis was sentenced to death, but the strong wish of the Queen
and Prince that the sentence should not be carried out was supported
by the Law Officers, whose advice was sought by the Cabinet. It was
very doubtful indeed whether the pistol had been loaded, and one
Judge, when consulted, gave it as his opinion that he had been a
member of the Jury he would have voted for acquittal. In these
circumstances Ministers found no difficulty in acceding to the
Queen's proposal that the death sentence should be commuted to
transportation for life. In Albert's papers there is a deeply moving
letter of gratitude from Francis's father for having spared his son.
Also, on the urging of the Queen and Prince Albert, new legislation
was quickly passed to deal with the crime of attempted assassination
of the Sovereign, and which did not include the death penalty. In an
age of public executions, which both the Queen and Prince
abhorred, and the widespread – if gradually diminishing – use of the
death penalty, this may be regarded with particular interest.

In July another shot was fired at their carriage by 'a hunch-backed
lad named Bean', and Peel was so distraught and his concern moved
the Queen so deeply that all her prejudices were removed, to the
point that she now described him as 'a great statesman, who thinks

but little of party, and never of himself'. Not long after, Peel's secretary was assassinated, in mistake for himself. This tragedy, also, made the relationship between Queen and Prime Minister even closer.[1]

In the summer and early autumn of 1843 Victoria and Albert discussed at length the possibility of buying a home of their own. The difficulties over Buckingham Palace were acute, with Ministers expressing concern at the constant requests for more funds for rebuilding and improving a Palace for which the Royal couple had little affection, but which they accepted must be their State residence in the capital. Whenever the Prince raised the issue of money Peel expressed 'extreme embarrassment', and on one occasion, in Prince Albert's account, Peel 'spoke for some time without in fact saying anything, with his eyes turned away.' The Prince's efficient stewardship of the finances of the Royal Family entitled him to raise the issue, which he did frequently, but with a meagre response.

But now that Lehzen and Uxbridge had gone, Prince Albert had been able to hand over the administration and reconstruction of Buckingham Palace and the Court to a new and capable Master of the Household, and his careful management and economies had so improved the Royal finances that the purchase of their own home was now a practical possibility.

Windsor Castle, for all its many attractions was, as the Queen wrote, 'beautiful and comfortable, but it is a *palace*', whereas what she and her husband wanted was a home. Also, Prince Albert's ambitions for designing, planting, gardening and farming were constantly frustrated by the fact that the real authority was vested in the Office of Woods and Forests, whose approval had to be sought for every change. Claremont, which they liked, had its disadvantages, and it remained the personal property of King Leopold. Albert's design of the Royal Dairy at Windsor was one of his most deeply satisfying and successful creations, and in addition to the management of the farm and the Duchy of Cornwall estates he immersed himself in examining the extraordinary Royal art collections, to which he was beginning to make his own contribution. It was largely the influence of Ludwig Gruner that drew him to the

[1] There were to be other more tentative attempts on her life. She was fired on by an Irishman called Hamilton on Constitution Hill in May 1849, although the pistol had no ball; she was hit by a stick wielded by Robert Pate in May 1850; an unloaded pistol was aimed at her in London in February 1872 by Arthur O'Connor; and a shot was fired at her in Windsor by Roderick MacLean in March 1882. In fact, none of these episodes, not even the last, were as serious as the endeavours of Oxford and Francis.

'primitives' of the Early Renaissance, but he also recognised the outstanding talents of Franz-Xavier Winterhalter, and he shared his wife's admiration for the skills of Edwin Landseer and George Hayter. One of his most charming initiatives was the decoration of a little garden pavilion in the grounds of Buckingham Palace, which Gruner described as 'picturesque and fantastic, without any regular style of architecture'. It contained three rooms and a kitchen, the principal one being an octagon, and Albert commissioned eight Royal Academicians to design frescoes for them. The result, although it delighted the Queen and the Prince, has generally been adjudged to be artistically disappointing; unhappily, it no longer exists, as it fell into such poor condition through damp and neglect that it was demolished in 1928, and we only have Gruner's record of its lightness and colour.

This was not, however, satisfying enough for a man of such exceptional and restless talents. Neither he nor the Queen liked the glittering extravaganza of King George IV's and Nash's master-piece, the Brighton Pavilion, indeed so much so that Queen Victoria wrote that her husband was rendered speechless when he first beheld it. The Pavilion was also manifestly highly inconvenient and unsuit-able for a young and growing family, and the rapid development of Brighton into a popular spa had resulted in much building in the vicinity of the Pavilion that shut off the view of the sea. In addition to these considerable disadvantages the Brighton crowds were so inquisitive and pressing when the Royal Family visited the town that they became seriously upset. 'We are more disgusted with Brighton than ever', Prince Albert wrote to Peel on February 8th 1845. 'We were mobbed this morning at our walk in too disagreeable a way'.

In these circumstances it was not surprising that the Prince did not appreciate at all the real qualities of the drama and romance of the Pavilion's design and decorations, and it was systematically stripped of its valuables, which were transferred to Windsor and Buckingham Palace, and public auctions disposed of what was not required by the Royal Family. The shell itself was due to be demolished until local sentiment and public protests prompted the Brighton Corporation to purchase and save it. Gradually it was restored to something of its former grandeur, and a lamentable act of vandalism was prevented. Prince Albert's indifference to the fate of the Pavilion may dismay later generations, but the complete unsuitability of this bizarre and wonderful creation as a Royal residence is obvious.

Thus, there was Buckingham Palace, bleak, formal, too large, and too official; Windsor, where complete privacy was difficult, and over which the Office of Woods and Forests held authority; Claremont, which was not theirs; and the hopelessly inadequate and disliked Brighton Pavilion. In the autumn of 1843 the Queen and the Prince spoke to Peel about their desire to have their own home.

The Queen and her mother had visited the Isle of Wight in 1831 and 1833, when they had stayed at Norris Castle, to the east of Cowes and occupying a dominant position over the Solent. The Isle was verdant, quiet, and thinly populated, and in her explorations with the Duchess of Kent the young Princess had been delighted by it. She would have bought Norris, but 'had not the means', and in the summer of 1843 she and Prince Albert visited the Isle, which revived her pleasure in it and aroused his strong interest. The transport revolution provided by the railway and the steam ferry no longer made it impossibly remote for the Household or for Ministers or communications with London.

Peel had fortuitously learnt that Lady Isabella Blatchford wished to sell Osborne House and its estate, which adjoined that of Norris Castle. The house itself first charmed the Queen, who described it happily as 'so complete and snug', but this was not the opinion of her husband, not that of Anson or other observers. But the estate, with eight hundred acres and a wonderful situation commanding a magnificent view of the Solent, perfectly suited the ambition of Queen and Prince for, in her words, 'a place of one's own, quiet and retired', and his for a real opportunity for design and farming and planting 'free from Departments, Crown, Woods & Forests etc', as he wrote to Stockmar.

Lady Isabella was a difficult and disagreeable vendor, and initially Osborne was rented, although eventually bought for £26,000, with an additional £20,000 to be paid in eighteen years for land purchased from Winchester College. The final Osborne Estate constitued 600 acres of parkland, 400 of woodland, and 700 of arable, and was finally over 2,000 acres.

This gave the Prince his setting, in which he and Thomas Cubitt created one of the most remarkable buildings of the nineteenth century. It was such a close partnership between the Prince, Gruner, and Cubitt that it is impossible to regard them other than as an inspired trio. The vision of an Italianate facade, with twin 'campaniles' and terraces, was Prince Albert's, as was the site. Cubitt provided his unequalled capacities of draughtsmen and technicians; Prince Albert and Gruner worked closely on the details that make Osborne so personal and original. Cubitt's hand is to be seen in the structure – strong, with the use of iron girders instead of wooden beams, an excellent and efficient heating system (a matter of indifference to Queen Victoria, but not to Prince Albert or the Household), and insulation that used crushed sea-shells – and Prince

Albert's in the façade and the private 'Pavilion', which is the heart of
the house. The tiled floor in the Marble Corridor clearly shows the
influence, and probably the hand, of Gruner, as do many of the
details, notably the door-furniture, that gives Osborne so much of its
charm.

The Pavilion, with its own 'campanile' tower, was built first.
Imposing on the outside, internally it is surprisingly modest. The
ground floor consisted principally of the drawing and billiard rooms
– the billiard table, with its slate top and, unusually, slate legs, was
designed entirely by Prince Albert – with large windows, and dining
room. The billiard room and drawing room are in fact one L-shaped
room, which was highly unusual and of particular interest to modern
architects, many of whom have assumed that such open-planning
was a creation of the present century. The dining room, which leads
immediately off the drawing room, has such wide doors that it, also,
forms part of the whole. Each room is admirably proportioned, and
at night – a touch of which Thomas Jefferson would have particularly approved – large concealed shutters with mirror glass on the
inside were drawn across the windows to make best advantage of the
light, particularly from the chandeliers designed by Gruner and
Prince Albert. Although very large and stoutly constructed, these
shutters can to this day be opened and closed at a touch, so perfectly
are they balanced.

The private rooms of the Queen and the Prince are immediately
above. On the landing there is a waiting room for pages, and then
two large and light dressing rooms for the Prince and the Queen,
with what was officially known as The Queen's Sitting Room
between them, but which was a private drawing room and study,
with a bow window leading onto a balcony from which, on summer
evenings, Albert would call to the nightingales and rejoice in their
responses. There are two bathrooms, with deep baths and running
water – luxuries as yet unknown at Windsor or Buckingham Palace –
and efficient water closets, again a significant rarity in the country
homes and Palaces of England. The principal and only bedroom,
which like all the other rooms is not large, faces due East to receive
the morning sun. On the West, next to the Prince's dressing room,
was the children's schoolroom and a sitting room for their Governess, while on the floor above were the children's bedrooms and
playrooms and Nursery, and accommodation for their staff.

This was the Pavilion, the real part of Osborne. The main wing for
official purposes contained on its ground floor an Audience Room, a
Council Room, a suite for the Duchess of Kent, and accommodation
for the Household, with family rooms above. On the ground floor
it was linked to the Pavilion with the tiled and pillared marble

corridor, and on the other floors with arcades, the open upper one earning a deserved reputation for extreme coldness until an ingenious removeable iron and glass protective screen was designed and installed. Over a century later it is daily praised by those who have to make the journey from the main wing to the Pavilion.

It is one of the remarkable features of Osborne that it looks much larger than it is, and Prince Albert's original design did not incorporate the Durbar Room – on whose merits opinions vary – and which was added long after the Prince's death. The texture is also deceptive. Osborne looks as though it is made of stone, when in fact it was built of brick with 'Roman cement' applied to the surface, and then lightly etched to give the appearance of stone, whose cost would have been prohibitive. So well was the deception achieved that only close inspection reveals it, and the problems of maintenance only arose many years later.

The siting, which required considerable moving of earth and new and deep foundations, is that of an artist, as are the apparently but in reality complementary towers. Almost all the now massive trees that visitors and experts so admire were chosen, planned, and planted by Prince Albert. It was also he who conceived the idea of the 'Swiss Cottage' for the children, in reality more of a large chalet than a cottage, brought over from Switzerland in components and erected in the Osborne grounds close – but not too close – to the house. It is the first pre-fabricated building of any size erected in Britain. Here, the children had their own working house and gardens, with their own tools, and the boys their own fort and model guns. Prince Albert also designed a small but delightful building on the beach which can hardly be described as a beach-hut where, protected from the prevailing winds, the Solent view could be particularly appreciated. A large bathing-hut for the use of the Queen was bought, and a special ramp built for its use.

It is impossible to exaggerate the importance of the design and building of Osborne on the lives of the Royal couple, and especially for Prince Albert. On May 12th 1845 Victoria wrote that 'It does my heart good to see how my beloved Albert enjoys it all, and is so full of admiration of the place, and of all the plans and improvements he means to carry out. He is hardly to be kept at home for a moment'. Albert described his life at Osborne in those early, very happy, years as 'partly forester, partly builder, partly farmer and partly gardener'. He was eager that the farms be as well managed and efficient as possible, and that he and the Queen be the best of employers. Like Jefferson, he was a farmer – once described by the highly outspoken head keeper of Windsor, in Albert's presence, as 'that damned farmer' – with a passionate, almost sensual, feeling for nature, its

9   Prince Albert, 1842, by Thorburn

10a   The façade of Buckingham Palace, by Nash
      Painted in 1846, immediately before the removal of the Marble Arch and
      the building of the new façade that linked the wings of the main
      courtyard

10b   Buckingham Palace Pavilion − the Octagon room

11a Osborne under construction, by Leitch, 1847
The Pavilion, the heart of the house, has been completed, and the top
terrace; the lower is under construction. On the left, the Household wing
nears completion

11b Osborne completed
Photograph taken in 1867. The Pavilion remains separated from, but
linked to, the Household wing

12a Osborne: the Drawing Room
This photograph was taken in 1885, but the room was as it had been in
Prince Albert's lifetime. A view is from West to East. To the right, out of the
picture, is the Billiard Room with no dividing wall. At the far end to the right
is the entrance to the Dining Room

12b Osborne: The Queen's Sitting Room
When working, Queen Victoria sat on the right hand chair, the Prince on
the left; This arrangement was identical at Buckingham Palace, Windsor,
and Balmoral

13a The Queen and the Princess Royal, 1844
This is the first known photograph of the Queen; the child is usually erroneously described as the Prince of Wales

13b Lord Palmerston, by Partridge

14a The Queen, Prince Albert, and the Princess Royal at Windsor, by
Landseer. The Prince is stroking his greyhound, Eôs

14b The Royal Family, 1846, by Winterhalter
The children are, from left to right, Prince Alfred, the Prince of Wales,
Princess Alice, Princess Helena, and Princess Victòria

15   Prince Albert, 1848

16a   The Crystal Palace from across the Serpentine, by Wyld, 1851

16b   The opening of the Great Exhibition, May 1st 1851, by Roberts

hazards, constant surprises, frustrations, and joys. He wrote to his eldest daughter many years later that 'the art of gardening' had had 'extraordinary attractions for me of late years, indeed I may say from earliest childhood', and his letter continued:

> In this the artist who lays out the work, and devises a garment for a piece of ground, has the delight of seeing his work live and grow hour by hour; and, while it is growing, he is able to polish, to cut up and carve, to fill up here and there, to hope, and to love.

That he was a very successful farmer became so well known that when he opened his speech to the Royal Agricultural Society in July 1848 with the words 'We agriculturalists of England' he was genuinely surprised by the thunderous applause which interrupted him. An invention of his own to convert raw sewage into agricultural fertiliser was so successful at Osborne that he became excited by its general application, bearing very much in mind the foetid horrors of the industrial towns and cities; unhappily, his invention depended upon a sharp fall of ground to be effective, and the special circumstances of Osborne could not be repeated elsewhere.

It was his purpose 'to make Osborne a smooth, easily worked, yet beautiful machine in which to live'[1], as had been Jefferson's at Monticello; unlike Jefferson, Prince Albert, Gruner and Cubitt got it right first time.

Psychologically, Osborne was crucial for the Prince. He could apply his energies, his frustrated ambitions, his mind and his imagination to the creation of something that was *his*. No Parliamentary money was involved, there was no need for the constant, irritating, demeaning and usually fruitless appeals to Ministers and officials to make Buckingham Palace habitable for a young family, and to defray the Royal expenses for their official duties. The fact that Osborne could be bought and built, at an eventual cost of some £200,000, was entirely due to the Prince's careful management of her estates, and particularly the Duchy of Cornwall. The income had been substantially increased, and the overheads drastically cut, and indeed it was from this source, and money from the inherited money of the infant Prince of Wales as Duke of Cornwall, that part of the original funds for Osborne were found.

He had now fulfilled an ambition that is very common and human, to create a home for his wife and children that was truly theirs. His own Early Renaissance pictures glowed in the principal rooms, and portraits of his family were in the corridors and in his

---

[1] J. H. Plumb and Huw Wheldon: *Royal Heritage*, p. 255.

own dressing-room. He designed the gardens, built an ice-house, and had a reservoir built on top of The Mound near the house, to be principally used for fire fighting in the event of a fire (it was, in fact, to be used once for that very purpose). Everywhere at Osborne one sees the evidence of the remarkable abilities of a man who was twenty-six years of age when he designed and built what remains his most revealing personal memorial.

Thus did the young Queen and her husband create for themselves and their children what was, in her words, 'a perfect little Paradise'. It was always to remain so for her, and it was at Osborne that she was to die, in their bedroom, with her husband's portrait and watch case, in which he hung his gold watch every night, beside her.

This capacity for achievement was also evident in his campaign to achieve the abolition of duelling in the Army, which was the direct result of Prince Albert's intervention, making use of considerable newspaper comment on a fatal duel in July 1843. Wellington, whose advice Albert sought, was content to leave the matter to public opinion, now becoming markedly hostile, but Albert proposed, as a first step, Courts of Honour on the French and Bavarian patterns, to resolve disputes between officers. The Duke was unenthusiastic, and the Master of the Ordnance and the Lords of the Admiralty were adamant in their opposition. Prince Albert stuck to the principle that it was an 'unChristian and barbarous custom [which] has been generally condemned, forbidden by law, and severely punished; but no substitute has been granted, and the officer, whose very existence is based upon his honour, is left to the alternative of either trespassing against the laws of religion and of the State, and becoming a criminal, or of losing caste in the estimation of his profession and of the world, and seeing that honour tarnished' (to Wellington, January 13th 1844).

His suggestion having met with such opposition, Albert proposed, with Wellington's approval, that the matter should be laid before the Cabinet. The Courts of Honour proposal did not find favour, but it was agreed to amend the Articles of War, which were issued in April 1844, and which in effect ended the practice completely. Prince Albert's achievement – a not inconsiderable one – did not raise him in the already low estimation in which he was held in the more reactionary elements in the Army and in the ranks of ex-officers. Another link with cherished English traditions of honour had been sundered by this youthful German, who had never served in the Army, was a foreigner, and had no comprehension of his adopted country's heritage. Thus, although he was absolutely right, his success brought him few thanks in the socially and politically vocal military establishment.

The Prince's dislike and distrust of the Duke of Cambridge and his brother, the King of Hanover, which had led him to the immediate conclusion that Oxford's murder attempt had been instigated by Hanover to destroy the Queen and the succession, were now significantly increased. They snubbed invitations to the Court, Cambridge was pestering for money, his son Prince George was regarded as dissolute and was the father of an illegitimate child, and when the engagement was announced of the daughter, Princess Augusta, in the Spring of 1843, Cambridge was swift to demand a large annuity for her from the public funds.

Prince Albert was immediately sympathetic to the determination of Peel to resist what the latter described in a letter to the Queen on April 19th as 'His Royal Highness' indefatigable perseverances'. She was also the recipient of these appeals, usually with somewhat menacing undertones, and Albert drafted for her a stiff letter to her uncle, which had little effect. Although, as Peel pointed out in a letter to Cambridge, he had already received £540,000 from the public purse at a time of national economic difficulty and much poverty and distress, Cambridge persuaded the M.P. for Lymington, W. A. Mackinnon, to propose in the House of Commons an annuity of £2,000 for Princess Augusta, to take effect immediately. 'It was with difficulty that Mr Mackinnon was prevented from publicly stating that he made his proposal with the Concurrence of the Duke of Cambridge', Peel wrote to Albert on June 13th, the proposal having been successfully resisted by Ministers.

The Royal brothers accordingly arrived at the wedding on June 28th in a foul mood. Their anger, long simmering, was the direct result of Queen Victoria's determination to increase her husband's status and position, and it was notable that each of the births of her first three children had been very advantageous to this ambition, as had the assassination attempts. After the birth of Princess Alice on April 25th, following a far easier confinement, Albert held the Levees in her place, she having ruled that 'Presentations to him were to be considered as equivalent to Presentations to the Queen herself.' This was not popular in the Court, and outraged Cambridge and Hanover, who refused to attend. They saw only too clearly how considerably, and relentlessly, Prince Albert's position was increasing in strength and influence, and they hated it, and him.

The King of Hanover had deliberately arrived late for the christening of Princess Alice, although Queen Victoria had asked him to be one of the baby's sponsors, and had been calculatingly offensive to Albert, and now he was determined to take precedence over him, on the grounds that he was a King, whereas Prince Albert was not. What ensued was described by Anson as 'rather a Bear Garden scene'. When the service ended Hanover hobbled to the Queen and told her that she must walk out with him; she refused; he insisted; Albert shoved him away; he nearly fell over, but was removed by the Lord Chamberlain 'by force, fuming with ire', in Anson's account. There was then a scene at the signing of the register, when Hanover again demanded precedence. The Queen seized the register, and he was thwarted again, but, persistent to the end, he now insisted on leading with her to the reception. Victoria resolved this problem brilliantly by giving precedence to the Queen of the Belgians and Albert, she and the furious Hanover walking second. To Prince Albert's immense satisfaction Hanover, after storming out, slipped and fell badly. Albert wrote to Ernest that 'I was forced to give him a strong punch and drove him down a few steps . . . he left the party in a great wrath. Since then, we let him go, and happily he fell over some stones in Kew and damaged some ribs.' Hanover, happily for all, left the story of Queen Victoria's life and Prince Albert's concerns. Until his death in 1851 he did his best to spread evil and malicious stories about Albert in Hanover and London, and his reputation as the least attractive of all the sons of King George III endured. The Queen's staunchness in backing her husband touched him very deeply. 'My wicked Uncles' had had their day.

The end of 1843 contained two events that were to prove of lasting significance in Prince Albert's life.

In October he and the Queen went to Cambridge for him to receive an honorary degree, when he first met the then Vice-Chancellor and Master of Trinity, Dr Whewell, and the scholar Professor Adam Sedgwick. The Prince was deeply impressed with Sedgwick's courteous wisdom, and the Professor was surprised by the maturity and intellectual ability of a man who had only recently celebrated his twenty-fourth birthday. The Royal couple was enchanted by Cambridge, which Albert considered far superior to Oxford, and their reception astonished them.

The Queen's original impressions of Cambridgeshire had been that it was 'frightfully ugly. No hedges, but ditches, no trees but willows, with ugly barren fields, and the whole county as flat as a table. The whole was more like Holland than England'. (Journal, September 21st 1835). This time, with her husband at her side, the impression was entirely different. 'The enthusiasm of the students was tremendous,' Albert reported to Stockmar, 'and I cannot remember that we were ever received anywhere so well as on the

road to Cambridge and in Cambridge itself'. This was to be the
beginning of an association of outstanding benefit and importance
for the Prince and for Cambridge University.

In December they visited Chatsworth, the imposing and glorious
mansion of the Cavendishes, where the Duke of Devonshire presided
over an estate and palace superior to any of the Royal residences
except Windsor. But what made the deepest impression on them was
the huge iron and glass Conservatory designed by the head-gar-
dener, Joseph Paxton. They visited it at night, when it was spectacu-
larly illuminated, and were astonished, the Queen describing it as
'the finest thing imaginable of its kind,' and Prince Albert was
enthralled by the conception and the genius of its execution; he
described it as 'magnificent and beautiful', which was high praise,
and sincerely meant. He never forgot Paxton and the Conservatory.
Seven years later Paxton was to come to his rescue in a dramatic
manner, but if Prince Albert had never seen the Chatsworth Conservatory there would never have been the Crystal Palace.

These visits, although somewhat tedious for the Queen and
especially for her young husband, were of value in Prince Albert's
growing understanding of the Britain that existed outside London
and Windsor. The Mayor of Birmingham, a vehement Chartist, told
him that 'he would vouch for the devoted loyalty [to the Monarchy]
of the whole Chartist body,' which Prince Albert never forgot. His
real skill and courage as a rider to hounds startled the county bloods
when they stayed at Belvoir Castle, to his wife's amusement. They
had expected a dull and intellectual German, and found that he was
a horseman of exceptional ability and spirit; the Queen's enjoyment
of the admiration he aroused for these accomplishments did not
extend to approval of what she regarded as a highly dangerous
pastime, and at her insistence he abandoned it. Anson considered –
and certainly rightly – that it was no sacrifice on his part. Except
very occasionally, he abandoned the hunting field for ever, having
made his point that not only Englishmen could be distinguished in it.
His shooting he never abandoned, but in this skill he also excelled –
again to the considerable surprise of those who had accepted the
reports from London of this solemn and rather dreary Coburg
Princeling.

1844 opened bleakly. Stockmar had warned Albert of the decline in
his father's health, but the death on January 29th 1844 of Duke
Ernest in his sixtieth year upset the Prince greatly. 'My darling
stands so alone', Victoria wrote to Stockmar, 'and his grief is so
great and touching'. 'Here [Windsor] we sit together, poor Mama,

Victoria, and myself, and weep', Albert wrote 'with a great cold public around us, insensible as stone'. He described his wife to Stockmar as a 'consoling angel', and 'the treasure on which my whole existence rests. The relation in which we stand to one another leaves nothing to desire. It is a union of heart and soul'. But the sense of being far away was intense, and was at least partly responsible for this outburst in the same letter (February 4th 1844):

> The world is assuredly not our true happiness; and, alas! every day's experience forces me to see how wicked men are. Every imaginable calumny is heaped upon us, especially upon me; and although a pure nature, conscious of its own high purposes, is and ought to be lifted above attacks, still it is painful to be misrepresented by people of whom one believed better things.

Five days later he wrote, rather more calmly, 'I have regained my composure . . . My youth, with all the recollections linked with it, has been buried with him around whom they centred. From that world I am forcibly torn away, and my whole thoughts diverted to my life here and my own separate family. For these I will live wholly from this time forth'.

The English Court went into deepest mourning, the Royal note-paper was heavily black-bordered, the little Royal children could not understand why their parents and everyone else had to wear black, and Albert's weeping gave Anson what Lady Lyttelton described as 'a violent attack of nervous headache'. 'One loves to *cling* to one's grief', Queen Victoria wrote to King Leopold, a profoundly interesting and prophetic remark. The memorial service at Windsor for the late Duke saw the lovely Chapel almost smothered in black. There was a general recognition at the Court that, although the Prince's grief was obviously absolutely genuine, this was somewhat excessive, and it was certainly a very considerable exaggeration for Queen Victoria to lament of her dissolute and improvident father-in-law, whom she hardly knew, that 'We shall never see his like again'.

With good cause, Albert and Stockmar looked with much nervousness at the alarming prospect of Ernest as the new Duke. He could be charming, although this was not a quality all would acknowledge, was engagingly cynical about himself and his unashamed hedonism, and was truly loved by his brother; but he was as improvident as his father and even more licentious, with a reputation that spread far beyond Coburg. This fact caused Albert constant alarm, and was often the subject of his letters to his brother. Albert was remarkably tolerant of Ernest's excesses, as he had been of his father's, but he understandably dreaded the real possibility of the Queen of England's brother-in-law becoming involved in a major public scandal that would certainly reverberate appallingly in England, and be the happy topic of many a scurrilous broadsheet, public innuendoes, and gleeful gossip in London, especially by those who disliked the new high-minded morality of the Court that Prince Albert had introduced and firmly maintained. There was also the question of money, with which Albert was becoming somewhat obsessed – and with good reason – at this time. The prospect of endless importunities from his brother was not one to be relished, and at the end of March he left England to visit Coburg and Ernest.

This was the first separation in their marriage, and one Victoria felt deeply, but Albert was a regular and loving correspondent on what turned out to be a particularly mournful expedition for him. Ernest made many pledges of good behaviour, but Albert was sceptical. The warmth of his reception in Coburg, the pathetic joy of his grandmother at seeing him again, and his visit to The Rosenau, in whose garden he picked flowers for his wife, moved, but also depressed him. Here was his real home, here were his real friends, here were his true roots. The loss of his father was both personal and symbolic of what he had given up, and all he missed in England. Coburg, The Rosenau, and the countryside was indeed, as the Queen knew and understood, 'the place he loves best'. He wrote to her from Coburg: 'Oh! how lovely and friendly is this dear old country, how glad I should be to have my little wife beside me, that I might share my pleasure with her!' On April 11th he wrote in his diary: 'I arrived at six o'clock in the evening at Windsor. *Great Joy*'. Victoria wrote of her 'immense joy' at 'being clasped in his arms'.

In the summer there was another break with the past when Albert's greyhound, Eôs, died, on which event Albert lamented to his grandmother: 'How many recollections are linked with her! She was my companion from the fourteenth to my twenty-fifth year, a symbol, therefore, of the best and fairest section of my life.'

On August 6th there was much joy when the Queen gave birth to her second son, christened Alfred, but known in the family as 'Affie'. Shortly after the birth there was the first visit of the Prince of Prussia to Windsor, with whom Albert developed a close and eventually important friendship, and in October Louis Philippe paid the first official visit of a reigning French monarch to England, which was, to the deep pleasure of the Queen and Albert, a remarkable and outstanding success. Their family was growing with a speed that pleased the Prince, but troubled the Queen, who had now produced two daughters and two sons in five and a half years of marriage.

The spring and summer of 1845 were cold and wet, but made delightful for Victoria and Albert by at last taking possession of Osborne. 'The weather is frightfully cold and disagreeable', Albert wrote on May 10th, but the pleasures of planning the new house and estate were even less to him than the visit he and the Queen paid to Germany, where they were entertained by the King of Prussia and Victoria saw Coburg and The Rosenau for the first time.

On their return they visited the French Royal Family at Eu. This was a political occasion, with the Foreign Secretary Lord Aberdeen in attendance, whose purpose was to ensure that neither the young Prince Leopold of Coburg nor any of the sons of Louis Philippe would be contenders for marriage to the daughters of the King of Spain. It appeared that full agreement had been reached on this matter, and that the prospect of a Franco-Spanish Royal marriage, with its uncomfortable political possibilities, had been averted.

They reached Osborne well contented 'after one of the most beautiful journeys we have ever made, or shall probably ever make', Albert wrote, in spite of the 'unceasing rain' which features prominently in the Queen's Journals.

In fact, it had not all been sweetness and light. There had been difficulties with the King and Queen of Prussia and criticism of Queen Victoria's manner, which dismayed and upset her, while the eminent naturalist Alexander von Humboldt took a strong dislike to Prince Albert. But there had been one outstanding result. A young German scientist, A. W. Hofmann, a research chemist at the University of Bonn, expressed interest to Sir James Clark in taking a temporary appointment at the new College of Chemistry in London. As the Prince was President of this new venture, Clark introduced Hofmann to him, and Albert personally arranged with the King of Prussia that Hofmann would not lose his place at Bonn. Hofmann came for two years, but stayed for twelve, Prince Albert again making the necessary arrangements. His laboratory and his students constituted the first school of research in England, with dramatic and long-lasting consequences for British science. In some respects this was the single most important intellectual contribution Albert made to his adopted country, perhaps even more significant than the revolution he was to effect at Cambridge.

Superficially it might appear strange that Prince Albert, so fearful of Queen Victoria's political partisanship, should now lay himself open to the same charge in his relations with Peel. Here, the attraction was personal in the first instance, but given Peel's uneasy position within the Conservative Party, of which Albert was fully aware, his genuine admiration for him and desire to assist him contained perils. The key point, often overlooked, is that Peel's character not only mirrored that of Prince Albert – there was much wisdom in Wellington's comment that 'it was the Prince who insisted on spotless character, the Queen not caring a straw about it' – but so did his politics. Commenting on Peel's unpopularity among the Conservatives to Anson in April 1843 Albert remarked that it was exactly this that made him admire Peel so greatly, as 'he was determined either to stand or fall by his own opinion, and the Prince felt that in such a man's hands *the interests of the Crown were most secure*'.[1] After Peel's death, in a tribute in a public speech in York in October 1850, Albert said of him with admiration that 'he was a Liberal from feeling, but Conservative upon principle', a man whose 'impulses drove him to foster progress' within established institutions, the maintenance of society, 'like organic growth in nature'. These are revealing words, as they absolutely represented Prince Albert's political views. In May 1846 the Gladstones dined with the Queen and Prince, after which Gladstone recorded that 'the Prince is very strongly Conservative in his politics and his influence with the Q. is over-ruling; through him she has become so attached to Conservative ideas that she could hardly endure the idea of the opposite Party as her Ministers.'

Thus, between the Prince and Peel there developed a relationship never equalled in his life between himself and an individual politician. They corresponded frequently on a very wide variety of subjects, met often, and even after Peel had ceased to be Prime Minister he remained the Prince's closest adviser on most matters, from political affairs to the reorganisation of Cambridge University and to the development of Osborne. Although Albert sought Stockmar's advice on domestic and foreign affairs throughout his life, Peel took his place as his real adviser and confidant in England. It was Peel who, in Albert's view, had given him his first real opportunity for public service as Chairman of the Fine Arts Royal Commission, for which he was deeply, and touchingly, grateful, as it gave him the chance to have the ready access to intellectuals, artists, musicians and scientists for which he craved, and whose absence – apart from his own private attempts – had been a significant cause of his depression and frustrations. For his part, Peel was an unstinting admirer of one whom he described to Charles Eastlake, the secretary of the Commission, as 'the most extraordinary young man you will have ever met.' It was this manifest and genuine respect for her beloved husband that gradually thawed the Queen's ingrained coldness towards Peel, although some reservations could not be completely effaced.

Some of Prince Albert's artistic ventures – notably the attempt to

[1] Author's italics.

revive frescoes in England by a public competition for the new
Palace of Westminster, now rising amidst incessant difficulties and
acrimony – the full genius of Barry and Pugin's masterpiece as yet
widely unrecognised – were not notably successful in themselves, but
attracted a surprising and heartening degree of public interest, the
fresco exhibition itself drawing very large crowds to Westminster
Hall.

Then, there was a very real and important intellectual sympathy
between the Prince and Peel. Albert once remarked to Queen Victoria
that 'to me, a long, closely-connected train of reasoning is like a
beautiful strain of music. You can hardly imagine my delight in it'. To
him, as to Peel, the latter's abrupt change of policies that characterised his career and was the chief cause of the intense mistrust felt for
him in his own Party were logical, necessary, and intellectually
coherent. In the harsher world of politics they were regarded as
evidence of opportunism, lack of principle, and arrogance. Peel was
certainly poor at cultivating people for whom he did not have much
regard, another characteristic he had in common with Prince Albert,
whose 'playfulness and good humour' that so attracted those who
really knew him was strictly reserved for private occasions.

The danger in this very close relationship between Prince and
Premier was that Prince Albert's popularity, although definitely
improved, was not very great, while suspicions of his political
influence were steadily growing. These attacks were particularly
frequent in the summer and autumn of 1845, to Queen Victoria's
anger and distress, not much lessened by Leopold's comment (October 10th) that 'to hope to *escape* censure and calumny is next to
impossible, but whatever is considered by the enemy as a fit subject
for attack is better modified or avoided'. The wisdom of this advice
was quickly to be demonstrated. Greville, whose position as Clerk to
the Privy Council gave him an admirable vantage point, saw the
signs. 'Anything that can be done to enhance the dignity of the
Prince is done', he noted, also – as did many others – that the Queen
had had 'a chair of State set up for him in the House of Lords the
same as her own, another throne, in fact. He is as much King as she
can make him; all this, however, does not make him any more
popular'. Neither Greville nor any one else apart from Victoria,
Stockmar and Melbourne knew of her desire to appoint him King
Consort, but the indications were clear.

In these circumstances the Prince's manifest admiration for Peel
demonstrated his own political immaturity. His successes, one
suspects, may have seriously misled him to over-confidence on his
political judgement, and if Anson's memoranda are accurate –
and there is no reason to believe that they are not – he wholly

underestimated the dank mists of jealousy, suspicion, and dislike that menaced him. When the Prince stayed with Peel at Drayton Manor in the autumn of 1843 he wrote that 'the visit made the Premier very happy, and is calculated to strengthen his position'. Admittedly, Albert was flushed with excitement and pleasure after a visit to Birmingham that had caused Ministers considerable apprehension, and yet which had passed off very successfully. Nonetheless, this is a revealing, and dangerous, comment. Royal patronage of a Prime Minister was not what it used to be.

Both, moreover, were becoming obsessed – and rightly so – by 'the condition of England question', which included that of Ireland, sinking rapidly towards unimagineable horrors. The Prince had read, and had been appalled by, the famous report on the employment of children in factories and mines, and had sought out its initiator, Lord Ashley, soon to become the seventh Earl of Shaftesbury. 'I have been horror stricken by the statements which you have brought before the country', Prince Albert wrote; ' ... The nation must be with you, at all events I can assure you that the Queen is'. This was not true. The Queen was strongly opposed to Ashley's Ten Hour Bill limiting the hours of workers in mills and factories, many of whom were children, which she considered harmful to British, commercial interests. She remained a Melbourne Whig, her husband was the pragmatic liberal Conservative reformer. He urged further action on the slave trade to the Foreign Secretary, Lord Aberdeen; he persuaded Ministers to pass special legislation to naturalise a German artist whom he wished to include in the patronage list of the Fine Arts Commission; his interest and involvement in European politics increased steadily, and Peel used him to convey British views on the Turkish *status quo* to the Tsar of Russia when he paid an official visit in the early summer of 1844. Having read Peel's letters to the Lord Lieutenant in Dublin he wrote:

> ... Your correspondence with Lord Heytesbury has very much interested me & much pleased me as proving the entire agreement & harmony of feeling existing between you & the steady purpose to adhere to a moderate liberal, equitable but firm course of policy. This is so rarely found that it is still more rarely recognised & therefore it will wait till it will, by its own weight, have penetrated through misconception & misrepresentation, but in the end you must be triumphant if you are left time to reap the fruits of your own work, which I hope will be the case for the Queen & Country's sake.

These enterprises, far from being evidence of what one of his biographers has called his 'ripening sagacity in public affairs' in fact demonstrated his increasing personal and political commitment to the Peel Administration.

The State visit of Louis Philippe in October 1844 was successful, the King of France was lavish in his praises, but the event was not generally popular. Prince Albert's two great European ambitions were the unification of the German States into one nation with a liberal constitution and institutions, and substantially improved relations between Britain and France. The phrase *entente cordiale* belongs to this, and not to a later, era, and figures often and prominently in the letters and memoranda of himself and the Queen. They had taken great trouble to ensure that the first State Visit of a French King to England would be as well-managed, warm, and successful as possible, but others did not share their ambitions. Suspicion and dislike of France and French designs were very deep in England, and Palmerston's view of France as his country's most dangerous and potentially hostile adversary was far closer to the popular judgement than that of Prince Albert.

'Now that France becomes every day more over-reaching, more overbearing, more insulting, more hostile', Palmerston was writing just before this visit, 'even the quietest and most peaceful among us are beginning to look forward to a war with France as an event which no prudence on our part can long prevent, and for which we ought to lose no time in making ourselves fully prepared'.

By this time, at the beginning of 1845, Victoria's admiration for her husband was total. 'Everywhere my dearest Angel receives the respect and honours I receive' she wrote in January 1845, but when a critical Member of Parliament again raised – in a hostile manner – the question of whether he was to become King Consort she wrote to Peel that 'The title of King is open assuredly to many difficulties, and would perhaps be of no *real* advantage to the Prince, but the Queen is positive that something must be done at once to place the Prince's position on a constitutionally recognised footing, and to give him a title adequate to that position. *How* and *when* are difficult questions'.

Stockmar warned him not to abandon 'your firm, lofty, powerful, impregnable position to run after trifles. You have the substance; stick by it for the good of your wife and children, and do not suffer yourself to be seduced even by the wishes of affection into bartering substance for show'. Prince Albert entirely agreed that, as he wrote in reply, 'it is power and not titles which are esteemed here', and Peel concurred with him that 'my [public] position is extremely good'.

But, was it? He was, after all, only 26. He intensely resented public criticism or mockery; his detailed and extensive Press cuttings, organised by Anson at his command, were perhaps too efficient and comprehensive for his peace of mind; and on one occasion after he had perused *Punch* and two broadsheets *The Satirist* and *The Age* he protested strongly to Aberdeen. A meticulous reader of newspapers, journals, and cheap broadsheets, which flourished mightily, he demonstrated his professionalism in one respect, but also his inexperience. To consider, as he genuinely did, that hostile comments in Germany on the English Royal Family were the result of lampoons in *Punch*, or that Peel's difficulties were solely the result of vicious journalists and political place-seekers – described with some fervour and injustice by the Queen as 'gentlemen who did nothing but hunt all day, drank Claret or Port Wine in the evening, & never studied or read about any of these questions' – reveals not only an excessive sensitivity to criticism but a marked, and growing, partisanship.

Few areas of public life escaped his eager attention or concern. He had, and expressed, strong views on the role of Bishops; they should 'abstain completely' from contemporary politics, but should give general support to 'the *Queen's Government*'. The Anglican Church should certainly support his own liberal attitudes to 'questions like Negro Emancipation, education of the people, improvement of the health of towns, measures for the recreation of the poor, against cruelty to animals, for regulating factory labour, &c., &c.', but, 'while they should come forward whenever the interests of Humanity are at stake' there must be recognised limits to such activities. A Bishop, he warned, should 'never forget that he is a representative of the Church of the Land, the maintenance of which is as important to the country as that of its Constitution or its Throne'. Albert regarded himself, with some justification, as a liberal, but, like Peel, within severe limits. To Samuel Wilberforce, the new Bishop of Oxford, his message was plain:

> Always be conscious that the Church has duties to fulfil, that it does not exist for itself, but for the people, for the country. Let there be no calling for new rights, privileges, grants, &c ...

Then, in the context of 1845, a most revealing passage:

> ... a Bishop ought to be a guardian of public morality, not, like the press, by tediously interfering with every man's private affairs, speaking for applause, or trampling on those that are fallen, but by watching over the morality of the State in acts which expediency or hope for profit may tempt it to commit, as well in home and colonial as in foreign affairs.

This was heavy stuff for a man of 26. He now devoured work, in his increasingly important position. The Queen's Ministers had no doubt of the importance and influence of the Prince, nor of his assiduity. In one year he read, annotated, and advised upon several thousand documents from the Foreign Office alone. He personally designed and developed a highly efficient filing system, with swift cross-references. All his correspondence of any importance was in his own hand, and he wrote copies of any of his own letters he regarded as significant. From Buckingham Palace, Windsor, and now Osborne, there came to Ministers a ceaseless flow of memoranda, comments, and advice usually in the name of the Queen, but whose true author was only too well known to the recipients. Most seriously of all, he had become, and was to remain, and was known to be, a 'Peelite'.

There are two ways of regarding all this earnest activity in the affairs of State. One is admiring, the other is more dubious. Certainly, the Queen needed assistance and advice, and the very heavy burdens of her official engagements were now augmented by the fact that she was the mother of four small children, while the sheer volume of the papers she had to read and the letters she had to write was very formidable. In these circumstances Prince Albert was the perfect Private Secretary and adviser, and the efficiency of their transaction of business was, in itself, quite remarkable, and commands the admiration of a twentieth century civil servant operating in the age of the typewriter, the telephone, and modern communications.

All this is to be applauded. What was more dangerous was that he was still very young, a foreigner with only five years' experience of the politics of his adopted country, in effect responsible for the Queen's political views and advice to her Ministers – advice that was always taken very seriously and was usually decisive. This was not accidental, nor was it the result of circumstances. Now that Prince Albert had achieved his position as the Queen's principal political adviser he intended to use it – with caution, it is true, but very definitely to use it. He had become, by deliberate intent, deeply and personally involved in contemporary politics. Ministers and ex-Ministers knew it; Members of the House of Commons knew it; the newspapers knew it. It was this knowledge that resulted in the criticisms of him which he and Queen Victoria so strongly resented, and it is impossible to avoid the conclusion that he was intent upon the maximum of political influence with the minimum of criticism – to be in the fray, yet seemingly above it. These are dangerous objectives to attempt to combine simultaneously.

By the autumn of 1845 Albert's hero, friend, and virtual colleague, was entering a crisis of desperate proportions from which he was destined never to emerge.

.   .   .

The cold and wet summer of 1845 ensured that the harvest, and particularly the grain harvest, would be poor. This was serious enough, but it was not to be compared with the potato disease which had originated in America in 1844, had carried to Europe, and in 1845 now spread catastrophically to England and to Ireland, where at least half the population of well over eight million[1] depended upon the potato crop for its survival. The potato was crucial, as it enabled large amounts of food to be produced from the small plots of land which had become characteristic of Ireland; the 1841 census revealed that 45% of holdings were less than five acres, and the great majority was very considerably smaller. There was remarkably little hardship or starvation in a country where an acre and a half would provide a family of six with food for a year, where heat from peat was plentiful and cost nothing. But this very precarious balance between existence and starvation depended absolutely upon the potato, and all warnings of disaster were ignored, in spite of the grim lessons of previous, and recent years, when local failures had been calamitous. But nothing had happened, even in the very dark years of 1839, 1841, and 1844, to compare with the total disaster of 1845 when the 'blight' which was ravaging England first arrived in the fields around Dublin. The human nightmare of what became tragically immortalised as 'The Great Hunger' was to result in over a million deaths in Ireland, the massive depopulation of the country through emigration, and a scar that remains livid and unhealed to this day. In England, the political consequences were traumatic, and dominated the rest of Prince Albert's life.

Peel's conversion to the arguments of the Anti-Corn Law League had been suspected for some time in the Conservative Party, and had been at least partly responsible for the formation of the Anti-League in 1843, whose whole purpose was the preservation of the Corn Laws and Protection for British agriculture. Not surprisingly, it had strong support in the Parliamentary Party, where fears of betrayal by its leader rumbled menacingly long before the disastrous summer of 1845 persuaded Peel to put all at hazard to advocate a policy diametrically opposed to that on which he had been elected in 1841. By October 15th he had definitely resolved that 'The remedy is the removal of all impediments to the import of all kinds of human food – that is, the total and absolute repeal for ever of all duties on all articles of substance'.

[1] The 1841 census figure was 8,175,124, but this was almost certainly too low, giving considerable justification for Disraeli's claim that Ireland was the most densely populated country in the world (C. Woodham-Smith: *The Great Hunger*, p. 31).

To attempt some appreciation of the passions aroused in the late autumn of 1845 and throughout 1846 it could be said that it were as though a Conservative leader in Britain or the United States in the 1980's suddenly pronounced himself in favour of massive nationalisation and penal taxation, or a Socialist leader in Office was dramatically converted to the total virtues of private enterprise and the iniquities of State management, coupled with the supreme virtues of the Christian reliance upon the all-dominant role of the individual in society. The religious analogy is important, because there was a fervent, and to its opponents singularly obnoxious, religious fervour behind the Free Trade movement. The Anti-Corn Law League was essentially urban, and Radical, its most persuasive and popular champions Cobden and Bright, but it had little sympathy or support in either political Party in Parliament until the Irish famine gave the League its opportunity. In Bright's own words, in his eulogy to Cobden many years later, 'Famine itself, against which we had warred, joined us'. The clamour to 'open the ports' to cheap foreign grain swept Ireland, the north of England, and its harsh echoes reverberated in Whitehall and Westminster. The Crusade now appeared to have been abundantly justified.

Much censure, then and subsequently, has been placed upon Peel for his reaction to this real and terrible crisis. He could easily, it has been argued, have dealt with the emergency with emergency measures. If he had become convinced that the high price of grain was certain to make the Irish crisis worse, why did he not suspend the Corn Laws temporarily, as he was fully entitled to under the existing legislation? Other historians – and many contemporaries –have justifiably pointed out that the repeal of the Corn Laws in itself could have done little to help the literally starving Irish. Nor did it. But the reality was that Peel had become intellectually and emotionally convinced of the strength of the Free Trade cause and the grave limitations of Protection. The Irish Famine merely accelerated a step that he would have taken sooner or later; it was this that revealed the full extent of his apostasy to his dismayed and demoralised colleagues and followers. He believed that he could carry them with him. He saw none in Parliament in his Government or Party who could match his Parliamentary or national experience, following, or skills. The Whig Opposition, feebly led by Russell, and with Palmerston in moody eclipse, presented few dangers. He had the full confidence and backing of Prince Albert and, through him, the Queen. 'The Queen thinks the time is come when a removal of the restrictions upon the importation of food cannot be successfully resisted', came the clear message from Osborne to Peel on November 28th 'Should this be Sir Robert's own opinion, the Queen very much hopes that none of his colleagues will prevent him from doing what it is *right* to do'. Peel had been through such storms before in his long career, and had triumphed. But this time, he gravely miscalculated.

The failure has been described with great clarity by Justin McCarthy:

> The influence of Peel at that time, and indeed all through his administration up to the introduction of his Free Trade measures, was limitless, so far as his party were concerned. He could have done anything with them. But Peel ... was a reserved, cold, somewhat awkward man. He was not effusive; he did not pour out his emotions and reveal all his changes of opinion in bursts of confidence even to his habitual associates. He brooded over these things in his own mind; he gave such expression to them in open debate as any passing occasion seemed strictly to call for; and he assumed perhaps that the gradual changes operating in his views when thus expressed were understood by his followers.

The crisis began in late November, when Peel was unable to persuade Lord Stanley and the Duke of Buccleuch to agree to repeal, and on December 5th the Ministry decided to resign. 'We were, of course, in great consternation,' Prince Albert wrote in a memorandum of December 7th. ' ... The whole country cries out: the Corn Laws are doomed'. Peel assured the Queen that he would support a Russell Administration on the repeal of the Corn Laws, and agreed to put this undertaking in writing. Russell, who was clearly seeing the political advantages of espousing Free Trade, and who had abandoned the fervent faith in the Corn Laws that still animated his predecessor Melbourne – who wrote to the Queen on December 9th that he 'would be very unwilling to come in [to any office] pledged to a total and immediate reform of the Corn Law' – was unwilling to accept the Premiership under such lowering circumstances, and with his own supporters so sorely divided. Prince Albert, although eager to see Peel continue as Prime Minister, regarded Russell's action as evidence of cowardice and weakness, and although his relations with Lord John remained formally correct, Russell had permanently forfeited his full respect. There was to be, of constitutional necessity, a *rapprochement*, and not least because Russell gradually developed a high opinion of the Prince. He noted, with evident approval, Peel's complaints of Russell's actions; 'He blamed the want of deference shown to the Queen, by not answering her call with more readiness.' Significantly, the Queen reported to Leopold (December 30th) that '*Joseph Hume* expressed great distress when Peel resigned, and the greatest contempt for Lord John Russell'.

When Russell threw in his hand, and passed what Disraeli described as 'the poisoned chalice' back to Peel, the couple were
relieved and pleased.

Peel resumed Office immediately,[1] and with conspicuous alac-
rity, informing the Queen that 'I want no consultation, no time for
reflection. I will be your Minister, happen what may. I will do
without a colleague rather than leave you in this extremity'. Stanley was the only Cabinet Minister who refused to join him, and the
Repeal of the Corn Laws was brought forward as the supreme
priority of the Government.

One very significant oddity must be noted.

Gladstone, of whom both Prince Albert and Peel had a very
high opinion, had resigned from the Presidency of the Board of
Trade over the issue of the Government's decision to increase the
annual grant to Maynooth, the Roman Catholic training college
in Dublin, from £9,000 to £30,000, on the grounds that he had
written a book – long forgotten by everyone save himself – opposing the principle involved. There was general astonishment, and
Gladstone himself subsequently wrote that his action was 'fitter
for a dreamer, or possibly a schoolman, than for the active purposes of public life in a busy and moving age'. But he did accept
the post of Secretary of State for the Colonies under Peel; under
the then electoral law – unchanged until 1918 – he had to submit
himself for re-election for his constituency of Newark, only to find
that his patron, the vehemently Protectionist Duke of Newcastle,
would not have him. Gladstone was therefore a member of the
Peel Cabinet without a seat in the House of Commons until he
was returned for Oxford University in 1847. Peel was thus deprived of the abilities and oratory in Parliament of one of the most
formidable debaters in the House of Commons at a critical point
in his fortunes, and Gladstone's absence was a major – although
probably not crucial – factor in the events of 1846. Prince Albert,
like everyone else, found Gladstone's attitude incomprehensible,
and temporarily lost faith in a politician he had regarded with
specially high esteem.

But Peel was in an exultant mood. 'I feel like a man restored to
life after his funeral service has been preached', he wrote on
December 26th. Even Wellington, who had agreed to put his
unrivalled prestige behind Peel, was unhappy. 'Rotten potatoes

[1] In fact, at the Queen's request, he had not formally resigned, so that she could
'keep his ministry until a new one can be got'. He remained Prime Minister while
the negotiations within the Opposition were continuing. As Russell had not
accepted the Queen's invitation to form an Administration this was perfectly
proper.

(

have done it all', he complained to Greville; 'they have put Peel in his
d--d fright'.

Queen Victoria, totally persuaded by her husband, all her previous hostility to Peel forgotten, wrote to Leopold on December
23rd:

> ... I have little to add to Albert's letter of yesterday, except my
> *extreme* admiration of our worthy Peel, who shows himself a man
> of unbounded *loyalty, courage,* patriotism, and *high-mindedness,*
> and his conduct towards me has been *chivalrous* almost, I might
> say. I never have seen him so excited or so determined, and *such*
> a good cause must succeed.
>
> We have indeed had an escape, for though Lord John's *own*
> *notions* were *very* good and moderate, he let himself be entirely
> twisted and twirled about by his *violent* friends, and *all* the
> moderate ones were crushed ...

Albert recorded on December 25th on the Privy Council of the
previous day that Peel had stayed at Windsor for over three hours
after the Council with him and the Queen and was 'in the highest
spirits ... It is to his *own* talent and firmness that Sir Robert will owe
his success, which cannot fail'. Peel described to them at length what
he had in mind, which Prince Albert admiringly recorded was '*that of
removing all protection and removing all monopoly,* but not in favour of one
class and as a triumph over another, but to the benefit of the nation,
farmers as well as manufacturers'. Peel spoke of a rural police force
on the same lines as his famous Metropolitan Police, the establishment of a State Public Prosecutor, new State commitment for the
relief of the poor, and what could be done to assist the railway
labourers when the rail boom ended. It was exciting, and the Queen
and Albert were entranced.

Peel's was an astonishing political metamorphosis, but not as out
of character as some historians have alleged, or Wellington believed.
In 1845 Benjamin Disraeli, a bitterly disappointed seeker after
Office in 1841, could not be regarded, even by himself, as a formidable politician. A gifted speaker and with a merited reputation as a
novelist and essayist of rare vividness of expression and colour, he
was widely regarded in the House of Commons, with good cause, as
essentially disreputable, blatantly opportunistic and unprincipled,
undeniably clever, but fundamentally a Jewish adventurer. No one
saw him, and he did not see himself, as the future champion of the
Tory agricultural interests, the Squirearchy from which he was
separated by a vast gulf of intellect, background, and attitude. But,
with his acute sense of political realities, their contempt and mistrust
of him were not shared by his for them, although he was certainly not

a natural nor obvious spokesman for their bewilderment and mounting anger at Peel's latest betrayal. Disraeli's hour had not yet dawned by the close of 1845 – he was, in fact, out of the country – but it is to him that we should look for the heart of Peel's complex personality: 'Instead of being cold and wary, as was commonly supposed', Disraeli later wrote of Peel in one of the few authentic classics of British political literature,[1] 'he was impulsive, and even inclined to rashness ... he was ever on the outlook for new ideas, and when he embraced them he did so with eagerness, and often with precipitancy'. In the case of the Corn Laws, Peel's inner conversion had been long made, but his public conversion gave the clear, if entirely incorrect, impression of an unappealing mixture of panic, eagerness for Office at whatever price, and total lack of remorse for having totally overturned the policies and principles on which he and his Party had stood in the 1841 election. In this harsh and acrid dispute the cause of it all –the starving millions in Ireland – was totally forgotten.

Albert and Victoria had been dismayed at Peel's resignation, and delighted at Russell's failure to form a Government. When Melbourne burst out with the comment that Peel's behaviour was 'a damned dishonest act' the Queen rebuked him with total effect. She, also, had become a partisan. 'We are glad in soul, as they say in Coburg', Albert wrote, 'or still more frequently, in high glee [*ganz fidel*] that we have survived a Ministerial crisis of fourteen days' duration, and are now standing exactly where we stood before'. Stockmar, however, was troubled by these events, and not convinced by Peel's professions of acting solely in the national interest: 'the most that can be said of him', he wrote to Albert with some bleakness on December 27th, 'is that he has not helped to make Royalty weaker than it was when handed over to him by Melbourne'. The Prince pointed out in his reply that at least there had been no public questioning of the Constitutional impartiality of the Queen in the crisis.[2]

This was not to be of long duration. When Parliament resumed on January 19th 1846 Peel informed the Commons that 'It is no easy task to insure the harmonious and united action of Monarchy, Aristocracy, and a reformed House of Commons', and on the 27th, with Prince Albert prominent in the Gallery, he introduced the Resolution to deal with the crisis, whose most momentous proposal was the total abolition of the Corn Laws within three years.

[1] *Lord George Bentinck.*

[2] There was another cause of happiness for him. Queen Victoria was pregnant again, and although Lady Palmerston noted that she was 'very large and looks drawn' she was 'in good spirits'.

On that day, immediately after Russell, Disraeli had struck his first blow against Peel, but it was from a most improbable source that there arose the true leader of the betrayed Tories. Lord George Bentinck was one of those people, more common then than now, and yet happily not wholly extinct, who enter the House of Commons for no particular reason, and certainly not from motives of personal ambition, and play little part in its political proceedings. The second son of the Duke of Portland, he had been in Parliament for eighteen years, hardly ever spoke, and although a celebrated and respected figure on the Turf, with a famous racing stable, had occasioned no notice or attention in the Commons beyond enjoying the respect accorded to a country gentleman of manifest integrity, wealth, and family prominence. What no one suspected, until he rose to speak in the debate on Peel's Resolutions on the twelfth day, was that he felt a man betrayed. For years he had been a strong supporter of Peel, and could have even been described as an admirer. All that was now finished.

Disraeli's speech immediately after Peel and Russell on the first day had been the most brilliant he had ever made, and stands as one of the best he ever made in the House of Commons. The images poured out, with Peel compared to the admiral who took his fleet immediately to the enemy's port 'so that I might terminate the contest by betraying my master', to a nurse who dashed out the baby's brains, and depicted as 'no more a great statesman than the man who gets up behind a carriage is a great whip'. The Conservatives who had listened to Peel in stunned silence had cheered Disraeli excitedly. Bentinck, who had never met nor spoken to him, had heard a kindred voice. But Disraeli, for all his brilliant and vicious oratory, could be safely ignored by the Ministry; Bentinck was another matter; and this unlikely combination was to spell political doom for Peel.

Prince Albert and the Queen identified themselves strongly with Peel against his opponents. She wrote to Peel to tell him (January 23rd, 1846) that his speech was 'beautiful & indeed *unanswerable*', while her husband noted with intense disapproval and distaste the 'violent invectives' of 'Mr D'Israely', 'calling him [Peel] a traitor & hypocrite, accusing him of overbearing vanity, want of purpose, time serving, etc, ridiculing his manner, etc, etc, etc, etc'. But although Albert regarded Peel's speech of February 16th as 'one of the finest he ever made', he noted with alarm that whereas the Prime Minister on January 30th was 'in good spirits on the whole & has received good accounts from the Country, where his measure is generally well received', there was a steady succession of resignations from the Royal Household on the issue, and also from the House of Commons. The latter included Ashley, who after his resignation decided not to contest the by-election. By February 11th Peel wrote to inform the Prince that 197 Conservatives would vote against his measure, and only 123 for it; he was, accordingly, totally dependent upon the Whig, Radical, and Irish Members for his survival. Prince Albert now saw the clear indications of disaster, writing on Peel's letter, 'This is of course a heavy blow for the Government'. What was difficult to realise, although it is evident that Albert was beginning to appreciate, was that the Conservative divisions were fatal for Peel and his Party.

Peel had grievously underestimated the fury that now fell upon him from his former supporters, and not even the bitter disputes over Catholic Emancipation in the 1820's – another 'betrayal' keenly remembered by the Protectionists – equalled the passions now unleashed.

This is not one of those political disputations of a distant past over which historians brood with such contentment to the bafflement of later generations. The issues involved may have centred on the repeal of the Corn Laws, but the real dispute was between two firmly entrenched and bitterly opposed faiths. That of Free Trade was to triumph in the late 1840's, and to hold sway until Joseph Chamberlain in 1903 was to question its very foundations, and to initiate again the schisms and arguments which, like the Irish Question, have had periods of abeyance, only to surge once again into the centre of political debate. For a politician of the 1970's and 1980's the debates of 1846 have an eerie familiarity. Then, as now, there was no middle ground.

Prince Albert's political judgement, which made him a strong supporter of Peel and a Free Trader, may have been correct in the national interest, and was certainly genuine, but drew him into the maelstrom. He had deliberately chosen to make his first appearance in the Gallery of the House of Commons on the first day of the debate to hear Peel's speech. This caused some critical private comment, but it was Bentinck who voiced it in his first speech on the issue, when he declared that 'I would take leave to say that I cannot but think he listened to ill advice when on the first night of this great discussion he allowed himself to be seduced by the First Minister of the Crown to come down to this House to usher in, to give *éclat*, and as it were by reflexion from the Queen, to give semblance of the personal sanction of Her Majesty to a measure which, be it for good or evil, a great majority of the landlord aristocracy of England, of Scotland, and of Ireland imagine fraught with deep injury if not ruin to them'.

Surprise, and strong criticism, of Prince Albert's presence in the Commons were not confined to Bentinck and the angry Tories, and the subsequent explanations by his official biographer that he merely attended 'from the impulse of natural curiosity' or by the Queen that he went 'for once to hear a fine debate' are defensive, lame, and wholly unconvincing. For one thing, there was no debate intended. Under the unwritten, but powerful, conventions of the House of Commons at that time the opening day of a debate without any time limit – the abomination of the Closure still thirty-five years ahead – was confined to the two principal speakers. If Disraeli had not seized his opportunity of a full House to launch the first of his assaults on Peel, there would only have been two speakers – Peel and Russell.

The fact was that Prince Albert totally supported Peel both personally and politically, and was determined to do all he could to assist him, as the deliberate visit to his home in 1843 had demonstrated. He was outraged that the Prime Minister, whose policies he warmly supported, was 'abused like the most disgraceful criminal'; he admired his 'boundless courage', agreed with him that 'he is at this moment playing one of the most important parts in the history of his country', and considered his possible defeat 'a great misfortune'. To accept that Prince Albert's prominent appearance in the Gallery was a casual occurrence of no political significance is to wholly misunderstand not only the extent of his commitment to Peel and his policy, but his belief in the importance of the evidence of public Royal support for the Queen's First Minister. It was a calculated symbol, was rightly seen as such, and could have had devastating consequences for the alleged impartiality of the Crown. It also showed how much Prince Albert had to learn about England and its politics.

By this stage the full horror of what Peel proposed had hit the Conservative Party in the House of Commons. At first, its members had assumed that his ambitions were confined to the Corn Laws, but they now realised that he intended to apply the principle to all manufacturers, and all commerce; the import duties on foreign cattle were to be abolished immediately; his purpose was the introduction of Free Trade by an elected Protectionist Government. Peel had totally miscalculated; in December he had felt, as Gladstone recorded, 'glee and complacency' and full confidence in carrying his Party. Now, assailed with unprecedented ferocity by Bentinck, Disraeli, and the Conservative Protectionists, his measures could only be carried in the Commons by the votes of the Whigs, the Radicals, the Manchester School, and the Irish.

Conservatives who supported Peel and, either through choice of the compulsion of their patrons, resigned their seats and stood for re-election in their constituencies fared badly. Captain Henry Rous, Royal Navy (retired), stood with great confidence in his Westminster constituency, only to find himself opposed by an official Whig candidate, a General Evans. Prince Albert wrote angrily on February 18th that 'It appears that Lord Palmerston was the instigator of the Party move, which led Evans to stand, that most of the Whigs disapproved the step. General Evans is [a] personal adherent of Lord Palmerston, who is very much in want of a few friends in the House of Commons. Evans pledged himself to the support of the Government measures now under discussion.' When Peel upbraided Rous for having given him false reports of his prospects and causing the Government such humiliation, Rous indignantly replied that 'Westminster can never again be won by a Tory except in extraordinary times of excitements during a presumed national grievance or during a general despondency. D'Israeli in full Dress Uniform – Lord John Russell in simple Toga, & a Leaguer in Rags met & polled together for Evans at the same booth. This is the key to the position'. Peel blamed Rous for being a fool, Prince Albert blamed Palmerston for being a cynical opportunist.

Lord Lincoln, appointed Lord Lieutenant of Ireland, ran into the ferocious wrath and opposition of his father, the Duke of Newcastle, when he sought re-election in South Nottinghamshire. Lincoln wrote to Peel that 'The nomination is over and I got the show of hands, but I fear many of them were too dirty to do me any further good – there being no votes under them'. This forecast turned out to be entirely accurate. Albert, noting that *The Times* had turned against the luckless Lincoln, wrote that 'The Duke of Newcastle had issued a most violent address against his son, calling upon the County to reject that swindler who had come to disturb the peace of the County! This of course had much weight with the Duke's tennants [*sic*]'. On top of these reverses there was another wave of resignations from the Royal Household as Tories either voluntarily, or under intense pressure from their parents, relatives, or colleagues, relinquished their posts.

Prince Albert followed the debates[1] and developments intently, and the correspondence with Peel became very substantial. To his

---

[1] These were extensive and detailed for the principal speakers, but somewhat harsh on the others. Thus, this report in the Corn Law debate: 'Lord Charles Churchill made his maiden speech, but it was not well heard. He was understood to claim protection on account of the peculiar difficulties to which the farmers of this country were subjected, compared with the facilities enjoyed by the foreign producer'. And that was all!

dismay, the analysis of the key vote on February 27th after 'a debate of unexampled duration' in which 102 Members took part, revealed that only 112 Tories had voted for Peel's motion, while 231 had voted against, with 28 absent. This, he wrote to Peel, 'does not look like a strong Government!', but he was hopeful that its *'moral strength'* would impress the country: 'Your position is an anxious one, but you have passed the worst day on Friday, I hope, & your Followers will soon increase'. This was not to be.

On the same day that the Corn Law repeal passed the Lords – June 25th – the hostile alliance against the Ministry, joined by the embittered Conservatives, swept Peel's Government aside on the issue of Irish Coercion by seventy-three votes. It had been a cruel and passionate debate, and Bentinck and Disraeli led into the lobbies over seventy Conservatives, while some eighty others abstained. Wellington called it 'a blackguard combination', but it was sufficient. Peel's Government was wrecked; his Party was shattered into angry and warring fragments for a generation; Russell and the Whigs were back in Office. Free Trade had triumphed, but at a heavy cost and with many victims, one of the most conspicuous of whom was Prince Albert.

It is now an accepted truism that, in the words of Cecil Woodham-Smith, the principle that 'the Crown is disassociated from party and above party, is Prince Albert's contribution to British politics',[1] but it requires some qualification. Albert's dominant purpose was not to reduce, but significantly to *increase*, the real power and influence of the Monarchy within the new conditions of British politics and society. It was his judgement in the winter of 1845–46 that the Corn Laws must be repealed, not only because of the crisis and the Irish famine but as a result of his internationalism, and deep feeling for the moral, as well as the strictly practical, arguments for Free Trade. This was to be the theme and inspiration for the 1851 Great Exhibition, with England as the leader in a crusade to destroy trade and fiscal barriers as evils in themselves, and obstructive of the ultimate goal of the community of nations. Thus, in this matter he was a keen partisan, although not linked to any political Party – Russell's conversion to Free Trade should, logically, have led him to support the Whigs – but to Peel personally, and to his Government. By making this so obvious, he made it evident that the Monarch was not impartial; by accepting Peel's over-sanguine estimates of his probable total success he made the same major miscalculation as did the Prime Minister of the passions that existed on the other side of the argument against the Anti-Corn Law League. Thus, he had

[1] Woodham-Smith, op. cit., p. 199.

become a participant in the utter disruption of the Conservative federation which Peel had so carefully created and had now destroyed. Out of this turmoil at least one lesson had been learned. Prince Albert never entered the gallery of the House of Commons again. But his political ambitions burned undimmed.

The Queen and Prince Albert, with their children and new baby went to Osborne at the beginning of July 1846 in considerable gloom,[1] not wholly relieved by the 'beautiful weather for this truly enjoyable place; we drive, walk, and sit out – and the nights are so fine', as Victoria wrote to Leopold on July 14th. Peel's valedictory speech in the Commons – 'a smothered volcano of emotions', the new Bishop of Oxford reported to Anson – had included a glowing tribute to Cobden which startled and upset Prince Albert, but when they spoke on the matter on July 5th, Peel, in Albert's account, 'was not inclined to enter upon the subject'. The Queen described the loss of Peel and Aberdeen as 'irreparable to us and the Country ... We felt so safe with them'. To Lord Hardinge she wrote that 'one of the most brilliant Governments this country ever had has fallen at the moment of victory!'

But there was sunshine, as well. On May 25th the Queen had given birth to her third daughter, Princess Helena. When her husband went to Liverpool in July to inspect the new Albert Dock he sent a loving letter to her, ending 'May we soon meet and embrace each other again!', and she wrote to Stockmar:

> I feel very lonely without my dear Master; and though I know other people are often separated for a few days I feel habit could not make me get accustomed to it. Without him everything loses its interest. It will always be a terrible pang for me to separate from him even for two days; and I pray God never to let me survive him. I glory in his being seen and loved.

In her Journal for June 8th she wrote that 'Really when one is so happy & blessed in one's home life, as I am, Politics (provided my Country is safe) must only take a 2nd place'.

[1] They had wanted – once again – to visit Ireland, but were dissuaded by Ministers, as in 1843.

SIX

CRISIS AND TRIUMPH

The lamented departure of Peel and the return of the Whigs meant that Queen Victoria and Prince Albert had to deal with a Prime Minister, Russell, whom they considered as diminutive in intellect and political courage as he was in physical stature, and a Foreign Secretary, Palmerston, whom Albert especially regarded with doubt, and of whom the Queen had never really approved. She had certainly not approved of his marriage with Melbourne's sister, Lady Cowper, and in spite of Melbourne's entreaties had not ever been able to write a letter of congratulation. But Palmerston's breezy manner, his political independence, his lecherousness, his acute desire for popularity, his close links with sections of the Press, and his brazen opportunistic populism and nationalism, all combined with great effectiveness to make him highly uncongenial to Prince Albert. The Queen had disliked his aggressive attitude in the 1840 crisis over Egypt and his unconcealed hostility to France in general and King Louis Philippe in particular. Albert considered Palmerston politically immoral, with a shallow understanding of Europe, and, although an ingrained Whig at home a dangerous flirter with liberal causes abroad – in short, the exact opposite to Prince Albert. Eventual German unity was to him, as to Stockmar, his great ambition, but he had no sympathy whatever for popular movements encouraged from outside that were intended to bring down constitutional monarchies. Palmerston gave the clear impression that he would welcome them.

Initially, Prince Albert had a greater regard for Palmerston than the Foreign Secretary had for him. In 1846 Palmerston was sixty-two, had an unrivalled experience of politics, and was not disposed to pay much attention to a German consort of twenty-seven, with whom he had little in common. Their relationship was to veer from cold suspicion to open animosity, and then back to mutual regard and respect. At this stage Palmerston considered Prince Albert with condescension, an attitude that he was subsequently to amend. Albert saw him clearly, but with a dislike which he was also destined to qualify, and his attitude during this time was clearly expressed in a letter to Russell:

'Lord Palmerston is an able politician with large views and an energetic mind, an indefatigable man of business, a good speaker; but a man of expediency, of easy temper, no very high standard of honour and not a grain of moral feeling'.

It was not an unfair assessment, but it omitted much. For his part, Palmerston did not realise that the Queen's husband was not only powerful in title and position, but also in knowledge and ability.

Aberdeen, a seriously underrated Foreign Secretary, had been much to Albert's liking. He was, like him, essentially a European and a pacifist. He wanted good relations with France, and had no sympathy for Palmerston's rasping and erratic methods. Prince Albert's unhappiness at losing Aberdeen was swiftly given justification.

After the meeting at Eu in the previous summer with Louis Philippe it had appeared that the Spanish Marriage issue had been satisfactorily settled, so that the British would not press the claims of Victoria's cousin, Prince Leopold of Saxe-Coburg-Kohary, as the husband of Queen Isabella, and Louis Philippe would not advance those of any of his sons. Now, in July 1846, within a few weeks of taking office, Palmerston coolly included Leopold's name in a list of possible husbands for the Spanish Queen, and naturally showed the dispatch containing the proposal to the French Ambassador, the Comte de Jarnac. Louis Philippe was enraged, there was a fierce Anglo-French storm, at the end of which Queen Isabella was married to the loathsome (and reportedly impotent) Duke of Cadiz, and her sister Fernanda married Louis Philippe's son, the Duc de Montpensier. It was a classic Palmerston venture, angrily denounced by Albert as a *bock* (blunder), and although Queen Victoria at first instinctively sided with Palmerston against the French, she quickly had her mind changed by her husband. Then, she discovered that Palmerston had little time for her cousins the King and Queen of Portugal and their government, and was willing to stir up trouble against them. As Albert described later in a particularly angry letter to Palmerston, this was representative of 'that species of angry, irritating, *Bullying* which has long characterised our relations with Spain, Portugal, etc.'.

This particular crisis passed, but it was deeply ominous. By this stage Prince Albert, with his modest team of Anson, Charles Grey and Charles Phipps[1] had a firm grip on foreign affairs, which he did not

---

[1] Anson was Treasurer and Private Secretary to the Prince until 1847, when he became Keeper of the Privy Purse to the Queen, while remaining Prince Albert's Treasurer, Phipps becoming the Prince's secretary. On Anson's death in 1849 Phipps succeeded him in both positions, and was succeeded by Grey as the Prince's secretary.

intend to relinquish. He conducted a voluminous correspondence with Stockmar, King Leopold, his brother Ernest and the King of Prussia. When Cracow was absorbed by Austria in the summer of 1846, the strong criticisms in England were met by Prince Albert himself, who arranged for a *Times* leader-writer, Henry Reeve, to write a lengthy defence of the Austrian action for the influential *Edinburgh Review*, the final version being edited and corrected by Albert himself. When the issue of the Duchies of Schleswig and Holstein arose Prince Albert supported their incorporation into the much coveted united Germany, while Palmerston supported the Danish claim. Palmerston was immensely sympathetic to the cause of Italian independence; the Prince was strongly hostile to the dismemberment of the Austrian Empire. Prince Albert believed in Anglo-French amity and the *entente cordiale*; Palmerston did not. The Prince was becoming seriously concerned about the condition and training and equipment of the British Navy and Army; Palmerston believed that they were quite adequate. Both on policy and in personality the gulf between them was substantial, and was remorselessly to widen. Lord Clarendon is an unreliable and embittered commentator, but there was some truth in his subsequent complaint that 'the Queen and Prince are wrong in wishing that courtiers rather than Ministers should conduct the affairs of the country. They labour under the curious mistake that the Foreign Office is their peculiar department and that they have a right to control, if not to direct, the Foreign Policy of England'.

This was an exaggeration, although only marginally so. What Prince Albert sought, and certainly had from Aberdeen, was the right for the Queen to be consulted, to be fully informed, to see all the important despatches, and to have the opportunity for influence. In principle, neither Palmerston nor Russell disputed any of this, but Palmerston had never brooked any interference by colleagues in his conduct of foreign affairs, and saw no good reason why Prince Albert should be a solitary exception.

In addition to having views of his own on the proper conduct of foreign policy, Prince Albert told Russell firmly that he disagreed 'totally' with the doctrine that the Queen could not and should not involve herself actively in the work and decisions of her Government. In his own words, the Sovereign had 'an immense moral responsibility upon his shoulders with regard to his Government and the duty to watch and *control* it'. This was a substantial, and very significant, claim. The real divide between him and Palmerston lay not so much in their characters and differences over foreign policy, important though they were, but in the fact that Palmerston did not accept this definition of Royal authority. From the earliest days of the Russell

Administration the Prince and Palmerston were on a collision course, and the difference in their approach can be clearly seen in this letter, in 1847, from Albert to Stockmar:

I am very anxious that England should declare in time that she will not allow independent states to be prevented by force from introducing such internal reforms as may seem to them good. This appears to me to be the right standpoint *vis-à-vis* Germany, Switzerland and Italy. We are often inclined to plunge states which have no wish for them into constitutional reforms – this I regard as quite wrong (*vide* Spain, Portugal, Greece) although it is Lord Palmerston's hobby horse. I, on the other hand, regard England's true position to be that of a protecting power for those states whose independent development may be hindered from without'.

The hard political fact was that Russell was weak, his Government was shaky, and Palmerston was by far his greatest political and personal asset. Russell was in awe of his formidable and popular Foreign Secretary, and although he often lamented Palmerston's impulsiveness and theatricality, and his capacity for getting the Government into dangerous and sometimes ludicrous situations, a Russell Administration without Palmerston seemed an impossibility. Thus, in his own words, the Prime Minister found himself 'as umpire between Windsor and Broadlands' (Palmerston's Hampshire mansion and estate), a hapless and somewhat undignified mediator between two men of strong will, high position, and unquestionable ability. Thus did matters stand at the end of 1846.

At this moment, Prince Albert became embroiled in an embarrassing and unwelcome political and academic maelstrom, yet which was to have momentous results for him and for English higher education.

The Chancellor of Cambridge University, the Duke of Northumberland, died on February 12th 1847, and with indecent speed a group of Fellows of St. John's at once publicly proposed the candidature of the second Earl of Powis, himself a John's man, a former Tory M.P. for Ludlow for twenty-three years, and a hero in certain quarters in the Universities for his vehement and successful opposition to the proposed merger of the Sees of Bangor and St. Asaph into a new Bishopric of Manchester. So intense had been the feelings aroused over this controversy that when Powis' campaign ended in victory over £5,000 was raised to him as a testimonial of gratitude. A High Churchman, a High Tory, the grandson of Robert Clive, a

Cambridge man, and a contemporary of Palmerston at St. John's, Powis was regarded by St. John's as a very strong candidate.

These manoeuvrings were viewed with intense distaste and dismay in Trinity College and elsewhere in the University, where the alleged merits of Lord Powis were regarded as positive disadvantages. Thus, on February 13th the Master of Trinity, Dr Whewell, wrote urgently to Anson to enquire whether the Prince would be willing to respond to an invitation to stand for the Chancellorship from a number of heads of College. It is not precisely clear who originally proposed Albert, but it is certainly the case that Whewell was the most active and determined of his supporters, and the chronic feud between Trinity and St. John's can hardly have been a totally insignificant factor.

The Prince, the Queen, and Stockmar were greatly attracted by the proposal, none being aware of the fact that the office was generally regarded as ceremonial and honorary. Albert agreed (February 15th) to accept if the invitation were indeed 'the unanimous desire of the University'. The Vice-Chancellor, Dr. Henry Philpott, Master of St. Catharine's, assured him – quite wrongly – that it was indeed the unanimous wish of the heads of College, and a deputation waited upon Prince Albert on the 17th. His acceptance of the invitation was, Whewell told Phipps, received 'with the most lively satisfaction throughout the University', and Lord Powis would now certainly withdraw.

Lord Powis, St. John's, and the High Tories had no intention whatever of withdrawing, and indeed a Tory M.P., F. H. Dickenson, publicly called for Prince Albert to withdraw in favour of Powis. Even worse, a Powis election committee was established in London after a dinner at the British Hotel, Cockspur Street which included the Master and President of St. John's, the President of Queen's, and the Public Orator. In these circumstances, and angered by the false information given to him by Whewell and Philpott, Prince Albert resolved to withdraw his candidature on February 18th. But his name was now in contention as a candidate, and his supporters were determined to persevere. Anson and Phipps were appalled by the prospects of 'a disagreeable Encounter, & one which those who support YRH ought not to have subjected you to', as Anson wrote to him on February 22nd.

Prince Albert wisely consulted Peel on February 22nd whether he should 'take a further step in order to stop the possibility of my name appearing in the Contest, and what ought that step to be? If I remain quiet, and my election is carried by a majority, am I to accept or refuse the honor proposed to me?' Peel, in a firm memorandum on the 23rd, advised 'strongly in favour of permitting the Election to take its course' and to accept the Chancellorship if elected. With considerable reluctance and unease, Albert accepted Peel's advice.

Meanwhile, Phipps and Anson were determined to protect their master, and when Whewell submitted his election circular on behalf of the Prince to Phipps for transmission to the Prince Phipps took it upon his own responsibility not to forward it on the grounds that Albert should have no knowledge of it nor of any campaign being waged on his behalf. With some reluctance, and surprise, Whewell accepted this decision on February 24th, about which Prince Albert did not know for some time.

The judgement of Anson and Phipps was very sound, as the contest was livening up in Cambridge. The Master of Clare Hall publicly called for Albert to withdraw, and Powis's committee stated 'that it is very desirable that the Chancellor of the University of Cambridge should have been educated at the University, in order that he may be acquainted with its interests and privileges, and that he should be a member of the Legislature, in order that he may watch over and maintain them in Parliament'. Earl Nelson now joined the list of activists on Powis's behalf, and Whewell further raised the temperature with a fiery pamphlet declaring that 'In Lord Powis we should only have a Chancellor of St. John's', which stung the Master of St. John's mightily.

Only senior members of the University could vote in the election, and urgent and elaborate measures were taken to alert and convey the scattered voters around the country to Cambridge on the three consecutive polling days. Those Cambridge members of the Government and others in high political station were strongly advised to interrupt their Parliamentary and other duties to travel to Cambridge to vote for Prince Albert; as the voting was public, this intimation of the certainty of grave Royal displeasure in a certain eventuality was perhaps superfluous to ambitious Ministers, but Lord Powis' friends were also very active in both Houses. Although the undergraduates could not vote they had also captured the election fever, and vociferously crammed the Senate House throughout the voting.

At the end of the first day of polling, Thursday February 25th, the voting was Prince Albert 582, Lord Powis 572, and well could Lord Ernest Bruce report to General Bowles that 'It is a *neck* and *neck* race ... I am rather an old hand at University elections, & I never saw anything like this ... the excitement beats anything I ever saw'.

The voting was conducted amidst scenes of considerable tumult and uproar. 'There were cheers and groans for everybody and everything', as *The Times* reported.

At 12 o'clock an immense number of voters arrived by the London train, and the lower part of the building presented an enormously dense appearance. The general wish seemed to be to get towards the front, to vote and have done with it, and to get back to Town in time. Some not very feeble barriers placed in front of the Vice-Chancellor's little hustings to keep back the flow of the tide, and the wands and staves of the attendants in office, shared the fate of all things fragile.

At the close of poll on the second day Prince Albert was still ahead, by 875 to 789, and on that day the Directors of the Eastern Counties Railway made a somewhat opportunistic intervention by announcing that 'In the event of the election of Prince Albert, the directors intend building a Royal carriage in a style of unsurpassed magnificence for the conveyance of His Royal Highness and suite to the University'. Lord Powis, it would appear, would have to make his own way in the event of *his* election.

The excitement of the Friday, *The Times* reported, was no less than it had been on the previous day.

The row was of a terrific character; missiles of all sorts were employed in assailing the voters, all of whom gladly retreated as soon as they had given in their voting cards, and some refrained from voting at all, after having travelled many miles for the purpose, rather than subject themselves to the fury of the storm raging within the Senate-house.

From afar, the Prince, the Queen, and the distraught Phipps and Anson could only observe and receive Press and personal reports from the turbulent battle-front, and Albert's grave doubts about having accepted Peel's advice were now greatly augmented. Clearly, his majority would be small, if there was to be one at all, and the frenzy, fierceness, and closeness of the contest had come as an unpleasant surprise to those without experience of the intensity of academic politics – in this case intermixed with real politics, as the Tory Cantabridgians streamed down to the University and fought to enter the hubbub of the Senate House to vote for Powis.

In the event, when polls closed on the Saturday evening, and the final count was announced, Prince Albert had triumphed by 953 to 837, but it was so modest a victory that he consulted Peel again as to whether he should accept the Chancellorship. Peel strongly advised him to do so: 'The acceptance of the office without reluctance or delay has about it a character of firmness and decision, of supporting friends instead of giving a Triumph to Opponents', and he submitted the draft of an acceptance speech to the Prince.

This would have appeared to have been decisive, although Prince Albert's own doubts were also robustly swept aside by the Queen, who recorded in her Journal that 'all the cleverest men were on my beloved Albert's side'. But perhaps even more significant in his final decision was the analysis of the voting, which revealed that he had obtained a clear majority of the heads of colleges, of the University Professors (16 out of 24), of the Senior Wranglers (19 out of 30), and of the Resident Members, who had voted three to one for him. On February 27th he conveyed his acceptance to the University.

The Inauguration of Prince Albert to accept the office of Chancellor of the University of Cambridge took place on March 25th in the Green Drawing Room at Buckingham Palace, when all the notables of the University – including the Master of St. John's – waited upon him with proper solemnity, and to whose Address Albert responded with one of modesty and gratitude. The assembly, in the words of *The Times*, then moved to 'a sumptuous *déjeûner*' with the band of the Life Guards playing throughout the feast. The University dignitaries may well have reflected that Powis Castle would have been a somewhat inadequate alternative. Although the new Chancellor criticised the Latin letter of invitation which described him as *dux de Saxe*, he was deeply honoured and excited: 'It is my first chance', he wrote to Ernest, 'to do something in my own name for my adopted country'.

Unhappily, it has to be recorded that Lord Powis was a bad loser. Prince Albert invited him to the Inauguration, but Powis declined, replying acidly that March 25th immediately followed the day announced by the Queen as 'a day of Prayer & Humiliation' and that he would, accordingly, be with his family. In the following January, while pheasant shooting on his estates, he was shot and killed by one of his sons.

In July 1847 Prince Albert and the Queen, in their roles as Chancellor and eminent Royal visitor, travelled to Cambridge, where the Prince read a formal address of welcome to his wife, which she described as 'almost absurd'. The Poet Laureate, Wordsworth, had composed an Ode of such dismal banality that it gave clear evidence of failing powers or possibly – being a St. John's man and a Tory – lack of personal commitment to his task. One evening the Royal couple walked together down the incomparable Backs – which the Queen, sadly, described as 'the waterside' – with Prince Albert in Chancellor's cap and a mackintosh over his formal clothes, with Queen Victoria in full evening dress but 'with a veil over my diadem'. Indeed, Cambridge had been astounded by her diamonds.

Their only complaint, as they wandered together, quite alone and in deep happiness, was of the absence of music and singing.

Each was twenty-eight years of age. She was the Queen of England, he had just been described – not felicitously – by Wordsworth as 'the chosen lord' of Cambridge. On that evening in Cambridge mid-summer they were a happy couple walking together by the Cam, deep in conversation. They laughed at the performance of the Heads of Houses when they had to kiss the Queen's hand, and how they had done so 'with an infinite variety of awkwardness', as she described the scene. 'It is very pleasant', John Brown said to Queen Victoria of her husband, 'to walk with a person who is always content'. The remark so struck her that she recorded in in her Journal, as she understood its truth so completely. It was certainly entirely appropriate to their walk along the Cambridge Backs in July 1847.

Even before Prince Albert was formally inaugurated as Chancellor he received from Whewell on March 8th a letter proposing to enlarge the activities of the University 'so as to include some of the most valuable portions of modern science and literature' and enclosed a detailed paper prepared by himself and the geologist, Charles Lyell,[1] which described the condition of the University in very critical, and justified, terms. The situation of Cambridge was, indeed, lamentable. The dominant purpose of the University was to train men for the clergy, and the contemporary comment that it was simply 'a vast theological seminary' was not at all unmerited. The only main studies were classics and mathematics, over half the students were at Trinity and St. John's, of which the Fellows were almost wholly clergymen; even the Professorships in the natural sciences tended to go to clerics, and their classes and lectures were virtually deserted. So low was the standard of tuition that the pernicious practice of private tutors had replaced it, and, as Peacock, a Fellow of Trinity and Dean of Ely wrote in a paper full of mordant and unsparing criticism requested by Albert, 'This unhappy system has contributed more than any other cause to the very general, &, in some respects, just complaints which have been made of late years of the paucity of works of learning & research which had issued from the University of Cambridge'.

Modest advances had been made in the 1820's, but the fact remained that 'the natural sciences, which were gaining a foothold in European and Scottish universities, only fitted into the Cambridge

[1] 1797–1875. Knighted, on Prince Albert's personal recommendation, in 1848.

pattern when they could be treated mathematically, and the moral sciences, languages, literature and history, which could not be so treated, were considered to have little educational value'.[1] Whewell regarded himself as a reformer, but was in fact deeply dedicated to the maintenance of the classics and mathematical domination of the University.

The position of Oxford was equally forlorn, where violent diatribes had been issued in denunciation of the British Association For The Advancement of Science, and which included the declaration of an Oxford divine that 'men who entertain such fears seem to forget that The Book of Nature and The Book of Revelation were both written by the same Author'. As Lyell caustically observed: 'After the year 1839 we may consider three-fourths of the sciences, still nominally taught at Oxford, to have been virtually exiled from the University. The class-rooms of the professors were some of them entirely, others nearly, deserted'.

The more that Prince Albert examined the Cambridge situation, and compared it with Berlin, Bonn, and Edinburgh, the more astonished he became. Whewell admitted the limitations of the University, but argued that internal reform was improbable, and lamely proposed special scholarships in Jurisprudence and Natural History. Indeed, Whewell's *Principles of University Education*, published in 1837, which particularly excited Lyell's condemnation, was an eloquent plea for the old order which the new Chancellor was resolved to end.

He began by inviting Professor Sedgwick to act as his personal and official secretary in Cambridge, and then asked Philpott to prepare and present to him a detailed list of 'studies & scientific enquiries pursued at Cambridge at this time'. The results were appalling. As Albert wrote to Lord John Russell, seeking his views, there were no studies in history, political economy, law, psychology, modern languages, geography, chemistry, art, astronomy, natural history, or science. The Professor of Oriental Languages, lecturing on Sanscrit, had only one pupil. The second year public examination was confined to Euripides, Cicero, St. Mark's Gospel in Greek, *Evidences of Christianity*, and Old Testament history. As Lyell rightly wrote, the student's 'highest hope of future preferment is not in the University, but in the Church'.

Prince Albert also consulted Peel, who fully shared Lyell's exasperation at Whewell's excessive caution, and wrote to him on November 2nd 1847:

[1] T. J. N. Hilken: *Engineering at Cambridge University, 1783–1965* (Cambridge, 1967), p. 17.

The Doctor's assumption that *a century should pass* before our discoveries in Science are admitted to the course of Academical Instruction exceeds in absurdity anything which the bitterest enemy of University Education could have imputed to its advocates.

Are the students at Cambridge to hear nothing of Electricity or the Speculations concerning the mysterious influence, its possible connection with the nervous system and with muscular action, till all doubts on the subject are at end? Will they be at an end after the lapse of 100 years?

If the Principle for which Dr. Whewell contends be a sound one it will be difficult to deliver a Lecture on Theology ...

In the new Vice-Chancellor, Robert Phelps, Master of Sidney Lodge, and in Philpott Albert had more encouraging and sympathetic supporters. Philpott explained to Prince Albert, in the latter's account to Russell, that 'the Heads of Colleges were such a nervous & essentially Conservative body that it required the greatest caution in proposing any improvement not to arouse an insurmountable opposition'. But this was tactical caution, and very different from the hostility of Whewell, and Albert accepted his wise advice to advance with discretion. In the meanwhile, with a reasonable amount of general approval in the University, Prince Albert instituted the Chancellor's Gold Medal for History. It was his idea entirely, and marked his first direct intervention in the University's affairs.

On December 30th 1847 Philpott wrote to Phelps to set out his proposals for reform, and particularly 'The exclusive character of our Studies which gives the University the appearance of a place of Education for candidates for Holy Orders only ... It would be a great calamity to the University & to the Nation at large if an opinion should gain ground among the higher orders of Society that the Studies of the University are not such as tend to fit a man for the active business & intercourse of life & promised to be useful to him in it ... There is no doubt that such an opinion does now prevail in some degree'.

Albert was delighted with the thrust of Philpott's revolutionary proposals – for such they were – and especially the emphasis upon the natural sciences and history. Philpott knew the Prince's mind, and was quite aware that his censures and proposals would be warmly welcomed by the Chancellor, but it must be emphasised that the actual proposals for which Albert – with justice – later received so much credit stemmed from the eminent Professor of Moral Philosophy.

Philpott proposed – and Prince Albert immediately accepted,

with great enthusiasm – a new Moral Sciences Tripos involving moral philosophy, political economy, modern history, general jurisprudence, and the laws of England. There would also be compulsory attendance at a much wider number and variety of lectures for all undergraduates, but the proposal that excited Albert even more was that for the establishment of a Natural Sciences Tripos. He was disappointed by Philpott's advice not to present his proposals to Senate until October, but accepted that much preparatory work, discussion, and negotiation would be needed in Cambridge if these extraordinary suggestions were to be accepted. He also saw the wisdom in attempting to win over the influential Whewell, a task to which he particularly addressed himself.

It was also proposed that there should be a new Board for Mathematical Studies, to consult together 'on all matters relating to the actual state of mathematical studies and examinations in the University' and to prepare an annual published report. In some respects this was to prove the most far-reaching proposal of all.

In the event, Prince Albert's prestige and position as Chancellor were sorely needed in the following months. With considerable reluctance Whewell agreed to support the proposals, but resistance elsewhere – and strongly supported in Oxford, where there was much horror at the implications of the Cambridge reforms – was stiff and enduring. The Senate eventually approved the reforms on October 31st 1848, but although Phelps described the majority as 'triumphant' the Prince noted the significantly high minority vote. Nonetheless, the reforms had been forced through, and drew unexpectedly lavish praise upon Albert's head from *The Morning Chronicle* and *The Times*. Oxford had little choice but to follow suit.

Prince Albert deeply resented the action of Lord John Russell in instituting a Royal Commission on the universities in 1850 without consulting him, and in a public letter clearly expressed that resentment. This was not enough for certain Cambridge personalities, who treated the Chancellor with studied offensiveness in matters small and large, 'the present Vice-Chancellor withholding all information from me on principle', as he noted on one occasion. But Sedgwick was a staunch supporter, and there were others who recognised and appreciated the Prince's profound and sincere commitment to Cambridge.

His concern for science, technology, and engineering formed only part of his interests; he wished Cambridge to become a place 'where the *savants* of this country may find a home which at present is absolutely denied to them, and they themselves being driven to join the mere money-making pursuits or to starve', and he wished this of all British universities. It was in his acute understanding of the crucial balance between the humanities and the new sciences that his genius as Chancellor and leader of thought resided. He was not only the greatest Chancellor Cambridge University has ever had, but he was the pioneer of the principles of enlightened scholarship and of the love of learning for its own sake.

Prince Albert's papers on Cambridge for the rest of his life and Chancellorship demonstrate his keen interest in the University, and his deep concern to improve the chronically bad relations with the Town. The University of Cambridge and Borough Act of 1856 was a serious endeavour to improve matters, including handing to the Town authorities the Vice-Chancellor's ancient right of granting Alehouse Licences, although Wine Licences were retained. He was the founder of the University Rifle Corps, and his advice and intervention frequently sought on a very wide variety of subjects, including the Petition by several Fellows of Clare Hall against its Master (Webb) in 1854. He was diligent in his official duties and visitations, which he enjoyed greatly.

But these services, important and onerous though they were, do not compare with the service he rendered not only to Cambridge but to British Universities by ending the lethargy of centuries and laying the foundations of a modern, relevant, and high quality University that was to develop rapidly from lassitude and ineptitude into one of the greatest Universities in the world.

There were to be many difficulties. The Cambridge University Act of 1856 was bitterly contested in the University, and it was not until 1871 that the pernicious religious tests – which had effectively debarred Roman Catholics, dissenters, and free-thinkers – were removed, and opened Cambridge to a new reservoir of talent for college Fellowships and University Professorships. It was Prince Albert's successor as Chancellor, the Duke of Devonshire, who built and equipped the Cavendish Laboratory at his own expense. But Albert had led the way, and charted the new course that others followed. The impact that he made upon Cambridge, and indeed upon the concept of British universities, is literally incalculable.

He indeed did achieve his ambition of doing 'something in my own name for my adopted country'.

Prince Albert and the Queen had never forgotten their visits to Scotland in 1842 and 1844, but political crises, the arrival of more children, and the building of Osborne combined to make another visit impossible until August 1847 when they cruised up the West Coast in the *Victoria and Albert* and made frequent and happy expeditions by carriage, horse, and foot. This visit was even more

successful than the first, being private and informal, and immediately on their return they discussed the possibility of buying a
house of their own, preferably in the Highlands, where the astringent
air and glens had made such a deep impression upon Albert. Both
suffered slightly from rheumatism, but there was also the factor that
the air in London was notoriously harsh on lungs and throat, the
dank Thames Valley did not make Windsor notably healthy, and the
air at Osborne, although gentle and unpolluted, was undeniably
soft. Nonetheless, although these were the reasons that secured Sir
James Clark's warm support for Highland air – which he described,
somewhat oddly, as very suitable 'for the peculiar constitution of the
Queen and Prince' – the most important attraction for Victoria and
Albert had been the Highland people they had met. Queen Victoria,
with her keen eye for beauty, admired their physique, and also their
quiet pride, independence, generosity and kindness. They were, she
wrote with admiration, 'never vulgar, never take liberties, are so
intelligent, modest, and well bred'. It was very refreshing for the
young couple to meet ordinary people, many of them very poor, who
were courteous without any hint of obsequiousness, not averse to
speaking their minds, and genuinely pleased to meet them. These
factors made the greatest impression of all, and it later became
legendary in Court circles that the Queen would put up with a
frankness in Scotland that she would not have tolerated in the Court.

In 1843 it had been Peel who had told them of Osborne; now it was
Aberdeen who suggested Balmoral Castle, on Deeside, near Balla-
ter, which had been designed and built by his late brother, Sir
Robert Gordon, and had the unexpired portion of a lease; Gordon
had died in 1847 and the lease, inherited by Aberdeen, had 26 years
to run. It so happened that Sir James Clark's son had stayed there
with Robert Gordon at the same time as the Queen and Prince had
been in the western Highlands, where 'the weather was most
dreadful', in the Queen's words, whereas that at Balmoral had been
excellent. On these recommendations, and after seeing some
sketches of the Castle, the Queen and Prince Albert bought the lease
from Aberdeen without further commitment at that stage.

They reached Balmoral for the first time on September 8th 1848.
Queen Victoria wrote that it was 'a pretty little castle in the old
scotch style', although it was, in fact, only recently built; they were
charmed by the position, rode and walked, sketched, went on
numerous expeditions, and Albert successfully stalked and shot his
first deer. 'We have withdrawn for a short time into a complete
mountain solitude', he wrote on September 11th, 'where one rarely
sees a human face, where the snow already covers the mountain tops,
and the wild deer come creeping stealthily round the house ... The

air is glorious and clear, but icy cold'. 'It was so calm, and so solitary', Victoria wrote, 'it did one good as one gazed around; and the pure mountain air was most refreshing. All seemed to breathe freedom and peace, and to make one forget the world and its sad turmoils'. But, again, it was the people who made an even stronger impact upon them than the glorious mountains, wild streams, and glens. The tenants and crofters took with much warmth to the young family, and when they sadly left they passed under an arch with the words, 'More beloved than ever, Haste ye back to your home of heather'.

The only practical difficulty concerned the Castle itself, which had limited space and inadequate facilities for a growing family and the needs of the Sovereign. Although Balmoral was intended to be another Osborne, a family home for retreat, it also had to accommodate the Sovereign's staff and have facilities for visiting Ministers and distinguished guests.

The purchase of the freehold from the Fife Trustees proved a lengthy and highly frustrating business, particularly as Albert had successfully bought the freehold of 6,500 acres of the Birkhall estate, and although the Gordon family would not sell the freehold of Abergeldi, the neighbouring estate to the east, they granted a lease for forty years, with the option of renewal. The Farquharson family would not sell the forest of Ballochbuie, which Albert also coveted, and which only became part of the Balmoral estate after his death, in 1878. These purchases, although wise, and on good terms, had little relevance while the 17,400 acre Balmoral estate and castle remained unavailable, and it was not until June 1852 that it at last became Royal property, at a cost of 30,000 guineas, and Albert could put into effect his detailed plans for the castle, its immediate garden and grounds, and the estate and its tenants. Until then, the Royal family were simply tenants, and every visit only increased their impatience to own it. But in 1852 the building of the new Balmoral could begin in earnest, and was first occupied in 1855.

In 1848 the couple had first met John Brown, the son of a local farmer employed at the Castle, with an exceptional knowledge of the area, a favourite of the children, and greatly liked by Albert. He became, in Victoria's own phrase, her 'particular gillie', and was a permanent and invaluable member of all their great 'expeditions'. Their understanding and affection was to become very deep, and after Prince Albert's death was to be the topic of much speculation, gossip, and allegations that went far beyond innuendo that he was her lover and even, in some reports, that they had secretly married. By this stage Brown had been brought to London and Osborne as 'the Queen's Highland Servant', where his brusque manners and heavy drinking were not generally appreciated, although matters of no consequence whatever to the Queen. He remained, with her devoted maid, Annie Macdonald, the two servants whom she especially trusted, and in Brown's case he had the outstanding qualification of having been discovered by her husband. Her perception of character may have been uneven, and certainly became more noticeably so after Albert's death, and she had her favourites who could do no wrong and those who, having once fallen into disfavour, had considerable difficulty in retrieving their lost position. But although these very human aspects of her personality had serious consequences in her political judgement before and after her marriage, her deep loyalty to, and dependence upon, John Brown should not be misinterpreted. He was, above all, the living reminder of the great discovery of Balmoral by Albert and herself; he had been their constant leader and adviser in their happy expeditions; he had been the Prince's choice as their companion and guide; he brought back all the happy memories of those perfect family autumns. That is all there was to it. Lady Longford has put the matter clearly and unanswerably:

> That the Queen was neither John Brown's mistress nor his morganatic wife should be clear from a study of her character.[1]

By the autumn of 1847 Prince Albert was becoming deeply concerned by the condition of Europe, and by the evident signs of imminent disaster to the established regimes. 'The political horizon grows darker and darker', he wrote to Stockmar on September 11th; 'Italy, Greece, Spain, Portugal are in a state of ferment', and Queen Victoria wrote to Leopold that 'the state of politics in Europe is very critical and one feels *very* anxious for the future'.

These apprehensions were fully merited. What neither Albert nor Victoria anticipated was the extraordinarily rapid extinction of the Orleanist government of Louis Philippe and its guiding genius, Guizot. As a result of a series of blunders exceptional even by French monarchical standards, a general resentment grew into an insurrection, and thereby rapidly progressed into an unplanned and unexpected revolution, from which Louis Philippe and his family barely escaped: 'there is an impression they fled too quickly', as the Queen tartly remarked.

Stockmar, characteristically, was not greatly surprised. He had written on August 1st 1847:

[1] Longford, op.cit., p. 333.

> Louis Philippe's ambiguous reputation as a master of the art of statesmanship has been most unequivocably ruined by the Spanish intrigue. If he lives long enough he can hardly fail to suffer some portion of the punishment which according to the laws of nature, he has incurred.

The revolution, and its completeness and suddenness, took almost everyone by surprise. Louis Philippe and his wife had to be hustled in disguise from Trouville to Newhaven, whence they were taken to refuge at Claremont. While Albert and the Queen were distressed and sympathetic to the predicament of the French Royal Family, and were glad to be of assistance, there was an evident coldness in their attitude. 'One does not like to attack those who have fallen', the Queen wrote, 'but the poor King L.P. has brought much of this on, by that ill-fated return to a *Bourbon policy*. I always think he *ought not* to have abdicated'.

This new French Revolution occasioned emotions of popular alarm and intense optimism in England and Ireland.

A letter by the Duke of Wellington of the previous January to Sir John Burgoyne was published in which he claimed that, after detailed examination of the coast from the North Foreland to Portsmouth 'excepting immediately under the fire of Dover Castle, there is not a spot on the coast on which infantry might not be thrown on shore at any turn of the tide, with any wind and in any weather, and from which such body of infantry, so thrown on shore, would not find within the distance of five miles a road into the interior of the country through the cliffs, practicable for the march of troops ... When did any man hear of allies of a country unable to defend itself?'

This was palpable nonsense, as any person conversant with the bleak and inhospitable, and virtually harbourless, English south-eastern coast can easily testify, but the military judgement of the Duke was unquestioned and unquestionable, and a great and unnecessary stir was occasioned, to which the timorous Government eagerly bowed. With wholly uncustomary celerity, the Russell Administration bounded into precipitate and patriotic reaction.

On February 18th Russell announced to the House of Commons an increase of £358,000 to the Military, Naval, and Ordnance Estimate, with a further £150,000 to form a Militia Force. But he also announced a Budget deficit of £3,346,500 to be met by renewing Income Tax (about to expire) for three years, and to raise it from 7d to one shilling in the £ for the next two years. Such was the uproar that within ten days the increases were withdrawn, 'In the country', Disraeli sardonically remarked, 'a menagerie before feeding-time could alone give an idea of the unearthly yell with which it was received'.

Prince Albert, obsessed by the crisis in Europe and the threat it posed to the institution of Monarchy itself, was baffled by the fact that London seemed considerably more concerned with the possible fall of the Government over this – to him – relatively minor issue than with violent Revolution on the Continent. His bewilderment emphasised his continuing difficulty in identifying himself with English attitudes; but we can now clearly see that the general indifference in England to the European storm was a highly encouraging political response.

The widespread European upheavals, initiated by the collapse of Louis Philippe, also spread to Germany. Albert hoped that Germans would see what Revolution had brought to France, where, he wrote to Stockmar, 'the dregs of the populace, who now *alone* may be styled the people, are to be the rulers; they are armed, and in a fortnight will be without bread, for all labour is at a standstill, the banks are failing, the capitalists getting out of the way'. 'The poor King of Prussia has made a sad mess', Stockmar commented on March 31st. 'Never has he made a move or a concession but it was too late, nay, when it would have been better had he done nothing'.

The Queen wrote to Leopold that 'Belgium is a bright star in the midst of dark clouds. It makes us all very happy', but to Stockmar on March 6th: 'I am quite well – indeed particularly so, though God knows we have had since the 25th enough for a whole life, – anxiety, sorrow, excitement, in short, I feel as if we had jumped over thirty years' experience at once. The whole face of Europe is changed, and I feel as if I lived in a dream ...'

You know my love for the [French Royal] family; you know how I longed to get on better terms with them again ... and you said, 'Time will alone achieve this, but will certainly bring it about'. Little did I dream that this would be the way we should meet again, and see each other all in the most friendly way. That the Duchesse de Montpensier about whom we have been quarrelling for the last year and a half, should be here as a fugitive, and dressed in the clothes I sent her, and should come to thank *me* for *my* kindness, is a reverse of fortune which no novelist would devise, and upon which one could moralise for ever'.

The forlorn French Royal Family sought succour in England, Louis Philippe arriving at Windsor on March 6th, while in Germany there were reports of violence and anarchy, which deeply troubled Albert. 'It is wonderful to see how my dear Prince bears up under so much anxiety and distress', the Queen wrote to Stockmar, 'for these one must feel, if one loves one's country and sees the awful state things have got into. But he is full of courage, and takes such a large and noble view of everything that he overlooks trifles, and looks solely to the general good'.

The Queen – advised by Albert and Russell – firmly took the view that hospitality for refugees should not be seen as political support for the old regime, and that the new one must be recognised and accepted. 'It will not be pleasant to do this', she wrote to Leopold, 'but the public good and the peace of Europe go before one's personal feelings'. Their hospitality was somewhat ill-rewarded. The French Royal Family and its retinue could not believe that their exile was likely to be permanent, and demonstrated a marked lack of appreciation for the considerable assistance and consideration shown to them, particularly by Albert, who rapidly became exasperated by these ungrateful and not particularly welcome guests. At a time of considerable concern for him, with Europe in turmoil and the sounds of revolution heard in several English cities, and his wife about to have another child, his irritation and impatience with the exiles was wholly understandable. They accused him of being 'hard and unfeeling', and continued to complain and quarrel with each other.

'Things are going badly,' he wrote on February 27th to Stockmar. 'I lose flesh and strength daily. European war is at our doors. France is ablaze in every quarter, Louis Philippe is wandering about in disguise, so is the Queen ... [yet] I am not cast down, still I have need of friends and counsel in these heavy times.' The death of his beloved surviving grandmother was an additional, and heavy, blow. Victoria wrote that he was 'pale and sad', and another observer – almost certainly Henry Reeve – wrote of him 'in these days of gloom with an expression on his face which was harrowing.'

In London, in spite of considerable tension and damage by wandering crowds, the authorities had little difficulty in controlling the somewhat aimless mobs, which received very little support. 'Our little riots here are mere nothings', the Queen wrote to Leopold on March 11th, 'and the feeling here is good ... but what an extraordinary state of things everywhere! *Je ne sais plus où je suis*, and I could almost fancy we have gone back into the last century. But I also feel that one must not be nervous or alarmed at these moments, but be of good cheer and muster up courage to meet all the difficulties'.

The Glasgow riots, beginning on March 5th, were much more serious, but were short-lived, and firmly met by special constables and the military. Other disturbances in Edinburgh, Newcastle and Manchester were swiftly and easily dealt with. 'I believe', Peel wrote to Stockmar, 'that the times are in our favour, that is, in favour of the course of constitutional freedom under the aegis of Monarchy'.

There were real fears, however, about what would happen when the Chartists carried out their intention of marching a vast procession from Kennington Common to Parliament on April 10th with

their monster national petition. It was an immensely difficult period
for the Royal couple. On March 18th Queen Victoria gave birth to her
sixth child, Princess Louise – named after Albert's mother – and it was
a particularly difficult and painful confinement. On top of these
strains there were now the fears about the situation in London, and
which naturally caused both considerable concern. 'I never was
calmer and quieter and less nervous', the Queen wrote to Leopold on
April 4th, with rather more bravado than veracity. '*Great* events make
one quiet and calm; it is only trifles that irritate my nerves'.

In fact, both were genuinely – and understandably – concerned
about their safety, and it was decided that the Royal Family should
leave London for Osborne. They left Waterloo station on April 8th,
and arrived at 'our dear Osborne' that afternoon.

In the event, this reasonable precaution turned out to be
unnecessary. The Duke of Wellington took charge, and massive troop
and artillery forces were introduced into London, kept well out of
sight, but readily available. There was a heavy enrolment of special
constables, but the Chartist crowd was hardly much more than
20,000, and the petition was conveyed to Westminster in three cabs
amid widespread derision and relief. Furthermore, the petition itself
proved to contain a large number of false names, not excluding those
of the Queen, the Duke of Wellington, Sir Robert Peel, 'and others of
equally Chartist proclivities'.

A telegram was sent to the Queen by the Government informing her
of the peaceful resolution of the threat. 'Thank God!', she wrote; 'the
Chartist meeting & Procession has turned out a complete failure; the
loyalty of the people at large has been very striking & their indignation
at their peace being interfered with by such worthless and wanton
men – immense'. 'What a glorious day was yesterday for England!'
Albert wrote to Phipps. 'How mightily will this tell all over the world!'
Greville recorded that 'In the midst of the roar of the revolutionary
waters that are deluging the whole earth, it is good to see how we stand
erect and unscathed. It is the first tribute that has ever been paid to our
Constitution, the greatest that has ever been applied to it'.

Prince Albert wrote to Stockmar on the 11th: 'We had our
revolution yesterday and it ended in smoke. London turned out some
hundreds of special constables; the troops were kept out of sight, to
prevent the possibility of a collision, and the law has remained
triumphant. I hope this will read with advantage on the Continent.
Ireland still looks dangerous'.

Ireland did indeed 'still look dangerous'. The conditions there were
now unspeakable, and the exodus of wretched and near-starving

Irish to England and Scotland brought to the country thousands of understandably embittered and desperate people. It was not surprising that Young Ireland should endorse revolution and the use of arms. *The United Irishman*, edited by John Mitchel, spoke in language that has become only too grimly familiar to the present day:

> Let the man amongst you who has no gun, sell his garment to buy one. Every street is an excellent shooting-gallery for disciplined troops; but it is a better defile in which to take them.

A deputation went to France to seek assistance to create the Irish Republic; *United Irishman* gave detailed instructions on streetfighting and missiles for maiming horses, to which 'revolutionary citizens add always boiling water or grease, or, better, cold vitriol, if available'. The French absolutely refused to be involved, and the Government asked Parliament for additional powers to deal with Irish insurrection, which were quickly granted. Meanwhile, dissent had broken out in Ireland itself between the remaining supporters of O'Connell and Mitchel and his allies, to the point where the latter had to seek police protection. Mitchel himself was sentenced to transportation for fourteen years, to the fury of the Irish, Chartists, and Repealers in the north of England. 'We have Chartist riots every night, which result in numbers of broken heads', Prince Albert wrote grimly at Buckingham Palace on May 6th.[1] 'The organisation of these people is incredible ... if they could, by means of their organisation, throw themselves in a body upon any one point, they might be successful in a *coup-de-main*'. He was, however, optimistic that the police could handle the situation without military force, as it transpired.

But it was an ugly, menacing, and frightening period. 'Commerce is at a deadlock', he wrote to Stockmar on April 29th, 'and manufacturers depressed; numbers of citizens are out of work, and the prospects of the revenue are gloomy'. 'Albert is my constant pride and admiration', the Queen wrote to Leopold, 'and his cheerfulness and courage are my great comfort and satisfaction; but, believe me, I am often very sad'. In another letter to him at this time she wrote of her husband that 'He has that happy gift of constant cheerfulness, which is a treasure in these times.' For the christening of Princess Louise, in the Private Chapel at Buckingham Palace on May 13th, he adapted a chorale he had written some years before to the hymn 'In Life's Gay Morn.'

In the lowering and difficult political circumstances of 1848, Prince Albert resolved to reassert his deep and genuine concern for what he

[1] The Royal Family had returned from Osborne on May 2nd.

described as 'that class of our community which has most of the toil, and least of the enjoyments, of this world'. His reading, his observations, and his discussions with Ashley and other concerned public men had made him profoundly worried by the poverty, abominable housing, and malnutrition that were the dark side of Britain's rapid and dramatic economic and industrial advance. 'It is dreadful to see the sufferings at this moment' he wrote to Phipps after inspecting housing conditions in London, and in the fevered atmosphere of April 1848 he bombarded Russell with complaints and appeals. 'Surely', he wrote, 'this is not the moment for the taxpayers to economise upon the working classes!'; he was shocked by high unemployment, and the fact that the number of people receiving poor relief was over four and a half million, some one-seventh of the entire population of the United Kingdom. He told Russell that the Government was 'bound to do what it can to help the working classes over the present moment of distress'. Lord John and his colleagues did not agree.

Frustrated by Ministers, Prince Albert now looked for a convenient and appropriate public platform from which he could express his feelings, and found it in The Society for Improving the Conditions Of The Labouring Classes, of which he had been President for four years. The Society had made little real progress, but the Prince eagerly took Ashley's suggestion that he should speak at a public meeting to support the Society's aims.

Ministers, when informed of the Prince's intentions, were hostile to them, and it became quickly evident that the gulf in attitudes between Prince Albert and the Cabinet was a very substantial one. Palmerston was adept at stirring the excitement of large audiences by his audacious nationalism, but his concern for the circumstances of the people was as minimal as that of Melbourne and Russell. But the Prince had got the measure of the Prime Minister, whose timorousness over Palmerston's activities had confirmed the low opinion of his political courage that Prince Albert had formed in December 1845.

In an attempt to dissuade the Prince, Russell sent him a copy of a tract assailing the Royal Family, which the recipient regarded as further evidence for the need for him to make his position clear. 'We (the Queen and I) may possess these feelings [of sympathy and interest] and yet the mass of the people may be ignorant of it', he wrote to Russell on April 29th, 'because they have never heard it expressed to them, or seen any tangible proof of it.' 'It will be difficult', he wrote to Ashley (April 23rd) 'to find another becoming opportunity for expressing the *sincerest interest* which the Queen and myself feel for the welfare and comfort of the working classes.' 'I conceive', he wrote bleakly but emphatically to Russell, 'that one has a *Duty* to perform towards the great mass of the working classes which will not allow one's yielding to the fear for some possible inconvenience'.

Thus, in total defiance of the advice and wishes of the Queen's Ministers, Prince Albert took the chair at the public meeting of the Society on May 18th, to express his apprehensions and put forward his remedies. He did so with the full support of the Queen; Ministers, their advice and warnings ignored, were powerless.

Today, the Prince's prescription for curing the ills which he depicted with impressive clarity and a strength of feeling that impressed his large audience may appear somewhat paternalistic, and certainly the theme of 'self-help' is very strong. But there were two features that startled his audience, and which were deeply significant. First, while strongly opposing 'any dictatorial interference with labour and employment, which frightens away capital, destroys that freedom of thought and independence of action which must remain to everyone if he is to work at his own happiness, and impairs that confidence under which alone engagements for mutual benefit are possible', he argued that it was the duty of those with capital to give practical assistance to housing, loan funds, and land allotments to those who wished to advantage themselves. 'The interests of classes, too often confronted, are identical, and it is only ignorance which prevents their uniting for each other's advantage. To dispel that ignorance, to show how man can help man, notwithstanding the complicated state of civilised society, ought to be the aim of every philanthropic person; but it is more peculiarly the duty of those who, under the blessing of Divine Providence, enjoy station, wealth, and education'.

The second argument, which was particularly and carefully attuned to the mood of the increasingly prosperous but still troubled middle-class, was to point out the long-term advantages of social advances in prosperity and housing for 'their poorer brethren'. 'God has created man imperfect, and left him with many wants, as it were to stimulate each to individual exertion, and to make all feel that it is only by united exertions and combined action that these imperfections can be supplied, and these wants satisfied. This presupposes self-reliance and confidence in each other'.

The speech, which was widely reported, had a considerable impact. It appalled those magnates and entrepreneurs imbued with Melbourne's still-pervading hostility to, and terror of, the potential power of the labouring masses; it deeply troubled Ministers, who had little confidence in the desire, or the capacity, of poor people to improve their lot peaceably; but it struck a real chord in enlightened businessmen, attracted political radicals – a far from revolutionary group – and, by the strange processes that often attend certain speeches, filtered through to a largely illiterate and despairing multitude. Indeed, it was a major episode in the development of the Monarchy into a genuinely popular and, in the best sense of the word, populist element. At a time when few politicians except Peel and Ashley seemed to care particularly about the circumstances in which millions of people barely survived, it was obvious to the immediate audience and those who read the speech, or heard of it, that he was not only concerned but was absolutely sincere. And so he was. To his brother Ernest he wrote in April 1849:

> At present the democratic and social evils are forcing themselves on the people. The unequal division of property, and the dangers of poverty and envy arising therefrom, is the principal evil. Means must necessarily be found, *not for diminishing riches* (as the communists want), but to make facilities for the poor. But there is the rub. I believe this question will be first solved here, in England.

Prince Albert's role as an enthusiastic patron of the arts and music, and the friend of artists and muscians as individuals, provided him with an essential outlet for that part of his complex personality that was so full of happiness, warmth, and enjoyment of life. In political matters and on formal occasions he was immensely serious, although not as solemn or cold as was often alleged, and his early and enduring dismay at the general gloominess of English life was very significant. As his family knew, he loved colour, laughter, and happiness, and Thomas Carlyle was not the only person to be surprised to meet, instead of an earnest and dull young German, someone 'very jolly and handsome'. His own music was notably cheerful, and although he was a far better judge of art than a practitioner – in which the Queen was much superior – his jewellery designs and his architecture have a lightness and delicacy that are revealing, as was his passion for the then much despised Early Renaissance artists. Far ahead of his time, he realised that the era of the private patron was over, and must eventually be replaced by the State.

In reality, a modest start had been made, following a Report by a Select Committee of the House of Commons in 1836 lamenting that 'the arts have received very little encouragement in this country. The want of instruction in design among our industrious population; the absence of public and freely-opened galleries containing approved specimens of art; the fact that only recently a National Gallery has even been commenced among us, have all combined strongly to impress this conviction on the minds of the members of the Committee.' From this there grew the School of Design in London – the direct progenitor of the Royal College of Art – and the establishment of seventeen local Schools of Design in the principal manufacturing towns. But it was a very modest beginning.

Prince Albert had become quickly and actively involved in encouraging such enterprises, but his predicament was that his net income of £29,000 was largely absorbed in family and estate expenses, and he was as a result unable to contribute personally as much as he wished to personal financial support for the arts. As he pointed out in a lengthy and detailed memorandum to Russell on December 30th 1849 his personal establishment cost £14,000 to maintain, the Queen was worse off than George IV and William IV, and he could not to be the 'protector & Patron of Literature, Science & Art'. Russell was adamant that any proposals for increased grants would be 'very unadvisable', and the matter had to be dropped. It was a poor response to a man who had consistently lived within his income, had managed the Queen's affairs with frugality and skill and refused to depend on her 'in money matters'. Russell saw the possibility of Revolution if the Royal grants were increased, and dwelt heavily on the awful precedents of the events of 1848. Prince Albert accepted the Prime Minister's view, while making the point that he considered himself to have been 'crippled in my means of usefulness to the Country & the Throne', and that if the nation wanted a Royal Family it 'will have to provide for them'.

He believed passionately that the glories of art and music should be opened to the public, and took his own lead in making the royal collections available to serious students, and in 1848 the pictures he had taken as security for a loan from Prince Oettingen-Wallerstein were made the principal part of an exhibition at Kensington Palace which was open to the public. He had attempted to interest the National Gallery in this collection, but without success; after his death, at his bequest, twenty-two were given to the Gallery. His endeavours to revive English frescoes may have been unsuccessful, but over a half a million people had visited the Westminster Hall exhibition in two months, and he was personally responsible for ensuring that 'The famous Obelisk called "Cleopatra's Needle"' was brought from Egypt to London and erected on the Embankment. He was a highly active, and enlightened, President of the Royal Society of Arts, and bought wisely for the Royal collections.

It should be remembered that all this took place simultaneously with his political responsibilities, which he regarded as the first call on his time and energies, the management of the Royal estates and the designing of Osborne, and then Balmoral, and the responsibilities as a husband and father, which he took with immense seriousness, although with great happiness.

He urged upon Ministers that Gaelic should be taught in the Highland Schools and the Welsh language in Wales, in which not successful endeavours he had the strong support of the Queen. He was insisting that Cambridge undergraduates should be compelled to attend – and answer in examination for this attendance – lectures on subjects outside their specialities. He continued to give every assistance he could to the revival of music, and to increasing its popularity. But he also found time to write a loving, funny, letter to his wife from Lincoln which ended: 'Last but not least (as they say in the after-dinner-speeches phrase) that he loves his wife, and remains Your Faithful Husband'.

When Anson died suddenly in September 1849 Lady Lyttelton recorded that 'The Prince and Queen in floods of tears, and quite shut up . . . The Prince's face is still so sad and pale and grave, I can't forget it'. Prince Albert was an intense, passionate, and highly sensitive man, with great capacity for love, gratitude, and loyalty, and also for those descents into grief and melancholy that also emphasised the acuteness of his feelings. He was realistic, calculating, and shrewd, and this was the aspect that was most often seen. The real man was gentle and vulnerable, affectionate and kind. He hated crisis, strains, and unhappiness, although these were too often his fate to endure. He seemed to triumph easily over them, but the attrition on a tense and febrile personality was severe.

At this point, almost – although not entirely – by chance he embarked upon a venture of exceptional difficulty.

The idea of establishing something on the lines of the Frankfurt Fairs, which he had so enjoyed as a child, had been with him for some time when Henry Cole, the assistant Keeper of the Public Records, returned in June 1849 enthused by the Paris *Exposition* he had just attended.

Cole was one of Albert's most notable discoveries in England, a man who fully shared his enthusiams for the arts, architecture, industrial design, and music, wrote excellent and popular children's books, published the first Christmas card, was dynamic and efficient, and had the precious quality of imagination. Officially the Assistant Keeper of the Public Records, he had helped to launch the

Penny Post, campaigned – again successfully – for the standard gauge railway track, was to be in charge of the South Kensington Museum for twenty years, and was eventually to be responsible for the Royal College of Music and the Albert Hall. He and Prince Albert constituted a most formidable combination of youth, ability, and capacity for work. Cole joined the Society of Arts in 1846, and the two worked together to create a series of exhibitions of manufactures, with particular emphasis on design. The first was held in 1847 – when the Society received its Royal Charter – and it and its successors were immediately successful, the number of visitors rising from 20,000 in 1847 to over 100,000 in 1849. The idea grew – and it is not clear whether it was the Prince's or Cole's – to hold a great National Quinquennial Exhibition in 1851, modelled on the successful French *Exposition* in Paris.

But when Cole returned, fired with enthusiasm for a similar enterprise in London, the key decision was taken at once by Prince Albert that it should be international, thus making it a substantially more ambitious and quite different venture to the French *Exposition*, and at the outset he decided that half the available space should be allocated to foreign exhibitors.

After the Exhibition had proved a brilliant success, claims were made – and are still repeated – that the real originator was Cole. His own account, and the letters in the Royal Archives, make it clear that Cole envisaged an English version of the French *Exposition*, although he was definitely interested in the possibility of making it international in scope. It was Prince Albert who, in Cole's words, 'reflected for a minute, and then said, "It must embrace foreign productions", to use his words, and added emphatically, "International, certainly"'. It was then Albert who devised its title – 'The Great Exhibition of the Works of Industry of all Nations in 1851'. Cole's contribution was to be invaluable, but the idea of the first international exhibition was that of Prince Albert, and it was not Cole, but the Prince's detractors, who have tried to prove otherwise.

The next stage was to discover what, if any, interest there was in British industry for such a project, and Cole and Scott Russell – the Society's secretary – were sent on tour, armed with a personal letter of authorisation from Albert, charging them 'to travel through the manufacturing districts of the Country, in order to collect the opinions of the leading manufacturers' concerning 'a great Exhibition of Industry of all Nations to be held in London in the year 1851'. Cole had wanted to move even faster than this, and on July 16th urged upon the Prince the immediate appointment of a special Commission to act as guarantor of sums raised by the Society, and for a deputation to see the Prime Minister for this purpose. Albert was already becoming concerned that the Society did not have the capacity to handle a project of such a scale as he envisaged. 'The undertaking appears to HRH to be one of immense magnitude and of very great national importance', Phipps wrote to Cole on the 17th: ' – it is a question so large that the Govt. would not in HRH's opinion be justified in committing themselves upon it without mature consideration in the Cabinet'. He added that Prince Albert considered that any dealings with Ministers must be done by him, as President of the Society.

There were also disagreements about Cole's wish to hold large public meetings to build up popular interest, but other counsels from Windsor prevailed, it being pointed out to Cole that London was full of 'Orators who object to everything, and would sacrifice any Undertaking to the pleasure of making a smart speech'.

Cole returned from his tour with ardour undimmed, and with reports of considerable enthusiasm, interest, and solid pledges of support. '5,000 influential persons' agreed to act as promoters.

The sheer magnitude of the undertaking was sufficient to persuade the Royal Society that it could not possibly cope with it, and Prince Albert formally invited the Government to appoint a Royal Commission; this was agreed to, as were all his proposals for its membership, including the fact that he was to be its President. He brought together a most remarkable group, including Ministers and the Prime Minister himself, other Members of Parliament, most notably Gladstone and Cobden, nine Fellows of the Royal Society, the Presidents of the Institute of Civil Engineering and of the Geological Society, and Charles Barry, the architect of the Palace of Westminster. The Commission was established on January 3rd 1850. Cole was an immensely active, prominent, and crucial member of the Executive Committee.

Hard though the Commission and its committees worked, the main burdens fell upon Prince Albert. He accepted them willingly, to the point that, for the first time in their marriage, Queen Victoria became worried about his health. This was not to be wondered at. His work on the Exhibition, which was arduous enough, had to be conducted simultaneously with his official and political concerns, which were especially intense and complex. Thus, on top of these, and family matters which included the building of Balmoral and the continuous task of administering the Royal estates, he was undertaking the first international Exhibition. He had barely more than a year to stage what Cole was later to describe as without precedent 'in its promotion of human industry', but which was also to be 'a festival' of internationalism and peace, and on which everything depended, in Albert's words, upon 'peace, love, and ready assistance, not only between individuals, but between the nations of the earth'.

Between the vision and the reality, and all to be done so quickly, lay practical problems that were awesome and intimidating. It is difficult to avoid the conclusion that these had been very seriously underestimated by everyone, including Prince Albert. The question of the site was quickly resolved; the Prince proposed Leicester Square, but Cole pointed out that this would be too small, and suggested Hyde Park, which Albert accepted at once. The Queen and the Commissioners agreed, but hostility grew rapidly in Parliament, fuelled by Albert's old foe Colonel Sibthorp, and by *The Times*. Brougham was another violent critic in public, although in private he wrote to Charles Grey to say that although he was 'a Hyde Park Heretick' he was not opposed to the Exhibition 'whereof I am a sincere well wisher – but only to the place – & perhaps in that I have a selfish feeling, for I doubt if London will be *habitable*'. The opponents loudly claimed that trees were to be cut down,[1] the Park defiled, vagrants, thieves, pickpockets, and prostitutes would abound; the noise would be unbearable, foreigners of very dubious character would create their own forms of unpleasantness – and for what purpose?

While the Commissioners and their committees were coping with problems such as the prizes – no money, but special medallions was the decision – and the juries to award them, the bodies that would make the selections of the exhibits, the hours of opening and entrance prices, whether refreshments should be available (no alcohol), and how the foreign entries should be judged, the Building Committee came close to wrecking the entire venture when it produced its design for the Exhibition Building, a turgid, huge, and obviously immensely solid and permanent edifice of brick and mortar, involving the use of nineteen million bricks. It was reproduced in the *Illustrated London News* on June 22nd 1850, and the storm broke.

The Times excoriated not only the design but the entire concept. Hyde Park was to 'be turned into something between Wolverhampton and Greenwich Fair', the whole thing was 'insanity'. Sibthorp was in top form, denouncing the Exhibition as 'the greatest trash, the greatest fraud, and the greatest imposition ever attempted

[1] I am indebted to Mr. Reginald Pound for giving prominence to these lines from *Punch*:

Albert! Spare those trees,
Mind where you fix your show;
For mercy's sake, don't please,
Go spoiling Rotten Row.

to be palmed upon the people of this country. The object of its promoters is to introduce amongst us foreign stuff of every description – live and dead stock – without regard to quantity or quality. It is meant to bring down prices in this Country, and to pave the way for the establishment of the cheap and nasty trash and trumpery system'. There is a strong temptation to quote more of Colonel Sibthorp's magnificent and absurd demagogery, richly enjoyed by the House of Commons and *The Times*, but not at all by Prince Albert, who resented it intensely.

So serious was the uproar that Albert seriously believed that the entire project would have to be abandoned, but a well-whipped Commons gave it their support, although opposition to the Committee's monstrosity did not diminish. When it is examined, this is not surprising.

At this point, Providence intervened in the form of Joseph Paxton, whose glittering Chatsworth Conservatory the Queen and the Prince had so much admired in 1843, and who had just completed the special Lily House at Chatsworth, also created out of iron and glass. Paxton was fortuitously in London for a trial session of the new House of Commons and its acoustics – which were terrible, and required major alterations which Barry would not accept – and, as he said later was 'afraid they would also commit a blunder in the building for the Industrial Building ... I had a notion in my head'. He found that the Executive Committee were prepared to accept another design; what started as 'a notion' became a rough sketch on his blotting paper while he was doodling during a railway board meeting at Derby, and after nine days and nights of intense activity with his very small staff he returned to London with his amazing plan, which was in essence a vastly enlarged version of the Lily House. It also had the outstanding merit of being easily put up and subsequently dismantled, thereby obviating the principal objection to the virtually permanent proposal of the Committee. But it was the concept itself that was so marvellous, the perfect combination of lightness, strength, and visual excitement that made it an immediate, and enduring, classic of modern architecture.

Paxton's design was so revolutionary and extraordinary that the luckless Committee, battered by the intense hostility and abuse aroused by their design, was in a turmoil of indecision. But Paxton proceeded to publish his plans in the *Illustrated London News* on July 6th, and there was immense and immediate enthusiasm for a magical concept that *Punch* described as 'The Crystal Palace'. Ruskin mocked it as a 'cucumber frame between two chimneys', but his was a very exceptional voice. Prince Albert at once recognised it as the masterpiece that it was, and his opinion was shared by most contemporaries and is endorsed to this day. 'Paxton's design', an eminent modern architect of conspicuous skill and sensitivity has said, 'has stalked the imagination of all architects, engineers and designers of any real ability from that day to this. It was *the* most advanced and wonderful building of the nineteenth century'. On July 15th Paxton's superb design was accepted, with the proviso – with Colonel Sibthorp very much in mind – that three giant elms should be roofed in; to meet this, Paxton produced the great vaulted transept which was the only significant change to his original design, the tender of the builders was accepted by the end of July, and the first foundations were laid in August. It subsequently rose with astonishing speed.

Paxton's glorious design was exactly what Prince Albert had wanted – 'truly a piece of marvellous art', he described it to Ernest. It was in itself a marvel of construction, using pre-fabricated mass-produced parts, covering sixteen acres with iron and glass, its length over three times that of St. Paul's Cathedral, with 293,655 panes of glass, over 4,500 tons of iron, and twenty-four miles of guttering. Paxton was not an easy man to deal with, and there was at least one sharp dispute between him and the Commissioners that so infuriated Albert that Paxton had to make a quick and handsome apology, but his achievement was phenomenal, and certainly merited his subsequent knighthood. The fact that he, a gardener's son, was neither a qualified engineer nor architect aroused vehement comment in the members of those professions, who publicly anticipated disaster for the bucolic amateur's creation, even the Astronomer Royal giving his view that it would assuredly fall down. Colonel Sibthorp publicly desired that it might be 'dashed to pieces', and railed against it as 'a piece of low, dirty, cunning ... a humbug from beginning to end'. He called upon the Almighty to destroy it. He had spirit. Even when the Exhibition was a manifest success, Colonel Sibthorp did not relent in his abuse, saying on July 29th 1851 that its results were 'the desecration of the Sabbath, the demoralisation of the people, a disunion of parties, and increasing poverty to a most serious extent'.

These forecasts of doom, added to the warnings of the arrival of what Brougham called 'Socialists and men of the Red Colour', so alarmed the King of Prussia that he was anxious that his son and heir and his wife should not attend. To these fears, Albert replied robustly:

Mathematicians have calculated that the Crystal Palace will blow down in the first strong gale, Engineers that the galleries would crash in and destroy the visitors; Political Economists

have prophesied a scarcity of food in London owing to the vast
concourse of people; Doctors that owing to so many races
coming into contact with each other the Black Death of the
Middle Ages would make its appearance as it did after the
Crusades; Moralists that England would be infected by all the
scourges of the civilised and uncivilised world; Theologians that
this second Tower of Babel would draw upon it the vengeance of
an offended God.

   I can give no guarantee against these perils, nor am I in a
position to assume responsibility for the possibly menaced lives
of your Royal relatives.

In spite – or, more probably, because – of this engagingly sardonic
account of the perils, the King gave his permission.
   Then, there was the fear that Roman Catholics would exploit the
occasion, neatly countered by Prince Albert who pointed out that the
Belgians had been prevented from sending a wax Pope and twelve
Cardinals (including Wiseman) for their stand. The Archbishop of
Dublin sent plans for a Universal Coinage, and the Liverpool Peace
Society wished to be involved; both were courteously rejected.
   The great building rose, with remarkably few difficulties, and was
completed by the end of March 1851, by which time it was the topic
of widespread praise and admiration, Colonel Sibthorp and the
angry professionals had lost their audience. But it had been an
alarmingly adventitious salvation. The exhibits – apart from the
Koh-i-Noor diamond – have virtually all been forgotten today; the
Crystal Palace has not.
   The Queen wrote in her Journal on February 18th 1851:

   After breakfast we drove with the 5 children to look at the
   Crystal Palace, which was not finished when we last went, and
   really now is one of the wonders of the world, which we English
   may indeed be proud of... The galleries are finished, and from
   the top of them the effect is quite wonderful. The sun shining in
   through the transept gave a fairy-like appearance. The building
   is so light and graceful, in spite of its immense size. Many of the
   exhibits have arrived. We were again cheered loudly by the
   2,000 workmen as we came away. It made me feel proud and
   happy.

Paxton had provided exactly what Prince Albert wanted – a
superlative mixture of colour, modern technology, glamour, grace,
and drama. The exhibits provided their own problems. They were
divided into six main parts – raw materials, machinery, textiles,
metallic vitreous and ceramic manufactures, miscellaneous, and

Fine Arts – with thirty classes within these main categories, each encompassing a dizzying range of products. The tests for the juries awarding prizes had to be carefully specified, with the overriding consideration 'to reward excellence in whatever form it is presented'. The selection, transportation and arrangement of over 100,000 exhibits constituted a major logistical problem. Indeed, the establishment of the Great Exhibition from Cole's discussion with Albert in June 1849 to its realisation on May 1st 1851 was the story of the surmounting of problems that most sensible people considered insurmountable. There were problems with the British and Foreign Bible Society, which applied late; there was The Great Wig Dispute, which particularly amused the Queen, when a wigmaker who had wanted to be in Fine Arts found himself, to his fury, in Animal Products; there were complaints about the expensive refreshments, and what one visitor described as 'the worst and smallest sandwiches I ever tasted'; another wrote to the *Morning Chronicle* about the absence of ale, and another about the fact that 'the young females at the refreshment tables ... would be greatly improved by a moderate use of soap'; there was much controversy over a statue of Bacchante in the French Section, 'rolling in a state of drunken excitement on a bed of vine leaves and grapes', which the jury considered evidence that the sculptor (Clesinger) had 'allowed his imagination to be perverted and degraded to the service of a low sensuality', but accepted and, on artistic grounds alone, praised. The annals of the Great Exhibition are not devoid of interest.

The result was magnificent, and enthralling. It was a wonderful achievement, but when Cobden said that no one 'has done one half the labours' as Prince Albert, it was only too true. For his part, the Prince praised others, especially Cole: 'You have been one of the few who originated the design, became its exponent to the public, and fought its battles in adversity, and belong now to those who share in its triumphs', he wrote to his friend and collaborator. Cole was later to write of Prince Albert as 'of pre-eminent wisdom, of philosophic mind, sagacity, *with power of generalship*'.

It would be possible, reading Albert's papers on the Exhibition, to take the view that he was over-obsessed with details, but the fact was that the details, however tedious, were crucial if the great concept itself was to succeed. That it did succeed owed everything to his leadership and application. At the age of 32 he had created the greatest popular spectacle and occasion in the history of the modern Royal Family. But the cost, in terms of personal anguish, concentration, hours of work, strain, and patience in a normally impatient personality was very considerable. Also, this immense burden had to be borne in a series of major political crises. 'All day some question

or other or some difficulty', Queen Victoria wrote in her Journal, 'all
of which my beloved takes with the greatest quiet and good temper'.
She wrote to Stockmar on January 25th 1851 that 'The Prince's sleep
is again as bad as ever, and he looks very ill of an evening'. But his
calmness was only superficial. To 'Grandmother Coburg' he wrote
on April 15th – two weeks before the opening:

> Just at present I am more dead than alive from overwork. The
> opponents of the Exhibition work with might and main to throw
> all the old women into panic and drive myself crazy. The
> strangers, they give out, are certain to commence a thorough
> revolution here, to murder Victoria and myself, and to proclaim
> the Red Republic in England; the plague is certain to ensue
> from the confluence of such vast multitudes, and to swallow up
> those whom the increased price of everything has not already
> swept away. For all this I am to be responsible, and against all
> this I have to make efficient provision'.

This was not a patient, or even whimsical, letter, but a bitter one.
There were to be more problems. On April 29th, two days before the
Official opening, he recorded: 'Terrible difficulties with the arrange-
ments for the opening'.

These 'terrible difficulties' had significant political consequences.
The Commissioners, led by Prince Albert, had decided that the
Doyen of the Diplomatic Corps should present a joint congratulatory statement on behalf of them all, which the Doyen had been
pleased to arrange. All seemed settled, but then the Russian Ambassador, Baron Brunnow, claimed that this was highly improper, and
that no individual had the right to speak for the representatives of
other nations, and canvassed successfully for support among his
colleagues. Prince Albert was intensely angry at this apparent snub
to him, as President of the Commission, and to the Queen of
England. Russell agreed with him that 'they are making great fools
of themselves' (Albert to Russell, April 24th) and the Prime Minister
blamed Lord Granville for mishandling the matter.
    The real and serious problem was that it was Palmerston, not
Granville, who was responsible, as he supported Brunnow. 'It
appeared to me to be inconvenient and objectionable to invest the
Foreign Ministers with a Corporate Character', Palmerston breezily
wrote to Russell on the 24th; he recommended that the suggestion
'should be dropped', and that the Diplomatic Corps should be
invited to attend the opening 'as *Spectators* and not as *Actors*'. To make
matters even worse, so far as his relations with Prince Albert were

concerned, both he and Granville then left London, '& one so pressed for time', as Albert wrote on the 26th. He wrote with some anger to Russell:

> ... Ld Palmerston is quite right in calling the proceeding unusual & unprecedented in this Country, but so is the occasion for it. It is not a purely English ceremony for an English object, but an international one, in which *all Nations* have taken an *active Part*: half the Building is in charge of foreign Authorities, half the Collection the property of foreign Countries, half the Juries are appointed by foreign Govts who have also defrayed the expenses of the foreign Part of the Exhibition. It would have been wrong, in my opinion, not to have given the Representatives of these foreign Nations the opportunity of taking an active part also in the opening Ceremony.

Parts of this letter have been quoted in previous accounts[1]; what has not been made clear is that it was written within five days of the opening.

Palmerston, although warned by Russell of the Prince's strong feelings, wrote to him somewhat casually on April 26th to say that he entirely agreed with Brunnow, and enclosed his letter, to which the Prince replied with tartness that 'Baron Brunnow's letter is entirely arguing upon the principles of the Etiquette of the English Court, which is not in the Russian Minister's keeping & therefore cannot properly form a ground of objection on *his* part'. But he unhappily accepted that the proposal must be definitely dropped, and the Diplomatic Corps be given a decorative and mute role in the proceedings. The episode did nothing to improve his already low opinion of Palmerston, who may have been technically in the right but who had dealt with the matter not only incompetently and rudely but with no apparent recognition that it mattered so much to the Queen and her husband. But this was not the first example of Palmerston's lack of interest in the project. On July 2nd 1850 Albert had written to Russell that 'I hope you will ask Ld Palmerston to say a few words in debate on the communications with Foreign Governments, & the disappointment they would justly feel at the overthrow of the Exhibition at the 11th hour', but Palmerston had not done so. The fiasco of the *Corps Diplomatique* marked another important point in the deterioration of Prince Albert's opinion of the Foreign Secretary, especially as it did not involve sincere differences of opinion on politics or the conduct of foreign policy, but on a matter of deep

[1] First in Martin, ii, 360, undated and not in full.

personal importance to himself and the Queen. Subsequent letters
from Palmerston of congratulation when the Exhibition was an
obvious success did nothing to improve matters.

Of equal – if not greater – importance was that Queen Victoria
was deeply mortified, as her personal appeal to the Corps – with
the barbed comment that 'Her Majesty is not able to compel the
Diplomatic Corps to accept a courtesy' – was rejected by Brunnow
and not supported by Palmerston. The biographer and historian,
confronted with new and largely unpublished material, must
always be cautious about its significance, simply because it *is* new.
But there is no question in my judgement that this was an important episode in the relations between Prince Albert and Palmerston.

Meanwhile, other problems haunted the final preparations. The
Austrians, Prussians, French and Russians became frantic about
possible assassinations, and there were many meetings about
security; then, only a week before the opening Russell wrote to
Albert expressing alarm that the firing of celebratory guns in Hyde
Park might shatter some of the windows and create panic, and they
had to be hurriedly moved to St. James's Park; the unexpected
problem of the sparrows in the great elms was, allegedly, mag-
nificently resolved by Wellington's simple remedy, 'Sparrowhawks,
Ma'am', but then tremendous uproar greeted the announcement
that the Queen would open the Exhibition in private, with only
officials and specially invited guests present.

The tumult in the newspapers – by now almost wholly ardent
supporters of the Palace and the Exhibition – was one thing. What
impressed the Prince was the formidable number of letters he
received from people he respected – Cole, Lyon Playfair, and
Granville among them – urging a change of policy. The Prime
Minister's concern, understandably, was the security of the Queen
and of the increasingly agitated foreign dignitaries, who were very
much in favour of as much privacy as possible, but on April 19th he
recommended to Prince Albert that only the possessors of season
tickets to the Exhibition, which had been on sale for some time at
three guineas for men and two guineas for women, and which had
had a limited popularity, would be admitted; the result was a
spectacular demand for the tickets, whose sale soared in ten days to
over 25,000. The nervous foreigners could only reflect – as they
glumly did – on the fact that their security fears had not been
allayed at all, but the decision had been made.

Up to the opening day there were many and complex problems

to be resolved, bruised feelings to be coped with, personality clashes to be dealt with; by the end of April Prince Albert was intellectually and physically totally exhausted, 'fagged out' in Queen Victoria's words. The actual opening itself on May 1st, which was of un-restrained joy to almost everyone else, was to him the culmination of months of worry, immense hard work, nervous strain, and apprehension. While everyone was ecstatic, his tired comment to Cole was simply, 'Quite satisfactory'. It was only later that he could relax, as he realised that it had been, after all, a triumph.

But although the public was enthralled, and was to flock to the Palace in numbers – over six million – that far exceeded expectations and left the Commissioners with a healthy profit of £186,000 even after reducing the entrance prices, Lady Lyttelton was writing that 'I believe it is quite universally sneered at and abominated by the *beau monde*, and will only increase the contempt for the Prince among all fine folk. But so would anything he does'. Wellington was sceptical of its value, although not its popular success, and Brougham was writing with some savagery that 'Prince Albert will be hated as much as ever prince was for this *Exposition* and the consequent invasion of the Park. A man in his very peculiar position should have the sense to know that repose and inaction is his only security against ridicule. But he must needs be disliked as well as laughed at'.

But, once again, the *beau monde* was proved wrong.

The opening, on May 1st, was described by Queen Victoria as 'one of the greatest and most glorious days of our lives, with which to my pride and joy the name of my dearly beloved Albert is for ever associated!' She described it to Lady Lyttelton as 'that *great & glorious 1st of May* – the proudest & happiest day of, as you truly call it, my "happy life"'. It was a day of triumph and sunshine, enormous and enthusiastic crowds, the first appearance of Royalty on Albert's balcony at Buckingham Palace, the evident discomfiture of the Diplomatic Corps, described with satisfaction by the Doyen as 'mute as fish [and] ... thoroughly ashamed of what they had done', and the odd appearance at the opening ceremony of a dignified Chinese, who made a very public and much-noticed obeisance to the Queen, but turned out to have no official status at all. According to Cole, 'he was a sea captain who brought his junk into the Thames for exhibition, and got a great deal of money'.

Two days later, with the Exhibition drawing over 60,000 visitors a day, Albert was the guest of honour at the Royal Academy dinner, where he received an ovation that greatly moved him, and gave him the opportunity of praising its new President, Eastlake, and denouncing excessive criticism of artists. On June 17th he undertook a more difficult assignment when he spoke at the 150th anniversary of the Society for Propagating the Gospel in Foreign Parts, and was able to move carefully across the current commotions concerning Tractarianism and anti-Papism. At the beginning of July he attended the meeting of the British Association at Ipswich, where he was much acclaimed, and then back to the work of the Exhibition Commissioners, which could now look with satisfaction, and some surprise, at the great commercial success they had already achieved. The City of London then gave the Queen and Prince a triumphal dinner at the Guildhall, and Queen Victoria recorded to Russell 'how enthusiastically we were received by an almost *fearful* mass of people in the streets; the greatest order prevailed, and the greatest and most gratifying enthusiasm', and Albert spoke at the Royal Agricultural Society at Windsor when he applauded increased mechanisation – which had been one of the principal features of the Exhibition, which he and Victoria had visited repeatedly. 'We go out of town tomorrow', she wrote to Stockmar on July 19th, 'and, though it is a great relief to us, still it pains me that this brilliant, and for ever memorable season should be past'.,

The Prince was invited by the French Government to a special celebration in Paris, but refused. He reacted strongly against a proposal to raise a statue to him to commemorate the Exhibition, and froze at its outset a well-intentioned attempt for a national subscription, limited to one guinea each donor, in his honour. The problem of what to do with the Crystal Palace and some of its exhibits had to be dealt with, and how the unexpected surplus should be used. At the Prince's insistence, the latter was used to begin his ambition of a huge scientific and technological complex in South Kensington by the Commissioners acquiring the site. His desire was that 'the Great Exhibition of 1851 should not become a transitory event but that its objects would be perpetuated.'

Cole became deeply involved in this project which, like the Exhibition itself, caused immense difficulties and frustrations. In 1852 Cole became General Superintendent of the School of Design, whose collection, now augmented with substantial additions from the Great Exhibition, was housed in conditions of considerable chaos at Somerset House. Prince Albert offered the loan of Marlborough House to accommodate 'the Museum of Manufactures' until the Prince of Wales reached his eighteenth birthday, when Marlborough House would become his official London residence. The offer was gratefully accepted, and Cole began his work of creating the internationally famous collection that was to become the Victoria and Albert Museum. In the process, there were many difficulties and controversies, but Cole – with the Prince's strong support and encouragement – persevered, and between 1856 and 1861 the first permanent buildings arose. But Prince Albert's dream was far from being fulfilled in his lifetime.

Perhaps the most lasting and significant results of the Great Exhibition were the new scholarships that were endowed, and the new and exciting encouragement to scientists, scholars, and designers. The great Palace, the South Kensington complex, and the special model dwellings, in which the Prince took a particular interest[1] were among the most important tangible results. But it is difficult to escape the conclusion that the most important aspect of all was the vision that had inspired 'The Great Exhibition of the Works of Industry of All Nations, 1851' – that it be truly international, and that it be for the enjoyment as well as the edification of the people. Wellington may have been right in being cautiously sceptical of its long-term importance, and while Roger Fulford is right to call it 'a festival of peace – a proof of international friendship' which proved to have little effect on international amity, its history is crucial in any understanding of Prince Albert's personality, application, internationalism, and vision. In contemporary importance, his popularity, in spite of the sneers of the Upper Ten Thousand, rose to an unprecedented height. He was swiftly to learn again the fickleness of that mood, but when crisis came this triumph was remembered.

Whatever reservations remained about the Exhibition, there were none concerning the Crystal Palace itself, later described with truth as 'an architectural triumph so overwhelming as to entitle the Palace to a place among the great epoch-inaugurating buildings of history'.[2] Paxton proposed that it remain where it was, as a permanent garden under glass, with tropical plants and birds – a kind of gigantic conservatory. In spite of public criticism, the Commissioners decided to sell it to a commercial company, which re-erected it at Sydenham, with some alterations. It became, Lady Eastlake wrote in 1854, 'a paradise of flowers and works of art'. It is one of the major tragedies of modern architecture that it was totally destroyed by fire in 1936, but the impact of Paxton's genius has survived its destruction.

· · ·

[1] These were designed by Henry Roberts as 'A Model Lodging House' and were originally built on the Cavalry Barracks, at the request of Prince Albert and with the permission and approval of Wellington, so as to be close to the Exhibition but not on what *Punch* described as 'Hyde Park's hallowed ground'. After the Exhibition they were re-erected at Kennington.

[2] John Steegman: *Consort of Taste*, p. 228.

It had been a gruelling year, but when Prince Albert reached Osborne at the end of July he plunged into more work and reading, and Queen Victoria wrote to Stockmar on August 17th, in a letter full of love and admiration for her husband – 'I must always stand amazed at his wonderful mind. Such large views of everything, and such extreme lucidity in working all these views out. He is very, very great'. 'He is,' she added, 'as usual, full of occupation'. Stockmar had detected the signs of extreme exhaustion in Albert, and urged rest. Prince Albert assured him that he had resolved 'to retreat into my shell as quickly as possible'. The fact was that it was not possible. Other crises were upon him, and the glory and happiness of the triumph of the Great Exhibition were to be of brief duration.

SEVEN

THE UNBLESSED PEACEMAKER

The creation, and eventual fulfillment, of the Great Exhibition had been achieved in the midst of domestic political crises and seriously deteriorating relations between Prince Albert and Palmerston. The Prince had had to move rapidly from the complex problems of the Exhibition to advising the Queen on how to handle an explosive religious crisis that arose at the end of 1850 when the Pope issued a Brief re-establishing the hierarchy of Roman Catholic Bishops in Britain, and the Ecclesiastical Titles Bill aroused Protestant passions which the Queen and Prince Albert deplored, but which indirectly brought down the Russell Government in February 1851; a coalition of Whigs and Peelites was attempted, but proved impossible, and Russell returned to office after a brief but fierce political crisis. So, to the deep regret of Albert, did Palmerston. 'One conviction grows stronger and stronger with the Queen and myself (if it is possible), viz. that Lord Palmerston is bringing the whole of the hatred which is borne to him – I don't mean here to investigate whether justly or unjustly – by all the Governments of Europe upon England, and that the country runs serious danger of having to pay for the consequences', was one typical letter from the Prince to Russell (May 18th 1850); ' ... for the sake of one man the welfare of the country must not be exposed'.

Accordingly, the triumph of the Exhibition afforded only limited solace in the autumn of 1851 as Prince Albert gloomily contemplated the national and international political scenes. Relations with Palmerston had so remorselessly declined since 1847, to the point that the Queen was frequently informing Russell that she 'is highly indignant at Lord Palmerston's behaviour' and seeking his removal. Palmerston's conduct in the torrid summer of 1848 had opened a wide gulf of attitude between himself and the Queen and Prince Albert. The Schleswig-Holstein dispute, which continued until 1852, was a particular source of friction and disagreement, but it was the spread of unrest to Italy that had caused the real rift.

The correspondence and memoranda on this matter are characterised by increasing alarm from the Queen and the Prince at the successes of the Italians against the Austrians and ill-concealed satisfaction by Palmerston, who then attempted to improve the internal condition of Spain, with the result that the British Ambassador was thrown out. From the Royal couple had come this unmistakeably Albertian comment:

> When the Queen considers the position that we had in Spain and what it ought to have been after the constitution of the French Republic, when we had no rival to fight and ought to have enjoyed the entire confidence and friendship of Spain, and compares this to the state into which our relations with that country have been brought, she cannot help being struck how much matters must have been mismanaged.

Russell, caught in the middle, temporised, apologised, occasionally rebuked Palmerston mildly, and hoped for happier days. But on almost every issue, important or small, Prince Albert and the Foreign Secretary were in dispute. On Italy the Queen wrote to Palmerston a letter drafted entirely by her husband, stating that 'She cannot conceal from him that she is ashamed of the policy we are pursuing in the Italian controversy, in abetting wrong, and this for the object of gaining influence in Italy'. There were frequent complaints that the Queen was not being adequately informed, that Palmerston lacked courtesy and consideration, that 'vindictiveness is one of the main features in Lord Palmerston's character', and that 'The Queen must say she is afraid that she will have no peace of mind and there will be no end of troubles as long as Lord Palmerston is at the head of the Foreign Office'. For his part, Palmerston increasingly resented this interference and the tone of the Royal letters to him and the Prime Minister. The Queen told Russell bluntly that she wanted Palmerston – now called 'Pilgerstein' by Albert – to leave the Foreign Office in as early as September 1848; the unhappy Prime Minister said that he sympathised deeply, but it could not be done. When the Austrians triumphed in Italy, and Palmerston's letters to the Queen became notably evasive, there were further protests. Palmerston's strong sympathy with the Hungarian revolution – again, not shared by the Queen and the Prince – could not prevent its overthrow, but when the Russians demanded from Turkey the refugees that had fled there, he backed the Turks not only with words but with an Anglo-French fleet to the Dardanelles. 'With a little manly firmness we shall successfully get through this matter', Palmerston wrote to Russell, and so it proved, but the venture was not approved of by Albert, who regarded it as another example of the recklessness of the Foreign Secretary. Meanwhile, exchanges continued on a consistently acrimonious level on trivial issues.[1]

The difference of attitude towards Europe by Palmerston and Albert was, as has already been emphasised, absolutely fundamental. The Prince, although himself in many respects far more liberal than the Foreign Secretary, was horrified by the prospect of widespread violent revolution and anarchy across the Continent, while Palmerston saw considerable advantage in seizing opportunities to strengthen Britain's interests and concerns. Palmerston had wanted a swift resumption of diplomatic relations with the new French Republic; he supported the Danes over Schleswig-Holstein, the Italians against the Austrians, and the Hungarians against the Russians, in total contradiction to Albert's views. His policy had a real pattern, but it contained considerable dangers. Prince Albert saw too much of the dangers, Palmerston minimised them excessively. If their personal relationship had been better, each might have realised that the other did have valid arguments. As it was, they moved from coldness to hostility and suspicion, and then – certainly on Prince Albert's side – to real and deep enmity.

Palmerston did not comprehend the traumatic effect upon Albert of the Year of Revolution in Europe. In most English eyes – and certainly in Palmerston's – the collapse of despotism and the advance of liberal reform in Europe, especially as England had remained splendidly free from such difficulties and dangers, were both to be welcomed – within certain limits. To a German Prince and a fervent European the proximity of anarchy, violence, civil wars, and the destruction of the *status quo* through bloody revolution was a nightmare. Palmerston considered the events of 1848–9 as having been, in the main, satisfactory; to the Prince, they had been deeply frightening.

There were also physical factors. The Prince was grossly overworking and unwell, and the fact that the crisis with Palmerston coincided with the intense strain involved in the preparation of the Great Exhibition was of real significance. He was oppressed with worries at home and in Europe, worked very long hours on official papers, and seemed incapable of relaxation, even at Osborne. 'It is anxiety that wears out the man', Sir James Clark wrote with concern. 'Anxiety is the waster of life'. He was only 32, yet looked far older, and the graceful figure and luxuriant hair had disappeared. Peel was the only politician of substance with whom he had a complete understanding and trust; Gladstone might well have taken

---

[1] It is an immensely large correspondence, of which a substantial proportion was used in Brian Connell's *Regina v. Palmerston* (1962).

his place in Albert's estimation, but he was not yet able to do so. He admired Aberdeen and liked the young Granville, but he saw no one in public life comparable to Peel, and never again had such a close relationship with any other politician.

Albert's temperament was not nearly as placid as most believed, and his self-control and patience were formidably tested over the birth of the Exhibition. Thus, a political relationship with Palmerston that might have been possible, despite deep differences of perception of the European situation, was at least partly destroyed by Prince Albert's chronic exhaustion and worry on other matters. He did far too much, was excessively conscientious on quite minor matters, had – apart from Phipps and Gray – no personal assistance, and never delegated any matter of substance. The loss of Anson was especially grievous, for he had lost his daily and wise confidant who had been with him from the very beginning. The Queen wrote to Leopold in February 1852 a particularly sad letter:

> Albert becomes really a *terrible* man of business; I think it takes a little off from the gentleness of his character, and makes him so preoccupied. I grieve over all this, as I *cannot* enjoy these things *much as* I interest myself in *general* European politics; but I am every day more convinced that *we women*, if we *are* to be *good* women, *feminine* and *amiable* and *domestic*, are *not fitted to reign*; at least it is *contre gré* that they drive themselves to the *work* which it entails.

Palmerston should have realised, because the signs were quite unmistakable, that the Prince was under intolerable strain, but he did not. What he saw was his own immense and rising popularity in the country, his command over the House of Commons, the apprehensions and excitement his name aroused throughout the European Powers, and the sheer enjoyment of being Foreign Secretary of a very powerful nation with a strong and feared Navy. He considered himself indispensable to the weak Russell Administration. He was not proposing to surrender his freedom of action and real power to a young Prince of so little comparable political and international experience. In short, each misunderstood and underestimated the other.

The Don Pacifico crisis in the early summer of 1850 marked another major advance towards the complete rift. The Foreign Secretary supported the claim of the Gibraltar-born Portuguese Jew, Don Pacifico, against the Greek Government for very considerable compensation for alleged losses when his house in Athens was pillaged. To the general astonishment, Palmerston ordered the Fleet from the Dardanelles to the Piraeus and blockaded Athens. Greece appealed for support from France and Russia, Palmerston insisted on full reparation for Don Pacifico, the Russian note of protest was in very strong terms, and the French Ambassador to London was abruptly recalled. For a few weeks it seemed that Europe was on the brink of war over this absurd episode, and Queen and Prince again pressed Russell hard for Palmerston's removal from the Foreign Office. When Russell suggested the Leadership of the Commons for him Albert responded that this might give Palmerston even greater political influence, and Russell's suggestion of his father-in-law, Lord Minto, as Foreign Secretary was dismissed as impossible by the Prince and the Queen.

A more unnecessary European crisis could hardly have been imagined, and the Prince wrote tartly to Russell on May 15th that 'We are not surprised, however, that Lord Palmerston's mode of doing business should not be borne by the susceptible French Government with the same good humour and forbearance as by his colleagues'. The Don Pacifico issue was viewed by him as an intolerable example of Palmerston's belligerent and irresponsible conduct of his office. He had written to Russell on April 2nd with cold anger that 'at a moment and in a conjuncture in which England ought to stand highest in the esteem of the world, and to possess the confidence of all Powers, she is generally detested, mistrusted, and treated with indignity by even the smallest Powers'.

It seemed that this time Palmerston had gone too far, even for his most fervent supporters and popularity. On June 18th, after a debate of rare quality, the Lords passed a motion that in effect condemned the Government's policy, but the Commons debate that began on June 25th was even more remarkable, in which Gladstone, Disraeli, Cobden and Peel took part. Palmerston seemed doomed – describing the debate 'as a shot fired by a foreign conspiracy, aided and abetted by a domestic intrigue' in a letter to his brother – but in an amazing speech of four and a half hours described by Gladstone as a 'gigantic intellectual and ·physical effort', he routed his critics and caused a national and international sensation with the declaration that 'as the Roman in days of old held himself free from indignity when he could say *Civis Romanus Sum*, so also a British subject, in whatever land he may be, shall feel confident that the watchful eye and the strong arm of England will protect him against injustice and wrong'.

To the deep regret of the Queen and the Prince this saved the day for Palmerston and the Whigs. 'The Queen has no more confidence in Lord P. now than she had before', Prince Albert wrote in a lengthy memorandum of which he sent a copy to Russell; 'the debate has not shown her anything that she did not know before, though it was silent on many things that she did know ... Foreign governments

distrust and foreign nations hate Lord P. now as much as before –
Lord P. himself is not likely to change his nature in his sixty-seventh
year on account of a vote, which is calculated to gratify his vanity
and self esteem'.

But worse was to follow. On June 27th the Queen was attacked
and badly bruised by one Robert Pate who hit her repeatedly with a
cane when she was leaving Cambridge House, and then came the
news that Peel had had a grievous riding accident the day after the
Don Pacifico debate, and sustained injuries from which he never
recovered.

The Queen and Prince Albert had been severely shaken by Pate's
assault, were unhappy at Palmerston's reprieve, and now had lost in
Peel a staunch supporter and friend, and one to whom they had
looked upon as certain to return to the Premiership when the
unhappy Whig interlude ended. Also, Albert had lost a valued
champion of the Exhibition, now being vehemently abused, and was
in such despair at Peel's death that he recorded on July 3rd that 'we
are on the point of having to abandon the Exhibition'. In fact, so
strong was the impact of Peel's death and his known advocacy, that
on the next day the Commons overwhelmingly defeated the Exhibition's critics and endorsed its purposes. This was some, although
little, consolation for a loss that Prince Albert felt very deeply. Peel
had been the one English politician whom he regarded as being of
real moral and intellectual stature; he felt himself beholden to him as
his 'benefactor'; and he had lost his friend and close adviser. In these
melancholy circumstances his attitude to Palmerston hardened
further.

The fundamental problem was how to remove Palmerston without giving him the opportunity to implicate the Queen in his
downfall. Prince Albert even raised with Russell in July the question
of Palmerston's morals, and his attempt to seduce one of the Queen's
ladies at Windsor several years before.[1] Russell, to whom the
episode came as no surprise, did not regard it as an acceptable
reason for dismissing the Foreign Secretary. Albert knew enough of
Palmerston to appreciate that he would not depart pacifically, and
his henchmen were already hinting broadly in Parliament and in his

[1] This had been in 1837, and the lady involved was Mrs. Brand, later Lady Dacre.
Fortunately, Stockmar was also staying in the Castle, and was able to impress
upon the enraged husband the absolute necessity of avoiding a major scandal.
The Queen was not told, but a memorandum by Anson on December 13th 1841
after a description by Stockmar of what had occurred reveals that even by then
the Queen had not been told, whereas Prince Albert had been. The Prince,
therefore, kept this information to himself for ten years before using it, in very
strong terms, as an additional reason for Palmerston's dismissal.

favoured newspapers at 'whispers of mysterious influence' and 'backstairs intrigue'. The Queen had written to Russell (the letter drafted, as usual, by her husband) that 'she cannot allow a servant of the Crown and her Minister to act contrary to her orders, and this without her knowledge'. The Don Pacifico affair had prompted Prince Albert to describe Palmerston as 'our immoral one for foreign affairs' to Ernest, adding that 'We are still more weakened by it, we and all those who advise Christian straightforwardness, peace, and love'.

For a Sovereign to summarily dismiss a Foreign Secretary would have been difficult in any event, but one riding a crest of patriotic popularity, and upon whom the Prime Minister considered himself totally dependent, was a practical political impossibility. Stockmar produced the answer. Palmerston had consistently denied information to his Sovereign on vital matters, had acted on several occasions without her knowledge, had treated her with deliberate casualness, and must now heed his ways or face legitimate dismissal as her Secretary of State. This was the genesis of the memorandum that the Queen sent to Russell from Osborne on August 12th, which related Palmerston's deficiencies and omissions, and set down the rules for the future. It was, in reality, the product of Stockmar and Albert.

Palmerston's reaction was to ask for a personal interview with Albert, which took place on the 14th. The Prince was startled that Palmerston 'was very much agitated, shook, and had tears in his eyes', but when he expressed his pain at the severe rebuke he had received he was coldly reminded of 'the innumerable complaints and remonstrances which the Queen had had to make these last years'. Sticking closely to the theme of the memorandum, Albert said that the fact that the Queen disagreed 'almost invariably' with his policies was one thing, and not insignificant; what was wholly intolerable was that she was inadequately informed. The discussion then moved to the raging conflict over Schleswig-Holstein, but did not lead to any closing of the gulf in attitudes between them. It was not a satisfactory discussion, but at least Palmerston had expressed his regrets for his treatment of the Queen, and seemed to accept the validity of the memorandum.

It was not a happy summer. In spite of the Commons vote the problems of organising the Exhibition remained incessant and heavily burdensome, there was a Royal visit to Edinburgh, where Victoria paid the first Royal visit to Holyrood since Mary, Queen of Scots, and Albert laid the foundation stone of the National Gallery. He remained dismayed by the bitter war over Schleswig-Holstein, and by the condition of Germany, which, he wrote to Stockmar on August 25th, 'appears to me to be going utterly to the deuce under the miserable policy of its rulers, and to be becoming a still readier toy for the next revolution. Are there no longer in it men of heart and head, who might avert the disaster? It is altogether too sad'. The death of Louis Philippe on the next day was a chilling reminder of the mortality of monarchies and monarchs.

But Palmerston was incorrigible. In September General Haynau, popularly depicted in sections of the English Press as the 'Butcher of Austria' and 'General Hyaena', and certainly with an evil reputation for the suppression of the Hungarian revolution, unwisely visited London and was mobbed when he was recognised at Barclay's Brewery. Indeed, having narrowly escaped to refuge in a nearby public house he was only rescued from possible lynching by the police. Palmerston seized the popular mood by a letter of formal apology to the Austrian Chargé d'Affaires that was notably insulting about Haynau, all his works, and the illiberal Empire he served. By the time the Queen and Prince read it, it had already been sent.

This was a clear breach of the August Memorandum, and for once Russell showed some spirit and demanded the recall of the Note. Palmerston threatened resignation, Russell insisted, and it was Palmerston who climbed down. Albert was accordingly once more deprived of his quarry, but again it had been Palmerston and not he who had judged the public mood correctly. As he and Victoria recognised, 'General Hyaena' was not a popular cause. Nonetheless, another major international uproar had occurred, and the Queen had been slighted again.

The Queen and the Prince could have been forgiven for believing that Palmerston was determined to precipitate his removal. When the Hungarian leader, Kossuth, arrived in London it was on Russell's insistence – strongly supported by the Queen – that he should not be officially received; Palmerston complied reluctantly, but then received a Radical deputation that presented him with an address of thanks for accomplishing Kossuth's freedom and which also contained some withering observations on the tyrannical rulers of Austria and Russia, with which Palmerston patently did not disagree. Then he proceeded to express approval of the *coup d'état* of Louis Napoleon in France who had proclaimed himself Emperor, and this was a last straw for Russell. To the delight of the Royal couple and to the astonishment of all in politics, Palmerston was asked for his resignation.

What had happened was that Palmerston considered that Louis Napoleon had prevented an Orleanist counter-coup, and told the French Ambassador that he approved. The British Ambassador in Paris, Lord Normanby, was highly indignant to be informed of this by the French Foreign Minister, and gave the details to his brother,

Charles Phipps, who immediately alerted Albert to this latest
example of Palmerston's perfidy. 'What an extraordinary and
unprincipled man Lord P. is', Victoria wrote, 'and how devoid of
every feeling of honour and consistency'. On December 20th she
received 'great and most unexpected news' at Windsor that Russell
had at long last acted decisively. 'Our relief was great', the Queen
wrote, 'and we felt quite excited by the news, for our anxiety and
worry during the last five years and a half, which was indescrib-
able, was mainly, if not entirely, caused by him! It is a great and
unexpected mercy, for I really was on the point of declaring on my
part that I could no longer retain Lord Palmerston, which would
have been a most disagreeable task, and not unattended with
danger, inasmuch as it would have put me too prominently forward'.

The appointment of Granville in Palmerston's place was one of
the factors that led Palmerston not to appear in person at Windsor
to surrender the Seals. For the whole of the afternoon of December
26th the Royal couple and Russell waited for him at Windsor,
making conversation with Lord Lansdowne and Granville, but 'no
Lord Palmerston appeared'. They then discussed whether it was
possible for the Queen to receive the Seals – sent separately to
Windsor – from another Minister. Russell, who at one stage had
left to check the railway timetables, had a useful precedent, and so
formally handed them over to the Queen on Palmerston's behalf.
She did not particularly mind Palmerston's deliberately insulting
behaviour, so relieved was she and Prince Albert to see him gone.

They believed, as did everyone else, that this was the end of
Palmerston, and the *annus mirabilis* of 1851 ended with great, but
premature, rejoicing at Windsor.

Prince Albert had made for himself a very formidable enemy. The
word was swiftly put out that the popular and courageous Foreign
Secretary had been brought down by the Court, and specifically by
the Prince. Politicians and newspapers particularly supportive of
Palmerston began by hinting at excessive Royal influence, Court
intrigues, and Prince Albert's malign role. 'Lady Palmerston says
she can neither eat nor sleep', Greville recorded, 'and they raise
already the cry of "Foreign influence"'. She did not conceal her
view that the Queen and the Prince wanted her husband's removal
and Granville's appointment 'because they thought he would be
pliable and subservient and would let Albert manage the Foreign
Affairs, which is what he had always wanted'. The trouble was that
there was some truth in the charge.

Palmerston swiftly humiliated his former colleagues by defeating the Government in the Commons on the grounds that defence proposals were inadequate – 'I have had my tit for tat with John Russell', he commented with satisfaction, having effectively and so quickly proved that he had been indispensable after all – and an extremely weak Government led by Derby and dominated by Disraeli was the consequence. Palmerston lost no opportunity of defending his record, either covertly through anonymous articles or the arranged support of his friends in the Press and Parliament. One very long article in the *Westminster Review* rhapsodising Palmerston's policies – and whose true author was only too obvious to the Queen and Prince – particularly enraged the latter, who wrote searing comments, notably on the clear indictment of the inability of the Sovereign to adopt 'a passive indifference' because of the 'high interests' of the Coburg family. On this, the Prince minuted:

> Nowhere does the Constitution demand an indifference on the part of the sovereign to the march of political events, and nowhere would such indifference be more condemned and justly despised than in England. There was no interest of the House of Coburg involved in any of the questions upon which we quarrelled with Lord Palmerston, neither in Greece nor Italy, Sicily, Holstein, Hungary etc.
>
> Why are Princes alone to be denied the credit of having political opinions based upon an anxiety for the national interests and honour of their country and the welfare of mankind? Are they not more independently placed than any other politician in the State? Are their interests not most intimately bound up with those of their country? Is the sovereign not the natural guardian of the honour of his country, is he not *necessarily* a politician? Has he no duties to perform towards his country?

Few documents that Prince Albert wrote are more revealing than this. What had been at stake had been the position and authority of the Queen, put in the position of being considered either to support Palmerston's words and actions, whatever his judgement, or constitutionally too weak to influence them, 'both suppositions equally derogatory to her honour and dignity'. Thus, it had all been a challenge to the political authority of the sovereign, a battle that had to be won.

But it had been won very dearly. The Prince had never been widely popular until the Exhibition, but even then his public position could not be compared to that of Palmerston, the Liberal Patriot and Defender of the Realm. An extraordinary national panic about a possible French invasion by the new Emperor Napoleon was given greater apparent emphasis by the death of Wellington in September 1852, lauded by Tennyson as 'the last great Englishman', and whose funeral was a martial and patriotic parade of great emotion. Prince Albert and Cole were responsible for the design of Wellington's elaborate funeral carriage, and the Prince for the music at the service. But Tennyson intoned:

> Remember him who led your hosts;
> He bade you guard the sacred coasts.

The Derby Ministry had little chance, and eventually fell in December when Gladstone destroyed Disraeli's Budget in a speech that established his already impressive reputation. The political situation was so confused as to be chaotic, but it was obvious that a Whig-Peelite coalition was the only one that had the possibility of survival, and would be impossible without Palmerston. His position was now so strong that he could successfully deny Russell the Premiership on the grounds that he would not serve under him. There was nothing that the Queen and the Prince could do to prevent Palmerston's return, but even he recognized that he could not become Foreign Secretary so soon after the bitter battles with the Royal couple and which had left such deep wounds. Thus, Aberdeen became Prime Minister, Russell went to the Foreign Office, Palmerston was Home Secretary, and Cabinet places were found for Sir James Graham and Gladstone. The Prince hopefully noted that 'Lord Palmerston looked excessively ill, and had to walk with two sticks', and he and Queen Victoria were reconciled to his very unwelcome return by the consolation that he was not Foreign Secretary and was so obviously old and ill.

Once again, they had misjudged their man. He hurled himself into the work of the Home Office with enthusiasm and dedication. But dark clouds were gathering, and Palmerston's eyes never lost their attention on the looming crisis in the East.

Prince Albert believed in the value of reason, and its capacity to resolve most difficulties. He was a realist, and also a passionate and impatient man by character, but the romanticism that inspired the Great Exhibition, his music, and his artistic and architectural enthusiasms did not extend to politics, and especially to European politics. Where others – notably Palmerston – saw excitement and opportunities, he saw dangers. When popular feeling became bellicose, he was pacific. He now entered the darkest and most difficult period of his life.

The Tsar of Russia, informing the British Ambassador that the Ottoman Empire was 'a sick man, a very sick man' in January 1853, swiftly followed this statement by moving Russian troops into the Turkish principalities of Wallachia and Moldavia. The British fleet was dispatched to the entrance of the Dardanelles. The Four Powers – England, France, Austria, and Prussia – submitted a Note to the Russians from Vienna which was accepted by the Russian Government, but not by the Turks. Lord Stratford de Redcliffe, the British Ambassador at Constantinople, conducted a persistent and dedicated role as an implacable opponent of Russian ambitions, and engaged in a detailed and elaborate battle of wills with his Russian counterpart, Prince Menschikoff. The British Government, urged on by Palmerston, slithered inexorably into an indeterminate commitment to Turkey. In October Turkey declared war against Russia.

The Queen and the Prince were appalled at these ominous developments. They asked for de Redcliffe's immediate recall, but Aberdeen replied that 'he could not answer for the effect it might produce in the country, and in the Government' – particularly meaning Palmerston, who was calling for the English fleet, supported by the French, to move from the entrance to the Dardanelles to the Black Sea; as a timorous compromise, it was sent to the Bosphorus. Palmerston later wrote that 'We crossed the Rubicon when we first took part with Turkey and sent our squadrons to her support'. Although nominally Home Secretary he was back in his element: 'We must help Turkey out of her difficulties by negotiation, if possible', he wrote, 'and if negotiation fails we must, by force of arms, carry her safely through her dangers'. The Prime Minister became justifiably alarmed by the near-certainty of the Turks provoking conflict 'in the presence of the British fleet', but then he was completely overtaken by events and out-manoeuvred by Palmerston. As Graham remarked of the Aberdeen Government: 'There are some odd tempers and queer ways among them'.

'No doubt', Aberdeen wrote to the Queen on October 6th, 'it may be very agreeable to humiliate the Emperor of Russia; but Lord Aberdeen thinks that it is paying a little too dear for this pleasure, to check the progress and prosperity of this happy country, and to cover Europe with confusion, misery, and blood'. This was all very well, but in Cabinet he was weak, and Albert became deeply alarmed: 'The Queen', he wrote in a memorandum at Balmoral on October 10th, 'might now be involved in war, of which the consequences could not be calculated, chiefly by the desire of Lord Aberdeen to keep his Cabinet together; this might then break down, and the Queen would be left without an efficient Government, and a war on her hands'. The bellicose tones of de Redcliffe's dispatches 'exhibit clearly on his part a *desire* for war, and to drag us into it' the Queen wrote to Aberdeen on November 5th.

But the tide of Russophobia was proving too strong for the Prime Minister and the increasingly worried Royal couple.

On November 30th the Russian fleet achieved an overwhelming victory over the Turks off Sinope. This was a legitimate act of war between belligerents, but was inflamed by Palmerston and a significant element of the Press into a disastrous and outrageous massacre of the innocents. Albert had foreseen the perils of encouraging the Turks to move their ships into the Black Sea by the arrival of the British warships: 'This can only be meant to insult the Russian fleet', he had written warningly, 'and to entice it to come out in order thereby to make it possible for Lord Stratford to bring the fleet into collision'. Palmerston's own newspaper, the *Morning Post*, was notably outraged, and *The Times*, now under the editorship of the remarkable and highly influential J. T. Delane, began to shift its anti-Turkish position.

On the same day that it announced the Turkish defeat at Sinope (December 16th) it also carried the traumatic news of the resignation of Palmerston.

The issue had been a draft Reform Bill that Palmerston allegedly found impossible to accept; the true cause was deeper, and had everything to do with the crisis in the East. The Queen and Prince were glad to see him go, although they had taken no direct part in his resignation, and the Queen was strongly opposed to his return in any capacity, as a result of 'his unscrupulous dexterity'. But after Sinope, and the consequent anti-Russian uproar in Parliament and the newspapers, the Aberdeen Government joined with the French in a hostile Note to Russia about the action of the Black Sea fleet, Palmerston declared his satisfaction, and returned to Office with greater popularity than ever.

By this time all the major newspapers – *The Times*, *Manchester Guardian*, and *Globe* – had changed their previous pacific approach, and anti-Russian fervour in their columns was reflected in Parliament. The *Morning Post*, carefully informed by Palmerston, announced that his resignation was not concerned with Reform at all, and charged that his removal was the result of 'a *rapprochement* between the Courts of Vienna and England'. The *Daily News* referred to 'Courtly distastes and Coburg intrigues', and *Reynold's Weekly* – which had a circulation of some 50,000 – attacked 'the Prince Prime Minister'. Palmerston was back in triumph, and an extraordinary storm of abuse fell upon Prince Albert.

Palmerston, having initiated his campaign, tried to check it when it went far beyond anything he had anticipated, but for a while Albert was denounced in vicious broadsheets, in newspapers, and at public meetings with a ferocity that would be unimaginable for a modern member of the Royal Family. He was described as the chief agent of 'the Austrian-Belgian-Coburg-Orleans clique, the avowed enemies of England, and the subservient tools of Russian ambition'. Wild rumours that he had been impeached for treason and sent to the Tower of London circulated. It was a terrible period.[1]

Albert, although astonished, angered, and deeply upset, outwardly maintained a calm attitude. 'The Government is a popular Government', he wrote, 'and the masses upon which it rests only feel, and do not think. In the present instance their feeling is something of this sort: "The Emperor of Russia is a tyrant, and the enemy of all liberty on the Continent, the oppressor of Poland. He wanted to coerce the poor Turk. The Turk is a fine fellow; he has braved the rascal, let us rush to his assistance" '. To Stockmar he wrote that 'The public here is furiously Turkish and anti-Russian', and to Ernest that 'I am not giving up hope that we may be able to enforce peace, and yet the folly of both Russians and Turks is unbelievable'; this was written immediately after Palmerston's resignation, when he rejoiced at the departure of 'One warlike element' and 'The great Liberal bully', but that had been shortlived. 'The state of politics here is quite insane', he wrote to Stockmar on December 23rd, warning him that he also – although in Coburg for over six months – was part of the 'Coburg plot', being 'in assiduous attendance on the Prince Consort'; 'one almost fancies oneself in a lunatic asylum'.

The reality was that he and the Queen were outraged, and deeply wounded. On this occasion the remarkable efficiency of his Press and broadsheet collection organisation was rather too efficient, as he and Victoria read daily, with mounting anger and incomprehension, the torrent of abuse and vilification directed at them personally. Stockmar shared their anger totally, describing hostile Tories as 'simply degenerate bastards' while the Whigs 'stand in the same relation to the Throne as the wolf does to the lamb'. 'If our courage and cheerfulness have not suffered', Albert wrote, 'our stomachs and digestions have, as they commonly do when feelings are kept long upon the stretch'.

Victoria's feelings were even more intense than those of Albert, who wrote to Stockmar on December 27th that 'the stupidest trash is babbled to the public, so stupid that (as they say in Coburg) you would not give it to the pigs to litter in'. Indeed, his correspondence at this time contains the strongest language he committed to paper. He had considered the Cabinet's dispatch of the Fleet as 'morally

---

[1] Kingsley Martin: *The Triumph of Lord Palmerston* (1924) and revised edition in 1953, remains the best analysis of Press opinion and influence.

and constitutionally wrong,' as it had been done without the Queen's approval, and now he judged that Britain had been perilously committed as 'auxiliaries to the Turks'. His warnings and protests had been unheeded, now he was the object of intense attack. 'The nonsense and lies which the public have had to swallow with respect to my humble person within these last three weeks have really exceeded anything I could have imagined', he wrote to Lord Hardinge.

A foolish proposal to erect a statue to him in honour of the Exhibition could not have been more ill-timed, and produced another outpouring of patriotic denigration. In fact, he had deplored the well-intentioned suggestion of the Lord Mayor and Aldermen of the City of London, and wrote to Granville (November 3rd) that:

> ... I can say, with perfect absence of humbug, that I would much rather not be made the prominent feature of such a
> · monument, as it would both disturb my quiet rides in Rotten Row to see my own face staring at me, and if (as is very likely) it became an artistic monstrosity, like most of our monuments, it would upset my equanimity to be permanently ridiculed and laughed at in effigy ...

This characteristic good humour was sorely tested by the ordeal he now had to endure. The Queen was enraged, and wrote to Aberdeen on January 4th 1854 that she intended to make her husband Prince Consort – the title he had not formally received, but by which he was now generally known – and that if she thought that the attacks on him represented the real views of her people 'she would LEAVE a position which nothing but her domestic happiness could make her endure, and retire to private life – leaving the country to choose another ruler after their own HEART'S CONTENT. But she does *not* think so ill of her country, though she must say that these disgraceful exhibitions will leave behind them *very bitter* feelings in her breast, which time alone can eradicate'.

The Queen had written to Aberdeen as early as October 11th 1853 – the warning drafted by her husband – that 'we have taken on ourselves, in conjunction with the French, all the risks of a European war, without having bound Turkey to any conditions with respect to provoking it'. This was exactly true, but in the war-fever, and with a Prime Minister who was equally helpless in the storm, wisdom and caution of this nature were profoundly unpopular. Bulwer Lytton was right when he wrote that 'Palmerston is Mamma England's spoilt child, and the more mischief he does the more she admires him. What a spirit he has! cries Mamma, and smash goes the crockery!' Albert considered the prospects of a European war as 'a terrible calamity', and had little faith in 'the ignorant, barbarian, and despotic Mussulman' (Memorandum to Aberdeen, October 21st 1853). The gulf was total.

The storm, although fierce, was brief. The Queen threatened not to open Parliament in person to demonstrate her anger, but there had been a reaction against the abuse. Aberdeen wrote apologetically to Albert that it had been 'a signal example of popular delusion, and, although we consider ourselves to be an enlightened people, I know of no greater instance of stupid credulity than has been exhibited in the disgraceful proceedings of the last few weeks'. Palmerston, having achieved his object and his revenge, hastened to make some amends. Ministers and Members of Parliament were ardent in their eulogies of the Prince; the Press clamour faded as quickly as it had begun; when he inspected the Guards on February 22nd 1854 he was 'much cheered'.

But this episode had left deep, and ineradicable, wounds. He was not prone to self-pity, and although he often looked nostalgically to his childhood and to Germany, he was happy in his marriage, for all its occasional tempestuous storms – 'What are you really afraid of in me?' he wrote to her in one especially sad moment shortly after this episode – and he had rendered extraordinary service already to his adopted country. He loved Cambridge, and was proud of its rapid revival; his work for art and music was admired by those whose admiration he appreciated; the Exhibition and its aftermath gave him pleasure; he had created Osborne; Balmoral was rising rapidly; the Royal estates were being managed with unprecedented efficiency; he was greatly respected as an exceptionally qualified expert in agriculture by people not ready to bestow their respect; he loved his growing family. In twelve years of endeavour he had established himself in England in every area in which he had involved himself. And now, after all this endeavour, he was being widely portrayed not only as an interfering foreigner, but an enemy of England.

The Queen had been totally staunch during this crisis, and supported him vehemently. Of her husband she wrote to Stockmar on January 19th 1854, that he 'treats it with contempt, but with his keen and very high feeling of honour he is wounded, hurt, and enraged by the attack on his honour, and is looking very ill, though his spirits do not fail him'.

Stockmar, although distressed and angry, characteristically argued that there was a good side to this experience. 'I cannot wish, hard as you may have been hit by them, that you should have been spared this experience. It is only in war, under its threatened or real wounds and bruises, that a real soldier is formed'. Stockmar's relish that his protégé had thus been tested was not echoed by Albert, whose reply (January 24th 1854) is deeply significant. He was no longer looking forward.

A very considerable section of the nation had never given itself the trouble to consider what really is the position of the husband of a Queen Regnant. When I first came over here I was met by this want of knowledge and unwillingness to give a thought to the position of this luckless personage. Peel cut down my income, Wellington refused me my rank, the Royal family cried out against the Foreign interloper, the Whigs in office were only inclined to concede to me just as much space as I could stand upon.

The Crimean War broke out in March 1854. It was as the Queen wrote to Leopold, 'popular beyond belief'. The series of disasters that overtook the Allied forces gave Palmerston his ultimate, and total, political triumph. What the Queen described as 'our eternal government hunting errand' resulted in Palmerston as Prime Minister. After much unnecessary tragedy, the war was technically 'won', its only genuine and enduring triumph achieved by Florence Nightingale in nursing the wounded and by *The Times*' correspondent, W. H. Russell, in bringing to the British public the full horror of the adventure on which they had so enthusiastically and casually embarked. By one of the supreme ironies of Prince Albert's life, the one result of the war was the breaking of the links between Austria and Russia which led to the unification of Germany and the liberation of Italy. Otherwise, in the words of H. A. L. Fisher, it was 'a contest entered into without necessity, conducted without foresight, and deserving to be reckoned from its archaic arrangements and tragic mismanagement rather among medieval than modern campaigns'.

Once the war was begun, the Prince immersed himself totally in its prosecution, often reflecting with some anger on politicians who neglected the armed forces in peace and then embarked upon wars in which their deficiencies were blamed upon others. His activity, not always appreciated by Ministers, was intense, and it was entirely due to him that they accepted his proposal for a new medal to be awarded for acts of supreme valour in the face of the enemy, to be open to men of all ranks. This, in itself, was a striking novelty, and the genesis of the Victoria Cross is to be found in this memorandum by the Prince:

1. That a small cross of merit for personal deeds of valour be established.

2. That it be open to all ranks.

3. That it be unlimited in number.

4. That an annuity (say of £5) be attached to each cross.

5. That it be claimable by an individual on establishing before a jury of his peers, subject to confirmation at home, his right to the distinction.

He not only instituted, but designed, the Cross – from that day to this the highest decoration for valour in the British armed forces.[1]

He and the Queen followed the war anxiously, and often with anguish. 'You can form no conception of the fatigue which just at this moment this treadmill causes me', he wrote to Stockmar. His personal views were not dissimilar to those of Carlyle, who wrote 'Never such enthusiasm among the people; seems to me privately that I have hardly seen a madder business'. Of the war, Prince Albert recorded: 'Ich mag ihn nicht' – 'I do not like it myself'.

---

[1] See also M. J. Crook: *The Evolution of the Victoria Cross* (1975).

EIGHT

HUSBAND AND FATHER

Queen Victoria and Prince Albert had known little of each other when they became engaged, and although their love was intense and profound it developed through shared experience and difficulties into a marriage in which they attempted to balance the heavy responsibilities of Sovereign and Consort with those of parents of a rapidly growing young family. Almost, although not entirely, by chance they created a pattern of living that embraced the formalities of Buckingham Palace, the more relaxed atmosphere of Windsor, the peacefulness of Osborne – 'the children catch butterflies, Victoria sits under the trees' he wrote of one day – and the more bracing environment of Balmoral, but where they felt particularly happy, remote from the political and official world, and with their children. Above all, Osborne and Balmoral were their creations, not only physically but in atmosphere.

Prince Albert was a devoted, loving, and amusing husband and father, and although his patience was tried on several occasions by his wife's variable temperament they were deeply happy together. In Gladstone's noble phrase, 'He was to her, in deed and truth, a second self'.

Victoria and Albert had nine children in seventeen years, and the regular arrivals of Royal babies were the topic of a certain popular ribaldry and political criticism, and it was a long time before the Queen's intense dislike at 'this occupation', became known. Many years later she wrote to her eldest daughter:

> What you say of the pride of giving life to an immortal soul is very fine, dear, but I own I cannot enter into that; I think much more of us being like a cow or a dog at such moments; when our poor nature becomes so very animal & unecstatic.

But these events gave immense pleasure to Albert, who doted on his children – and none more than the firstborn, Victoria ('Vicky'). The others were Albert Edward ('Bertie') (born 1841), Alice (1843),

Alfred ('Affie') (1844), Helena ('Lenchen') (1846), Louise (1848), Arthur (1850), Leopold (1853), and Beatrice (1857). To their parents' dismay and distress Leopold was a haemophiliac, the Queen being the 'carrier' of this grievous affliction, but the others were healthy and lively children. Albert greatly enjoyed their company, ordered the special cottage for them at Osborne, and made Christmas – as he always did – a particular time of family enjoyment and happiness, his purpose being to provide, as far as was possible in their circumstances, a happy, well-ordered, and normal childhood. 'The greatest maxim of all', Queen Victoria wrote, 'is that the Children should be brought up as simply and in as domestic a way as possible; that (not interfering with their lessons) they should be as much as possible with their Parents, share and place their greatest confidence in them in all things'. This memorandum, probably drafted by Albert, remained their policy.

The exception was, and perhaps had to be, the Prince of Wales, the Heir to the Throne, the future King, and the repository of Albert's ambitions for the future of the Monarchy. The assassination attempts on them both gave to the task of raising and educating the future Sovereign an additional urgency, and one to which he applied himself with characteristic thought, resolution, and care. So much misunderstanding has arisen about what then happened that it is important to relate the story in considerable detail, as it throws much further light on the character of Prince Albert.

The genius of Stockmar and Prince Albert lay in their clear understanding not only of the political limitations, but the considerable political potentialities, of the British Monarchy. As Albert wrote to Stockmar in January 1846, 'the exaltation of Royalty is possible only through the personal character of the Sovereign. When a person enjoys complete confidence, we desire for him more power and influence in the conduct of affairs. But confidence is of slow growth'. Stockmar had now played a brilliantly successful role twice – in the tragically ended education of Leopold, and in the development of Prince Albert into a cautious, serious, but intuitively skilful Consort and man of influence. In spite of the storms that often swirled about the Prince, and the continuing denigration of his alleged dullness, stiffness, and admitted German-ness, he had gradually established himself not only in the heart of his highly intelligent and volatile wife, but in the respect, however grudging, of most senior politicians. By them, he was becoming recognised as being himself a politician of the first rank, and most of them detected, as only politicians can, the ambition and sense of power that lurked under the courteous façade.

It is against this background of political success already achieved, and ambition for the future, that the eventually futile endeavour to mould the eldest son into the perfectly equipped heir to the Throne must be seen – a fundamental point which has eluded several biographers and historians.

Albert Edward – always called 'Bertie' in the family – had been born on November 9th 1841 after a particularly difficult confinement; he was created Prince of Wales on December 4th, and christened amid great pomp in St. George's Chapel on January 25th 1842, the Duke of Wellington carrying the Sword of State, and the service meticulously planned and organised by Albert. The event was not without its practical difficulties. Melbourne was anxious to avoid 'the risk of cavil or motions of enquiry' into the cost, and found that the resources of the department of the Lord Steward could assist with £2,500 or even £3,000, to which Albert wrote in reply that 'even £2,000 will be very gratefully accepted'. In the event, the final bill was £4,991 16s. 5d., charged to the Lord Chamberlain's department. Then, the Duke of Coburg was angry that the name Ernest did not find favour with the couple, and even angrier when the King of Prussia was invited to be a godfather. 'He has reproached me severely', Albert wrote to his brother, but on both points he and the Queen successfully resisted his father's pressures, and the new Prince of Wales was christened in appropriate style. The young parents then took counsel about the upbringing of the future King.

There is something infinitely touching about the devotion with which they approached their task. Very mindful of the deficiencies of their own childhoods, and somewhat awed by the heavy responsibility of educating Queen Victoria's eventual heir, they discussed the subject at great length, and often, and inevitably turned to Stockmar for guidance. He, for his part, advised them to take counsel from others. The results were somewhat unhelpful and sycophantic, the Bishop of Oxford portentously writing that 'the great object in view is to make him the most perfect man', although Melbourne was a characteristic refreshing exception, writing to the Queen: 'Be not over solicitous about education. It may be able to do much, but it does not do as much as is expected from it. It may mould and direct the character, but it rarely alters it'.

This was emphatically not the view of Stockmar. 'A man's education begins the first day of his life', he had written sternly to Albert on October 1st 1840, 'and a lucky choice [of a governess] I regard as the greatest and finest gift which we can bestow on the expected stranger. Suffer me, apropos of this subject, my dear Prince, to pause a moment, and to ask you to consider, first, *how much* we have already gained step by step, and, secondly, to take courage

from success, and to give to Providence the thanks that are due!'
Stockmar, as has been remarked, was not disposed to leave matters
to Providence, and when the heir was born he hastened to write to
Albert: 'Sleep, Stillness, Rest, and the exclusion of many people from
her room are now the essentials for the Queen. You cannot be too
guarded on these points. Thus, be a very Cerberus'. It was due to his
advice that Lady Lyttelton was appointed governess of the nursery,
which was a very happy and successful choice. But, as Stockmar
emphasised, this was only a first step. On September 18th 1843 he
wrote to Prince Albert:

> ... Pray give renewed attention and serious reflection to what is
> necessary for the training and education of the Prince of Wales.
> The present nursery staff is no longer adequate. As the Swiss
> governess may take the special charge of the Princess Royal, so
> a German governess might take the Prince of Wales for a time
> under her special care, until perhaps an English one is found
> who might look after him till his 5th or 6th year, when he might
> be transferred to manly hands ...

It was over the management of the nursery that, as has been
already related, Albert and Victoria had had their first notable, and
most vehement, quarrel, but the issue of nursery management had
been subordinate to the deeper differences between them over the
character and role of Lehzen. Nonetheless, the future of the heir to
the throne was a major factor, and one on which Albert fought and
won his most important victory over his wife. Also of significance
was the question of security, and Lady Lyttelton was to write of
'various intense precautions, suggesting the most hideous dangers,
which I fear are not altogether imaginary, and make one shudder'.
Chief among these apprehensions was that of the Princess Royal and
the Prince being kidnapped, and although such fears may have been
exaggerated by the young parents and their advisers, their concerns
can be appreciated. The result, inevitably, was a degree of supervision and segregation for the Royal Children that was only gradually,
and then only moderately, relaxed.

Stockmar's essential purpose, as he emphasised to the Royal
parents, was to produce 'a man of calm, profound, comprehensive
understanding, with a deep conviction of the indispensable necessity
of practical morality to the welfare of the Sovereign and People'.
While the parents enthusiastically agreed, the difficulty was that
Bertie, even as a small child, was proving difficult and temperamental, with fits of frustrated anger and temper that left him limp and
exhausted, 'as though he were asleep with his eyes open', as Albert
reported to Stockmar with some concern. Lady Lyttelton described

him, at the age of four, as 'uncommonly adverse to learning and requires much patience from wilful inattention and constant interruptions'.

It was also evident that he was less intelligent and pleasing to the parents than Princess Victoria, on whom Albert's complete devotion was bestowed early and never faded. This love is one of the most moving events in his life, but it inevitably had some effect upon the small boy who was the recipient of the immensely detailed and thorough plans of his parents and Stockmar. Lady Lyttelton was immensely struck by Albert's devotion to his children, and his 'patience and kindness' to them, and some of Victoria's most warm Journal entries describe him 'noisily and eagerly managing a new kite with his two elder sons', playing hide and seek with Vicky and Bertie with the gusto of a boy, and teaching Bertie how to turn somersaults. 'He is so kind to them and romps with them so delightfully, and manages them so beautifully and firmly'. 'There is certainly a great charm, as well as deep interest in watching the development of feelings and faculties in a little child', he wrote on February 16th 1843, 'and nothing is more instructive for the knowledge of our own nature than to observe in a little creature the stages of development which, when we were ourselves passing through them, seemed scarcely to have an existence for us. I feel this daily in watching our young offspring, whose characters are quite different, and who both show many loveable qualities.'

But although Albert loved his son dearly, he saw him also as the future King on whom would fall immense responsibilities and powers, and his determination to ensure that nothing should be spared nor overlooked in his preparation for his great destiny inevitably made Bertie 'different' from his sister and his subsequent brothers and sisters. As Lady Lyttelton wrote, he was, after all, '*l'infant d'Angleterre*'.

> ... Your Royal Highness can *never* rate too highly the importance of the life of the Prince of Wales, or of his good education; for your own interests – political, moral, mental & material are so intimately and inseparably bound up with those of the Prince that every neglect in his training and culture is certain to be avenged upon his father ...

Thus Stockmar wrote, perhaps unnecessarily, on November 27th 1843 to Prince Albert, while adding his concern at the lack of firm supervision when Lady Lyttelton was absent: 'The great thing to be looked to is not the learning of a foreign language but the moral and physical superintendence which ought not to be entrusted to uneducated persons'..

It was Stockmar who drew up the Nursery Regulations and who, after interview, had recommended Lady Lyttelton, while also advising special facilities at Buckingham Palace and Windsor for herself and her daughters, a special carriage for her, and a footman to assist her and accompany her carriage. It was also Stockmar who drew up the overall Plan on March 6th 1842:

> The Child is born with natural dispositions to good and to evil.
>   The object of Education is to develop and strengthen the good, and subdue or diminish the evil disposition of our Nature.
>   Good Education cannot begin too soon.
>   'To neglect beginnings', says Locke, 'is the fundamental error into which most Parents fall...'
>   The beginnings of Education must therefore be directed to the regulation of the child's natural Instincts, to give them the right direction and above all *to keep its Mind pure* ...

Emphasising the need for early teachers of 'good, of virtuous, and intelligent Persons', Stockmar continued:

> Good Education is very rare, because it is difficult, and the higher the Rank of the Parents the more difficult it is. Notwithstanding, good Education may be accomplished, and to be deferred from attempting it, merely because it is difficult, would be a dereliction of the most sacred Duties. This can neither be the intention of our good and right minded Queen nor the Prince, but it is quite evident that on account of their Youth, they must lack that knowledge, maturity of judgement and experience, which are requisite to a successful Guidance of the Education of the Royal Infants. It becomes therefore their sacred Duty to consult upon this important subject honest, intelligent, and experienced Persons and not only to consult them but to follow their advice.
>   The first truth by which the Queen and the Prince ought to be thoroughly penetrated is that their position is a much more difficult one than that of any other Parents in the Kingdom. Because the Royal Children ought not only to be brought up to the moral character, but also fitted to discharge successfully the arduous duties which may eventually devolve upon them as future Sovereigns. Hence the magnitude of the parental responsibility of Sovereigns to their Children; for upon the conscientious discharge of this responsibility will depend hereafter the peace of mind and happiness of themselves and their family, and as far as the prosperity and happiness of a

Nation depends upon the personal character of its Sovereign the welfare of England ...

. After a somewhat unnecessarily bleak appraisal of the deficiencies of George III as a parent, and the lamentable consequences, Stockmar went on to warn Victoria and Albert about the 'delusion' that they could actually superintend the education of their children. It was essential that this task should be delegated fully to 'a person of rank', as 'the English, so aristocratic in their notions, feelings, and habits would not relish a deviation from the established rule'.

This description certainly covered Lady Lyttelton, who reported daily on the children's progress, but plans were laid early for the next stage, when the Prince of Wales could be moved from the nursery to the attentions of a male tutor. Again, as Stockmar urged, there must be full delegation, and no parental interference once the choice of tutor was made. Again, the parents fully complied.

One may note at this point a certain dichotomy in Stockmar's approach. While urging delegation, he was also writing to Albert that the Governor of the Prince of Wales was 'the man of the highest rank in the Kingdom – His Royal Highness the Prince Albert' a view warmly shared by the Queen, who wrote that 'I wish that he should grow up entirely under *his Father's eye*, and every step be guided by him, so that when he has attained the age of sixteen or seventeen he may be a real companion to his father'. Thus, Stockmar saw Albert as the overseer with the ultimate responsibility, but without responsibility for the actual teaching. By the beginning of 1846, with Bertie only five years of age, his parents and Stockmar were seriously disappointed by his physical and mental progress. Although he detected some advance, Stockmar submitted a somewhat sombre analysis of the boy in an undated memorandum to Albert early in 1846, which glumly observes that 'I must perceive that the Prince remains up to this hour essentially a nervous and excitable child with little power of endurance or sustained action in any direction, and that the utmost care and judgement will be required in his physical and mental training to improve his stamina and develop his faculties to their full extent'. Fortified by the opinion of a Doctor Combe to the effect that Bertie needed 'a dry bracing air ... to give tone to the nervous system and also to the nutritive functions', Stockmar urged 'well regulated exercise with an appropriate regimen', while 'taking care not to go so far at any time as to weaken by fatigue, nor to stop short too soon, so as not to admit the attainment of any increase of strength. In this respect Harm may result equally from pushing mental stimulus too far and from applying it too sparingly or in a wrong direction ... '

Stockmar's principal concern, however, was 'the judicious moral management of the Prince'.

> ... it follows that every irregularity of mental action, every excitement of temper or impatience, every minute of fretting or repressed feeling, every attempt to gratify curiosity or effect a purpose, and even every exhibition of right and amiable feeling too strongly excited, all tend to act more or less injuriously on a brain already so susceptible ...
>
> The one thing needful above all others with the Prince of Wales at present is as far as possible to promote the uniform, equable, and sustained action of his feelings, affections, moral sentiments and intellectual processes. To do this requires a very favourable combination of good sense, kindliness, firmness, readiness and activity of mind, great tact, thorough control of temper and unwearied patience. A real interest in the trust must also be felt ...

The search for a suitable tutor to this complex and affectionate, if temperamental, child was conducted with immense seriousness by Stockmar and the parents. In a refreshingly candid memorandum by Stockmar on July 28th 1846 he denounced 'Utopian' plans of arduous study drawn up on the mistaken assumption that 'the Prince is to be a paragon – a youth of universal genius, in whom the highest moral activity and the greatest powers of application will be combined, with the best endowment of every physical, moral and intellectual quality'. It was already clear that any such expectations were unlikely of fulfilment, and Stockmar not only cautioned flexibility but also made the significant point that national and social circumstances would change so considerably before he ascended the throne that an upbringing based on the contemporary *status quo* could easily create prejudices and anomalies which, in the words of Lord Mahon, would be 'at variance with the reason and moral perception of enlightened men'. In one of his most deeply interesting analyses of the contemporary social scene, Stockmar continued:

> The extraordinary wealth and luxury of a comparative small proportion of the inhabitants of the British Isles, and the appalling poverty and wretchedness of many among the labouring classes, is another 'anomaly' which is at variance with our natural sentiments of humanity and justice, and finds its chief precedents in the history of ancient Rome, when she was tottering to her fall. Can this condition of things permanently endure in Great Britain?

Stockmar accordingly urged that the Prince's education should 'prepare him for approaching events' rather than to educate him to resist change, while avoiding the other extreme of making him 'a demagogue or a moral enthusiast, but a man of calm, profound, comprehensive understanding, imbued with a deep conviction of the indispensable necessity of practical morality to the welfare of both Sovereign and People.

'The proper duty of the Sovereigns of this Country is not to take the lead in change, but to act as a balance wheel on the movement of the social body ... ' Thus, the Prince must be trained to have 'freedom of thought, and a firm reliance on the inherent power of sound principles – political, moral, and religious, to sustain themselves and produce practical good, when left in possession of a fair field of development'. The Prince should steer a careful course between religious bigotry and 'conventional hypocrisy', and all should beware of 'the sexual passion (which) is very often the source of innumerable evils to young men' until 'the proper time of life', and emphasised his view that the Prince's tutor should not be a clergyman, a point to which he often returned. Eventually the Queen and Prince Albert prepared a joint Memorandum on January 3rd 1847 which opened with the words 'It is necessary to lay down a positive plan for the future management of the Children's education', and which was devoted to the different problems and requirements of the four stages of their childhood 'from the first month after their appearance in this world' until the final one which would require 'a person to introduce him into life & the world'.

This is not a solemn nor at all an unsympathetic or unkind document. The couple warmly agreed that for the first six years of life 'The chief objects here are their physical development, the actual rearing up, the training to obedience. They are too little for *real* instruction, but they are taught their language & the two principal foreign languages, French & German, as well to speak as to read ... Children at this age have the greatest facility in acquiring languages'. It should not be thought that Vicky was an easy or docile child. After her marriage she received this letter from her mother: 'A more insubordinate and unequal-tempered child and girl I think I never saw! The trouble you gave us all was indeed very great. Comparatively speaking, we have none whatever with the others. You and Bertie (in very different ways) were indeed great difficulties'.[1]

---

[1] 28th July 1858 (Kronberg Papers, quoted in Andrew Sinclair: *The Other Victoria* (1982).

The actual programme for the Prince of Wales can be seen from one entry by his governess, Miss Hildyard, for a day in January 1848:

From 20 minutes after 8 until 9 – Arithmetic, Dictation, Writing
$\frac{1}{4}$ past 11 to $\frac{1}{4}$ past 12 – French
1 to 5 minutes before 2 – German
4 to 5 – Reading, Geography, Writing on the Slate
5 to 6 – Dancing
On other days Chronology & History read aloud Poetry
After 6 read some story book
Play with the map of History or with counters.

The search for the Tutor was eventually resolved by the appointment of Henry Birch, a Cambridge graduate and Eton tutor, but only after much anguish and difficulty.

Birch was recommended by Sir James Clark, to whom he wrote with a certain smugness on May 30th 1848 that 'I boast of no other place of Education but Eton, where I came from home at about 10 years of age and rose to be Captain of the School', but both Prince Albert and Stockmar were concerned – and rightly, as it transpired –by Birch's evident ecclesiastical ambitions. Albert was particularly worried that he might have been 'contaminated' by the teachings of Pusey, and received assurances from the Bishops of Ely and Chester, to whom he referred the point. Peel, after discreet enquiries, endorsed Clark's recommendation, and Stockmar, after interviewing Birch, was satisfied, and the latter added that no false economies should be made in salaries or holidays for the staff attending the Royal children, and particularly the Prince of Wales.

Albert had been contemplating a high salary for the Prince's tutor, which was a very handsome emolument, but Birch proved a hard bargainer. The moment it was clear to him that he would receive the appointment he informed Prince Albert that his fees at Eton were substantially greater, and Albert hastily revised the proposed fee to equal this very considerable amount. In the event, Birch received even more than this and it is difficult to escape the conclusion that the Prince had taken Stockmar's strictures about excessive economy rather too much to heart, and that Birch was selling his services at a singularly high level.

But this was not all. Birch's personal ambitions went beyond money. On April 12th 1849 Albert set out the Prince's programme of tuition and added that 'Sunday is to be kept as a day of recreation & amusement in which the Prince will be glad to see a little more of his brother & sisters than the occupation of the week will allow', but Birch saw his role as something more than a temporal tutor. He was courteously indignant about Royal comment on his attendance at services and obvious indications of his remorseless movement towards Holy Orders. He demanded an assistant 'taken from a comparatively humble station in life' and enquired of Stockmar (December 13th 1849) 'If the Prince of Wales is to become eventually the Head of the English Church, how is he to be trained, but in the plain unadulterated scriptural teaching of that Church?'

Birch's letters to Stockmar and Albert obviously gave them concern, and Queen Victoria became so worried that she set out a detailed memorandum about the Prince's education to Birch, which included the point that 'no corporal punishment without report to the decision of the Prince Albert' would be permitted, and eventually a formal 'Final Agreement' between the Royal parents and Birch was prepared by them and revised by Stockmar on the issue of religious instruction and influence.

From this voluminous correspondence it is clear that the parents felt that they had little choice but to accept the recommendations concerning Birch, but that they were increasingly perturbed by Birch's evident ambition and religiosity. These concerns did not go as far as challenging the universal recommendation, and the couple were loyal to Birch, in spite of their added dismay when he insisted upon his intention of eventually taking Holy Orders.

Birch instituted a firm regime of six day a week tutoring, with limited holidays, and a daily report to the parents. He found Bertie 'extremely disobedient, impertinent to his masters, and unwilling to submit to discipline', selfish, short-tempered, and extremely sensitive. He considered that the boy's temperament was uneven, that he was naturally rebellious, and often refused to answer questions which he knew perfectly well. Some indication of Birch's character can be gleaned from a note to himself in April 1849 in his papers about the Prince of Wales:

He must obey – I must command – His temper must yield – His affection must be won. How one and the same hand is to effect this, I know not. I must see Baron Stockmar.

In an undated letter, but probably of the same time, he wrote to Prince Albert:

Sir,
     The conduct of the Prince of Wales begins to frighten me. I begin to search myself and see if my ingenuity can devise any other mode of dealing with him, but I seem to have tried every expedient, and I do hope that no feeling of delicacy towards myself will prevent Her Majesty and Your Royal Highness from

asking me to resign my charge into other hands, if you think that
a change would produce any better result at any time.

The moment that one attempts to teach anything arises the
difficulty – an unwillingness to give himself the slightest trouble
or exertion . . .

I will continue to do my best, but it seems of little avail.

Albert hastened to write to say that Birch had the full confidence
of himself and the Queen, but whether it was the result of the advice
of Stockmar or Birch, or, more probably, Clark, the parents resorted
to the extraordinary measure of asking the very fashionable phreno-
logist, the Dr. George Combe to whom reference has already been
made, to examine the unruly and difficult patient. On June 22nd
1850 he submitted his report on the boy, not yet nine years old:

> . . . The Prince of Wales appears to me to have improved very
> considerably since I saw him three years ago. He is in better
> health, his head has grown in all the regions, and the indications
> of excitability, through feebleness in the nervous constitution,
> generally have diminished. The intellectual organs have
> become larger absolutely, although perhaps not relatively to
> those situated in the posterior region of the brain. There are
> still, however, signs of a delicate constitution of the brain, the
> effects of which will probably be a degree of inaptitude for
> mental labour, and an aversion to it at particular times; and, on
> other occasions, an excess of activity, especially in the
> emotional faculties . . .
>
> It is a fundamental principle in Phrenology that no organs
> are in themselves bad. God, who instituted the brain and
> organised to every part of it certain functions, provided a
> legitimate sphere of action for each. It is, therefore, only activity
> in excess, or ill-directed, that leads to evil.
>
> In the Prince of Wales, the organs of Combativeness, Des-
> tructiveness, Self-Esteem, Concentrativeness and Firmness are
> all large. The intellectual organs are only moderately devel-
> oped; and in a child, one of the effects of this combination will be
> a strong self-will, amounting at times to obstinacy; a tendency
> to anger and opposition, and a temporary apparent insensibil-
> ity to the influence of reason and the requirements of duty . . .

The dismayed parents, reading this appalling analysis, could at
least console themselves that, in the judgement of Dr. Combe, the
Organs of Conscientiousness, Benevolence, and Veneration were
impressively large, although that of Cautiousness was 'only moderately developed'. It was also open to question whether Dr. Combe

17a   Balmoral under construction, 1855

17b   Balmoral: the Drawing Room, 1857, by Roberts

18a   Prince Albert, 1854

18b   The Queen and her
children at Windsor, 1854
Left to right: The Prince of
Wales, the Princess Royal,
Princess Alice, the Queen
and Prince Alfred

19a   Prince Albert, 1855

19b   The Queen and Prince
       Albert, 1854

22a   The Prince Consort, 1859

22b   A Group at Coburg, October 8th, 1860
Left to right: Princess Alice, Princess Frederick William and Prince Frederick William of Prussia, Ernest II, Duke of Saxe-Coburg-Gotha, Queen Victoria, The Prince Consort, Alexandrine, Duchess of Saxe-Coburg-Gotha

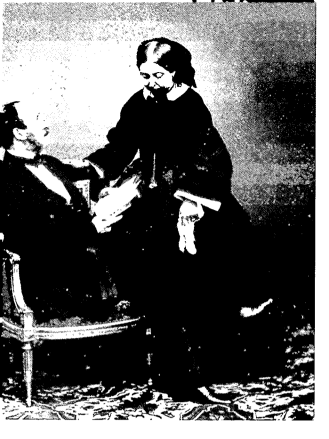

23a The Queen and the Prince
     Consort, 1860

23b The Queen and The Prince
     Consort, 1861

24   The Prince Consort, March 1861

was being particularly helpful when he observed that 'Every fit of obstinacy or passion should be viewed not as an act of voluntary disobedience, but as a physiological manifestation or indication of a certain cerebral condition'. Moreover, Dr. Combe recommended the appointment of a tutor whose own cranium had been exposed to the same ruthless examination, and who would be prepared 'to study Phrenology and to submit to be trained to apply it ... The public sentiment in favour of Phrenology is advancing: In twenty or thirty years hence, a new generation may ask why was the Prince of Wales denied the advantages of its application? And it may be difficult to find a satisfactory answer ... '

One would like to think that the parents saw through this pseudo-scientific nonsense; in any event, the prattlings of Dr. Combe blessedly and abruptly disappear from the voluminous archives on the Prince of Wales' upbringing that Albert meticulously filed and preserved.

To Stockmar he confided his concerns, who replied on August 4th 1849:

A letter received yesterday from the Queen again depresses my hopes in reference to the progress of the Prince of Wales. I therefore beg you will from time to time let me hear from you with the results of your own observation on the state of things. There can be no theorising as to what it may be necessary, possible, and therefore judicious, to do in this business. Nothing but experience, acquired by close observation of actual facts, can give us indications how to proceed, and form a sure guide to the course to be persevered in ...

Albert's observations were, simply, that the Prince of Wales remained highly strung, emotional, warm-hearted and devoted to his parents, and – to modern eyes strangely – fond of the tedious and sanctimonious Birch, but also rebellious, irritable, and clearly very unhappy. His parents were baffled and troubled, particularly when Bertie was compared with the adored Vicky, but they faithfully followed Stockmar's instructions of not interfering with Birch and his tutors, while hovering very uneasily around what was clearly a major breakdown of the grandiose Plan. Birch had the great quality that Bertie deeply liked him, and the feeling was wholly returned. The Queen wrote that 'I never felt at my ease with Birch. There always seemed to be something between us', and one difference may be seen in Birch's final report, which condemned the boy's enforced segregation from his contemporaries, blamed his 'peculiarities' on this fact, and concluded that Bertie 'will eventually turn out a *good* and, in my humble opinion, a *great* man'.

Unhappily, matters deteriorated when Birch was replaced in 1852 by Frederick Gibbs, a lawyer and former Fellow of Trinity College, Cambridge. Birch's schedule of work had been formidable enough, but Gibbs immediately increased it, and added lessons in riding, drill, and gymnastics. Not altogether surprisingly, the condition of the subject did not improve.

By this stage Albert and Victoria were becoming seriously troubled by the evident failure of the Plan. Their affection for Bertie was considerable, and he was to them a delightful, amusing, and charming son. In other circumstances they might have realised that his particular quality – and one not to be under-estimated – was a remarkable ability to get on with people, and a questing intelligence and understanding of humanity that marked him out as a truly precocious and exceptionally sensitive boy. But they could never forget that he was the future King of England, and while Prince Albert was tolerant and patient, the Queen kept comparing her young son unfavourably with her husband. And, in the Coburg background, there was the constant drum-beat of Stockmar's high-flown estimates of what a Prince and future King should be. And thus, with the very best of intentions, and with an earnestness and love that is usually underestimated, the young parents laid the foundations of a grievous tragedy for themselves and their son.

The greatest problem of all was Victoria's ardent desire to see Bertie develop as a second Albert, and the realisation that the boy's personality and intelligence were very different from those of his father was the principal cause of her acute disappointment. Immediately after his birth she had written to Leopold that 'I *hope* and *pray* he may be like his dearest Papa', and her impatience with him, which developed early and which was to endure throughout her life, were in contrast to Albert's immense patience and care for his son. She never really deviated from the ambition expressed at Bertie's birth that 'You will understand *how* fervent my prayers and I am sure *everybody*'s must be, to see him resemble his angelic father in *every, every* respect, both in body and mind. Oh! my dearest Uncle, I am sure if you knew *how* happy, how blessed I feel, and how *proud* I feel in possessing such a perfect being as my husband, as he is, and if you think that you have been instrumental in bringing about this union, it must gladden your heart! How happy should I be to see our child grow up like him!'

The father, despite many disappointments, became more realistic, and was evidently very pleased by a favourable report from Stockmar in 1860:

That you see so many signs of improvement in the young gentleman is a great joy and comfort to us; for parents who watch their son with anxiety and set their hopes for him high are in some measure incapable of forming a clear estimate, and are at the same time apt to be impatient if their hopes are not fulfilled.

Greville came to the view that the Queen 'does not much like the child', and there is strong supporting evidence for this view from other observers. Of Prince Albert's devotion and determination to fulfil his view that education was the finest legacy a father could bequeath to his children – a remark which explains his devotion to his wayward father – there is no doubt, and throughout his life his son spoke of him with a love and respect that is evidence in itself. But Albert never wrote to his son as he did to Vicky when she married:

I am not of a demonstrative nature and therefore you can hardly know how dear you have always been to me, and what a void you have left behind in my heart: yet not in my heart for there assuredly you will abide henceforth, as till now you have done, but in my daily life, which is evermore reminding my heart of your absence.

By now the Prince of Wales had been joined in his education by Alfred, and Victoria noticed with concern that there were clear signs of exhaustion in her sons as a result of Gibbs' regime. Dr. Becker, who taught the Princes German, was so worried that he sent Albert a long memorandum in January 1852, pointing out that Bertie's fits of rage and surliness were a perfectly natural reaction to such a regime. 'To anyone who knows the functions performed by the nerves in the human body', he wrote, 'it is quite superflous to demonstrate that these outbreaks of passion, especially with so tender a child as the Prince of Wales in his moments of greatest mental exhaustion, must be *destructive* to the child'. Unfortunately, Becker then, no doubt remembering the stern work ethic of his master, somewhat qualified his strictures, but added that what the Prince needed most of all was encouragement, and certainly not irony or mockery from his parents when he failed to meet their impossibly high standards. Thus, Gibbs, whom the Princes keenly hated, was permitted to continue on his course, and the wise warnings of Becker went wholly unheeded.

That Prince Albert loved his son deeply is absolutely without question, as is his concern for his welfare and future. But there is also no doubt that Bertie had become a severe disappointment, and it is very significant that Becker protested at Albert's use of irony or mockery in reprimanding him. Victoria wrote in her Journal that her

son 'had been injured by being with the Princess Royal, who was
very clever and a child far above her age. She puts him down by a
word or a look, and their mutual affection had been, she feared,
impaired by this state of things'. Many years later she took up this
matter again with Vicky, when she wrote (April 10th 1861) that 'you
did not quite set about making matters better, for you kept telling me
all his most stupid and silly remarks (said as he too often does –
without thinking – partly to tease you and partly to give vent to his
temper) and enraged me, low and wretched as I was – greatly. If one
wishes to pour oil and not to "keep the kettle boiling" one must not
repeat everything another who irritates has said – else it of course
makes matters much worse. He left on Monday. His voice made me
so nervous I could hardly bear it'.

   The fact that his elder sister was clearly his father's favourite, and
that he was often the victim of his rebukes and sarcasm, clearly left
its mark on his already faltering self-confidence.

   There was also the fact that the children could not fail to notice the
occasional – but violent – explosions of anger between their parents,
all the more frightening because they occurred so seldom but were so
intense. Indeed, by selection of their sparse correspondence when in
anger the wholly false portrait would be conveyed of an unhappy and
indeed embittered marriage in which harsh accusations of selfishness and worse were exchanged with an alarming vehemence and
passion. The reality was that they loved each other deeply – 'My love
and sympathy are limitless and inexhaustible' Albert wrote to her
after a particularly fierce difference in 1857 – but there were storms
in which Victoria seemed to lose all self-control and would turn on
Albert with a ferocity which made him write on one occasion to her
that 'Neither will I play the part of Greatheart and *forgive*, that is not
at all how I feel, but I am ready to ignore all that has happened and
take a new departure' after another unhappy episode, and, after
another, undated, but probably in 1861:

   You have again lost your self-control quite unnecessarily. I did
   not say a word which could wound you, and I did not begin the
   conversation, but you have followed me about and continued it
   from room to room. There is no need for me to promise to *trust*
   you, for it was not a question of trust, but of your fidgety nature,
   which makes you insist on entering, with feverish eagerness,
   into details about orders and wishes which, in the case of a
   Queen, are commands, to whomever they may be given. This is
   your nature; it is not against Vicky, but is the same with
   everyone and has been the cause of much unpleasantness for
   you. It is the dearest wish of my heart to save you from these and

worse consequences, but the only result of my efforts is that I am accused of want of feeling, hard heartedness, injustice, hatred, jealousy, distrust, etc. etc. I do my duty towards you even though it means that life is embittered by 'scenes' when it should be governed by love and harmony. I look upon this with patience as a test which has to be undergone, but you hurt me desperately and at the same time do not help yourself.

The Prince brought to his task of Bertie's education a remarkable enthusiasm and dedication. Throughout his eldest son's childhood he was himself immensely busy, impressing everyone by his prodigious appetite for work and the extraordinary width of his interests and knowledge. And yet, every day, he would carefully study the daily report from Gibbs on his sons' progress – or notable lack thereof – and discuss the problems earnestly with his wife. At no point that I can discover did he entertain serious doubts about his methods, although Stockmar did. In a fascinating comment to Gibbs, Stockmar described the Prince of Wales as 'an exaggerated copy of his mother', but that 'you must make it the business of your life to do the best you can. And if you cannot make anything of the eldest you must try with the younger one'. In the event, Alfred was to prove an even worse candidate for the Stockmar-Albert experiment. Stockmar, indeed, began to harbour suspicions that the bad blood on the mother's side was coming out in the sons, and particularly noted how the bad Dukes had taken 'the greatest pleasure in making mischief – in giving pain to people and in setting them one against the other'. An effort to acquaint the boys with contemporaries at Eton was a dismal failure. Starved of companionship all their young lives, with virtually no friends, their bewildered shyness and lack of confidence manifested itself in such rudeness that the Provost of Eton complained strongly to Gibbs about their conduct. In later life the Prince of Wales admitted that he had been intolerant and suspicious in his youth, and too willing to make use of his position.

One becomes very conscious of the fact that by the time he was in his early teens his father's concern for him had developed into impatience and disappointment, although love – deeply reciprocated – never faded. All the early plans that he and the Queen had discussed for giving her heir a significant role in government and giving him their confidence had long been abandoned. Victoria did have her doubts. 'You say no one is perfect but Papa', she wrote to Vicky in 1861, 'but he has his faults, too. He is often very trying in his hastiness and over-love of business, and I think you would find it trying if Fritz [Vicky's husband] was as hasty and harsh (momentarily and unintentionally as it is) as he can be!' One of his few permitted companions – the future Marquess of Lincolnshire – wrote that 'he was afraid of his father, who seemed a proud, shy, stand-offish man, not calculated to make friends easily with children. I was frightened to death of him'. And Queen Victoria did not exactly help with her repeated admonitions to her son to live up to the standards of a father 'so great, so good, *so faultless*'.

But in spite of all disappointments and frustrations, the father never stopped trying. He took his son to important occasions, introduced him to eminent men, taught him to shoot and fish, instilled in him Bertie's lifelong love of the Turf, and took him frequently to the theatre. Science, literature, music and art were drawn to the boy's attention and interest, and with permanent good effects. On this aspect, Albert's consideration and concern for his son were seen at their very best, and although they were deliberately undertaken to broaden the Prince's knowledge and understanding as part of the great programme, they were by far the most successful, and explain why the son, although often unhappy and resentful of his father's severity of standards, so revered and loved him. If there had been more emphasis on attracting the boy's interests and genuine talents, and less on subjecting him to relentless intellectual pressure that was far beyond his capacities, the results must have been very different.

In this sad story Prince Albert must bear the principal responsibility, but not the only one. Queen Victoria, although a totally adoring wife, was basically uninterested in her children until they became adults, whereas her husband, despite his attitude to his two elder sons, was genuinely devoted and sympathetic to all his children, and especially to Vicky. It is not without significance that the most intense strains in their marriage involved, either directly or indirectly, the health and problems of their children. 'It is indeed a pity', Albert wrote to her on October 1st 1856, 'that you find no consolation in the company of your children. The root of the trouble lies in the mistaken notion that the function of a mother is to be always correcting, scolding, ordering them about and organising their activities. It is not possible to be on happy friendly terms with people you have just been scolding'.

It is not at all unusual for a parent to have favourites among children, just as it is not at all uncommon for children to have a particular favourite in their parents, and the fact that Albert failed to understand his elder son and became progressively exasperated by him is quite understandable. It was the son's deep misfortune that, being the Heir, he was to be systematically moulded into near-perfection by methods that were wholly inappropriate to his essentially warm, relaxed, and affectionate personality. In retrospect, and not only in retrospect when one reads his tutors' daily reports, it is evident that even as a child there was no hope of bringing him remotely to the intellectual level that his father desired. His mind, although good, lacked any spark of that urgent thirst for knowledge and understanding of its practical applications that made Albert such an extraordinary man. Indeed, it is clear that Stockmar was absolutely right when he described Bertie as 'an exaggerated copy of his mother', but she, besotted by Albert, despite their frequent and sometimes violent, differences, had at this stage little real interest in her children, as she frankly recognised with characteristic honesty in a letter she wrote to the Queen of Prussia on October 6th 1856:

> Even here, when Albert is often away all day long, I find no especial pleasure or compensation in the company of the elder children ... and only very occasionally do I find the rather intimate intercourse with them either easy or agreeable. You will not understand this, but it is caused by various factors.
>
> Firstly, I only feel properly *à mon aise* and quite happy when Albert is with me; secondly, I am used to carrying on my many affairs quite alone; and then I have grown up all alone, accustomed to the society of adult (and never with younger) people – lastly I cannot get used to the fact that Vicky is almost grown up. To me she still seems the same child, who had to be kept in order and therefore must not become too intimate. Here are my sincere feelings in contrast to yours.

Here was the real problem. As Sir Philip Magnus has shrewdly, and rightly, observed: 'Unlike the Queen, the Prince Consort tried to treat his children as equals; and they were able to penetrate his stiffness and reserve because they realised instinctively not only that he loved them but that he enjoyed and needed their company. All, except the Princess Royal, were afraid of him, but in a very interesting conversation with Lord Clarendon in December 1858, Prince Albert expressed "something like regret or doubt" at what he termed the "aggressive" system that the Queen had followed. He explained that "he had always been embarrassed by the alarm which he felt lest the Q's mind should be excited by any opposition to her will; and that, in regard to the children, the disagreeable office of punishment had always fallen on him"'.[1]

The more one examines the correspondence, the detailed reports, and the stern admonitions, the more one realises how deeply Prince Albert cared for his children.

[1] Magnus: *King Edward VII*, p. 20.

So far as his relationship with Bertie is concerned, the more one is struck by the remarkable similarities between that relationship and that which subsequently existed between Lord Randolph Churchill and his son, Winston, who only subsequently appreciated how deeply his father had cared for him, and how remote and selfish had his mother been. Churchill's poignant remark, 'I loved her dearly – but at a distance', could have been uttered with equal fervour by the Prince of Wales about his mother. There is a certain significant coldness in her Journal comment on August 27th 1856:

> We took leave of poor Bertie, who was pale and trembling for some time before, and much affected, poor dear child, at the prospect of this first long separation, for he feels very deeply. Though it is sad, I am sure it will be for his own good.

Prince Albert's mounting uneasiness about the effects on his son of the regime which he had so enthusiastically endorsed, and had planned so carefully, now became gradually apparent. There was a marked relaxation, manifested in approval for a European tour – admittedly carefully controlled and monitored – and also in matters such as his personal allowance and freedom to buy his own clothes, a privilege marred for him by his mother's admonition not to 'wear anything *extravagant* or *slang*, not because we don't like it, but because it would prove a want of self-respect and be an offence against decency, leading – as it has often done in others – to an indifference to what is morally wrong'. The more one reads Queen Victoria's letters to her son the more does one appreciate why his reverence for her was never really translated into love. 'I feel very sad about him', she wrote bluntly and coldly in March 1858. 'He is so idle and weak. God grant that he may take things more to heart and be more serious for the future and get more power. The heart is good, warm and affectionate'.

But his backwardness emerges very clearly from his letters to his parents, although there is a particularly sad one written on August 25th 1859:

> My dear Papa,
>   I hope you will accept my best wishes for many happy returns of your birthday. May you live to see me grow up a good son, and very grateful for all your kindness. I will try to be a better boy, and not to give Mama and you so much trouble. Very many happy returns of the day.
> I am, my dear Papa,
>   Your most affectionate son,
>   Albert.

When he went on an unofficial, and largely incognito, tour of the country in 1857, his reports were noticeably superficial (thus, on Leeds: 'it is a very dirty town, & the inhabitants are very low people'), and those he sent to his father on trips to Europe in 1858 and 1859 drew pained and rather scathing letters and comments from his father. When Bertie met Metternich his report was simply that he was 'a very nice old gentleman and very like the late Duke of Wellington' (Metternich wrote of Bertie: 'Il avait l'air embarrassé et très triste'). Albert wrote that he was 'not pleased' with his son's letters, nor with the standard of the Journal that he instructed his son to keep. On reading them, one appreciates his concern. Thus, a letter from Nuremburg, January 15th 1859:

My dear Papa,
    The ball at Brussells went off very well & was very pretty, I enjoyed it very much. Uncle Leopold spoke a great deal about the affairs in Italy, & the probability of a war, he was very much alarmed about it. We left Brussells last Thursday at 9.30 & arrived at Cologne after a prosperous journey at 4 o'clock ...

Concerned by what to him appeared the extraordinary political naïveté of his son, Albert wrote to him at length an analysis of the European situation, and with particular reference to the crisis in Italy. All he received in return was a letter from Rome, on March 14th 1859, in which Bertie simply remarked: 'Many thanks for your long & interesting letter which I received this morning by Post. It is very kind of you to explain to me the politics of the different nations, which certainly seem very complicated'.

Meanwhile, Albert, having vetoed Bertie's desire to join the Army, agreed that he should sit for the military examination, and organised his preparation under Gibbs at White Lodge, in Richmond Park. A trio of supervisors – two of whom had won the Victoria Cross in the Crimea – was appointed after careful vetting, and given detailed instructions about how he was to be brought into manhood. The care and detail of Prince Albert's advice, covering 'Appearance, Deportment and Dress', 'Manners of Conduct towards Others', and 'The Power to Acquit Himself Creditably in Conversation, or whatever May Be the Occupation of Society' appear at first glance to be insufferably earnest and glum, but bear a second look. Admonitions about dress ('he will borrow nothing from the fashions of the groom or the gamekeeper, and whilst avoiding the frivolity and foolish vanity of dandyism, will take care that his clothes are of the best quality') are balanced by the recognition of the fact that whereas trivia such as gossip, cards, and billiards are deplorable 'some knowledge of those studies and pursuits which adorn society

and make it interesting' was essential. Furthermore, 'The manners
and conduct of a gentleman towards others are founded on the basis
of kindness, consideration, and the absence of selfishness' has an
authentic ring, and certainly left its mark. Albert's chronic shyness,
nervousness, and sense of duty often effectively concealed – but not
to his family and closest associates, a genuine kindness and gentleness. Throughout this apparently tedious memorandum there
shines a deep concern for his son, and an absolutely sincere desire to
help him.

    To the immense relief of Bertie, Gibbs was removed from his
arduous and singularly ill-conducted responsibilities in November
1858. The mother took comfort in 'his implicit reliance in everything
on dearest Papa, that perfection of human beings!' while the father,
although considering 'Bertie grown up and improved', was troubled
by his increasing fascination with clothes, and his lack of 'mental
occupation'. Thus, while the Queen continued to lament his
deficiencies and his inability to match up to the qualities of his
father, Albert was becoming more realistic. 'His manners have
improved very much and the best school for him is the external stress
of life', he wrote to his beloved elder daughter, while expressing
dismay at his son's continued erratic behaviour – at one moment
charming and impressive, and yet treating his servants so badly.
Unconsciously echoing Stockmar's comment, the Queen wrote to
Vicky that 'Bertie ... is my caricature. That is the misfortune, and,
in a man, this is so much worse. *You* are quite your dear, beloved
Papa's child'.

These events have immense significance in comprehending the
complex characters both of Albert and Victoria, and their marriage.
As the sad saga of Albert Edward, Prince of Wales, gradually unfolds
the observer is struck less by the imperfections of the father than by
the inadequacies of the mother. One can easily lament, and criticise,
what he and Stockmar tried to accomplish, but one can understand
why they attempted it just as easily as it is easy, with all the benefits
of hindsight, to realise why they failed. But it is remarkable that a
mother could have remained so indifferent to the obvious distress of
a child, and could have so freely accepted, over many years, a regime
that was obviously so unsuited to him. Her adoration of her husband
cannot be regarded as an adequate explanation, nor her reverence
for Stockmar. Thus, while she condemned her son as 'a thorough
and cunning lazybones' (January 1860), the Prince was delighted
when Stockmar or anyone else reported favourably upon him, and
there is a certain humour when he wrote of his son that 'usually his

intellect is of no more use than a pistol packed at the bottom of a trunk if one were attacked in the robber-infested Appennines'.

One is reminded again of Winston Churchill's relations with his father, and his account of how that relationship ended:

> To me he seemed to own the key to everything or almost everything worth having. But if ever I began to show the slightest idea of comradeship, he was immediately offended ... Just as friendly relations were ripening into an Entente, and an alliance or least a military agreement seemed to my mind not beyond the realms of reasonable endeavour, he vanished for ever.[1]

The removal of Gibbs was long overdue, and this delay may be regarded as a major error. Major Robert Lindsay, equerry to the Prince of Wales, wrote to Phipps that he considered that 'a continuance of the present system will not be beneficial to the Prince ... Mr. Gibbs has *no* influence. He and the Prince are so much out of sympathy with one another that a wish expressed by Mr. Gibbs is sure to meet with opposition on the part of the Prince ... Mr. Gibbs has devoted himself to the boy, but no affection is given him in return, nor do I wonder at it, for they are by nature thoroughly unsuited to one another. I confess I quite understand the Prince's feelings towards Mr. Gibbs, for tho' I respect his uprightness and devotion, I could not give him sympathy, confidence or friendship'. (July 27th 1858). Action was taken, belatedly, and Gibbs was retired. 'Mr. Gibbs certainly failed during the last 2 years entirely, incredibly', the Queen wrote to the Princess Royal. But although the Prince of Wales had proved a terrible disappointment to his mother, Prince Albert emphasised that 'Bertie has remarkable social talent', which he demonstrated in Berlin and on a highly successful and greatly praised official visit to Canada and the United States in 1859. Gibbs was replaced by Colonel Robert Bruce, brother of Lord Elgin, who received the formal title of 'Governor' to the Prince of Wales.

Meanwhile, however, the Prince of Wales's desire to enter the Army and make a career had been frustrated, he had been 'bored to death' at White Lodge, and his brief periods at Edinburgh, Oxford, and Cambridge Universities, where he was strictly segregated, were not happy. This segregation from his contemporaries was made even worse by his father's insistence that his son gave select dinner parties for eminent senior members of the Universities, and on being given the lists of guests. Not surprisingly, these were sombre and worthy, and one's heart aches for a young man presiding over dinners such as

---

[1] Winston Churchill: *My Early Life*, p. 46.

one he gave at Madingley Hall, where the guests were the Vice Chancellor, 'the aged Prof. Sedgwick', the Senior Tutor of Trinity, the Masters of two colleges, and the Public Orator, and one is not surprised to read Bruce writing of 'the poignant contrast between the portly grey-haired guests and the faintly epicene beauty of their adolescent host'. Even as a child, Bertie had given clear evidence of what proved to be a lifelong facility to become quickly bored, and his heroism, both at Oxford and Cambridge, in presiding over such glum and intellectual feasts to please his father deserved more praise than it received. His father greatly enjoyed the company of such men, and it was one of the reasons for his success at Cambridge as Chancellor. He found it impossible to comprehend that his son did not, and the latter's enduring distaste for intellectuals was perhaps the only real result of his brief and unhappy sojourns at these ancient Universities.

Bruce, having noted his success and social talent, counselled the parents that an early marriage was highly desirable. It was evident that the Prince, in spite of his closetted and unhappy education, had a natural and infectious charm, and as he emerged from his isolation and boredom into young manhood was increasingly – and understandably – attracted by the many pleasures which suddenly opened before him. While Albert lamented his son's fascination for clothes and taste, Bruce was more worried about other aspects of Bertie's developing hedonism. The only contemporaries he had truly appreciated at Oxford were a notably hard-drinking, hard-living, and hard-riding group of flamboyantly rich young aristocrats, and there had been an incident on the European tour when Bertie had much too much to drink and had embraced a lady (an event sonorously described by Gladstone as 'a squalid little debauch'). Prince Albert had detected the good side, that his son had 'remarkable social talent' and could be 'lively, quick and sharp when his mind is set on anything, which is seldom', but he returned from one visit to Oxford 'terribly anxious for the future'. Meanwhile, the subject of these earnest conclaves was in miserable isolation at Madingley Hall, five miles out of Cambridge, gloomy and frustrated, still appealing to his parents to be allowed to have a military career, and at least a period of service with the Guards.

But the sudden and unexpected flowering of their difficult, volatile, and temperamental son into a young man of great popularity and with a real personal style considerably disconcerted his parents, and made them very receptive to Bruce's arguments. Thus, the hurried search for a suitable bride began.

Having agreed that the Heir could only marry a Royal wife, the parents were startled by the discovery of how limited the field was.

Vicky, pressed into service on behalf of her parents and brother, was struck (December 21st 1860) by the 'great dearth of nice princesses at present', and on April 20th 1861 wrote again to her mother:

> What are we to do? Unfortunately, princesses do not spring up like mushrooms out of the earth or grow on trees ... I sit continually with the Gotha Almanack in my hands turning the leaves over in hopes to discover someone who has not come to light!

The facts that the future Queen must be a Protestant, a Princess, and from a country with whom Britain was in political amity gravely reduced the options. There was also the factor of Bertie himself, who, when he was informed of the industry being conducted on his behalf, protested strongly, and declared emphatically that he would marry only for love. While Albert's concern was for suitability, he appreciated that an arranged marriage with a plain and undesirable princess would hardly resolve Bertie's problems nor avoid the difficulties to which Bruce had so tactfully alluded. The Queen, while insisting on Royalty, was also very sympathetic on this point.

Vicky, after suggesting the beautiful and intelligent Princess Elizabeth of Wied (later Queen of Romania), to which proposal her brother did not respond favourably, came up with the sixteen-year-old Danish Princess Alexandra, a girl of great beauty, but whose family was unfortunately involved in the interminable Schleswig-Holstein question. An Anglo-Danish marriage to the daughter of the heir to the throne of Denmark would be regarded with great coldness in Prussia and Germany, with which Prince Albert had strong personal sympathies. To add to the already considerable complications, the Queen and the Prince disapproved of the Hesse-Cassel family of which Princess Alexandra's mother was a member.

Nonetheless, there was virtually no available alternative, as the Prince unenthusiastically remarked when he was presented with the photographs of the possible candidates, and his father was now so eager to see his son safely married that the German objections rapidly assumed a lower place in his considerations, and when he heard that the Tsar of Russia was also very interested in Alexandra for his own heir, his remaining reservations vanished. 'It would be a thousand pities if you were to lose her', he told his son, and wrote anxiously to Vicky that 'We dare not let her slip away'.

'What a pity she is who she is!' the Queen wrote on December 8th 1860, and, on February 25th 1861: 'The mother's family are bad – the father's foolish'. But these grave disadvantages were overwhelmed by Vicky's enthusiasm for her when she met Alexandra in May: 'Oh if she only was not a Dane and not related to the Hesses I should say yes – she is the one a thousand times over'.

Thus the matter was settled so far as the Royal parents were concerned. To Vicky the Queen wrote on June 19th:

> Dear Papa and I are both so grateful to you about all the trouble you have taken about Princess Alix. May he only be worthy of such a jewel! There is the rub! When I look at Louis[1] and at the charming, sweet, bright, lively expression of the one – and at the sallow, dull, blasé and heavy look of the other I own I feel very sad . . . The contrast pains me very deeply. Let us hope that certain prospects may make a great change.

Vicky and Fritz ardently promoted the match, in defiance of German nationalist feelings, and the protests of Stockmar and Duke Ernest were rejected with surprising brusqueness, Ernest being bluntly told by Albert to mind his own business and keep out of the matter. Bertie, who received a somewhat precise, but not unsympathetic, memorandum from his father on the subject of matrimony before his departure, went to Germany on the pretext of attending military manoeuvres, and met Princess Alexandra in the romantic context of a rendezvous in front of the altar in the cathedral at Speyer on September 24th. On the following day they met again, and Fritz reported that 'the reverse of indifference on both sides' had been demonstrated. On his return to Balmoral he spoke very approvingly to his mother of Alexandra. 'Bertie is extremely pleased with her', she wrote to Vicky, 'but as for being in love, I don't think he can be or that he is capable of enthusiasm about anything in the world'. As Bertie had met Alexandra only twice, very briefly, and was being propelled very reluctantly into matrimony at the age of nineteen, this comment may be justifiably regarded as both unfeeling and unfair. 'As for B's affair', his mother reported to Vicky on October 10th, 'it is not very prosperous. A sudden fear of marrying and above all of having children (which for so young a man is so strange a fear) seems to have got hold of him – but I hope he will see this in its right light ere long'.

Prince Albert was more understanding, although he wished the match to succeed, and wrote to his son about his desire for delay:

> That is quite reasonable and proper, and it would, unless you had actually fallen in love (which after this apparent hesitation

---

[1] Prince Louis, eldest son of Prince Charles of Hesse, and later Grand Duke of Hesse-Darmstadt, who married Princess Alice in July 1862.

can hardly be supposed to be the case) have been imprudent on your part to go further in the matter without due reflection.

Thus matters stood at the middle of 1861, with the Royal parents relieved at the prospects of a reasonably suitable marriage for their difficult and errant eldest son. The Princess Royal was happily married, Princess Alice was engaged, and their other children were thriving, with the sad exception of little Leopold when it became apparent that he was a haemophiliac, and thus an additional centre of the parents' concern.

With this exception, and after all the difficulties they had jointly experienced in their sincere and dedicated endeavours to achieve the best possible upbringing for their children, the Queen and the Prince could justifiably feel that they could be reasonably confident about the future of their large and growing family.

NINE

'SOMETHING GREAT AND GOOD'

The deep concerns of Prince Albert and the Queen about their
children, and the establishment of a pattern of family life at Windsor,
Osborne and Balmoral that they had gradually and personally
created, must be seen as interwoven with their daily concerns on
national and international political issues. Indeed, what is so
remarkable about their correspondence with friends and relatives –
and especially the latter – is the manner in which personal and
public matters were discussed in the same letters, so that they moved
easily and naturally from news of the children's health to the
condition of the weather, the fate of a Government, and the state of
European affairs. Prince Albert's pattern of work was to rise early,
and work by himself for two hours before the Queen joined him for
breakfast, and as his burdens, mainly self-imposed, increased inexorably, so did his hours of work. 'I get on pretty well', he wrote in
April 1857 to his grandmother, 'in spite of a weak stomach, with
which I came into the world, and which I shall take with me to my
grave'.

The width and depth of his interests, especially in the arts and
industry and in military matters, did not diminish. When it was
proposed to launch an Art Treasures Exhibition in Manchester he at
once offered to lend it pictures from the Royal Collection, and then
successfully persuaded other private owners to do the same by his
example – an unprecedented event, with a successful result. But he
was also writing to Palmerston with enthusiasm about 'so important
a new fact as submarine navigation' and exploring the mysteries of
flight, while always involving himself deeply in current national and
international politics. 'I am overwhelmed with papers', he wrote to
his eldest daughter, 'and can scarcely wrestle through them; therefore, even to you I must say farewell so soon'. 'Tired to death with
work, vexation, and worry' he confided to Stockmar on January 5th,
1860. The pace never slowed, and there was no reduction in
endeavour or commitment. But, ominously, there were now regular

references by himself, the Queen, and others to bouts of poor health, exhaustion, irritation, and despondency. But these seemed of little significance, especially when he was with his family at Osborne or Balmoral.

His formidable intellectual energy was combined with a continuing zest for improvements at Windsor and Osborne, and his enthusiasm for the Balmoral 'expeditions' with his family and the hunting about which Theodore Martin wrote that 'In these pursuits the latent fire and force of his character could find a vent, which elsewhere were of necessity held under rigid constraint'. But the shadows were gathering.

In retrospect, it can be clearly seen that Prince Albert's greatest political error had been to underestimate Palmerston. When the Crimean War broke out, the Prince was dominated by a sense of failure that he had not been able to prevent this unnecessary futility. His unhappiness was substantially increased by the fact that all of his concerns about the lamentable condition of the British Army, and especially its leadership, were grimly and totally fulfilled in the Crimea. 'The present administration of the army is not to be defended', he wrote to Leopold. 'My heart bleeds to think of it!' 'I hazard the opinion that our army, as at present organised, *can hardly be called an army at all*, but a mere aggregate of battalions of infantry, with some regiments of cavalry, and an artillery regiment', runs another memorandum submitted to Ministers. In the main his proposals were sensible, although one to raise a British Foreign Legion was publicly denounced in the Commons and Press as 'a foreign idea', and consequently made no progress. The fall of the Aberdeen Government early in 1855 was inevitable, and the appointment of Palmerston as Prime Minister took place in an atmosphere described by the Prince as 'quite crazy'. He headed a Royal Commission to establish a relief fund for the families of the dead, which raised over a million and a quarter pounds, but criticisms of his alleged malign involvement still continued, and the Radical M.P., J. A. Roebuck, even spoke of impeachment. On this amiable proposal the Prince wrote:

We cannot make people either virtuous or wise, and must only regret the monstrous degree to which their aberration is extended. I must rest mainly upon a good conscience and the belief that during the fifteen years of my connection with this country, I have not given a human soul the means of imputing to me that want of sincerity or patriotism. I myself have the conviction that the Queen and myself are perhaps the only two persons in the kingdom who have no other interest, thought, or desire than the good, the honour, and the power of the country; and this not unnaturally, as no *private* interest can be thought of which could interfere with these considerations.

'The *will* at least to injure me is never wanting in certain circles', he added, with some bitterness, 'and the gullibility of the public has no bounds'. Such criticism genuinely baffled and distressed him, although he was now wearily resigned to it. In 1847 he had written that 'I must console myself with the conclusion that from my heart I mean well towards all men, have never done them aught but good, and take my stand on truth and reason, the worship of which becomes daily more and more a matter of conscience with me'. His activities during the war and after, and which included the establishment of the camp at Aldershot, for which he designed the Royal pavilion and donated his personal substantial military library (still known as The Prince Consort's Library) and the foundation and design of Wellington College, with the donation of another library, and the creation of the Victoria's Soldiers Libraries, continued to be publicly denounced as 'the Prince's incessant meddlesomeness'.

The real problem was that he had a regular capacity to be right when the politicians, newspapers, and soldiers were wrong. It was an unhappy period.

What was surprising was that Palmerston, the Prime Minister, turned out to be very different from Palmerston, the incorrigible and reckless Foreign Secretary. Difficulties remained, but his former hostility to Prince Albert moved into cautious respect, and finally, considerable regard.

Palmerston's tenure of the Premiership had a brief interruption early in 1858 after he made a rare and uncharacteristic misjudgement of British opinion by his reaction to an assassination attempt by Felix Orsini on Napoleon in Paris, the bombs and conspiracy having been made in London. It was considered that he had responded too easily to French anger and pressures, and for a time, as Albert noted with amazement, was so unpopular that he was regularly 'hooted down' in the Commons. But the second Derby-Disraeli Ministry was no more durable than the first, and fell in June 1859.

A State Visit by Napoleon III was a substantial success – the Waterloo Chamber at Windsor being tactfully named the Music Room – and after the death of Tsar Nicholas, although the war continued, the search for a settlement began. What worried the

Prince was that this process might be hindered by thoughtless speeches and newspaper articles suggesting that the British were prepared to concede everything, and in a speech at a Trinity House dinner he perhaps went too far in making these views known, which gave the impression that he believed that despotisms had advantages denied to a democracy, and drew much criticism. This was not one of his happier speeches, but what had happened was, as he confessed to Stockmar, his notes had contained 'a qualifying clause, but it did not flow (why I know not) from the lips'. To depict Prince Albert as an admirer of despotism and hostile to liberal democracy was grotesque, but what was true was that he was becoming obsessed by what he regarded as the total irresponsibility of the Press, and particularly W. H. Russell's unsparing dispatches in *The Times*. The alleged statement by the new Tsar that the English Press 'has been most useful to us' made a particular impression upon him, and Russell became a 'miserable scribbler' who was 'despoiling the country of all the advantages which the heart's blood of 20,000 of its noblest sons should have earned'. To be fair to him, it was the first time that the dilemma of uncensored Press reporting in time of war had arisen, and as he compared the British situation with that in France and Russia, it was this that so troubled him. It is a dilemma unresolved to this day.

A highly successful State visit to Paris and the opening of Balmoral lightened the strains of 1855. The Queen became profoundly impressed by Napoleon's charm and handsome good looks – 'at once mystic and Lothario, looking like an opium eater, and speaking French like a foreigner', in the marvellous description of H. A. L. Fisher – but Prince Albert's feelings went from cautious acceptance to dislike and distrust, and, finally, to outright hatred, and fear of what damage the new Emperor could achieve.

One of Napoleon's most severe deficiencies in the eyes of Prince Albert was his hostility to German unification, and when in 1857 the Emperor proposed to him the revision of the 1815 Treaty of Vienna to amend its boundary provisions 'I begged him to open the book of history which lay before him', he recorded.

His verdict was to prove more sound than that of Queen Victoria, and it was an interesting example of how she appreciated male beauty and flattery; it also illustrated one of her most endearing qualities – her ability to forget completely that she was Queen and to respond to attentions given to her as a woman. This was one of the essential keys to the supreme happiness of her own marriage, and also to why, in later years, she turned against Gladstone and found in Disraeli a new Melbourne-figure.

But the happiest event was the engagement between Vicky and

Prince Frederick William, the only son of the Prince of Prussia.
Contrary to some allegations then and later, this was not an
arranged and calculatedly dynastic engagement, but a love match,
which began when the Prince took her to the Great Exhibition in
1851. As the Princess Royal was only 15, there was no question of
an early marriage, but Prince Albert wrote that 'the young people
are ardently in love with one another', although his pleasure was
shadowed by the prospect of losing his favourite child. The Prince,
known in the family as Fritz, then aged 24, was a young man of
great kindness and gentleness. The political possibilities of the
marriage were obviously considerable, and both families were
eager for it for many years, but there was more to it than cynical,
political considerations. Also, as events were to prove, Fritz was the
least calculating of men, and certainly not as strong-willed as his
wife.

These private pleasures were, unhappily, far overshadowed by
other events. Anxiety was making Prince Albert sleepless, and he
deeply resented the unending stream of private and public criticism.
Speaking in Birmingham in June 1857 he set forth again his burning
faith in the power of education in one of his best speeches. It was
widely praised – except in *The Times*. 'Never mind!' Stockmar wrote;
'it pleased *me* very much'.

Peace came slowly. Prince Albert upbraided the King of Prussia for
his neutrality, and Leopold received a firm and fair lesson on British
objectives from his nephew. He continued to submit detailed and
thoughtful memoranda to Ministers on military matters but was, as
Aberdeen shrewdly noted, 'decidedly pacific'. His relations with
Palmerston continued to improve dramatically into a most improbable but genuine friendship and trust, Palmerston admitting frankly
to a friend that until he became Prime Minister he had not appreciated the extent of Prince Albert's extraordinary abilities and
wisdom.

When peace at last came he wrote to Stockmar that he was hard at
work on establishing a permanent and effective military organisation. Florence Nightingale was invited to meet the Royal couple, and
was closely and sympathetically questioned. His other interests and
involvements did not abate. He was selective about which matters he
felt he could take up, but when he made a decision to interest himself
in a subject he did so with immense thoroughness. When the
unfortunate ballast heavers of the Port of London approached him
with their justifiable complaint that they could only obtain work at
the docks through corrupt owners of riverside public houses he

persuaded Ministers to insert a clause in the 1853 Merchant Shipping Act to end this abuse, and transformed their conditions of employment. When John Clabon came to him with his imaginative concept of Working Men's Clubs it was Prince Albert who urged that they be open on Sundays, that families be allowed to join, that dancing should be encouraged, and, when the vexed question of smoking was raised, said that it should certainly be permitted, and not in a separate room. It was with some reluctance that he agreed that the provision of alcohol was hardly consistent with the concept of 'a reformed public house', but he told the virtuous Clabon that his substitution of beer for whiskey at the Balmoral Gillie's Ball had been a great mistake: 'There was dissatisfaction; they did not seem to enter into the dancing with spirit'. He was, as those close to him knew, very human and very tolerant of the less important human frailties, but this came as a surprise to people like Clabon who had only seen the distant façade. The Queen and Prince Albert still resented that he did not have any title, but once more, the politicians said that it was premature to discuss such matters. At a speech in Salford in May 1857 he was able to correct the unfortunate impression given by the Trinity House Speech, and on July 25th Queen Victoria achieved her purpose when, at her command, the Privy Council ordained, by Letters Patent, the creation of the title of Prince Consort. Ministers had, again, been doubtful of passing an Act of Parliament to achieve this, particularly as they expected – wrongly – strong controversy over the proposed dowry to the Princess Royal on her marriage. Exasperated, but careful to wait until the dowry issue was resolved, the Queen made firm use of her prerogative. He had been generally known as the Prince Consort for so long that it seemed superfluous for some, but it meant a great deal to him and to the Queen. *The Times*, again, was highly critical.

On one matter he had to concede to defeat, although not without a spirited battle.

Prince Albert's loathing of the English Sunday had not diminished, and he and the Queen strongly supported a proposal for military bands to play on Sunday afternoons in Kensington Gardens. The opposition by what the Queen angrily depicted as 'the incomprehensible blindness and mistaken piety of the so-called "Evangelical Saints"' made Ministers abandon the plan, fearful of defeat in Parliament, to the deep dismay of the Prince, whose hand is clearly seen in this letter from the Queen to Palmerston:

She really thought that the disgraceful scenes in Hyde Park last year would have opened the eyes of those who act most injudiciously in thinking, by depriving the poor people from

intellectual and innocent amusement on Sunday, they make
them religious! It is very well for those people who have no hard
work during the week to go two or three times to church on
Sunday and to remain quiet for the rest of the day, but as
regards the working classes the practice is a perfect cruelty.

Throughout the detailed record of his activities, which remained
awesome, his concentration upon the arts, the National Gallery, and
the new scientific site at Kensington figure conspicuously, and
especially his delight at the new appreciation of the popular importance of art in the great Provincial cities. But the condition of
education continued to appall him, as did the continuance of child
labour. Of the nearly five million children between the ages of three
and fifteen in England and Wales, he pointed out in a speech to a
national conference on education, nearly three million received no
schooling or instruction whatever, and child labour was 'an evil
which lies at the root of the whole question'.

Military affairs then supervened again, with the outbreak of the
Indian Mutiny. His marriage had coincided with a war in Afghani-
stan and a great British disaster – redeemed the following year – he
had had to endure the strains and abuse during the Crimean War,
and now this most pacific and so well informed of men had his
attention abruptly drawn to a quite unexpected, and particularly
grim, war. 'India', he wrote, 'is a torture to us both'. 'The position of
the Queen's army is a pitiable one', the Queen wrote to Palmerston,
and she and Albert – principally the latter – returned constantly to
the theme of naval and military weakness: 'The Queen is relieved at
seeing the Government now becoming anxious', runs one letter to
Palmerston. The successful ending of the Mutiny, after much blood-
shed and misery, and which opened the way for the complete
absorption of India to British rule, increased rather than diminished
the Prince's concern for the condition of the armed forces, and
especially the lower ranks, still abominably treated in the eyes of
himself and the Queen.

At a time of passionate denunciations of Indian barbarism and
calls for savage revenge uttered, as Lord Canning the Governor-
General, wrote to the Queen, 'loudest by those who have been sitting
quietly in their homes from the beginning, and have suffered little
from the convulsions around them, unless it be in pocket', he and the
Queen strongly supported Canning's policy of conciliation, for
which he was much excoriated as 'Clemency' Canning. The hand of
Prince Albert was very strong in the Royal Proclamation establishing the new administration of India, he and the Queen rejecting the
Government's draft and proposing another so that it 'should breathe

feelings of generosity, benevolence, and religious feeling, pointing out the privileges which the Indians will receive in being placed on an equality with the subjects of the British Crown, and the prosperity following in the train of civilisation'. And thus it was done, the Proclamation declaring that 'we disclaim alike the right and desire to impose our [religious] convictions on any of our subjects'. The Queen wrote to Canning – now the first Viceroy of India – on December 2nd 1858 that 'It is a source of great satisfaction and pride to her to feel herself in direct communication with that enormous Empire which is so bright a jewel in her Crown, and which she would wish to see happy, contented, and peaceful'.

As has been emphasised, the Queen and the Prince were a team, and it is wrong to apportion credit or blame to either individually for their political actions unless there is clear evidence – as there often is – of the principal author. In this case they were both emphatically on the side of tolerance, justice, and forgiveness in India, and wholeheartedly in support of Canning's generous instincts and policies while others were literally calling for blood. It was to their immense credit.

The marriage of the Princess Royal depressed Prince Albert, parting from her 'in tears and snowdrift', and the references to tiredness, illhealth, and indisposition become regular in his own papers and those of the Queen. He escaped a typhoid epidemic at Windsor, but was plunged into gloom at its ravages, having, as the Queen noted, 'a horror of fever'. 'We are over head and ears in work, all kinds of business which is peculiar in that it never brings anything agreeable', runs one letter in February 1859. 'I am tired and dull' states another. The birth of their first grandson – the future Kaiser Wilhelm – was a pleasure, and so were the visits to Balmoral. Osborne had become more formal and Court-like than he had intended, but Balmoral became a place of freedom and happiness.

European politics continued both to fascinate and perplex him, and he was now immersed in plans for a repeat of the 1851 Exhibition, to be held in 1861, but then postponed to the following year. The dream of a united and liberal Germany never faded, in spite of all vexations and disappointments. His opening speech to the British Association for the Advancement of Science was widely regarded as a triumph. But the burdens remained intense, the programme of work immense and increasing, and he seemed unable to emerge from a mood of almost perpetual melancholy; the Queen considered that he took things 'too much to heart', and this was true. There was a visit to Coburg in the summer of 1860, when he was injured in a serious accident, and, on visiting The Rosenau with Ernest, suddenly wept, and told his brother that he would never see the scenes of his childhood again.

He returned to England bitterly to ponder the duplicity of Napoleon, and the significance of reports of a large French naval building programme, urging upon Ministers a British programme of ironclads to ensure parity at sea. Of Napoleon he wrote that 'he has been born and bred a conspirator', and to Ernest that 'May God forgive the man who wantonly between sleep and waking is bringing so much unhappiness into the world'.

He had wisely noted in 1854 on the Emperor that 'He is bound to keep the spectacle, and, as at fireworks whenever a pause takes place between the different displays, the public immediately grows impatient'. As Napoleon flirted with a Franco-Russian *rapprochement* against Austria, espoused Italian aspirations against Austria, advocating revision of the 1815 border treaties, and, while professing undying devotion to Britain, built up the French Navy and the Cherbourg fortifications, Prince Albert's hostility grew more marked. To a courteous warning (April 28th 1857) about the effect on public opinion in France and England of a possible Franco-Russian pact, the Emperor replied 'why disquiet oneself about the mistakes of public opinion?'

He found serious difficulties in accepting the arguments of Palmerston and Russell that Britain should actively support Napoleon against Austria over the issue of Italian independence, once again a major European issue, and one that aroused much passion in England. Fearful of another unnecessary war, or at least responsibility for starting one, Prince Albert urged restraint, but although he complained of Palmerston that 'He has taken towards the Crown quite his old position of 1851 before he was dismissed by Lord John, has again written pamphlets against me and the Coburg influence in order to bear down all opposition', there was no serious rupture.

Oppressed as he was by evidence of his continued unpopularity in certain circles, the paradox was that he was in fact generally now more highly regarded than ever. *The Spectator*, not a notably friendly journal, described him with admiration in 1857 as 'the first gentleman in our commonwealth'. Alexis de Tocqueville, whose *L'Ancien Regime et la Révolution* the Prince greatly admired, wrote after he had met the Prince Consort that 'I have seldom met a man as distinguished'.

In his speeches and memoranda on social questions he had to be careful not to cross the very thin line between expressing his genuine outrage and appearing to be condemning the Government of the day. But his outspokenness whenever he did speak on these matters was remarkable, and his obvious sincerity was beginning to give to the Monarchy that true populism which was to make it so trusted and even loved by people who were the victims of the worst effects of the British industrial and commercial revolution. Even in Ireland, the crowds were large and enthusiastic. Palmerston had become a complete convert, loud in his praises. The regular gunfire from *The Times* and *Punch* was now becoming more sporadic. In the small but increasingly influential world of the arts, architecture, literature and education he now had no critics of any consequence. He had reached, after so many tribulations, an extraordinary pinnacle of achievement and, for the first time since the brief interlude of 1851, real popularity as well as respect; as Leopold later wrote, 'he had reached the difficult point of being fully acknowledged [for] what he was – the superior man of all'. It was true that there many who still regarded him as dull and cold, and Walter Bagehot, a warm admirer, made a fair point when he wrote of Prince Albert that 'he had not the knack of dropping seed without appearing to sow it'. There were also many who believed – and with strong justification – that his heart remained in Germany.

But a remarkable change had occurred in perceptions of his real personality. This was partly the result of Palmerston, who now spoke of the Prince to his friends in politics and the Press with admiration and warmth, and as Palmerston had now reached a position of adulation unparalleled since the death of the Duke of Wellington, this was more important than it might otherwise appear. 'His knowledge and information are astonishing', Granville remarked, and Lady Ponsonby subsequently wrote that 'The qualities of the Prince's character would place him, I think, on a far higher level than those of his mind. Unselfish, patient, kind-hearted, truthful and just, one felt it was possible to rely upon him as upon a strong rock'. In a strange manner that defies historical analysis, this had become widely recognised and understood.

There is, in reality, no mystery in this transformation. It often happens in modern politics that a man is characterised falsely, and it is when people actually meet him that a more true assessment is reached. Indeed, when that characterisation is inaccurately hostile, the counter-reaction is exceptionally strong. Not only artists and musicians found Albert an amusing and stimulating person, but the people who met him in the Isle of Wight and in the Highlands, on his walks and 'expeditions'. His love of children, and his happiness in their company, was genuine and obvious. His wit tended to the sardonic, and his devastating mimicry was confined to the family circle; and although his regrettable enjoyment of puns ('Richard Coeur de Cotton' on Cobden was one example) was not universal, the remark of Lord Malmesbury that Prince Albert had 'a great fund of humour *quand il se déboutonne*' was well known in his ever-widening circle of acquaintances.

This was the point. For twenty years he had travelled to most parts of the country, and the sneers had gradually faded when people actually met him. The British do not object to decency and ability, even though these qualities may make them uneasy. They certainly do not object at all to genuine achievement and courage, and after the assassination attempts the fact that the Queen and Prince went through the country, and in Ireland, virtually unprotected was not unnoticed. His wife was not an impartial commentator, but when she wrote that 'my perfect and beloved Albert' had 'raised monarchy to the *highest* pinnacle of respect, and rendered it popular beyond what it *ever* was in the country' her opinion was generally endorsed by the crowds and enthusiasm they experienced not only wherever they went together, but also when he went alone.

But only he seemed unaware of this subtle but crucial change in his public fortunes. He found the spring of 1860, as he wrote to Vicky, tarnished and blemished by 'some many things that remind me of the world of miserable men', and went on:

> The donkey in Carisbrooke, which you will remember, is my true counterpart. He, too, would rather munch thistles in the Castle Moat than turn round the wheel at the Castle Well; and small are the thanks he gets for his labour.

Prince Albert's physical constitution had never been strong, and although weakness in childhood often proves a surprisingly poor guide to future health, in his case he was often unwell and never enjoyed the robust and remarkable constitution of his wife. Increasingly, he worked obsessively long hours, was impatient of meals, tired easily, took too much trouble over details, and cared too deeply over vexations, frustrations, and criticisms. Indeed, there is a clear connection between his severe stomach disorders and sleeplessness and moments of particular strain, of which that between the attacks on the Queen and himself over the prelude to the Crimean War and his physical illness at the time was only one example. In addition he had attacks of severe rheumatism which he described to Stockmar as 'the long nights of sleeplessness and pain'. The Queen, who had been warned by the faithful and concerned Anson as early as in 1844 of the, even then, severe burdens upon his master, was sympathetic, and noted how he was 'torn to pieces with business of every kind', but like most people with excellent health she was often somewhat impatient with her husband's weakness, as she had been as a girl at his habit of falling asleep after dinner and disliking late functions. She wrote to Vicky on February 13th 1861 when Albert was suffering from a raging toothache that 'dear Papa never allows he is any better or will try to get over it, but makes such a miserable face that people always think he's very ill. It's quite the contrary with me always ... His nervous system is easily excited and irritated, and he's so completely overpowered by everything'.

Now, private sadnesses such as the death of his devoted valet, Cart, affected him deeply. The international scene constantly depressed him, and with good reason. The immense work involved in the preparation of the Great Exhibition and its 1862 successor had taken a far greater toll than anyone fully appreciated. Stockmar was in Coburg, an old man. Albert's narrow escape during the ill-fated Coburg visit had upset him very badly. His brother wrote that it was 'only too evident on this occasion how greatly the Prince's nervous system is shaken. When Stockmar ... observed his deep despondency and melancholy, he said to me "God have mercy on us! If anything serious should ever happen to him, he will die" '.

This may have been the turning point. From this moment the references to his poor health and spirits in the Queen's journals and the writings of himself and his staff are constant. In December 1860 he suffered from violent sickness, shiverings, and vomiting, an attack so serious that it caused his doctors considerable anxiety, and which may well have been – as he believed it to be – a mild attack of cholera. The death in a railway accident of his friend and doctor, William Baly, was a particular shock; his successor as Royal Physician was Dr. William Jenner, a very skilled doctor, but a stranger.

The winter of 1860–61 was of exceptional severity, and Christmas Day recorded the lowest temperatures for fifty years throughout the country, and this followed a year of uniformly cold and bad weather. The Prince's recovery from his illness was very slow, and was not hastened by the death of the Duchess of Kent in March 1861. Albert's devotion to her, and the total reconciliation he had achieved between mother and daughter, in some respects one of his most remarkable achievements, made the event especially melancholy. The Queen recorded that 'Albert lifted me up and took me into the next room, himself entirely melted into tears, which is unusual for him, deep as his feelings are, and clasped me in his arms. I asked if all was over; he said, Yes!'

Victoria herself, overwhelmed by her loss, wrote with truth to Leopold that 'Dearest Albert is dreadfully overcome – and well he may, for *she* adored him!' Furthermore, as the Duchess's skilled and loyal Secretary and Comptroller had died two weeks before her – an event that might well have hastened her own death – Albert became her sole executor. Thus was added another burden to many others, and Queen Victoria's prolonged and intense grief meant even more attention to public affairs and papers. Little Prince Leopold caused his parents great and constant concern. Thus, it was a bleak, sad period, which must have seemed to the tired and unwell Albert a succession of misfortunes and tragedies. At what was to be his last official public appearance, the opening of the Royal Horticultural Show in London on June 5th – 'this accursed thing', the Queen called it – it was widely commented upon that he looked wan and exhausted. 'Am ill, feverish, with pains in my limbs, and feel very miserable', he commented. To Ernest he wrote in the summer that 'I know that I dare not stop for a moment to relax. Like the hawk, I must not sleep, but be for ever on the watch'.

Victoria wrote in her Journal on Albert's birthday on August 26th that 'Alas! so much is different this year, nothing festive; we on a journey & separated from many of our children. I am still in such low spirits'.

The traditional autumn holiday at Balmoral was, as always, recorded by Queen Victoria in considerable detail, but in 1861 their anonymous and rather arduous expeditions were undertaken mainly in very wet and cold weather. 'We had travelled sixty-nine miles today, and sixty yesterday', the Queen wrote on October 9th. 'This was the pleasantest and most enjoyable expedition I *ever* made; and the recollection of it will always be most agreeable to me, and increase my wish to make more!' On the 16th, at the end of their travels, 'which delighted dear Albert', she wrote:

> The moon rose and shone most beautifully, and we returned at twenty minutes to seven o'clock, much pleased and interested with this delightful expedition. Alas! I fear our *last* great one!

Normally, the Prince arrived at Balmoral tired and pale, yet recovered quickly and was enormously refreshed by the great 'expeditions' by day, the pleasure of staying at modest inns, the blessed anonymity, the deer stalking, the days of shooting, the meetings with the Balmoral tenants and farmers, and the careful examination of progress and change in the estate and in the Castle gardens. But for once the combination did not have its usual restorative effect. It was noticed that he had a poor colour and tired easily, while the Queen certainly did not. She commented rather briskly that her husband was 'as usual desponding, as men really only are when unwell – not inclined himself ever to admit he is better'. On October 8th she wrote that 'With the help of an umbrella, and waterproofs and a plaid, I kept quite dry. Dearest Albert, who walked from the time the ground became boggy, got very wet, but was none the worse for it'. This was doubtful. As they prepared to leave, John Brown wished them well, and expressed the hope that 'above all, you may have no deaths in the family'. The Queen took this as a reference to her still-lamented loss of her mother, but subsequently regarded it as evidence of Brown's gift of second sight.

The Prince was also becoming very concerned about Bertie, who spent the Cambridge Long Vacation on a training course at the Curragh, near Dublin. His father had not been at all enthusiastic, but had reluctantly agreed. When he and the Queen went to Ireland on an arduous official visit in August and early September the Prince of Wales was marching in the review, but the reports on his progress by his commanding officers were unflattering, and indeed severe. But worse was to come. At the end of a riotous evening some friends smuggled a young actress called Nellie Clifden into his room. This incident could be regarded as harmless, had not Miss Clifden boasted of her conquest, flaunted it, and the rumours began to circulate. Stockmar heard of them, and Lord Torrington brought them to Prince Albert's attention. They turned out to be only too true.

The vehemence of Albert's reaction has been ascribed too much by some biographers entirely to the state of his health. It was, admittedly, very poor. He was clearly also suffering from depression, increased by the sudden death from typhoid of the twenty-five-year-old King Pedro V of Portugal on November 8th. He had been particularly close to Prince Albert, who regarded him as a son; Albert was shocked and distressed. The distress cannot be under-estimated. He wrote to Vicky on November 13th that Pedro 'was qualified to effect infinite good for a degraded country and people, and also to uphold with integrity the monarchical principle and to strengthen the faith in its blessings, which unhappily is so fre-quently shaken to its foundation by those who are its representa-tives'. The Queen, probably rightly, discerned another factor when she wrote to Vicky (November 16th) that 'It has been a terrible blow to us – and to dearest Papa, who found in him one entirely worthy of himself – which he, alas! does not find in those where it was most expected and wanted'.

Nonetheless, Prince Albert's reaction to his eldest son's esca-pade was not entirely the result of these additional misfortunes.

His son was the Heir to the Throne, and virtually engaged to

be married. The fact that the story of Nellie Clifden was all over
London and had even reached Coburg made it more than possible
that it would become a public scandal which was bound to damage
the Monarchy, and this was a poor return for the care and
endeavour which his parents had devoted to him. Also, the
achievement of making the Royal Family morally respectable and
admired was now at hazard, and Albert was haunted by the perils
of heredity – on his wife's side by the amorality of her family, and
on his own by the example of his father and brother, whose pre-
marital sexual excesses and consequent venereal disease had made
him impotent and his marriage childless, yet another frightening
example very much in his mind. The precedents were, in brief, not
heartening. And one should never forget his letter to Stockmar of
January 6th 1846: '... the exaltation of Royalty is possible only
through the personal character of the Sovereign. When a person
enjoys complete confidence, we desire for him more power and
influence in the conduct of affairs. But confidence is of slow
growth'.

Thus, he envisaged Nellie Clifden becoming pregnant, and, if
his son denied paternity, seeing him taken to Court where 'she
will be able to give before a greedy Multitude disgusting details of
your profligacy for the sake of convincing the Jury, yourself cross-
examined by a railing indecent attorney and hooted and yelled at
by a Lawless Mob! Oh horrible prospect, which this person has in
her power, any day to realise! and to break your poor parents'
hearts!'

This was a terrible letter of denunciation, written 'with a heavy
heart upon a subject which has caused me the greatest pain I
have yet felt in this life'. That the letter is absolutely sincere is
unquestionable, and he was right to be deeply worried by the
public implications. It is much too severe to say that 'on the
subject of sex, the Prince Consort was unbalanced',[1] but the
extent of his genuine horror was clearly at least partly the result of
his ill-health, depression, over-work, and unhappiness. But the
Queen's reaction was even more intense: 'Oh! that boy – much as
I pity him I never can or shall look at him without a shudder'. It
is significant that Bertie's abject and heartfelt contrition made
amends so far as Albert was concerned, but his mother was not to
be so forgiving.

Prince Albert was now in a condition of utter, and alarming,
dejection, 'low and sad', as the Queen noted on November 14th. He
had told Ernest in tears at Coburg that he would never see the

---

[1] Woodham-Smith, op. cit., p. 416.

countryside of their childhood again. Now he alarmed his wife by telling her that 'I do not cling to life. You do, but I set no store by it ... I am sure that if I had a severe illness I should give up at once, I should not struggle for life. I have no tenacity for life'.

That this was the case is obviously true. Stockmar and Ernest had noted it with concern the previous year.

As every doctor knows, there *is* such a thing as the will to live, which is medically unquantifiable but does exist and which does enable people to conquer illness which might otherwise be fatal. But its absence puts even the best physician at a severe disadvantage, and there is no question that by November 1861 Albert had lost the will to live. Perhaps it might have been but a phase which afflicts most people of sensitivity at some stage of their lives. It had been, after all, a terrible year, and constant ill-health, overwork, disappointment, difficulty in sleeping, and nervous strain would have brought low even the most optimistic of spirits. But Prince Albert's personality at this time could not be described in this term, and one notices the absence of references in the Queen's journals to the cheerfulness and enjoyment he had previously brought to their marriage and children. Vicky's absence was certainly a major contributor to his melancholy, and his wife's almost unnaturally lengthy period of grief and virtual retirement after her mother's death cannot have helped. He became increasingly concerned by her constant dwelling upon what she called 'a life sorrow', which even the traditional Balmoral holiday failed to remove entirely. 'For your Mama', he wrote to Vicky, 'who lives much in the past and future, perhaps more than in the present, it is a spiritual necessity to cling to moments that are flown and to recollections, and to form plans for the future'. To her she wrote mournfully on August 26th that 'I think *so* much of dearest mamma, and miss her love and interest and solicitude *dreadfully*; I feel as if we were no longer cared for'. Lord Clarendon commented to the Duchess of Manchester on the Queen's 'morbid melancholy', and there are several indications of Albert's impatience. Their love was not affected at all. 'How many a storm has swept over our marriage', he wrote to Stockmar, 'and still it continues green and fresh and throws out vigorous shoots'.

In this low condition of mind and body he went to Sandhurst on November 22nd to inspect the buildings for the new Staff College and Royal Military Academy. This was another product of his imagination and zeal, and another monument to the extraordinary width of his interests and concerns. But it was a day of pouring rain and cold – *'entsetzlicher Regen'* ('terrific rain') he wrote in his diary; he returned to Windsor wet, cold, and complaining of rheumatic pains.

He contracted a severe feverish cold, and found great difficulty in sleeping at all. On November 24th he wrote in his diary: 'Am full of rheumatic pains, and feel thoroughly unwell. Have scarcely closed my eyes at night for the last fortnight'. Nonetheless he journeyed to Madingley on November 25th for what he regarded as an essential, if painful, meeting with Bertie. On a bitterly cold day he walked for a long time with his son. He returned again utterly exhausted and 'greatly out of sorts'. *'Bin recht elend'* ('Am very wretched') his diary records. The Queen wrote to Vicky on the 27th that 'I never saw him so low'.

But his last meeting with his son had given pleasure to both. Albert was impressed by Bertie's genuine contrition and his refusal to name the officers who had been responsible for his disgrace. 'It would have been cowardly to sacrifice those who have risked themselves for you, even in an evil deed', his father wrote approvingly. 'We did not intend to prosecute the inquiry into their detection ... The past is past. You have to deal now with the future'. In this loving letter, the last he wrote to Bertie, he said:

> You *must* not, you *dare* not, be lost. The consequences for this country, and for the world, would be too dreadful!

Jenner became seriously concerned, but at this point the trouble seemed to be a classic combination of a feverish cold, utter exhaustion, and nervous strain.

But the burdens of State remained as onerous as ever, and the width of his interests and concerns still remained remarkable, the Horticultural Society, the plans for the 1862 Great Exhibition, the merits of the breech-loading rifle – 'As for Prince Albert's rifle mania', Cobden declared, 'that is pure Germanism in the disguise of British patriotism' – the future of the Volunteers, the condition of the Government, his profound worries over another wave of intense anti-German feeling in the English Press – notably *The Times* – the problems of Prussia, and the American Civil War that had opened in January and now threatened to involve England. In his last letter to Stockmar he wrote: 'How are you? It is useless to ask, for you will not answer, yet an answer I should very much like to have. To be forced to be so wholly without interchange of thought with you is to me a great privation'.

The American Civil War had brought considerable public and political support for the Confederacy in England, and in November the British Government, informed that there was a possibility of the

British ship *Trent* being boarded by a Federal warship to remove representatives of the Confederacy voyaging to England, warned the American Minister – Charles Francis Adams – of the serious implications of such an action. Nonetheless, the action was taken, and when the *Trent* arrived at Southampton and the story became known the public and Parliamentary reaction was of an intensity only too reminiscent of the mood just before the Crimean War.

Palmerston and Russell[1] responded to this mood by preparing a memorandum listing a series of demands of the Northern Government, which, if not acceded to in full would result in the severing of diplomatic relations within seven days. Furthermore, the Admiralty issued instructions to the Navy which could only be interpreted as preparations for war.

Ill though he was, the Prince saw the incendiary nature of the *Trent* memorandum, but he also saw a possible escape. Two of the passengers on the *Trent* averred that the boarding officer had said he was doing so on his own initiative, without instructions from Washington. Using this, Prince Albert prepared for the Queen a masterpiece of diplomatic and political sense. The main point of the British protest – which was quite justifiable – was not abandoned, but the Americans were given the opportunity of expressing their regrets and freeing the four passengers 'with suitable apology'. Palmerston and Russell at once agreed to the vital changes in language and tone, and the Americans gladly seized the compromise. It is hardly to exaggerate that a totally unnecessary major crisis was thereby averted, which could easily – indeed, almost certainly – have resulted in conflict.

The episode was instructive and important for other reasons. The first was that the Queen had been as vehemently outraged by the American action as had her Ministers, and had no disagreement at all with the belligerent memorandum, whose theme she warmly endorsed. The Prince Consort was swiftly able to persuade her that she was wrong, and that the policy must be changed. Then, the Government, so fiercely warlike, succumbed to his reason with immediate agreement. Never was Russell's tribute to Albert – 'an informal but potent member of all Cabinets' – so totally justified. It was an extraordinary example of the extent to which the reality of his influence and power had expanded since the Crimean War, to the point when he could now overturn the policy of Ministers, the

[1] Lord John Russell had become Earl Russell in July, on which event Albert wrote to Stockmar on July 29th that he 'will perhaps be surprised when he sees his influence in the country damaged. However, the atmosphere of the Upper House may perhaps have a soothing influence upon him'.

attitude of the Queen, and the surge of Press opinion. It was to be his last, but one of his greatest, services to his adopted country.

Prince Albert had been so unwell when he prepared the Queen's proposals on the *Trent* memorandum that he could hardly hold his pen. His illness now gathered, and now the Queen became seriously worried for the first time, although, on December 4th she wrote to Leopold that his ailment was only 'a regular influenza, which has pulled and lowered him very much ... you know how he is always *so* depressed when anything is the matter with him'. The doctors were not alarmed, but when he calmly told her that he would not recover a knell sounded. To Princess Alice he simply said that he was dying. On December 9th Sir Henry Holland and Dr. Thomas Watson joined the team. Palmerston, who was very worried indeed, urged additional medical advice, and although the Queen curtly dismissed the suggestion she wrote in her Journal that she was in 'an agony of despair about my dearest Albert and crying much, for saw *no* improvement & my dearest Albert was so listless and took *so* little notice'. On December 5th she wrote that 'he did not smile, or take much notice of me, but complained of his wretched condition, and asked what it could be, and how long this state of things might last ... His manner all along was so unlike himself, and he had sometimes such a strange wild look'.

Two bad days and nights followed, and Phipps reported to Palmerston on December 7th that his situation had deteriorated and 'that it requires no little management to prevent her from breaking down altogether'. Palmerston, who had considerable regard for Watson, urged Phipps on December 10th to seek additional advice at Watson's discretion: 'This is a matter of the most momentous national importance, and all considerations of personal feeling and susceptibilities must absolutely give way to the public interest'.

The decline now became remorseless. There seemed to be a slight improvement on the 10th and 11th, but on the 12th Phipps warned Palmerston by telegram and letter by special messenger that the situation was now grave; they came upon Palmerston, in his own words, 'like a thunderbolt'.

After wandering around the Windsor corridors in his thick quilted dressing gown, Albert had now settled into the Blue Room, an ominous choice, as it was in this room that both George IV and William IV had died. The doctors told the Queen that the cause of the illness was 'great worry and far too hard work for long', and that 'the fever must run its course'. The patient was restless, feverish, and irritable. His mind was now fitfully wandering, and he believed that he was back at The Rosenau. The Queen wrote: 'I went to my room & cried dreadfully & felt oh! as if my heart must break – oh! such agony as exceeded *all* my grief this year. Oh God! help me to protect him!'

Dr. Watson had at once realised that Albert was very ill indeed, and the first public bulletin was issued to state that the illness was 'of a more serious nature than was at first anticipated'. It is not clear whether Watson, who enjoyed a deservedly high reputation, had yet diagnosed that he had typhoid fever, although a reference to the fact that 'the malady is very grave and serious in itself' points to the possibility that he suspected.

After what appeared to be a slight improvement, the patient's condition abruptly declined. The Queen became distraught outside his room, but calm and loving inside it. Bertie was summoned – not by his mother but by his sister Alice – and the family gathered.[1]

The bulletins became more sombre. December 14th opened more hopefully, as the Queen recorded:

> Sir James Clark was very hopeful – he had seen much worse cases. But the breathing was the alarming thing, it was so rapid. There was what they call a dusky hue about his face and hands, which I knew was not good. I made some observation about it to Dr. Jenner, and was alarmed by seeing he seemed to notice it.
>
> Albert folded his arms, and began arranging his hair, just as he used to do when well and was dressing. There were said to be bad signs. Strange! as though he were preparing for another and greater journey.

Inexorably, and without any perceptible struggle, he slipped away, and died peacefully in the evening of December 14th.

Phipps wrote to Palmerston:

> ... The Queen, though in an agony of grief, is perfectly collected, and shows a self control that is quite extraordinary. Alas! she has not realised her loss – and, when the full consciousness comes upon her – I tremble – but only for the depth of her grief. What will happen – where can She look for that support and assistance upon which She has leaned in the greatest and the least questions of her life?

· · ·

---

[1] Four of the children – Alfred, Leopold, Vicky and Beatrice, aged four – were not present. Alfred was at sea, Vicky was told too late of the critical state of her father, Leopold was at Cannes, and Beatrice was deliberately kept away from the scene.

Prince Albert's body was temporarily placed in the Royal Vault in St. George's Chapel, and then, on December 18th 1862, eventually laid to rest in the Royal Mausoleum at Frogmore in Windsor Park, designed by his old friend, Ludwig Gruner. His grieving wife commissioned a moving effigy, designed by Carlo Marochetti, of him and her, lying together on top of the tomb in which, in due course thirty-nine years later, her effigy and body joined his.

The funeral obsequies were elaborate, and for several years Queen Victoria seemed inconsolable. How she gradually emerged from this terrible period, re-created her life, and departed from her husband's caution and political impartiality but successfully concealed this from her increasingly admiring subjects, belongs to her biographer and not to his. Her total devotion to his memory concentrated upon the less profound of his qualities; this created a general misunderstanding of his personality, which although remarkably enduring, is sadly inadequate. Less emphasis has been given to the impact of his death upon their children, and particularly the Prince of Wales. Several years later he was overcome with tears when attempting to speak of his father at an official public banquet, and his first statement when he became King Edward VII contained a moving reference to Prince Albert – 'ever to be lamented, good and wise', a tribute so heartfelt that it startled and moved all who heard and read it. Vicky, also, was especially bereft. 'Why has the earth not swallowed me up?' she wrote on her father's death. She was to endure other heart-breaks, but this, the first, was perhaps the most terrible of all. The others, even 'the baby' Beatrice, felt a lifelong sense of personal deprivation.

No assessment of this remarkable individual, perhaps the most astute and ambitious politician of his age, can ignore the simple but vital facts that he was a highly intelligent and acutely sensitive man whose fate was that he had to deal with men of power whose knowledge, experience, and intelligence were often inferior to his, and who were, moreover, aliens. Perhaps he did not greatly like, or certainly did not always understand, the English. This amiable, brave, emotional, selfish, easy-going, and lackadaisical people, with their contempt and distrust for brains and their insularity, grated deeply upon a man of such width of comprehension and knowledge, vision, sensitivity, internationalism, and self-destructive capacity for work. It was this slow-dawning realisation of the gulf of attitudes which existed between himself and his wife's country that inexorably created the melancholy and despair which made the end of his life so sadly shadowed.

It is perhaps fruitless to dwell on what might have happened had Prince Albert lived considerably longer. It is reasonable to speculate that the fortunes of Gladstone and Disraeli would have been considerably different, so far as their relations with the Queen were concerned, and it is possible – although in my view improbable – that the cause of German liberalism against Bismarck, whose full dominance began a year after Albert's death, might have been strengthened by his wisdom and experience, and Fritz – who became Crown Prince in 1858 – and Vicky would certainly have benefited from his knowledge and advice. But the forces that Bismarck assembled to defeat the German Anglophile liberals were so powerful that it is questionable whether Prince Albert's influence could have changed the eventual result. What is certain is that the manner in which German unification occurred, and the spirit is which it was led, would have been seen by Prince Albert with dismay and misery. There had been many times when he had deplored, and often angrily, the independence and unreliability of the British Parliament; he believed in a strong and influential monarchy; but he never envisaged anything on the model of what emerged in Germany – a Parliament with no control over the army, no role in policy, and without the power to make or unmake governments. What happened in Germany was the negation of everything he and Stockmar had believed in and worked for.

Obviously, all his achievements were founded upon his marriage, and had he not been the husband of the Queen of England his influence, whether in politics, the arts, architecture or industry, could not have been one fraction of what it became. But he took that opportunity to develop a role unprecedented by any consort of any English monarch, and in the process guided and assisted Queen Victoria through the difficult first years of her eventually triumphant reign. But there was more to this than just guidance and wisdom. As has been related, it was a marriage not without difficulties, but one founded upon a genuine and profound love whose intensity and endurance remain deeply moving. 'How many a storm has swept over it, and still it continues green and fresh and throws out vigorous shoots' he wrote within months of his death, and she wrote of him on his last birthday that 'This is the dearest of days, and one which fills my heart with love and gratitude and devotion'.

There are no false notes here. It remains one of the most moving, as well as the most important, marriages in modern history. Under all difficulties, and in the face of many disappointments, that love not only endured but strengthened. 'It is *you* who have entirely formed me', she told him, and of him she had said to Peel with moving simplicity and truth 'he is so good, and loves me for myself'. If he brought to her a more mature judgement and a better intellect, she contributed to him a warmth, common sense, and passion that gave him not only strength but a happiness and joy which is better reflected in his music and jewellery than in his letters, although the reference to 'flying with you through that lovely ballroom' reaches down the years, and warms the cold paper that lies upon the biographer's table. This was the real thing.

No one could have toiled harder at his many tasks. His childhood had not been without its sadness, but there had been much sunshine and laughter, and the joy of expectations. Thereafter, the sunshine had become more spasmodic, and less frequent, until by the end there was little laughter, much weariness when there had been intense and zestful activity, sadness in place of joy, and few hopeful expectations. But the sunshine of love remained.

It is impossible to improve upon the judgement of Justin McCarthy, written in 1910, that 'A marriage among princes is, in nine cases out of ten, a marriage of convenience only. Seldom indeed is it made, as that of the Queen was, wholly out of love. Seldom is it even in love-matches when the instincts of love are not deceived and the affection grows stronger with the days. Everyone knew that this had been the strange good fortune of the Queen of England. There was something poetic, romantic, in the sympathy with which so many faithful and loving hearts turned to her in her hour of unspeakable distress'.

As Rosebery said of Burns:

It was not much for him to die so young ... After all, in life there is but a very limited stock of life's breath; some draw it in deep sighs and make an end; some draw it in quick draughts and have done with it; and some draw it placidly through four-score quiet years; but genius as a rule makes quick work with it. It crowds a lifetime into a few brief years, and then passes away, as if glad to be delivered of its message to the world, and glad to be delivered from an uncongenial sphere.

During his last illness Albert heard one morning some winter birdsong, and thought it was The Rosenau dawn chorus. He spoke to his wife and family only in German, and asked incessantly for Stockmar, who only survived him until July 1863. In Grey's words, written truly, 'Surely no man was ever endowed with a stronger feeling of love for all the recollections and associations of his youth, and of his native place'. And, at the end, as his life faded, so did the memories of his childhood dominate all others, and his mind moved tranquilly to the soft Coburg hills and valleys, the keeper's house near the little inn, where he and Ernest had created their own garden, and had decorated the little summer-house. 'Never can I forget', Victoria wrote in her account in 1872, 'how beautiful my Darling looked lying there with his face lit up by the rising sun, his eyes unusually bright, gazing as it were on unseen objects & not taking notice of me'.

Stockmar's reaction to the news of Albert's death was his epitaph, as well as that of the Prince:

> Here do I see crumble before my eyes that edifice which I have devoted twenty years to construct, prompted by a desire to accomplish something great and good.

In her acute grief and agony, the Queen wrote to Florschütz:

> *You* know his pure, grand, and great soul ... You saw this great soul in its development and you may be proud of having educated *him*! He, my angel – Albert – my life, the life of my life. He was husband, father, mother, my support, my joy, the light in our deprived home, the best father who ever lived, a blessing to the country ...
>
> I thought of you and how sad you would be.
>
> Pray for me and be assured of my friendly feelings, which will last for ever.

REFERENCES TO DOCUMENTS QUOTED

FROM THE ROYAL ARCHIVES

p 81   Ibid 10 October 1839, 4 June 1836, and 11 October
              1839.
pp 82–3   Ibid 15 October 1839
p 85   RA Z 272/3 (Duke Ernest to the Queen, 19 December
              1839)

CHAPTER FOUR

p 89   The Queen's Journal, 1st January 1840
p 90   Ibid
p 92   RA Z 273/3 (Prince Albert to Lord Melbourne, 20
              December 1839)
p 93   RA Z 273/4 (Lord Melbourne to King Leopold, 23
              December 1839)
p 93   RA Z 273/8 (The Queen to Prince Albert, December
              1839)
p 94   RA Z 273/9 (King Leopold to Lord Melbourne,
              December 1839)
pp 95–6   RA Z 273/11 (Lord Melbourne to Prince Albert, 29
              December 1839)
pp 97–98   RA Z 273/12 (Prince Albert to Lord Melbourne)
p 101   The Queen's Journal, 10 February 1840
pp 111–2   RA Z 272/32 (Prince Albert to Duchess of Coburg)
p 103   RA Y 54/1 (Anson's Memorandum, 19 February 1841)
p 104   RA Y 54/2 (Anson's Memoranda, February and
              March 1840)
p 105   RA Y 54/3 (Anson's Memorandum, 15 April 1840)
p 107   RA Y 54/16 (Anson's Memoranda, 17 February 1841
              and July 24 1840)
p 112   RA Z 272/33 (Prince Albert to Duke Ernest, 21 June
              1840)
p 113   RA Y 153/6 (Stockmar to Prince Albert)
p 119   The Queen's Journal, 23 November 1840

CHAPTER FIVE

p 122   RA Y 54/23–46 (Anson's Memoranda, May 1841)
              The Queen's Journal 17th May 1841
p 123   RA Y 54/ (Anson's Memorandum, 14 June 1841)
pp 123–4   RA Y 54/51 (Anson's Memorandum, 12 June 1841)
p 125   RA Y 54/96&98 (Anson's Memoranda, 12 October,
              19 November, 5 December 1841)
p 126   RA Y 54/100 (Anson's Memorandum, 26 December
              1841)
              RA Add U/2/4 (Prince Albert to the Queen, 16
              January 1842)

p 127   RA Add U2/2 (Prince Albert to Stockmar, 16 January
          1842)
          RA Add U2/1 The Queen to Stockmar, 17 January
          1842
          RA Add U2/4 (The Prince to Stockmar, 18 January
          1842)
          RA Add U2/6 (Stockmar to the Queen, 19 January
          1842)
p 128   RA Add U2/7,8 (The Queen to Stockmar, 19 and 20
          January 1842)
p 129   RA Y 54/20 (Anson's Memorandum, April 26 1841)
          RA M 22/72 and 73 (Prince Albert to Duchess of
          Kent, Duchess to the Prince, 12 January 1843)
p 130   RA M 22/74 (Prince Albert to Duchess of Kent,
          January 1843)
          RA M 22/75 and 71 (Duchess of Kent to Prince
          Albert, 23 March 1843 and 10 January 1843)
p 132   The Queen's Journal, December 1841
p 133   Ibid 15 September 1842
p 133 (footnote) RA A 13/12, 13, 18, 82, 83; B6/48, 50
pp 136–8 RA M 67 ('Attempts on the Queen by Francis and
          Bean 1842, their trial and consequent alteration of the
          law'; memorandum and papers by Prince Albert)
pp 140/144 RA PP Osborne
pp 145–6 RA M 22 (Miscellaneous Family Papers; documents
          relating to Duke of Cambridge and correspondence
          with Peel)
p 146   Princess Victoria's Journal, 21 September 1835
p 151   RA Y 55/10 (Anson's Memorandum, April 30 1843)
p 159   RA C 44/16 (Memorandum by Prince Albert, 7
          December 1845)
          RA C 44/29 (Prince Albert to King Leopold, 30
          January 1846)
p 161   RA Y 92/36 (The Queen to King Leopold, 23
          December 1845)
p 163   RA C 23/14 (The Queen to Peel, 23 January 1846)
          RA C 23/27 (Memorandum by Prince Albert, 30
          January 1846)
p 166   RA C 23/81 (Memorandum by Prince Albert, 18
          February 1846)
          RA C 23/92 (Memorandum by Prince Albert, 25
          February 1846)
p 167   RA C 23/102 (Prince Albert to Peel, 1 March 1846)
p 168   The Queen's Journal, 8th June 1846

CHAPTER SIX

p 170   RA C 17/55 (Prince Albert to Russell)
pp 172–181 RA F 32–35a (Papers relating to Cambridge
             University Chancellorship)
pp 184–5   RA Y 197/27 (Stockmar to Prince Albert, 1 August
             1847)
pp 190–1   RA C 16/52 (Prince Albert to Russell, 29 April 1848)
p 193   RA L 23/1 (Prince Albert to Russell, 30 December
             1849)
pp 194–207 RA F 24–28 (Prince Albert's papers relating to The
             Great Exhibition)

CHAPTER SEVEN

p 209   RA C 17/67 (Prince Albert to Russell, 18 May 1850)
pp 213–4   RA A 79/32 (Prince Albert to Russell, 15 May 1850)
p 215   RA Y 54/99 (Queen Victoria to Russell)
p 217   The Queen's Journal, 26 December 1851
p 218   RA A 81/32 (Memorandum by Prince Albert, 14 July
             1852)
p 225   RA 149/87 (Prince Albert to Stockmar, 24 January
             1854)

CHAPTER EIGHT

p 228   RA Y 148/1 (Prince Albert to Stockmar, January
             1846)
pp 229–30   RA Y 153/9 (Stockmar to Prince Albert, 1 October
             1840)
p 230   RA Y 153/11 (Stockmar to Prince Albert, 21
             November 1840)
             RA Y 153/46 (Ibid to the same, 18 September 1843)
p 231   RA Y 153/48 (Ibid to the same, 27 November 1843)
p 232   RA M 12/20 (Ibid to the same, 8 April 1842)
pp 232–3   RA M 12/14 (Memorandum by Stockmar, 6 March
             1842)
p 233   RA M 12/42 (Stockmar to Prince Albert, 1846)
p 234   RA M 12/40 (Stockmar Memorandum, undated)
pp 234–5   RA M 12/43 (Stockmar Memorandum, 28 July 1846)
p 235   RA M 12/55 (Joint Memorandum by the Queen and
             the Prince)
p 236   RA M 12/66 (Miss Hildyard's Programme)
             RA M 14/3 (Birch to Sir James Clark, 30 May 1848)
             RA M 14/56 (Stockmar to Prince Albert)
pp 236–7   RA M 14/37 (Prince Albert to Birch, 12 April 1849)

p 237   RA M 14/55 (Birch to Prince Albert, undated)
               RA M 14/56 (Birch to Stockmar, 13 December 1849)
               RA M 14/61 (Memorandum to Queen Victoria)
               RA A5/23 (Birch papers, April 1849)
pp 237–8   RA M 14/116 (Birch to Prince Albert, 1846, undated)
pp 238-9   RA M 14/107 and 113 (Dr Combe's Reports)
p 239   RA Y 153/101 (Stockmar to Prince Albert, 4 August
               1849)
p 246   RA Z 461 (Prince of Wales to Prince Albert, 25
               August 1859)
               The Queen's Journal, 27 August 1856
p 247   RA Z 461/35 (Ibid to the same, 10 May 1857)
               RA Z 461/86 (Ibid to the same, 15 January 1859)

CHAPTER NINE

p 268   RA Z 141/94 (Prince Albert to the Prince of Wales, 16
               November 1861)
p 270   RA Z 141/95 (Prince Albert to the Prince of Wales, 21
               November 1861)
pp 272–3   RA Z 142 (Memorandum by the Queen, entitled
               'Account of my beloved Albert's fatal illness from
               November 9 to December 14 1861, written from my
               journal.')

Selected Bibliography

Those works from which quotations have been made are marked
with an asterisk.

*ALBERT, PRINCE CONSORT: Principal Speeches and Addresses (John
  Murray 1862)

Winslow Ames: PRINCE ALBERT AND VICTORIAN TASTE (Chapman and
  Hall 1967)

*Princess Beatrice: IN NAPOLEONIC DAYS: Extracts from the private
  diary of Augusta, Duchess of Saxe-Coburg-Saalfeld. (John
  Murray 1941)

*Daphne Bennett: KING WITHOUT A CROWN (Heinemann 1977)

*A. C. Benson and Viscount Esher: THE LETTERS OF QUEEN VICTORIA,
  First Series (John Murray 1908)

*Hector Bolitho: ALBERT, PRINCE CONSORT (Max Parrish 1964)

*Hector Bolitho: THE PRINCE CONSORT AND HIS BROTHER (Cobden-
  Sanderson, 1933)

Asa Briggs: VICTORIAN PEOPLE (Oldhams Press 1954)

*David Cecil: LORD M. (Constable 1954)

*Henry Cole: FIFTY YEARS OF PUBLIC WORK (G. Bell and Sons 1954)

W. Coningham: LORD PALMERSTON AND PRINCE ALBERT (Effingham
  Wilson 1954)

*Brian Connell: REGINA V. PALMERSTON (Evans Brothers 1962)

*Ernest II, Duke of Saxe-Coburg: MEMOIRS (Remington & Co
  1988 – 4 vols. 1880–90)

Viscount Esher: THE GIRLHOOD OF QUEEN VICTORIA (John Murray
  1912)

F. Eyck: THE PRINCE CONSORT (Chatto & Windus 1949)

*Roger Fulford: THE PRINCE CONSORT (Macmillan 1945)

*Roger Fulford: DEAREST CHILD (Evans & Evans 1964)

H. and A. Gernsheim: QUEEN VICTORIA (Longmans 1959)

*Sir Charles Grey: THE EARLY YEARS OF THE PRINCE CONSORT (Smith,
  Elder 1869)

Christopher Hibbert: GEORGE IV (Allen Lane, 1975)

Hermione Hobhouse: THOMAS CUBITT, MASTER BUILDER (Macmillan 1971)

*K. Jagow: LETTERS OF THE PRINCE CONSORT (John Murray 1938)

*Elizabeth Longford: VICTORIA R I (Weidenfeld & Nicolson 1964)

*(Sir) Philip Magnus: KING EDWARD THE SEVENTH (John Murray 1964)

*Kingsley Martin: THE TRIUMPH OF LORD PALMERSTON (Revised Edition, Hutchinson 1963)

John Matson: DEAR OSBORNE (Hamish Hamilton 1978)

*(Sir) Theodore Martin: LIFE OF THE PRINCE CONSORT (Five volumes, Smith, Elder & Co 1875–80)

*(Sir) Owen Morshead: WINDSOR CASTLE (Phaidon 1947)

*J. H. Plumb and Huw Wheldon: ROYAL HERITAGE (BBC Publications 1977)

Reginald Pound: ALBERT (Michael Joseph 1973)

Joanna Richardson: MY DEAREST UNCLE (Jonathan Cape 1961)

Jasper Ridley: LORD PALMERSTON (Constable 1970)

A. Rimmer: THE EARLY HOMES OF PRINCE ALBERT (Edinburgh 1883)

John Russell; BUCKINGHAM PALACE (Nelson 1968)

*John Steegman: CONSORT OF TASTE (Sidgwick and Jackson 1950)

*Baron E Von Stockmar: MEMOIRS OF BARON STOCKMAR (Longmans 1872–3)

*Lytton Strachey: QUEEN VICTORIA (Chatto & Windus 1921)

*Queen Victoria: LEAVES FROM THE JOURNAL OF OUR LIFE IN THE HIGHLANDS 1848–61, (Smith, Elder & Co 1868) (ed. A. Helps)

INDEX

In this index A = Prince Albert V = Queen Victoria

Aberdeen, George Hamilton Gordon,
  4th Earl of, 64, 79; and the Spanish
  marriage, 150; urged by A to take
  further action on slave trade, 153; A
  protests to about Press criticism,
  155; V and A's admiration for, 168,
  170, 212; allows V's right to be
  consulted, 171; V and A buy
  Balmoral from, 182; Prime Minister,
  219; and the Crimean War, 220–1; in
  storm over Press attacks on A,
  223–4; his Government falls, 255
Adams, Charles Francis (American
  minister), 271
Adelaide, Queen; as Duchess of
  Clarence, 19, 132
Age, The, 155
Albert of Saxe-Coburg and Gotha,
  Prince Consort, 7, 24, 37, 40, 57, 63,
  71, 73, 77, 122, 157; his earlier
  biographers, ix–x; as a child of
  post-Napoleonic German
  Enlightenment, 3; birth, 19; his
  legitimacy, 21–3; and 'Grandmother
  Coburg', 25–6; and Florschütz, 26,
  28; and separation from his parents,
  26–7; his shyness, 28–9; a happy
  childhood, 30; visits Uncle Leopold
  in Brussels, 31; his early education,
  31–3; and religion, 34; and music,
  34–5; his essay on German thought,
  36; influence of Leopold of the
  Belgians, 36; Stockmar's assessment
  of, 41–2; meets V, 45–8; V loves him
  and Ernest more than her other
  cousins, 49; with Baron von
  Wiechmann in Brussels, 50; at the

University of Bonn, 50–1; rumours of
  an engagement, 52; 'The Queen has
  in no way altered her mind', 53; not
  invited to V's coronation, 54, 63;
  separation from Ernest, 54; in Italy
  with Stockmar, 55–6; and his
  enduring affection for Ernest, 58–9;
  possible marriage 78–9; lack of
  enthusiasm for V, 80; at Windsor,
  81; a declaration from the Queen, 82;
  'my future has its dark side', 83;
  correspondence with Stockmar, 84;
  in love, 85; with Leopold and
  Stockmar, 86; reported to be a
  Catholic, 87; letter to V on his
  Protestantism, 88; storms over his
  income and rank, 88–90; 'the people
  of England not pleased', 91;
  arguments over the composition of
  his household, 91–8; departure from
  Gotha, 99; the wedding 100–1;
  isolation and distrust, 102–3;
  relations with Anson, 104, 107;
  initial misunderstanding of British
  politics, 105; his unpopularity, 106,
  152–3; and Baroness Lehzen, 107;
  his interest in a Tory Government,
  108; on the slave trade, 109, 153,
  155; studies British politics, 109; his
  relationship with Melbourne, 110;
  objectives of, 111; and the question
  of regency, 111, 113–14; describes
  assassination attempt, 111–12; as
  administrator, 114–15; and the
  English Sunday, 115, 259;
  reorganisation of Buckingham
  Palace, 115–17; and the Duchy of

A NOTE ABOUT THE AUTHOR

Robert Rhodes James, the biographer of Lord Randolph Churchill and Lord Rosebery, and the author of *Churchill: A Study in Failure, 1900–1939* and *Gallipoli,* has been a Fellow of All Souls College, Oxford, a senior officer of the House of Commons, and a principal officer in the Executive Office of the Secretary-General of the United Nations. He has been a member of Parliament since 1976. His work has been awarded the John Llewellyn Rhys Memorial Prize and the Heinemann Award of the Royal Society of Literature, and he is a Fellow of the Royal Historical Society. His most recent book is *The British Revolution, 1880–1939.*

A NOTE ON THE TYPE

This book was set in a digitized version of Baskerville, originally a recutting of a typeface designed by John Baskerville (1706–1775). Baskerville, a writing master in Birmingham, England, began experimenting about 1750 with type design and punch-cutting. His first book, set throughout in his new types, was a Virgil in royal quarto published in 1757, and this was followed by other famous editions from his press. Baskerville's types were a forerunner of what we know today as the "modern" group of typefaces.

Composed in Great Britain.
Printed and bound by
The Maple-Vail Book Manufacturing Group,
York, Pennsylvania.